Endorsements

This study of the political economy of agrarian change in what is now the Federal Democratic Republic of Nepal is an extraordinarily ambitious and impressively comprehensive piece of work. Leaving aside the distinctive regions of the Kathmandu Valley, the northern mountains and the trans-Himalayan plateaus (which are nevertheless briefly addressed), the authors have provided a very detailed description and analysis of agrarian change - in the hills and the plains (the Tarai) where the majority of Nepalis now live - from the earliest times to the present. Drawing on a wide range of secondary sources and the fieldwork that each of the three authors have themselves undertaken in different parts of the country, the study adopts a theoretical framework that is broadly based on a Marxist approach to the analysis of agrarian evolution and transformation, which recognises the complex interaction (or articulation) of modes of production in space and time. This is undoubtedly a path-breaking work, which will be a must read, not only for those concerned to understand the history of agrarian change in Nepal and those concerned to identify possible future developments (in response to climate change and other factors) in this particular country, but to all those interested in agrarian change, wherever and for whatever reason.

David Seddon,
former Professor of Politics and Sociology.
University of East Anglia.

This book, written in the most scholarly genre by deploying "mode of production" as the conceptual framework of the radical anthropology tradition, is useful for anyone interested in understanding Nepal's long global tradition of scholarship on the "agrarian transition" of more than 500 years from pre-capitalist to capitalist systems. In addition, the book has also contributed to unravelling regional agrarian histories, which have been glaringly missing in the scholarship on Nepal's agrarian studies. The high academic rigour of authors is duly reflected in their powerful and original analysis of changing structures of inequality and resource distribution over time, and this, as per their evidentiary claim, is mediated by both internal and external processes on an economic, cultural, political, and ecological level. The book, in a nutshell, has empirically demonstrated that the pattern of change, throughout Nepal's agrarian history, has been incremental rather than transformative. This monumental work has enriched Nepal's discourses and debates on the peasantry and their divergent trajectories of change in each region of Nepal.

Laya Prasad Uprety
Professor in Anthropology

The Agrarian History of Nepal

The Agrarian History of NEPAL

The Political Economy of
Agro-ecological Change

Fraser Sugden, Suresh Dhakal
and Janak Rai

VAJRA
Publications Inc.Pvt.Ltd.

Published and Distributed 2025 by
Vajra Publications Inc.Pvt.Ltd.
Jyatha, Thamel, P.O. Box 21779, Kathmandu, Nepal
Tel.: 977-1-5320562
e-mail: vajrabooksktm@gmail.com
www.vajrabookshop.com

© Author, 2025. All rights reserved.
*No part of this book may be reproduced in any form or
by any means electronic or mechanical,
including photography, recording, or by any information storage
or retrieval system or technologies now known or
later developed, without permission in writing from the publisher.*

ISBN 978-9937-624-54-1

Printed in Nepal

Contents

Acknowledgements — xiii

CHAPTER 1
INTRODUCTION — 1

Towards a documentation of Nepal's Agrarian transition — 2
Unravelling regional histories — 6
Methods to trace agrarian history — 12

CHAPTER 2
UNCOVERING NEPAL'S AGRARIAN HISTORY PRIOR TO THE GORKHALI CONQUEST — 15

Mode of production in the Tarai-Madhesh prior to the Gorkhali conquest — 17
   Early settlement and state formations — 17
   Understanding the mode of production — 25
      Adivasi Mode Of Production - Collective Rather Than Individualised Relationships With Land — 25
      Adivasi mode of production – redistribution rather than accumulation of surplus and collective labour — 29
      Extent of the Adivasi mode of production and processes of dissolution — 30
   Mode of production within caste Hindu domains and other areas under sedentary farming — 32

Mode of production in the hills prior to the Gorkhali conquest	35
The Kathmandu valley – a system apart	37
Western Nepal: Transition from Adivasi to peasant mode of production	39
The Central and Eastern hills	45
Co-existence of Centralised feudalism and Adivasi mode of production	45
Hill Adivasi mode of production: Shifting cultivation and transhumant agro-pastoralism	51
Hill Adivasi mode of production: redistributive ethos and collective labour	58
Cropping systems prior to the Gorkhali conquest	61
The introduction of agriculture and emergence of the rice and wheat cultivation in the plains	61
Cropping systems in the hills and the mode of production	62
History of rice and wheat production in the hills and terraced sedentary farming	64
Upland and unirrigated cropping systems	67
The Colombian exchange and other crops	69

Chapter 3

Gorkha conquest (1750s – 1900s) and Early Rana Rule — 71

Mode of production and tax collection hierarchy in Tarai-Madhesh	74
The tax collection system and land tenure	74
Land grants	78
Tax collection and the mode of production in the long-settled tract	82
State appropriation of surplus on raikar lands	82
Appropriation of surplus on birta and other private estates	84
Tax collection and the subordination of the Adivasi mode of production in the forest belt	86
Onset of Rana rule in Tarai-Madhesh	93
Birta grants during the Rana era	99

Cropping systems in Tarai-Madhesh (1750s-1900s)   101
Mode of production and tax collection hierarchy in hills in areas under sedentary peasant and feudal modes of production   105
   Tax collection hierarchy and mode of production in areas under sedentary cultivation   105
   Taxable raikar lands in the hills   106
   Birta and jagir lands in the hills   110
   Caste and landownership   113
   Internal migration in hills   114
   Forced labour and slavery   116
   Subordination of Adivasi modes of production   120
      Creation of functionary class   121
      The protection and dissolution of customary tenure   123
      Alienation of Adivasi lands and Land grants   132
      Debt, differentiation and the emerging landlord class   133
      Search for new land and Adivasi internal migration   135
      End to shifting cultivation   136
      Uneven dissolution of the Adivasi mode of production   137
   International Migration   143
Cropping systems in the hills   143
   Rice-wheat cropping system and irrigation in western Nepal   144
   Rice-wheat cropping system and intensification of agriculture in central and eastern Nepal   147
   Coarse grains and other rainfed crops during the Gorkha and Rana era   149
   Cash crop production   151
Late rana era: Rise in owner cultivation and local landlord-tenant relations   153
   Emergence of private property rights for raikar land   155
   Monetisation of and declining value of land tax   158
   Impact on the mode of production   159
   Early resettlement schemes and rising owner cultivation   161

Chapter 4
1951-1991: Early democratic period and Panchayat era — 163

- Land reform — 163
- Impact of land reforms — 168
  - Tenancy rights — 168
    - Land redistribution — 169
- Centralised planning and agricultural development — 172
  - Foreign aid and development plans — 172
  - Persisting agricultural crisis — 177
  - Resettlement programmes — 178
- Agrarian structure in Tarai-Madhesh during Panchayat era: feudalism and the rising owner cultivating peasantry — 184
  - Three domains of settlement — 184
  - Increase in the peasant mode of production in the newly settled tract — 185
  - The Transitional zone and Adivasi-settler interaction — 189
  - The mode of production in the long-settled tract – persisting feudalism and failed land reforms — 197
    - The agrarian structure in the Caste Hindu Heartland — 198
    - Demise of Tharu landed class in Adivasi belt and inter-ethnic transfer of resources — 201
    - Dispossession of land amongst small landowners — 204
    - Hill nationalism and exclusion from land — 205
- Agrarian structure in hills during Panchayat era: Differentiated owner cultivation peasantry and pockets of landlordism — 207
  - Monetisation and market integration — 207
  - The impact of land reform and persisting inequality in the hills — 215
  - Three trajectories of change — 216

Areas of land scarcity and intensifying or persisting inequalities in the central and eastern hills	217
Growing land scarcity and internal differentiation within owner cultivating peasantry	217
Localised feudalism	221
Areas of the central and eastern hills with abundant land and delayed subordination of Adivasi mode of production	222
Mode of production in the western hills	227
Convergence in the mode of production by end of the Panchayat era	231
Growing dependence on wage labour	232
Local wage labour	232
Migrant labour	234
Cropping systems: 1951-1991	236
Primary crops during the Panchayat era	236
Productivity and yields trends	239

CHAPTER 5
LIBERALISATION, AGRARIAN STRESS AND CAPITALIST INTEGRATION: THE 1990S TO THE PRESENT

	245
People's War	246
Agricultural development policy	247
Agrarian stress	252
Rural monetisation and rising demand for cash	252
Climate and agrarian stress	259
Growing articulations with capitalist sector through wage labour	260
Migration, new stresses on agriculture and mechanisation	265
Land reform failures	268
Contemporary Agrarian structure and mode of production	270
Feudalism and owner cultivation in the Tarai-Madhesh	272
Feudalism in flux?	280

Owner cultivation, growing inequality and feudal relics in the hills	283
Customary tenure and relics of the adivasi mode of production	286
Shifting cultivation and pastoralism	288
Capitalist agriculture and commercial production	290
Cropping patterns and current trajectory of agricultural development	296
Cropping patterns	296
A complex picture	296
Change in cereal production	297
Cash crops and commercial production	302
Irrigation expansion, agricultural intensification and climate stress	305

Conclusions:
Learning from the Past to Shape the Future — 311

The importance of land	311
The relationship between the spatial and temporal	314
Policy questions	316
References	319
Index	357

Acknowledgements

The idea for this book emerged from our shared interest in Nepal's agrarian history. All three of us have been engaged in grassroots research on agrarian relations across Nepal throughout the last two to three decades. Over the years, we have discussed the option of pulling together the threads of these many studies to develop a more comprehensive analysis of Nepal's multiple agrarian transition pathways. The opportune moment to achieve this goal emerged through the CGIAR initiative *Transforming Agrifood Systems in South Asia (TAFSSA)*, through which the International Water Management Institute (IWMI) commissioned a series of studies on the history of agri-food systems in South Asia – for which the three of us conducted a study on Nepal. This book is a much-extended version of the original report produced from this study, and we are very grateful to IWMI for supporting this work. We would particularly like to extend our gratitude to Shreya Chakraborty and Aditi Mukherji for guiding us and providing critical feedback. We would like to extend gratitude to all funders who supported this research through their contributions to the CGIAR Trust Fund: https://www.cgiar.org/funders/. The views and opinions expressed in this publication are those of the authors and are not necessarily representative of or endorsed by CGIAR, centers, our partner institutions, or donors. We would also like to thank all the participants of the Expert Multistakeholder Consultation on the Historical Evolution of the Agri-food System in Nepal on 11th September 2022, in Kathmandu, where we presented the preliminary outlines of the study, and were able to take on board diverse yet constructive feedback.

We are indebted to Prof. Laya P. Uprety for his guidance and consistent encouragement, with whom one of us (Suresh Dhakal) is privileged to coedit the book, *Peasant Studies in Nepal*. We would also like to express our gratitude to Prof. David Seddon, with whom one of us (Suresh Dhakal) co-authored a book, *Rural Unrest in Nepal*. We thank him for his continuous encouragement, through a series of engaging discussions and exchanges of ideas through emails over the years, to support our analysis of agrarian studies in Nepal. We would also like to pay our tribute to the economic historian, the late Mahesh Chandra Regmi, for his phenomenal work, which has laid a solid foundation for contemporary research on the land and agrarian history of Nepal.

We would like to offer special thanks to Prachanda Pradhan, Kathryn March, David Holmberg, and Corneelle Jest for providing us with many of their photographs from the Panchayat era and early 1990s, for inclusion in this study. We are also equally indebted to Madan Puraskar Pustakalaya for allowing us to access its archival resources and giving permission to use some of the photographs in this book. I (Fraser) would also like to thank the late Stephen Biggs for his commentary and sharing of papers at an early stage – he is greatly missed.

Importantly, as well as secondary and archival sources, this study builds upon a large amount of primary research conducted by the authors over two decades, including smaller-scale personal research projects as well as research carried out under larger multi-team consortia. For this, we have included, where possible, references to already published sources, but have at points also used primary unpublished field notes or data. Several larger research projects which I (Fraser) was involved in contributed field notes and data to the study. These include the following: (i) a series of studies conducted by the International Water Management Institute (IWMI), mostly via the erstwhile CGIAR Research Program on Climate Change and Food Security (CCAFS) and CGIAR Research Program on Water Land and Ecosystems (WLE) – for which I would like to extend my thanks to Ashok Rai, Niki Maskey, Upendra Khawas, Sujeet Karn, Krishna Sah, Tula Narayan Shah and Jenisha Maharjan who all contributed to the primary research; (ii) The EU funded project *Leaving something behind - Migration governance and agricultural & rural change in 'home' communities:*

comparative experience from Europe, Africa and Asia (grant agreement number 822730), and a particular thanks goes to the research team Arjun Kharel and Shalini Gupta; (iii) two ACIAR funded projects, *Sustainable and resilient farming systems intensification in the Eastern Gangetic Plains (SRFSI)* and *Improving Dry Season Irrigation for Marginal and Tenant Farmers in the Eastern Gangetic Plains (DSI4MTF)* – and a particular thanks goes to the research team for Nepal, which includes some of those mentioned above, as well as Ram Bastakoti, Manita Raut, Yaman Sardar, Lalita Sah, and Narayan Prasad Sah.

Similarly, I (Suresh) would also like to thank all those individuals and institutions who have been supportive over the years in pursuing land and agrarian relations-related research. I would particularly like to mention the Community Self-Reliance Centre (CSRC) for entrusting me with several studies carried out by the organization over the past two decades. Jagat B Deuja, the Executive Director of CSRC, Ganesh P Bhatta and Janak R Joshi at the Ministry of Land Management, Cooperative and Poverty Alleviation, whom I had opportunities to work with on several occasions, have always helped provide ideas and information whenever I approached them with a request. Data on shifting cultivation used in this book was initially collected as part of my MPhil study, funded by the University of Bergen, Norway, for which I would like to recall the support and guidance of Prof. Gunnar Haaland and Prof. Randi Haaland.

Suresh spoke to several individuals in person to gather primary information while drafting the initial manuscript. I would like to express my gratitude to them all. Thanks to the Central Department of Anthropology, Tribhuvan University, where I work, for entrusting me to coordinate with CSRC to organize a conference on peasant studies in Nepal, which later turned out to be a book project.

Some of the ideas for this text also emerged from I (Janak's) long-running research with the Dhimal of the eastern Tarai. I would like to thank all the Dhimal people who have shared their stories and experiences of land and agrarian changes with us.

More broadly, all three of us would like to once again extend our gratitude to the farmers and other community members across rural Nepal, whose invaluable knowledge has supported us in all the research, which contributed to this book.

Finally, we appreciate the support of Lokesh and Bidur Dangol of Vajra Books for their keen interest in our work and for supporting us through the publication process, and their enthusiasm and patience.

Fraser Sugden
Suresh Dhakal
Janak Rai

June, 2025

Boudhanath Stupa and village surrounded by fields, Kathmandu Valley, 1963 AD.
Photograph © Dr. Corneille Jest/Mémoires de l'Himalaya

Harvest in paddy fields and a farmer wading his ducks across the Bagmati River, Gokarna, Kathmandu Valley, 1960 AD
Photograph © Dr. Corneille Jest/Mémoires de l'Himalaya

Barley harvests in the Tarap Valley, looking towards Tokyu, Dho Tarap, Dolpo, 1963 AD
Photograph © Dr. Corneille Jest/Mémoires de l'Himalaya

Post-harvest activity in Dhanusha, Madhesh: Harvest being transported from the field to the home.
Phot credit: Suresh Dhakal

Chapter 1

Introduction

Today is a pivotal moment for Nepal's agrarian economy. Following three decades of economic liberalisation, the peasantry of Nepal has more than ever before become integrated into the global capitalist economy (Uprety, 2021). The expansion of transportation infrastructure and growing monetisation throughout the country means that farming households are increasingly buying and selling in global and regional markets. At the same time, the peasantry is also integrated into capitalist labour markets, both in the local non-farm sector in rural towns, in urban areas, and overseas via migration. This is also a time of unprecedented agrarian stress. Climate change is a real and imminent danger for Nepal's farmers, and it risks offsetting decades of technological improvement in agriculture through irrigation and improved inputs. The capacity for farmers to adapt to ecological and water stress is meanwhile, hampered by the rising costs of inputs in global markets and a term of trade which is increasingly stacked against agriculture.

However, importantly, the peasantry of Nepal do not exist in a vacuum, and how they respond to these growing challenges cannot be disentangled from the deeply complex and regionally specific matrix of evolving agrarian relations which shape the distribution of resources – including most notably land and the surplus which it yields, but also labour, capital, water and other agricultural inputs. To understand the regional diversity in agrarian relations, or as we will term it 'modes of production', and the long-term trajectory of change in Nepal's agricultural sector, it is critical to understand its history. This involves a deep analysis of changing structures of inequality and resource distribution over time, and how this is mediated by both internal and external processes on an economic, cultural, political and ecological level.

Towards a documentation of Nepal's Agrarian transition

Rather than being a conventional 'history' manuscript, this book builds upon a long global tradition of scholarship on agrarian transition. This is a genre of writing originally concerned with the transition from pre-capitalist to capitalist economic systems, although in a broader sense, agrarian transition denotes any shift from one 'mode of production' in agriculture, to another. Agrarian transition has been an area of academic interest since the times of Marx, although one of the first systematic empirical studies was Lenin's *Development of Capitalism in Russia* (Lenin, 1960 [1899]). Later historical studies includes debates over the European transition from feudalism to capitalism (Hilton and Hill, 1953, Takahashi and Mins, 1952, Sweezy and Dobb, 1950), and the mode of production debate in South Asia which debated whether India was still 'semi-feudal' (see Bhaduri, 1973, 1977, Prasad, 1973, Chandra, 1974, Sau, 1975), or making the transition to capitalism (see Rudra, 1974).

Scholarship on Nepal has been relatively more limited. There has been extensive research on agrarian history in the broadest sense, particularly from Mahesh Chandra Regmi (Regmi, 1972, 1976, Regmi, 1978d) and other scholars (e.g. Yadav, 1984, Sharma, 2015). However, this has generally focused on a single time period, particularly from the Gorkha conquest until the fall of the Ranas (although Sharma focused on the medieval period). This differs from the agrarian transition approach we take in this book, which is to understand historic agricultural formations in multiple different eras over the last 500 years, and how they have evolved to shape the lived reality of farmers today.

There have been some analyses from Nepal with a specific agrarian transition angle. This includes the classic studies of central Nepal by Blaikie, Cameron and Seddon (Blaikie et al., 2001, 2002a, b, Seddon, 1987), as well as Feldman and Fournier (1976). However, other than a small restudy in the 1990s (Blaikie et al., 2002b), the focus was primarily on the transition taking place in the 1970s and 80s, albeit with useful historical chapters. There have also been macro-level analyses of the larger Nepalese economy by Baburam Bhattarai (2003a), largely focusing on the 70s and 80s, and Chaitanya Mishra (2007)[1], which focuses on the post-war era. While the focus of these studies was of national level political economy rather than agrarian transition at the grassroots, they do echo the mode of production debates in India with Bhattarai gravitating towards the position that rural Nepal is largely feudal, and Mishra suggesting it is closer to capitalism. Other important recent texts include Laya Uprety's (2021) manuscript on the peasantry under capitalism in Nepal, which draws together a wide range of primary and secondary sources. It draws upon many themes raised later in this book around the penetration of capitalism into rural Nepal – although rather than being a historical manuscript, the focus is largely on the decades after economic liberalisation.

This study takes a much longer view than the studies cited above, by exploring Nepal's agrarian transition over centuries rather than decades. It focuses in particular on the last 500 years. The book is thus organised according to the main epochs in Nepal's political-economic history within this timeline, looking further into the past where possible. These eras are firstly, the pre-Gorkha period whereby we focus on the time of the Sen Kingdom in the east and Baise/Chaubisi Rajyas (22/24 principalities) in the west, through to Gorkha and Rana rule, and then on to the Panchayat era of absolute monarchy, followed by the post 1990s period – the decades marked by the restoration of democracy and economic liberalisation.

The book moves beyond the economic metrics which tend to dominate some agrarian transition scholarship, and combines insights from the radical anthropology tradition, in attempting to offer a more nuanced analysis of the interplay between economic, cultural and political processes which are driving change in agriculture. Important studies in this genre include the anthropological research on articulations of modes of production in West Africa (Meillassoux, 1981, van der Klei, 1985) and

---

[1] This is an edited volume of essays, although the chapter 'Development and Underdevelopment: A preliminary sociological perspective' is relevant.

Southern Africa (see review by Hall, 1980) and more recent iterations from South Asia (Singh, 2007, 2023) – all of which are grounded in the Althusserian tradition of political economy. Supporting our approach is a vast body of post-1950s anthropological literature on Nepal which we cite extensively in this book. While very little of the anthropology on Nepal deals with agrarian transition explicitly, it does shed light on the agrarian formation at the historical and geographical conjuncture when fieldwork was carried out.

In terms of the conceptual framework of the radical anthropology tradition, which we utilise in this book, a central analytical tool is that of the 'mode of production' (Althusser and Balibar, 1968). This refers to the social relations and technologies through which production (in this case agricultural production) takes place. It includes three interconnected elements – (i) the means of production i.e. land and agricultural equipment; (ii) the individuals who actually labour on the land (iii) and finally the individuals who appropriate any surplus produced from the land, (with the latter two, i and ii, frequently being the same in the context of a peasant society). These three elements are structured by two 'connections': (i) the relation between the labourer and the means of production, which refers in an agrarian context to the technology (e.g. irrigation, mechanisation) and cultivation methods used to farm the land or 'the *forces of production*; and (ii) the property relation which defines how any surplus from the land is appropriated and how it is put to use, or the *relations of production*'; (Althusser and Balibar, 1968). Importantly, modes of production never exist in isolation, but coexist and articulate with others at specific historical junctures within a larger entity, termed a 'social formation', within which one mode of production may be dominant (Ibid.).

Modes of production and their articulation are not reproduced through economic processes alone, yet instead are overdetermined by various political and ideological processes (termed as the 'superstructure' in Marxian parlance) – including local cultural processes and political struggle on the one hand, and the state and its ideological apparatus on the other (Althusser, 1969). At its most extreme in Nepal's case, the state and mode of production have converged, such as under the centralised feudalism of the Rana era, which was famously termed by Mahesh Chandra Regmi as 'state landlordism'. However, there have been many instances in Nepal's history whereby the mode of production has been almost entirely decoupled from the state – particularly in the context of Adivasi groups who have carried out indigenous agricultural practices with relative autonomy. A recurring theme in this book is the role played by the state in driving change as it exerts its authority over otherwise autonomous economic, cultural and political formations.

A remaining question is why the "mode of production" is a useful analytical tool in the first place? Agrarian transition research, which has its origin in the analysis of the historical European experience, has long been concerned with the development of capitalism in agriculture. The latter refers to an economic system where land is concentrated into the hands of a capitalist class, where production is oriented towards profit, and whereby the labour force is separated from the land and work for wages. This is arguably a form of agriculture which is the exception rather than the norm in Nepal, and in the wider region. It is on this basis that the 'mode of production debate' outlined above, was of huge political significance in South Asia, as it brought the *pre-capitalist* to the fore. Rather than pre-capitalist systems being studied in passing while discussing the emergence of capitalism, a modes of production analysis allows one to explore in detail what makes different pre-capitalist forms of agriculture unique in their own right (Sugden, 2019a, Tilzey and Sugden, 2023). It also offers a structural framework through which one can understand the relative stability of particular phenomena over time within Nepal's agricultural history – including the distribution of surplus, the opportunities for accumulation, labour mobilisation, the cropping choices and the role of technology.

Importantly, the book finds – in part because of this inherent stability – that 'modes of production' and cropping patterns have evolved from one epoch to the next, rather than experiencing 'transformative' change. The expansion and contraction of successive state formations with their internal struggles over resources – combined with interactions between diverse cultural groups, external pressures associated with expanding capitalist markets, global geo-political shifts and climate change – have at each stage, resulted in unique trajectories of agrarian transition at the grassroots. These changes include, amongst others, shifts in the land ownership and management practices, as well as changes in the distribution of the agrarian surplus, the choice of crops, and the associated technologies. Importantly, these trajectories are not linear across Nepal, nor are they shaped by a pre-ordained evolutionary framework drawn from theory (e.g. from feudalism to capitalism) – instead they are unique in their own right, and have unravelled unevenly across time and space. There are nevertheless, certain overarching themes. One relates to the importance of the state in shaping the trajectory of change, and a closely related theme is that of the enduring link between control over land and political power – and these will be analysed at length in the subsequent chapters.

Unravelling regional histories

Another valuable gap in scholarship that this book hopes to fill is with regards to the regionalisation of Nepal's agrarian history. There are many specific historical studies which explore various forms of economic (including agrarian) history in particular regions or populations (e.g. Caplan, 1970, Holmberg et al., 1999, Burghart, 2016, Sharma, 2015).

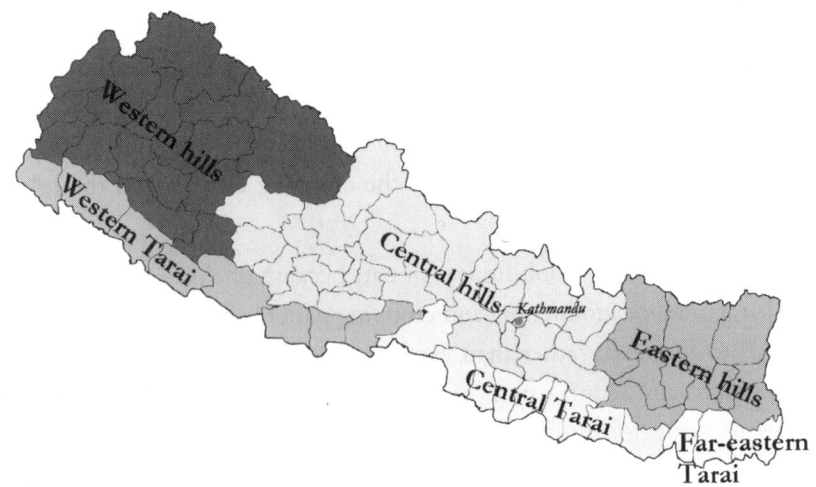

Figure 1: Map of Nepal's regions as discussed in this manuscript

There are also a large number of studies where the nation-state of Nepal is the unit of analysis. This includes not only Mahesh Chandra Regmi's vast portfolio of research on economic history, but also historical works with a broader scope such as Stiller's (1975) political history of the Gorkha state, or more general histories of Nepal (e.g. Whelpton, 2005, Vaidya, 2020). This latter scholarship lacks a systematic attempt however, to identify the locally unique and often divergent trajectories of change in each region.

This book thus attempts to map the regional trajectories of agrarian transition in different parts of Nepal (see Figure 1). While this can by no means be comprehensive, and a long-standing theme of this book is that change unravels unevenly, even within regions, we have been able to identify six regions across the country where there are more commonalities than differences in the local trajectory of change.

In terms of how we selected regions, these have very little correspondence at all with recent political boundaries. The old 'development regions' and zones, established during the Panchayat era, combined diverse ecological domains with no consideration of local history, culture or economy. Similarly, the new provinces, rushed through during the 'fast-tracked' constitution drafting process in 2015, are similarly unhelpful units of analysis. All but one combine vastly different hill and plains regions, with borders being drawn based upon political vested interests rather than being designed to correspond with ethno-linguistic history or agro-ecology. In fact, it has been argued that they were designed specifically, to deliberately divide regions with a shared history and culture in order to undermine regionalist ethno-political movements (Lawoti, 2019, Mørch, 2023).

We therefore have created our own regions shaped by three overlapping spatial layers. The first is the presence of the different historical state formations across particular territories. The second is the existence of indigenous modes of production and associated ethno-linguistic markers, which have operated in particular regions autonomously from the state. The third layer relates to the unique geomorphology and ecology of the different regions. Our regionalisation thus more closely aligns with economic, ecological and cultural realities – including their history prior to the formation of the kingdom of Nepal by the Gorkha dynasty in the late 18th century as well as subsequent social and political changes.

The **eastern hills** refer largely to the areas west of the Likhu and Kamala basins, which includes the historic ethnic domains of *Wallo Kirat, Majh Kirat* and *Pallo Kirat* (Limbuwan). These regions were all historically home to Kirat populations who maintained relative autonomy from the central state, although these lands were once under the influence of pre-Gorkhali eastern Vijayapur branch of the Sen Kingdom. This is a high rainfall region, albeit with localised micro-climates. The annual average rainfall in the easternmost districts of Ilam and Panchatar, and much of the higher foothills and Himalaya is >2000mm. It rises to >2500mm in some locales, while in the lower river valleys between the Himalaya and Mahabharat range it drops to between 1000 and 2000mm (Khanal et al., 2007).

The **central hills**, refers to the areas stretching from the Likhu/Kamala and the West Rapti and Gandaki river basins, which is historically home to the Tamang, Gurung and Magar. This also aligns with the political borders of the old Khas/Rajput ruled alliance of petty states, known as the Chaubisi Rajya (24 principalities). This includes the western branches of the Sen kingdom based in Palpa, and importantly, that of Gorkha, the historic homeland of the Gorkhali dynasty. The central hills also encompasses the former Malla city states of the Kathmandu valley, including Newar tributary states such as Dolakha, and the offshoot Sen kingdom of Makwanpur. While the Kham Magar country of the Rapti basin is often associated with 'western' Nepal as per old administrative divisions, it has far more in common with the Adivasi domains of the central hills than the rest of the western hills.

State formations in the central hills, have been historically stronger, and the Adivasi groups within this domain had arguably less autonomy than in the east, yet as will be shown, there were considerable localised differences within this region. The rainfall is also high in the central hills. Annual precipitation is over 2500mm in the foothills of the Annapurna range (with the exception of the trans-Himalayan district of Mustang) at times increasing to <3000mm. For the rest of the Gandaki basin, as well as in the foothills of the Manaslu, Ganesh Himal and Langtang Himalaya it is 2000mm-2500mm. Like in the east there are lower valleys between the Mahabharat range and higher hills where it drops to between 1500-2000mm (Khatri-Chhetri et al., 2017, Khanal et al., 2007).

What we refer to as the **western hills** refers largely to the western half of the country encompassing the Bheri, Karnali, Seti and Mahakali river basins. This region has a common identity as the homeland of the *Khas* who, following waves of westwards migration, went on to become the dominant group in Nepal, classified in the 2015 constitution as *Khas-Arya*. Much of what we refer to as western Nepal aligns with the borders of the historic Khas/Rajput allied principalities, the so called Baise Rajya (22 principalities), and encompasses all of contemporary Karnali province, the hill part of Sudharpaschim province, and part of Province 5. This region also has a history of relatively strong state formations, in spite of its perceived geographical remoteness today and distance from Kathmandu. Biophysically it also differs from the rest of the uplands. The west has large areas of elevated plateau above 2000m, poorer soil, and lower rainfall, a point echoed by Regmi (1978d) who noted the uniqueness of this region. While precipitation trends are complicated by local microclimates[2], in general the climate is drier than the east. There are only a few high elevation areas of the Mahakali basin where annual precipitation exceeds 2000mm, and rainfall in much of the west is between 1400 and 2000mm, dropping to 600-1400mm in the Karnali basin (Khanal et al., 2007). It does however, see more rain during the winter[3] (Madhura et al., 2015), and this has supported the rice-wheat cropping system which has been central to the sedentary agriculture of the Khas castes who live in this region.

---

[2] Precipitation is generally drier the further west you go, although also significant is the aspect and altitude (e.g. higher south facing slopes receive the highest rainfall) (Nayava, 1980, Karki et al., 2017)

[3] The 'western disturbances', a non-monsoonal precipitation pattern originating in Europe during the winter, brings rain to western Nepal. It is estimated that it makes up 40-45% of the precipitation in some parts of the generally drier western Himalaya and is thus particularly important for winter crops such as wheat and mustard (Madhura et al., 2015).

With regards to the plains, the **far eastern Tarai-Madhesh**, refers to the historically Adivasi region east of the Koshi river, forming the lowland part of contemporary Koshi Province, which is quite distinct from the caste Hindu domains west of the Koshi – having more in common with adjacent areas of North Bengal and the lower Brahmaputra valley. This is a highly fertile belt, with rainfall generally above 2000mm, making it uniquely suitable for jute and bamboo cultivation (Khanal et al., 2007).

The **central Tarai-Madhesh** refers to the area between the Koshi river and Chitwan valley, which are (with the exception of Chitwan itself) predominantly home to Maithili and Bhojpuri speaking castes, and today form much of the historic, Mithilanchal region, as well as the Bhojpuri belt – with much in common with the larger Eastern Gangetic Plains in terms of culture and social structure. It is drier than the districts east of the Koshi with few perennial rivers, and rainfall is mostly between 1400-2000mm, dropping to below 1400mm in the drought prone districts around Janakpur (Khanal et al., 2007).

The **western Tarai-Madhesh** refers to the districts west of the Chitwan valley – an area with a longer history of forest cover, including much of the Tharu heartland and pockets of caste Hindu and Muslim Abadhi speaking communities with cultural links to the central Gangetic Plains. The western Tarai-Madhesh was historically under the influence of hill principalities, while the western most districts, were for a short period under the British empire, being returned to Nepal after the 1857 rebellion – the so called Naya Mulak (including present day Banke, Bardiya, Kailali and Kanchanpur). The rainfall pattern and climate are similar to the central Tarai (Khanal et al., 2007), albeit with slightly elevated winter rainfall.

This book explores the agrarian history of most of Nepal, yet there are two areas which are touched upon, but receive less focus. The first is the Kathmandu valley (see Figure 2). While this region has a complex and rich agrarian history, and we touch upon this history for comparative purposes, we largely focus on the areas beyond the valley fringe where the vast majority of Nepal's farmers live today. This is because there is already outstanding existing ethnographically grounded scholarship on agrarian history in the valley (see for instance Raj, 2010, Sharma, 2015), and a

Introduction

Figure 2: Barahi Manahara, Kathmandu valley in early 20th century. There is already an extensive literature on the agrarian history of the valley, and thus this will not be a focus of this book.
Photo: Madan Puraskar Pustakalaya, Reproduced with permission

range of broader historical works which touch upon the economy of the valley from as far back as the medieval period and earlier (e.g. Regmi, 1952). Furthermore, the valley is an outlier in terms of agrarian history due to its complex peri-urban social formation, and it could potentially merit a separate book given the volume of data on this unique locality.

Another region where there is less focus is the Himalaya and trans-Himalayan region – i.e. the high glacial valleys above 3000m bordering onto the Tibetan Autonomous Region. While we also touch upon these domains at times for comparative purposes, this region is home to a very small share of Nepal's population and is itself a unique social formation with an economy dominated by high altitude pastoralism, trade and tourism – with agriculture often playing a secondary role in livelihoods. It would merit an entirely separate study to explore the unique agrarian history of this region. Therefore, when we refer to the Eastern, Central or

Western hills, we are indeed referring to the *hills* rather than the high Himalaya.

Methods to trace agrarian history

This book is primarily based upon a review of the extensive academic scholarship in Nepal since the 1950s, as well as selected archival sources. There have been few, if any, attempts to map the agrarian history of Nepal and its complex diversity across the country. There is however, a vast scholarship on rural Nepal which can be roughly categorised under four broad and overlapping typologies. The first is that of classic ethnography, which is generally focussed on a particular community or ethnic group and explores themes around cultural, religious, kinship, and economy. These studies tend to include some historical aspects (e.g. oral histories) and touch upon the agricultural economy, although this is rarely a focus. Older ethnographies, particularly the many which were produced during the Panchayat era however, are a valuable historical source in their own right – offering a snapshot of life in the particular spatio-temporal context of rural Nepal in the 1960s and 70s. The second type of scholarship includes policy focused or applied research on agricultural and rural development, which can often offer important insights into cropping practices, and again, old sources offer insights into the agrarian system at the times they were written. The third type of scholarship we engage with is more economic focused, and engages with themes around regional development and political economy, although there are few village level case studies. The final academic resource for this book are the actual historical studies. While some, such as the extensive work of Mahesh Chandra Regmi are specifically focussed on economic and agrarian history, others focus more broadly on political history.

This book has sought to extract data from each of the four types of scholarship, to try to piece together the mode of production in agriculture and the associated cropping patterns as they have evolved from one era to the next. As we developed our argument, we also supplemented our analysis with reviews of archival sources including the Regmi archives, which are by far the most important repository of historical agricultural data, the Hodgson collection from the British Library, as well as republished colonial era sources, Government of Nepal statistics, policy reports, strategies and five-year plans. Finally, we made use of a selection of primary data. This includes our own unpublished data – including a series of interviews carried out in Dhanusha and Morang in 2012 by co-author Fraser Sugden which compiled oral histories on changing land ownership patterns (supported by the International Water Management Institute), interviews carried out in Panchatar, Manang, and Sindhupalchowk in 2001 which were funded by GLTN in the course of a study on land tenure typology, and customary tenure. Similarly, interviews in Morang by co-author Suresh Dhakal were carried out over a number of different years since 2008 for several research projects, and reference to these studies are provided as and when they are incorporated. Some raw data was also integrated from a study on shifting cultivation which was carried out in Sankhuwasabha district in the eastern hill in 1997-98; and later different districts, namely Taplejung, Dhading, Makwanpur, and Nawalparasi in 2006, and was funded by ICIMOD, both by co-author Suresh Dhakal.

We also conducted primary interviews at the time of the study (2022-23) with various stakeholders including senior social and agricultural scientists. A preliminary idea and outline of this writing project was shared among the experts on different fields, including agricultural scientists, irrigation experts, crop researchers, economists, land and agrarian rights activists, and researchers during a stakeholder consultation in Kathmandu in September 2022, which provided a valuable input to carry the study forward. Inquiries were made in several occasions during the study period with senior agriculture scientists at NARC, the Department of Agriculture, and the National Planning Commission to obtain the information on various aspects on land, agrarian and crop history of the country. Unfortunately, no comprehensive data on any crop, its expansion and diversification is available from the period prior to the 1960s, so understanding cropping system change often involved the incorporation of often disparate isolated secondary sources from different parts of the country.

Chapter 2

Uncovering Nepal's Agrarian History Prior to the Gorkhali Conquest

Uncovering the agrarian history of Nepal prior to the Gorkha conquest is a challenging process, particularly if one wants to look beyond the city states of the Kathmandu valley, given the very limited historical records. While there has been some research on the Sen Kingdom, Baise and Chaubisi Rajya, most scholarship is on administration and political intrigue, and not on the nature of agriculture or how land and labour was managed. What limited knowledge there is of the economy is restricted to the areas well within the political control of the state, and not the peripheries. Piecing together the historical mode of production across the rural hills and plains thus requires an analysis of the limited archaeological scholarship, as well as accounts of the agrarian system immediately after the Gorkha conquest, for which extensive records are easier to come by.

While it is impossible to map the sheer diversity of agrarian formations, one can establish three dominant modes of production which were at different temporal-spatial contexts dominant prior to the Gorkha conquest, and would continue to play an important role in subsequent decades. The first is grounded in shifting cultivation (also known as swidden farming) or transhumant agropastoralism, dominated by the cultivation of coarse grains and root crops on unterraced land, which was generally under customary (often communal) tenure. This will be termed the **Adivasi mode of production** (see Singh, 2007).

The second is oriented around sedentary cultivation dominated by a rice-wheat cropping system, with the land being cultivated by peasants who are farming fixed plots of land – although situated within a larger **feudal mode of production**. While the use of the term 'feudal' is contested, it has been defined elsewhere as a mode of production dominated by (i) sedentary peasant units of production; (ii) concentration of land amongst a landlord class; (iv) appropriation of surplus via rent or labour tribute, often involving coercion, and (v) the reallocation of surplus into elite consumption rather than productive re-investment (see discussion in Tilzey and Sugden, 2023, 33-34). Feudalism within the deep history of Nepal, however, has taken on two forms. The first, which we term **localised feudalism**, involves peasant proprietors/title holders who pay rent to a local landlord – in a classical landlord-tenant relationship. The second more complex form, which we term **centralised feudalism**, (although was described by Mahesh Chandra Regmi as 'state landlordism') involves independent peasants who are proprietors/title holders to plots of land, paying tax or labour tribute to the state. At various times in history these peasants could be considered as owner-cultivators, depending on whether or not their titles are considered 'private' property, although in other cases they could be considered as de facto tenants for the state. Either way, a significant share of the surplus would be absorbed as tax, and thus they were still fundamentally part of a centralised feudal mode of production. A third formation, is a genuine **independent peasant mode of production**, whereby much of the surplus remained with a peasant owner-cultivator. This may have emerged during certain periods of history whereby the peasantry was able to avoid the administrative reach of the state. However, in reality, it was only to become widespread across Nepal during the late Rana era – when the tax burden dropped and surplus remained within the farm.

It will be shown in subsequent pages how the interface between the feudal economic formation on the one hand, and Adivasi on the other, appears to align strongly with the influence of historic state formations which have expanded and contracted across the current territory of Nepal throughout the last two millennia. This is an important observation, as while the Adivasi mode of production may at various points in history have paid some revenue to – or been situated within the territory of a feudal state, the persistence of this mode of production largely depends on it retaining relative political and economic autonomy. It is the full subordination to the feudal state which has invariably contributed to its dissolution.

The first part of this chapter focuses on the Tarai-Madhesh, a frontier zone which has a contradictory history – having been the site of early Vedic state formations, while also having at various points in history being sparsely populated and under dense forest cover. Over the last millennia it appears that much of the Tarai was indeed under forest and home to diverse indigenous groups integrated into an Adivasi mode of production. However, there were substantial tracts of the plains (particularly further south) which were in effect a cultural and economic extension of the Indo-Gangetic plains, with sedentary peasant/feudal production taking place primarily in the context of either smaller principalities or larger states to the south.

The second part of the chapter focuses on the hills. While much of the hills beyond the Kathmandu valley was arguably part of an Adivasi mode of production at some stage in history, the western hills made a transition from the latter to a feudal formation much earlier due to the influence of the medieval Khas kingdom. This stands in contrast with the linguistically Tibeto-Burmese indigenous groups of the central and eastern hills. The subsequent eastward migration of the Khas combined with emerging hill principalities paralleled an extension of sedentary peasant farming and feudalism in the centuries leading up to the Gorkha conquest. The final part of the chapter looks at cropping patterns throughout this period, and the links to the economic formation on the ground.

Mode of production in the Tarai-Madhesh prior to the Gorkhali conquest

Early settlement and state formations

The Tarai-Madhesh has a complex history – as it has long been a frontier between the kingdoms of the Gangetic plains to the South (including the Mughal empire), and the smaller principalities of the hills to the north –

and at different periods of time has fallen under the influence of state formations from both regions. The region has been the centre of ancient kingdoms of its own such as Kapilvastu (5th and 6th centuries BC), the home of Prince Siddhartha Gautam, or Buddha, and nearby Ramgram in present day Kapilvastu district (Tuladhar, 2002). These kingdoms emerged following the introduction of new varieties of rice and improvements in transplantation techniques, which supported a growth in population, as well as the rise in trade and emergence of towns. This facilitated a transition from smaller Vedic chieftaincies with lineage based land tenure, to larger more hierarchical social systems based upon the ideology of kingship and with early notions of private land ownership (Whelpton, 2000). However, these ancient kingdoms underwent decline at the end of the so called Vedic era (1500 – 500 BC) and large parts of the region were reclaimed by forest (Whelpton, 2000; Kafle, 2022).

This latter statement however, does come with some caution. While there is a popular narrative that the eastern and western Tarai-Madhesh was a forest wilderness between the collapse of the Vedic kingdoms and the Gorkhali conquest in the late 18th century onwards, this has been challenged by many scholars of the region (Burghart, 1978; Krauskopff, 2000; Warner, 2014; Guneratne, 2002). The Tarai was indeed for a large part of the previous two millennia, a frontier zone between the plains-based kingdoms to the south and hill-based principalities to the north – with the forest acting as a natural buffer between both. This supported a population of Adivasi communities such as the Tharu, a large number of whom carried out shifting cultivation/swidden (see below).

Nevertheless, not all the region was a wilderness at all times, and it is clear that both the area under forest, and the frontier between sedentary and shifting cultivation, expanded and contracted along with the rise and fall of different state formations. As Krauskopff (2000, 35) emphasizes:

> "Old kingdoms have risen and fallen there [Tarai-Madhesh] for at least 2000 years. The forest retreated when farming expanded under prosperous political conditions; jungle took over in times of instability and conflict. Reading today the journeys of the Chinese pilgrims from the 5th and 6th

centuries in search of Buddhist shrines gives a sound idea of the impermanent landscape of the Tarai-Madhesh. It seems after that several centuries after the Buddha's birth in the Sakya kingdom of present-day Kapilvastu, a previously well-developed area had partly reverted to wilderness."

In the western Tarai, it appears that hill-based principalities had nominal control over the region throughout the Middle Ages. The Tharu domains of the Dang valley for instance, was under the control of the Khas kingdom (Bouillier, 1993), and records suggest it was given by the Khas-Malla kings as *birta* (a form of land grant, which will be discussed below) to one Jayakar Pundit in 1393 (Sharma, 1988). The valley later retained some autonomy following the kingdoms' collapse in the 15th and 16th centuries (Mishra, 2007), when it came under the control of a king linked to the Rajput Chauhan dynasty based in Tulsipur. This principality was later one of the allied Baise Rajyas. Much of the remainder of the western Tarai was under the influence of both the Baise and Chaubisi Rajya between the 15th and 17th centuries, and each of these petty states at least nominally controlled a tract of land to the south of the hills, which at the time of the Gorkha conquest was around 20 miles across (Hamilton, 2007 [1819]). The level of political control held by these principalities is unknown, although some such as Dang, Makwanpur and Palpa likely had stronger influence in the lowlands as they were centred on the boundary between the hills and plains itself, where the kings would rule from throughout the winter, only retreating to the hills in the monsoon (Warner, 2014).

In the central and eastern Tarai there is evidence of larger state formations which would have had significant areas under settled agriculture. This includes the state of Tirhut, centred on Simraungadh, in present day Bara district close to the border. The city was founded in 1097 but was destroyed by Muhammad bin Tughluq in 1325 (Cimino, 1986). In later centuries it appears that the centre of political gravity moved south, and the border region of the Tarai would have fallen under the control of larger Gangetic Plains kingdoms. This includes for instance the

Oinavara dynasty (14th-16th century) of Mithila[1], centred on present day Madhubani district of Bihar.

Nevertheless, this does not mean that the rest of the central Tarai was a forested wilderness. There are ruined temples which resemble relics from the 10th century (Darnal, 2012) and 13th century (Das, 2014) across Saptari, suggesting the presence of more complex state formations at various points in the middle ages (see Figure 3). With reference to the Janakpur region, Burghart (2016) notes that while it was a heavily forested belt at the time of its 'rediscovery' by ascetics in the early 18th century after which it emerged into a religious site, it has a much longer history of permanent settlement than commonly thought. He cites evidence of numerous medieval era ruins of temples and mounds which long predate its so called rediscovery (Burghart, 1978, Burghart, 2016). Burghart (1978) links many of the medieval ruins in the Dhanusha region to independent chieftaincies, home to Hindu castes, with settled agriculture, some production of agricultural surplus and a ruling elite. For example, the chieftaincy of Mahottari west of Janakpur, was led by an Anivar Brahmin. It was captured by the army of Lohangga Sen in the 17th century along with a number of smaller chieftaincies, as described in Hamilton's (2007 [1809]) account.

In the Tarai east of the Koshi during the medieval period, Subedi (2005) suggests that this region fell under the influence of Koch kings from Cooch Behar, with a kingdom centered on Vijayapur (present day Dharan) which ruled in collaboration with *Kirat* chieftains from the hills, the borders of which extended as far as Jalpaiguri in present day West Bengal on the banks of the Tista river. This kingdom likely also had some administrative tax appropriation capacity and a ruling elite, with Vijayapur itself being what appears to be a well-established settlement with a fort - although in the absence of written sources, one can only speculate.

---

[1] What was to become the Nepal-India border at least in the case of the central Tarai was established following a split in the Karnata dynasty in the 12th century and it is likely that particularly prior to this, dynasties in the South had a strong influence over the region (Chaudhary, 1964).

It appears however that the most significant state formation in the central and eastern plains in the centuries prior to the Gorkha conquest was that of the Palpa based Sen kingdom. This was one of the more powerful principalities of the Chaubisi Rajya, and already controlled parts of the western Tarai (Kapilvastu, Rupandehi and Nawalparasi) from the 13th century onwards (Malla, 1979, Das, 2014). However, over time it had moved eastwards to encompass the Makwanpur region south of Kathmandu, which itself split from the rest of the Sen kingdom in 1553[2]. Lohanga Sen of Makwanpur subsequently expanded the kingdom further east along the Tarai and foothills and by 1609 had conquered the older Vijayapur kingdom. The origins of the Sen kingdom has been disputed (Beine, 2012). While the common narrative suggests that the Sen's (like the rulers of many of the other principalities of the Baise/Chaubisi Rajyas) could trace their ancestry to Chitaur in Rajasthan, and were Rajputs fleeing the Muslim invasions (Burghart, 2016; Biene, 2012; Stiller, 1975), Das (2014) suggests they originated in Bengal[3]. Regardless of origins, it was clear that the Sen Kingdom was a Hindu polity with influence over a large area. Khas and Rajputs played a central role in the administration (Hamilton, 2007 [1819]; Stiller, 1975), with Brahmins managing ritual affairs (Pradhan, 2009). Das (2016) implies that it was never an administratively strong unit. The influence of the dynasty was likely not continuous, and the borders of political influence were in continuous flux. Nevertheless, it appears from archival sources to have had a relatively sophisticated administration apparatus (Hamilton, 2007 [1819]).

In light of the discussion above, it is no surprise that by the time of the Gorkhali conquest, extensive areas of the Tarai were already cleared of forest and under permanent cultivation, with established trading and administration centres. For instance, colonial correspondences analysed by Regmi (1978a) from the late 18th century suggest that parts of Kapilvastu

---

[2] This took place when it was divided up between sons following the death of Mukunda Sen

[3] Das (2014) suggests that following the collapse of the Sena empire in Bengal itself in the 13th century the descendants of its rulers created new principalities in Nepal. They went on to form what is more commonly known today as the Sen dynasty with its capital in Palpa.

Figure 3: The Churia Hills near Kanakpatti of Saptari is said to be home to numerous ruins.

Photo: Fraser Sugden

and Rupandehi in the western Tarai were as well cultivated as Bihar and the Banares region (Uttar Pradesh). This is backed up by accounts of the central Tarai for instance by Kirkpatrick (2007 [1793]), writing in 1793, just years after the Gorkha conquest, who makes reference to emerging towns and large areas under settlement. The travelogue (which appears to pass northward from the border through Bhareh fort, approximately 10-15km north of the border[4]), makes reference to a mix of farmland and forest extending north of the border, before one enters what he terms the 'great forest', a likely reference to the larger east-west Tarai forest belt. Referring to this forest belt he states that "it is not of course equally close or deep in every place; some parts having been more or less cleared away, especially those which are situated most favourably for the commerce of timber, or in the vicinity of flourishing towns. To the eastward some considerable tracts are reported to be quite clear" (p17).

---

[4] 'Barah' fort is a likely reference to Baragadhi today in contemporary Bara, given the reference to other nearby sites such as Simraungadh.

It has been established that the Tarai was not a forested wilderness out of reach of the state – particularly in the central plains. However, even in the tracts which were under forest, these were by no means uninhabited. Firstly, for centuries the forested plains were used as pastureland from itinerant pastoralists, particularly from the south, including movement from Purnea to Morang (Hamilton, 2007 [1819]) and Avadh to Dang (Warner, 2014), and most of these seasonal migrants were taxed by the various state formations with control over these tracts (Ibid.).

More significantly however, a crucial aspect of the Tarai's history is that of its Adivasi communities – whose livelihoods were intricately connected to the region's forest ecosystem. They likely lived in relative autonomy from the various state formations across this region for many centuries in the run up to the Gorkhali conquest (Krauskopff, 1989, Rai, 2015, Muller-Boker, 1999). By far the largest group was the Tharu, who were dominant across the western Tarai, with subgroups including the Rana (present day Kailali and Kanchanpur in the far west), Kathariya (present day Kailali and Banke), and Danguara (Dang valley and present day Kapilvastu and Rupandehi). The Chitwan Tharu also were the main group in the Chitwan valley, while the Kochila Tharu resided across the central Tarai as far as the Koshi river (Guneratne, 2002, Krauskopff, 1989) (likely to the north of the more settled areas under caste Hindu influence). The Tarai districts east of the Koshi, which we refer to as the Eastern Tarai, were arguably the most diverse (see Figure 4) due to the frequent interchange of populations between Nepal's far-eastern plains and the diverse Adivasi cultures of the Brahmaputra valley. This region was home not only to the Tharu (known as Morangiya or Lampuchiya, see Guneratne, 2002), but also to Koch-Rajbanshi, Dhimal, Meche, Bantar, Gangai and other ethnic communities (Hamilton, 2007 [1819], Grunning, 2007 [1911]).

One can surmise therefore that in the centuries prior to the Gorkha conquest, the Tarai was home to two unique agrarian and political-cultural formations. Firstly, those of the small principalities or chieftaincies which were the domain of Hindu castes. These were likely further south towards

Figure 4: Traditional design of Bantar house (top) and Tharu house (bottom) in Morang, which emerged as one of the Tarai's most diverse districts
Photo: Fraser Sugden

the present-day border, and particularly in the Mithila belt of the central Tarai. Secondly there were those of the Tarai's Adivasi groups who lived deep within the more forested tracts of the lowlands which were beyond significant state influence – although the latter would over subsequent years make a transition to settled agriculture in a spatially and temporally uneven process. We will seek to understand the mode of production in these two domains in the subsequent sections.

Understanding the mode of production

Adivasi Mode of Production in the Tarai-Madhesh - Collective Rather Than Individualised Relationships With Land

As noted above, the lack of written records makes it extremely difficult to reconstruct the historical 'mode of production' of the Tarai's Adivasi groups, although several features stand out. The first was a *collective* rather than individualised relationship with the land, a phenomenon grounded in the type of agriculture (shifting cultivation) and the cultural/ritual relationship with a larger territory and ecosystem rather than to individual holdings. Within this context there were no legalised concepts of private property. Shifting cultivation in particular has been central to the Adivasi relationship with land, and has played an important role in the history of Nepali agriculture (Dhakal, 2000). It is generally accepted as an early stage of agricultural evolution (Rowley-Conwy, 1981). It involves felling vegetation on a plot of land, letting it dry, and then systematically burning it off. This technique serves to clear the field and enrich the soil with nutrients from the ash. Prepared fields are generally used not more than two years at a time, and after that, the land is left fallow for some years depending upon the availability of land and the rate of its ecological regeneration.

Shifting cultivation has been recorded as the historical agricultural system amongst the Tharu across the Nepal Tarai (McDonnaugh, 1989, Gurung, 2003, Müller-Böker, 1991a), as well as in the Tarai of Uttarakhand (Singh, 1989). One of the largest ethnographic studies of the Tharu of the western Tarai-Madhesh by Krauskopff (1989) notes how the Tharu traditionally cultivated rice through a form of shifting cultivation, diverting water from streams, with archival sources from the colonial era suggesting communities in Kanchanpur changed site every few years. With reduction in the available land and increased influence of the state (e.g taxation), they would decrease the length of the cycles, and eventually move further north into less settled tracts. According to Müller-Böker (1991a) the agricultural economy of the Tharus in the Chitwan valley was also dominated by shifting cultivation, alongside pastoralism hunting, fishing and gathering.

With regards to the eastern Tarai-Madhesh, this was also a largely Adivasi domain, but has a more diverse cultural-economic history. It was part of a larger cultural continuum which extended into the North Bengal Tarai skirting the Sikkim and Bhutan Himalaya, and into present day Assam. Accounts by Brian Hodgson (1880 [p1847]), the British resident in Kathmandu during the 19th century, suggest that the socio-cultural formation across this eastern sub-Himalayan lowland belt which included both Nepali and Indian territory was deeply complex, with multiple Adivasi groups including the Tharu, Rajbanshi, Dhimal, Meche and Bantar. Hodgson implied that certain sub-groups resided within the forest and pursued a semi-nomadic livelihood – which included shifting cultivation. Some would venerate forest and clan deities, whereas others appeared to have undergone Sanskritization (and likely with it, a shift towards sedentary agriculture). The latter likely included those living near the edge of (or just outside) the forested belt, in the sphere of influence of state formations such as that of the Koch kingdom (of Cooch Behar, present day West Bengal), who were the first to take up the name Rajbanshi, rather than Koch to assert their perceived higher status (Ibid.).

It appears however, from Hamilton's (2007 [1819]) account shortly after the Gorkhali victory from Morang, well within Nepali territory, that the regions in which he travelled were heavily forested and sparsely populated with an economic system akin to Tharu communities in the western Tarai. He reported that the indigenous Rajbanshi (also known at the time as Koch) and Gangai were engaged in slash and burn agriculture (shifting cultivation) with the use of the hoe rather than the plough, and there was a periodic movement of fields (Hamilton, 2007 [1819]), although no information was provided on the length of the cycles. Further insights can be gained from parts of the culturally similar North Bengal

Tarai (or Dooars) on which there are more records. Ray (2002) suggests that agriculture prior to the colonial period immediately to the south of the hills was characterised by shifting cultivation (known locally as *jhum*) by the indigenous Meche and Garo communities who lived in small settlements, led by a *Mandal* or headman. After cultivating a plot for three years, they would leave it fallow for several years, while settlements themselves would be shifted every 7-8 years. As one moved further south (particularly into areas under the political influence of the Koch-Rajbanshi state (echoing Hodgson, above) – agriculture became more settled, with sedentary cultivation in forest clearings of paddy, tobacco and mustard cultivation and residence in permanent villages (Ray, 2002).

Further insights on the role of shifting cultivation amongst Tarai-Madhesh Adivasi groups can be gained from anthropological research on the Dhimal of Morang and Jhapa in the east, who were engaged in shifting cultivation until relatively recently. They were not primarily farming people until they were forced to take it up by the emerging external political order (the Gorkhali state) and its regimes of extractive taxation in the later part of the 19th century (Rai 2013, 2015). The forested ecology, the threats of wild animals which would destroy the crops, and the prevalence of epidemics of malaria and cholera, would force Dhimal to move from one place to another following the deaths of villagers. This all made relying on farming fixed plots of land less desirable and practical.

Importantly, shifting cultivating Adivasi communities likely had a cultural and ritual relationship with a larger territory, its forest and other natural resources, rather than an individualised attachment to a given plot, as one would expect in a classic sedentary peasant society (see Shanin, 1973). Rai (2013) notes how the Dhimal maintained a culturally embedded relationship with the land which provided them their sustenance through limited farming, foraging, hunting and fishing, rather than a formal legal relationship with a particular plot. Forests, rivers, and soils which provided this sustenance, and associated deities were honoured during rituals (Rai, 2013). Linguistic evidence includes the lack of an indigenous term for 'plough', and conflation of the term for felling forest with that of agriculture itself. Rai (2015, 77) also points to a Dhimali term "*jaya kheraka*", which refers to the clearing of bushes to plant wild millet – emblematic of shifting agriculture or *jhum*[5].

In terms of the actual property relations, the means of production was likely to have been common property rather than being owned by individual households or lineages. Shifting cultivation based agricultural systems in the hills of Nepal have generally depended on customary communal tenure whereby a clan or lineage would enjoy communal rights to a tract of land (Caplan, 1970, Gaenszle, 2000). This may have applied also in parts of the Tarai-Madhesh, although even if land was not under any formal 'customary tenure', it was likely de-facto common property – particularly in the context of forest dwelling communities where livelihoods were semi-nomadic and for whom the means of production were extensive. Rai's (2015) ethnography of the Dhimal observes that with no concept and practice of land as fixed, owned property, there was no need for "communal ownership". More fundamentally however, Rai (2015) suggests that in this context the Dhimal had no concept of land as something one could own, control, or have property rights over. In the first scholarly account of Dhimal from India, Brian Hodgson (1880 [1847]) described them as "migratory cultivators of a soil in which they claim no proprietary or possessory ownership, but which they are allowed to till upon the easy terms of quit-rent and labor tax, because no others will or can enter the malaria guarded unit (p: 119)". Similarly with regards to the North Bengal Dooars during the pre-colonial period, Ray (2000) notes that the uncultivated forest lands were extensive and thus the means of production was essentially common property rather than being owned by individual households or lineages.

---

[5] In the first scholarly writing on Dhimal, published in 1847, Hodgson (1880 [1847]) mentions that at that time Dhimal possessed no word for "plough," and "agriculture" was described by the term "felling" or "clearing the forest" (p: 103).

Adivasi mode of production in the Tarai-Madhesh – redistribution rather than accumulation of surplus and collective labour

Historical studies of Adivasi communities elsewhere in the sub-continent, and in particular, the seminal study by Singh (2007)[6], also points to two important features of the Adivasi economic formation. Firstly, it is driven by the survival and reproduction of the clan rather than accumulation of wealth. This does not mean there is no internal differentiation or 'accumulation' internally, as most Adivasi communities will have chiefs or even petty kings[7]. However, there is a tendency for accumulation which does take place to be balanced out by redistributive systems. With regards to the Tarai, Rai's (2015) study of the Dhimal pointed to a strong cultural ethos of exchange and reciprocity. Though they had a customary leader or *Majhi*, this was not a vertically ranked social position. It was instead rooted in a moral economy based upon robust kinship bonds and mutual support within the clan. Even following the gradual dissolution of the Adivasi mode of production in later years, the Majhi would play a role in redistributing food and resources to those who needed it (Rai, 2013).

Singh (2007), in his conceptualisation of the Adivasi social formation, also points to lateral rather than vertically segmented mechanisms to manage labour, noting how the working age population would engage in labour on a collective rather than household basis (e.g. youth participating in collective hunts). While communal labour regimes have been well documented amongst hill Adivasi groups (Macfarlane, 1976, Campbell, 2018), there is less research in the plains. Nevertheless, it is highly likely that similar forms of collective labour were mobilised from the plains also

---

[6] According to Singh (2007) the *adivasi* social formation in India traditionally produces little surplus product and the imperative of this economic formation is the survival of the larger lineage rather than accumulation of wealth. Any accumulation which does take place is redistributed. He argues, like Rey, that it is only taxation and other coercive measures of capitalism and/or feudalism which can restructure this mode of production, as this paper will go on to argue.

[7] For instance a Katharia Tharu talukdar or tax administrator in Kailali, when it was still under the control of the Nawab of Oudh was designated as a 'raja'(Johnson, 2023), although whether this was a consequence of the subordination of the Adivasi mode of production, or predates subjugation to the state, is unknown.

– and they certainly featured in oral histories from the region (Sugden, 2025).

Extent of the Adivasi mode of production and processes of dissolution

In sum, it can be surmised that the Adivasi mode of production had two loose elements – (i) a collective rather than individualised relationship with land, with an absence of private property, and use of communal or customary land for agriculture, largely oriented around upon shifting cultivation; (ii) Redistribution of surplus rather than accumulation, along with a relatively non-hierarchical, clan based political organisation and labour mobilisation. Across South Asia however, these two elements have over time, been gradually undermined or dissolved, primarily by the emergence of centralized state formations, which has facilitated a transition towards or growing articulations with both feudalism and capitalism (Singh, 2007).

Three processes in particular have been significant throughout Nepal's agrarian history: (i) Taxation of the peasantry; (ii) creation of an indigenous functionary class (and intensified internal inequalities), and (iii) clearing of the forest frontier (Sugden, 2017b). These will be explored at length in chapter 3. Exactly when this transition began in the Adivasi domains of the Tarai-Madhesh is difficult to assess. Hamilton (2007 [1819]) suggests that the Chaubise and Baise Rajyas who controlled the westernmost Tarai tract, extracted some tax from the settlements deep in the forest, as well as using the forests for natural resources such as wild elephants and timber. However, there was limited interest in clearing the land and expanding cultivation to maximise revenue extraction given that the forest offered a valuable natural buffer for defence purposes (Ibid.).

Historical studies of the central and Eastern Tarai following its conquest by Lohanga Sen of Makwanpur in the century prior to the Gorkhali annexation of the region also contain recorded evidence of an administration system with feudal tax appropriation capabilities (Regmi, 1970c), although this may have existed earlier, given the long influence of the Sen dynasty in the Tarai (Das, 2016). Following the Sen conquest, the kingdom was split once more into three branches, the Vijayapur kingdom east of the Koshi (centred in present day Dharan), the Chaudandi kingdom to the west of the Koshi (centred on present day Udayapur), and beyond, that of Makwanpur itself (Kafle, 2022). These three Sen states introduced a taxation system based upon that used by the Pathan rulers in northern India prior to the rise of the Mughal Empire (Regmi, 1970, Burghart, 2016). Tax was appropriated from the peasantry by the Sen rulers, with tribute paid to Nawabs of Bengal (Acharya, 1973).

Documents compiled by Tej Narayan Panjiyar, a Tharu historian (see analysis by Krauskopff, 2018) suggest that Tharu chieftains were given tax collection and land reclamation roles in Saptari during the time of the Sen kingdom, alongside Hindu petty chieftaincies further south (see below). The documents also suggest that the land was well cultivated (and possibly under sedentary cultivation) and that these functionaries also potentially held large areas of land – pointing to early stratification within the Tharu political structure (Ibid). Guneratne (2002) uses this evidence to suggest that the Tharu were far from being a self-governing 'tribal' society, as some colonial reports implied. Nevertheless, what this more likely shows is that the dissolution of the Adivasi mode of production was uneven, and had already occurred in Saptari under the Sen state. The fact that the Tharu in Saptari have been long known to be more Sanskritised and follow ritual rules around caste, also points to much earlier stratification and alignment with the values of their caste Hindu neighbours (Guneratne, 2002). One would expect that significant revenue generation and the associated increase in stratification, would have been limited to parts of the central Tarai with a longer history of settlement. The degree to which the state was able to infiltrate remote forest dwelling communities, particularly in the more sparsely populated far eastern and western Tarai is questionable.

The western Tarai for example, as noted above, came under the influence of the hill principalities of the Baise and Chaubaise Rajya, which emerged following the collapse of the medieval hill based Khas kingdom (Kafle, 2022), including the principalities of Salyan, Palpa, Dang-Deukkhuri and Dullu (Shah, 1989). Some areas such as the plains below Palpa were actually leased by the rulers of Oudh. However, while these domains offered state formations to the north and south a source of natural resources such as elephants and fish (Shah, 1989), there is limited evidence that these areas were extensively settled or under the direct administrative control of the state – (although this doesn't preclude some modest collection of revenue from forest dwelling herders or cultivators - as discussed in later chapters).

The presence of shifting cultivation until relatively recently – until into the 20th century in areas such as the Dang valley – (McDonnaugh, 1989, Gurung, 2003) suggests that subordination to centralised states likely occurred much later here. This is supported in part by the high prevalence of malaria, which the Tharu had relative immunity to, when compared to settlers from outside[8]. Rajaure (1981) narrates the history as, "in those days there was a shortage of manpower for farmwork since normally no person, other than Tharus, dared to stay in that malarial valley. Persons who became Tharus, according to the informants, were encouraged to clear and cultivate some of the forest land in their vicinity" (p 171). The Dhimal, Rajbanshi and Meche of the far-eastern Tarai were also known to have relative immunity to malaria (Campbell, 1841).

Mode of production within caste Hindu domains and other areas under sedentary farming

As noted above, it was likely that parts of the Tarai-Madhesh were under the influence of small principalities and home to Hindu castes. These likely correspond with the areas of the Tarai which are today associated with Maithili and Bhojpuri speaking caste Hindu society.

It is difficult to assess the mode of production in these principalities but it was likely quite different to their Adivasi counterparts. Burghart (1978) suggests they were home to Hindu agriculturalists, organised politically into petty kingdoms, carrying out (likely sedentary) peasant farming. Relics of idols in temple ruins point to the religious traditions of Maithili Brahmins, who likely ruled these small states. There was a sizeable agricultural surplus which could be mobilised to build the many brick

---

[8] This has been backed up in medical studies. One paper found for instance that prevalence of malaria was seven times lower amongst Tharu when compared to non-Tharu (Terrenato et al., 1988)

temples and other structures – the ruins of which can be seen today (Burghart, 1978). The cornering of surplus implies that there would have been moderate inequality. Given that culturally, the residents of these principalities were an extension of the Maithili and Bhojpuri speaking caste society of the Eastern Gangetic plains (Burghart, 2016) (as one sees today) – one would expect that inequalities were stratified by caste (unlike their more egalitarian Adivasi counterparts). The economic formation was thus most likely a form of localised feudalism – dominated by cultivation by a differentiated peasant proprietor class who would pay some kind of tribute to a local ruler – although the status of property rights, and whether surplus was appropriated in the form of rent or tax is not known.

However, settlement and revenue administration likely increased after the conquest of these small principalities by Lohangga Sen in the 17th century and the boundaries of revenue administration aligned with the petty chieftaincies which had been brought under centralised control (Burghart, 2016). A functionary known as a Chaudhari (who would remain in place after the Gorkha conquest) was placed in charge of revenue collection, and they would collect tax from a village level headman or *mokuddam* (Hamilton, 2007 [1819]). Each would be responsible for a *parganna*, an official revenue generation unit, or otherwise their authority would be restricted to the land between two rivers, an area known as a *khari* (most of which run on a north to south basis) (Ibid). Tharu headmen whose villages had already been subordinated to state control (particularly in the Sen domains of Saptari) were also included in this state apparatus (Krauskopff, 2018).

Each district was under the control of a revenue officer or *diwan* and a civil officer or *fouzdar* who would be a kin of the royal family and would jointly channel revenue to the Royal Treasury in Makwanpur (Burghart, 2016). In Mahottari and Saptari the *fouzdar* had the added responsibilities of allotting waste land for cultivation to settlers and collection of revenue (Regmi, 1970a). There was notable migration of Hindu castes (and at some stage Muslim peasants also) from the Gangetic plains to the south during this period. For example, large tracts of land were given to the newly established temples in Janakpur – partially as a way for the Sen kings to consolidate their claim to the newly conquered territory. These encouraged peasants from the South to migrate into the area, clear the forests and work as tenants (Burghart, 1978).

Greater state control and taxation will have inevitably contributed to deepening inequalities and the emergence of a distinctive landlord class – like in Bihar to the south, which is a cultural continuum with the central Tarai-Madhesh in terms of linguistic and caste relations. In the Indian parts of Mithila for instance, the rigid caste system combined with the long history of revenue administration for the pre-Mughal and Mughal state formations – meant that there was a distinct landlord class as early as the 13th century (Chaudhury, 1964). Politically powerful upper caste landowners, extracted a portion of the crop from the peasants to channel to the state as tax, retaining a portion for themselves for diversion into luxury consumption. As many had more land than was needed for their own needs, excess lands would be rented out, with surplus being extracted as rent from tenants on these lands (Chaudhury, 1964). This points to an emergence of localized feudalism whereby landlords appropriate surplus via rent, alongside the more centralised variant whereby surplus was appropriated via tax.

In the Central Tarai-Madhesh, given the later history of settlement, concentrations of land may not have been as pronounced as in the well-established landlord economy of Bihar further south. Regmi (1978d) does however note the presence of 'zamindars' like their counterparts in India in the settled tracts of the Tarai-Madhesh around the time of the Gorkhali conquest who had customary rights over the peasantry and a tax collection role, with widespread tenancy. The fact that the Mughal term *zamindar* was used in government records relating to landlords in Mahottari and Saptari from the late 19th century (just after the conquest) is significant as it implies that these individuals had control over significant areas of land (possibly whole villages).

The distribution of tax free *birta* grants to influential families was reported from this period – and likely consolidated the localised emergence of a more powerful landlord class. The Sen king of Makwanpur for instance, granted 93 bighas of land to a Maithili Brahmin (Regmi, 1978d), and the Sen's of Vijayapur distributed *birtas* in Morang (Pradhan, 2009). Lands on these early *birta* estates were most commonly rented out to tenants on a sharecropping basis with the landlord extracting half of the annual crop (Regmi, 1972), a system which would come to define localized feudal agrarian relations in later years. Regmi (1972) also suggests that there were established private property rights to land in the eastern plains, which would have supported the reproduction of these landlord-tenant relationships. However, whether land tax extracted from the peasant title holders to land, or rents taken from tenants, were the primary mechanism of feudal exploitation, is not known – although as Regmi (1972) notes, this question was of little significance to the peasant who would see any surplus beyond their minimum subsistence needs appropriated by either the state or landlord.

Mode of production in the hills prior to the Gorkhali conquest

The agrarian system in the hills bears parallels with the Tarai-Madhesh, whereby there is a juxtaposition of indigenous Adivasi forms of economic and political organisation dominated by shifting cultivation and various forms of communal rights to land, alongside independent peasant or feudal modes of production oriented around sedentary farming on fixed plots. There were, however, also notable differences. The Adivasi mode of production in the hills had notable differences when compared to the Tarai, particularly given the importance of clan based customary tenure in the uplands. Similarly, the complex topography and the division of the hills into many smaller states, led to far greater diversity in agrarian relations on the ground.

Nevertheless, the division (albeit a fluid one) between these different agrarian systems, corresponds roughly with the primary cultural faultline in modern Nepal. Modern identity politics has differentiated between two distinct ethno-linguistic groups in the hills. The first are the Adivasi groups such as the Rai, Limbu, Gurung, Tamang[9] and Magar (known more often

---

[9] We refer to present day classifications of the regions indigenous groups, although note that how these communities collectively identified in history is likely complex. For instance, the term Tamang as a group identity came into widespread use in the early 20th century (Tamang, 2008). During the Licchavi period, Tamang (2008)

in the hills as *janajati*)¹⁰ who speak Tibeto-Burmese languages, and traditionally lived across the eastern, central hills between the Koshi and West Rapti basins. The second are the *Khas* or *Parbatiya* groups who speak the Indo-European language, Nepali. The latter migrated into Nepal from the west, assimilating with various Adivasi groups, while themselves assimilating waves of caste Hindu migrants from the Gangetic Plains (Pradhan, 2009). The majority have adopted a Hindu Brahmin and Chettri identity, with a smaller population of Dalit occupational castes. They have since migrated across Nepal, and include the founders of the modern Gorkhali state, the Shah dynasty.

This division is however not necessarily clear cut, and Sharma (1978) notes a tendency for anthropologists and early western observers in Nepal such as Francis Buchannan Hamilton to over-emphasise the cultural fault lines between 'tribal' and 'Hindu' societies. The boundaries are blurred by historic inter-marriage between hill Adivasi, Khas and Rajputs (which led to various changes in social and caste status), and two-way exchange of cultural and social practices (Sharma, 1978, 1977). Furthermore, during the peak of Nepal's ethnic federalism debate in the 2000s and 2010s, some Nepali speaking Chettris and even Brahmins claimed 'indigenous' identity as *Adivasi* or *mulbāsi* (original inhabitants) (Adhikari and Gellner, 2016). Another complexity in the division emerges from the historical evidence that some hill communities which today identify as Chettris from the Khas community, particularly in the mid and far west, were once integrated into an agrarian system and culture with closer resemblance to that of South Asia's tribal or 'Adivasi' communities than their caste Hindu counterparts in the plains (see Luintel, 2013). Sharma (1978) in this context, prefers to consider Khas society historically as a 'transitional', with

---

suggests that all of the groups outside the Kathmandu valley were known collectively as 'Bhota', by the Sanskritized inhabitants of the valley who would later be known as Newar. This included communities who are today known as Tamang.

¹⁰ While the Newar of the Kathmandu valley are also considered janajati/adivasi, the historical mode of production within which they were integrated is quite different from both other Adivasi domains of the hills and Nepali speaking caste Hindu communities, and thus this region is not included in our conceptualisation of Adivasi domains (see discussion below).

communities differentially situated on a continuum from 'Hindu' to 'tribal' depending on the temporal-spatial context.

Bearing in mind this complexity and fluidity – when we refer to Adivasi modes of production in the hills, we are referring to an economic formation, as discussed above, dominated by collective rather than individualised relationships with land, with itinerant livelihoods oriented around by shifting cultivation or transhumant agro-pastoralism, as well as a relatively egalitarian social structure, with collective labour and some redistribution of surplus. While this is commonly associated with the Tibeto-Burmese ethnicities in the hills, we argue that the mode of production has much deeper roots in the human landscape of the Himalaya and many communities identifying as Hindu 'castes' today, may have at some point in the past been part of this mode of production. Indeed the transition from 'tribe' to 'caste' alongside the process of Hinduisation has been a common phenomenon in the history of Nepal (Whelpton, 2005) and of South Asia more widely (Beteille, 1980).

This economic formation stands in contrast to the modes of production which are oriented around sedentary cultivation on fixed plots of land. The latter includes localised feudalism dominated by rent paying tenants, or the centralised feudalism of the state involving tax paying peasant proprietors[11]. It also includes (in later years) an independent peasant mode of production whereby owner-cultivating peasants retain their own surplus. While the above three sedentary modes of production are more commonly associated with caste Hindu populations, we accept that most indigenous groups have up until today become part of both.

The Kathmandu valley – a system apart

While the Kathmandu valley is not a focus of this book, it is worth touching upon the unique agrarian history of this region – to highlight how it stands apart from the rest of the hills. The valley has a very long history of centralised state formations dating back to the Lichhavi era from

---

[11] While Adivasi mode of production may still involve payment of tribute to a feudal state, as will be shown, this is generally more limited and they often retain relative political and economic autonomy.

400 to 750 AD, characterised by a hierarchical social formation. In the Lichhavi era, agriculture was sedentary, and there was even evidence of animals being used for ploughing as well as dams and canals for irrigation. In terms of the relations of production, land was all owned by the state, although there were three systems of tenure (Yadav, 1986). The first was land belonging to the monarchy. The second was land linked to religious organisations, which often included land used for public utilities – a possible precursor to the *guthi* land system prevalent in Nepal even today. The third was land belonging to a peasant proprietor/title holder, who would pay tax to the state.

The mode of production was hierarchical in character, with a large landlord and aristocratic class – many of whom had received land grants. There were emerging concepts of private property – although the degree to which ownership was private, or still bestowed ultimately to the state is debated (Yadav, 1986). Sharma (2015) suggests that land was owned ultimately by the state, and also provided the administration its primary source of income through taxation. It was only around the time of the 12th century that individuals were able to buy and sell land. There was some continuity in this agrarian system under the Newar Malla kings who ruled the valley in the 12th - 18th century (Regmi, 1976). The mode of production was almost certainly feudal in character, as described elsewhere (Narayan, 1986), with the combination of centralised (tax paying peasant proprietors) and localised (rent paying tenants) forms, although there were complexities also due to the important role of religious institutions and *guthi* tenure which operated differently from both. Also of note was the complex role of caste and lineage in shaping access to the means of production. Given the uniqueness of the Kathmandu valley and the much wider range of documentary sources – it could merit an entire study in its own right and there are indeed extensive studies on the agrarian, cultural and economic history of this region (Sharma, 2015, Raj, 2010, Gellner and Quigley, 1995). Much of the subsequent analysis will therefore focus on the regions outside of the valley which would later be subsumed within the emerging state of Nepal.

Western Nepal: Transition from Adivasi to peasant mode of production

Immediately prior to the Gorkhali conquest, Nepal was made up of a cluster of fragmented political domains, these included the Malla city states of the Kathmandu valley, and the Sen Kingdoms of Makwanpur, Vijayapur and Chaudandi in the east. Further west Nepal was fragmented into two intermittently allied clusters of petty kingdoms – including the Chaubisi Rajya (24 kingdoms)[12] (amongst which is the older Sen state of Palpa), which took up much of the Gandaki basin, and the Baise Rajya, or (22 kingdoms), which took up much of the Karnali, Bheri and Mahakali basins (Vaidya, 2020).

However, the Baise Rajya in the west, which spanned from the 15th to 18th centuries and makes up much of what we refer to as the western hills, was built upon an older state formation. This was the much larger Khasa empire from the 11th to 14th century (see Figure 5), centred on Sinja of Jumla (Vaidya, 2020, Campbell, 1978), which extended at points to include a large swathe of the western Himalaya (Bista, 1991). There is some evidence that prior to the development of this empire, the Khas people were part of a more egalitarian agrarian system, akin to the Adivasi mode of production described above. Luintel (2013) suggests that this included an absence of caste stratification, as well as shifting cultivation and transhumance (seasonal movement between summer pastures and villages). It was suggested that Khas farmers produced millet, wheat and corn rather than rice (see Figure 6), and lands near rivers (which could be irrigated) were often uncultivated (Cameron, 1998b). The Khas likely practiced an indigenous religion oriented around clan deities[13].

However, the development of the Khasa empire, which was in the centre of trans-Himalayan trade networks, changed this. Around this time, high altitude paddy was introduced, (supposedly from Kashmir) in the 13th or 14th century, which depended upon terracing and fixed fields.

---

[12] Which included the older Palpa branch of the Sen dynasty.

[13] It has been suggested that Khas followed an indigenous religion, with evidence provided by contemporary ritual practices of Nepal's Chettris, including veneration of clan or family tutelary deities and the use of shamans (Bista, 1991).

Figure 5: The Sinja valley of Jumla (2008). While today this is a peripheral region, it was once the centre of the vast Khasa empire

Photo: Fraser Sugden

Figure 6: Millet production in Dolpa. Many of the so called Matwali Chettri in the higher altitude locales were dependent traditionally on rainfed cultivaiton, particulalry of coarse grains

Photo: Fraser Sugden

This intensified the sedentarisation of agriculture, as well as differentiation grounded in ownership of land (Luintel, 2013)[14]. The drive to clear lowland valleys for agriculture may have been intensified by environmental pressures, given the drier climate and poorer soils in the western hills, particularly the Karnali.

As noted above, while the original Khas population had moved into these hills from further west and likely assimilated with local Adivasi (possibly Tibeto-Burmese speaking) groups before the emergence of the Khas kingdom (Fortier, 1995), they also absorbed migrants from the plains (Pradhan, 2009, Campbell, 1978). It has long been suggested that the latter includes upper castes such as Brahmins and Rajputs fleeing the Muslim conquest (Cameron, 1998b, Bista, 1991, Mishra, 1987)[15], who went on to hold positions of political power within the Malla state (Stiller, 1975).

Brahmin and Rajput migrants were generally welcomed in the domains where they settled due to their social rank and talents in statecraft, and they integrated into Khas society, adopting the language which would become Nepali while retaining their caste identity (Ibid.). Importantly, it has been speculated that this migration contributed to Sanskritization of the pre-existing Khas population and Pradhan (2009) suggests that the Khas were fully under Brahmanical influence by the 13th century, with the Khas empire utilising Brahmin priests (Campbell, 1978). Upper caste migrants also brought with them occupational castes, supporting the formation of a caste system in the western hills (Cameron, 1998b), which would later extend across Nepal.

---

[14] Although Cameron (1998b) suggests that paddy and associated irrigation techniques were brought by migrants from the plains. See discussion on cropping systems below.

[15] The topic of Rajput identity is controversial. There had been a tendency for the Thakuri Chettris (who went on to become the kings of Nepal) to claim Rajput descent, although some anthropologists such as Bista (1991) suggest that these claims were for the purpose of enhancing the status of the ruling clan – suggesting instead that most Chettris in Nepal were Khas pursuing an indigenous religion, who slowly underwent a process of Hinduization. These processes will thus always be open to debate.

Part of the process of Sanskritization of the older Khas population entailed the latter taking on Chettri (Kshatriya) caste identities (Stiller, 1975, Sharma, 1977). How this was realised in practice is unclear, but Sharma (1978) suggest the Chettri family title was often adopted following the marriage between a local person of lower social rank with a Brahmin or Thakuri (an identity later used by those who claim Rajput descent). Regardless of the mechanisms through which it took place, it is evident that most of the pre-existing Khas were integrated into the caste system (largely via adopting Chettri identity) throughout the medieval period. The 'Chettri' subgroup further swelled in subsequent centuries with intermarriage between various Adivasi[16] and upper caste groups (Sharma, 1978).

The limited evidence suggests that the Khasa kingdom was feudal, like the later Gorkhali state, appropriating a share of the agricultural surplus from the peasantry as tax. The land grant charter of the kingdom mention various kinds of taxes, which were collectively known as *Chattiskar*, (or 'thirty six taxes') (Adhikari, 1988). As occurred in the lowlands, a tax appropriation apparatus generally depends upon a network of intermediaries – thus driving social stratification – and this may have intensified the differentiation of the now largely sedentary peasantry.

Evidence of this shift can be observed in the Karnali basin today, whereby the so called *matawali* Chettris or *pawai*, identify as Chettri and are now classified as *Khas Arya* under the new constitution, yet reside at a higher altitude, and participate in a culture and agrarian system which is more akin to Adivasi groups. This includes a dependence on rainfed agriculture and transhumance, and veneration of folk deities such as *Masto* (Luintel, 2013, Campbell, 1978). It has been suggested by Luitel (2013) that this represents the pre-12th century culture and economy of the Khas prior to the emergence of the Khasa kingdom. Due to their residence at higher altitudes in more remote locales beyond the rice growing belt, where there is abundant land for pastoralism, they had been partially insulated from the process of sedentarisation, stratification and

---

[16] There is evidence that the adoption of Chettri title extended to inter-marriage with Tibeto-Burmese speaking communities such as the Magar in later years (Sharma, 1977, 1978).

Hinduization which the Khas experienced in the lower valleys (Luintel, 2013). They could be considered therefore not a separate ethnic group, but a sub-set of the Khas who had not undergone the same levels of assimilation into the Hindu fold and feudal society (Campbell, 1978).

The Khas kingdom disintegrated around the 16th century (Bista, 1991), with much of it becoming part of the loosely aligned Baise Rajya (22 principalities). The Malla state itself was made up of smaller princedoms, and the Rajputs, who held power at a local level, tended to strengthen these smaller polities (Stiller, 1975). This contributed to an inherent trend for fragmentation of political entities, due to tension between local nobility and central overlords (Ibid). It was Rajputs therefore, who founded many of the emerging petty kingdoms (Cameron, 1998b).

It is probable that there was some continuity in the land taxation system of the Khasa kingdom by the Baise Rajya principalities, with a similar mode of production on the ground. With the exception of the *Pawai* domains, much of the western hills was home to a form of feudalism oriented around sedentary peasant proprietors paying tribute to the state. Adhikari (1988) notes that land taxes used to be the main source of revenue for the principalities across western Nepal, and would have been the primary form of surplus appropriation. Tax was usually a share of the harvest, although at times it may have included cash (Regmi, 1972), and the peasantry had a range of other tribute obligations to pay to the local nobility (Subedi, 1998). In addition to the regular land tax known as *kut*, there was a tax called *mauni*, which was levied on seasonal agricultural produce such as vegetables and fruits (Adhikari, 1988). The peasantry were also expected to contribute *jhara* or unpaid labour tribute, to work on the lands of the nobility or to build defences (Stiller, 1975, Fortier, 1995).

Interestingly, Regmi (1972), suggests that unlike the central and eastern hills, farmers were recognised as the de facto owners of their plots – suggesting that the Khas heartlands of the western hills were one of the first parts of Nepal to have a proto private property regime. Records report an active market for land in Dullu and Dailekh prior to the Gorkha conquest, with sale and mortgage of plots becoming widespread (Regmi,

1972). Regmi suggests that the legacy of the unification of these regions under the Khas kingdom supported this development of property rights across the west. Some of the peasantry could even therefore have been considered as what we may term today owner cultivators, although as surplus was still drained away as tax, the mode of production was still fundamentally a form of centralised feudalism.

There may have been more localised forms of feudalism also via classic landlord-tenant relations, with Regmi (1978d) suggesting that there was a notable landed class, and widespread tenancy in the Baisi Rajya region by the late 18th century. Government directives from the late 18th century, shortly after the Gorkhali conquest refer to some landlords as *zamindars*, like their counterparts in the Tarai (Regmi, 1972). In the Karnali region for instance, there were multiple types of land, which facilitated the emergence of a landed class. *Aalo* was irrigated paddy land owned and cultivated by the peasantry. Rajibar was land cultivated by the peasantry by paying a tax to the king. *Birhauto* refered to newly cleared land, usually claimed by clearing the forest, where land taxes were waived for the first five years (likely to encourage expansion of the cultivated area). *Gaucharan* referred to grazing land for domestic animals, while *banbutyan* was forest and shrub land (Subedi, 1998). However, there was also land bestowed to powerful individuals. *Sero* was untaxable irrigated land owned or used by the King or royal family. The local peasantry would be expected to work on this land and harvest the crops for them as labour tribute. However, there was also *birta* - untaxable land which was donated by the king or nobility to political elites, including Brahmins (see also Adhikari, 1988) and *guthi*, which was (like today) trust land which was under the ownership of temples, and was also un-taxed. Tenants on these lands were obligated to not only pay rent, but also provide corvée (labour tribute) to landlords. In the case of Guthi land, the one who cultivated the land (usually tenant farmers) had to pay some rent, usually the grain, to the temples or the caretakers of the trust (Ibid.).

Regmi (1972) notes that the emergence of private property rights meant that it was in the interests of powerful families to accumulate large holdings, including wasteland (Regmi, 1972). This suggests that even economically powerful families who had not received 'grants' may have been able to accumulate land later through purchase.

A unique feature of the Western Hills in the decades preceding the Gorkha conquest was the relatively high levels of monetisation (Regmi, 1978). Cash was not only a medium through which to buy, sell and mortgage land, wages on state projects would also be paid in cash. For instance, the construction of the Royal Palace in Jumla in 1751 required a sum of Rs9000 – which was raised through a cash levy, while workers were paid in cash and cloth (Regmi, 1972).

The Central and Eastern hills

Co-existence of Centralised feudalism and Adivasi mode of production

In the central and eastern hills, the population composition, which included a large share of Nepal's Tibeto-Burmese speaking ethnic groups, meant that Adivasi modes of production likely played a much more critical role in the agrarian history of the region. Having said that, it would have coexisted with sedentary farming by peasant proprietors. This emerged in the context of considerable westward migration of Nepali speaking castes (Khas Chettris, Rajputs, Brahmins and occupational castes), into the central hill region between the 13th and 16th centuries, driven by the poorer soils, drier climate and rugged terrain in their homeland in the far west of the country (Pradhan, 2009). Evidence of this migration can be observed in the split in Nepali language between the earlier variant spoken in the Khas heartland in the Sinja region of Jumla, and the contemporary version of the language which is the dominant dialect in Nepal today. This variant developed amongst these settlers in the central hills (Pradhan, 2009). Suggestions that the medieval Khasa empire once extended to Gorkha itself and even raided the Kathmandu valley in the 13th century under king Jitara Malla (Shah, 1989), may also contextualise this eastward movement of the Nepali speaking castes (Campbell, 1978). The extent to which the migration of the Nepali speaking castes extended into eastern Nepal is not known, although past research generally acknowledges the presence of Khas and Rajput settlers and administrators in the former domains of the Sen kingdom in the east (e.g. Stiller, 1975; Pradhan 2009), which will be discussed below.

In the central hills, particularly the Gandaki basin, these settlers went on to establish the petty principalities of the Chaubisi Rajya (24 principalities), including the principality of Gorkha itself, which rose to become a regionally important state in the 16th century, and annexed several of the neighbouring principalities prior to conquering the rest of Nepal a century later (Pande, 2014). While these principalities were predominantly ruled by Brahmin, Rajput and Chettri castes, there is a suggestion that the Magar played an important role in some principalities – particularly in the military (Hitchcock, 1965).

The mode of production in the areas within the administrative reach of the state in these principalities, was dominated by a sedentary, tax paying independent peasantry under centralised feudalism. Rice appears to have been the dominant crop, cultivated in the lower valleys – although actual settlements were higher up given the prevalence of endemic malaria in the valleys[17]. Stiller (1975) suggests that ownership of land in the petty principalities belonged to the raja, and the peasant was simply a tenant who would pay them tax. They were also not bound to a particular plot as a serf, and were free to migrate or withdraw from farming – and the mobility of the peasantry contributed to a relative uniformity in living standards across regions. This implies there were some differences with the Baise Rajya further west, where private property rights appeared to have been established[18]. The state would also generate revenue from mines in

---

[17] Jesuit traveller Ippolito Desideri noted in the early 17th century in the hill country south of Kathmandu how rice was cultivated by the *parbatiya* (whether this refers specifically to Khas or was used as a general term for hill people isn't known), although he noted that the fever or *aul* (which today has been identified as malaria) was endemic and people would avoid the valleys at night as a result or would reside there only in the winter.

[18] Stiller (1975) refers to the Baise Rajya, Chaubisi Rajya and Sen principalities as a single entity in his analysis, which likely glosses over regional differences in land tenure. As noted above, Regmi (1972) cites evidence of a more fixed relationship between the peasant and his plot, including private property rights, in his discussion of the Baise Rajya, when compared to the principalities further east. This would imply that Stiller's assertion of full state ownership of land is more relevant to the Chaubisi

the territories, as well as appropriating revenue on land and forest products from Tarai territories that they controlled (Ibid.).

While the tax paying sedentary peasantry in the central hills were likely disproportionately from the Hindu Khas, Brahmin and Thakuri population who settled in these emerging principalities, it is likely that some Adivasi groups within these domains such as southern Magar communities had become settled tax paying peasant farmers also (Hitchcock, 1965), unlike their swidden farming counterparts in more remote northerly areas. This is backed up by Regmi (1978d) who reported that the agrarian system in large tracts of the Chaubisi Rajya (those within strong administrative reach of the state) consisted primarily of small peasants who were sedentary self-cultivators of allotted paddy lands. Customary laws ensured that peasants had access to land so long as they paid the relevant rents or tributes to local landlords or the nobility (Regmi, 1978d).

There was a landed class with political power – for instance, the so called *Tharghar* in the Gorkha kingdom, referring to upper caste landlords from six clans, who supported local administration (including keeping check on the power of the generals and judges who were all from the ruling family) (Warner, 2014). Regmi (1972) suggests that within the common peasantry, there was relatively equitable distribution of holdings across the central hill principalities given the high rates of taxation and limited market for land. Nevertheless, subdivisions of plots within families, and the ability of larger families to mobilise labour to clear new fields would have contributed to some differentiation over time. Regmi suggests though that this differed from the western hills and central Tarai-Madhesh, where as noted above, lands could be held as private property, regardless of need (Ibid.). In the Chaubisi Rajya, there were also land grants in the form of *birta* (tax free grant) or *jagir* (land paid as salary, generally to the military) in some locales (Stiller, 1975). These two tenure systems will be described in more detail later on.

Rajya, including the state of Gorkha which went on to apply this land ownership system across Nepal. This may have also applied to the principalities under the Sen dynasty.

There was some monetisation of economic relationships also in the domains of the central hills within the reach of the state – although perhaps not to the same extent as in the west (Regmi, 1972). This included payment of tax in cash, but also included a rise in money lending. The rise in usury meant that King Ram Shah of the Gorkha principality enacted legislation to limit the interest on cash loans to 10%. Whether cash was minted locally or originated in the Malla city states or India, is not known (Ibid.). There is also a dearth of knowledge as to whether there was a market in land – although Regmi (1972), suggests it was far more limited than in the western hills.

Whether the contact between Khas in these emerging principalities and Adivasi polities, resulted in subordination of the latter at this early stage is unclear. Messerschmidt (1976) notes for instance that while the Gurung had been in contact with Khas migrants since at least the 15th century, they tended to populate different agro-ecological zones on the northern or higher altitude fringe of the new principalities – and thus political autonomy and indigenous livelihood systems such as shifting cultivation persisted. This likely applied to many other areas of the central hills home to Adivasi communities, and the associated Adivasi mode of production will be discussed at length below. However, some Gurung, like their Southern Magar counterparts described above, started cultivating lower valley land as sedentary peasants and producing paddy long before the Gorkha conquest (Messerschmidt, 1976).

The history of state formations to the east of the Kathmandu valley is hazier, particularly prior to the 16th century. More powerful states before this included the Newar principality of Dolakha (Shah, 1989), and beyond this in the eastern hills was the Koch Vijayapur kingdom (Subedi, 2005, Pradhan, 2009). However, while the latter appeared to have administrative control over parts of the lowlands, it has been suggested that the Kirat communities of the hills maintained autonomy, being ruled by chieftains or *Hang* for the Vijayapur kings – known as *Dewan* or *Roy* to the rulers (Subedi, 2005).

Like in the Tarai, after the fall of Vijayapur in 1609, the Sen dynasty was to later form one of the largest state formations in the pre-Gorkha era – and the hill territory from Kathmandu eastwards was split into three branches of the dynasty – one in Makwanpur, one in Chaudandi in Udayapur and another in Vijayapur in the far east. The Sens likely had control over the southern part of the hills around their respective capitals and in proximity to the important trading towns such as Chainpur (Hamilton (2007[1819]). Areas of the north were under Tibetan influence, and there was nominal overlordship by Sikkim for the far eastern region of Pallo Kirat or 'Limbuwan' (Pradhan, 2009). The presence of Khas, Rajputs and Brahmins in the Sen administration, as noted above (Pradhan, 2009; Stiller, 1975) implies that the same upper caste groups ruling the Chaubisi and Baise Rajyas also held dominance in the Sen controlled principalities, and both Stiller (1975) and Pradhan (2009) suggested that some of these castes who had settled in the region, unhappy with the political control locally exercised by the non-Hindu Kirat, went on to later support the Gorkha invasion[19].

The mode of production in areas under the control of the eastern Sen rulers paralleled the Chaubise Rajya, and Stiller (1975) suggests that the state was the ultimate landowner, with a tax paying peasantry. The *dewan* was in charge of revenue collection, and this post was the most lucrative in the government. Under the *dewan* a *subba* was placed in charge of each revenue collection unit in the hills, supported by *zamindars* who received a land grant for their services as well as the right to cultivate additional waste land without a further tax burden (Ibid.).

Like in the Chaubise Rajya, Hamilton (2007 [1819]) also makes reference to land grants to high-ranking members of the military under the Sen kingdom (as well as smaller principalities such as Dolakha[20]), which likely contributed to the formation of a landed class. *Jagir* grant

---

[19] This includes for instance Harinanda Upadhaya Pokhrel, a Brahmin who clandestinely supported the Gorkhas. His forefathers had migrated from India to Dullu (Dailekh), before moving eastwards into the Sen domains where they worked as priests and received *birta* grants. He offered logistical and financial support to the Gorkha army, with promises of further land grants following their victory (Pradhan, 2009).

[20] The distribution of both tax free *birta* and *jagir* grants to the aristocracy was also reported with regards to the medieval Newar principality of Dolakha (Bajracharya and Shrestha, 1974), alongside a tax paying peasantry on other lands (with tax collected in cash from whole villages).

distribution, whereby an assignment of land was bestowed to members of the army in lieu of salary was widespread – and Hamilton suggests that large swathes of the territory in the lower hills was under this tenure system. Stiller (1975) suggested that regular soldiers, many of whom were Kirat[21], were also paid in *jagirs* and thus it was likely these were regular peasant plots rather than large estates. However, the *sardars* who were commanders in the army and who were responsible of distributing these holdings would keep a consignment of land for themselves (Hamilton, 2007 [1819]) and these would have been considerably larger than plots held by regular soldiers. Hamilton suggests that a lot of these *jagir* lands and other estates of functionaries were rented out to sharecroppers (Ibid.).

Pradhan (2009) is sceptical as to how many of the larger *jagir* and *birta* grants were offered in the hills, suggesting that most records of such bestowments were of Tarai lands to the south – even if they were bestowed to hill people. A more likely scenario however was that grants were given on the more fertile valley land within the administrative reach of the state.

Nevertheless, it is important to emphasise that the Sen kingdom was not a unitary entity. While some areas were directly under the control of the state as described by Stiller (1975), there were also areas which maintained relative political autonomy – most notably the Kirat[22] (Rai, Limbu and Sunwar) domains. Pradhan (2009) suggests that in spite of their important role in the Sen military, the Kirat had a high level of autonomy, aided by the fact that the priority of rulers at the time was control over a territory through strategic forts rather than full occupation. This meant that many communities beyond these centres of state power lived outside of the day-to-day administrative reach of the state and had limited contact with any political authorities other than their own tribal chiefs (Stiller, 1975; Gaenzle, 2000). Limbu and Rai chieftains continued to manage local affairs (Vansittart and Nicolay, 1915). Nevertheless, they

---

[21] English (1983) suggests that the Limbu were central to the Sen army in the Vijayapur state, yet in the Chaudandi state further west, the numerically dominant Rai had a more marginal role, with Magar making up a larger share of the military.

[22] Kirat is a collective term which refers to the three main indigenous ethnic groups in the eastern hills which share some cultural similarities – the Rai, Limbu and Sunwar.

still paid some kind of tribute to the state, and an indigenous *subba* was in charge of revenue collection (Pradhan, 2009). However, this was likely a relatively modest payment. In the North tribute was being paid to the Tibetan rajas rather than the Sens (see also Pradhan, 2009). The Sen state were happy to uphold this political and economic independence for the Kirat, as a compromise given their dependence upon them for military support (Gaenzle, 2000). It is likely therefore that much of the eastern hill country was under an Adivasi modes of production – and it is to this which we now turn.

Hill Adivasi mode of production: Shifting cultivation and transhumant agro-pastoralism

It is now time to understand in greater detail, the Adivasi mode of production which likely prevailed across much of the eastern and large tracts of the central hills in the pre-Gorkha era. While there were similarities with the Adivasi mode of the Tarai, there were also unique features.

Like in the Tarai-Madhesh, shifting cultivation has been central to agriculture in hill Adivasi communities for generations, and has various local names, such as *khoriya*[23], *bhasme, lhose,* and occasionally *jhum* (in eastern Nepal) (Dhakal, 2002, 2000)[24]. The transition between shifting cultivation and sedentary terraced agriculture has been a near universal process in Nepal (and large swathes of upland South and Southeast Asia) throughout the last 300 years (going alongside the gradual dissolution of the larger Adivasi mode of production). At the time of the Gorkhali conquest, this form of agriculture would have been widespread across the Adivasi domains of the central and eastern hills. For instance, amongst the Kirat as of the mid-19th century Hodgson (1880 [1847])suggests that

---

[23] In this study, the local term *Khoriya*, and the general term shifting cultivation, are used often interchangeably.

[24] In the Nepali context, shifting cultivation, does not refer to crop shifting, i.e., a different crop being cultivated each year on the same plot, nor, the settlement shifting as in the case of nomads who keep on moving from one place to another finding new cultivation area along with the new settlement – it simply refers to the periodic movement of the cultivated area.

villages were fixed yet agriculture was mobile, with farmers clearing new fields once one area becomes exhausted. The plough was rarely used, and they would cultivate maize, buckwheat, millet, peas, dry rice and cotton.

As shifting cultivation persisted in remoter domains until well into the twentieth century (see Figure 7), there is reasonable literature which has touched upon the role of this form of cultivation in indigenous agricultural practices. Studies have covered hill Adivasi groups such as the Gurung (Messerschmidt, 1976) (Macfarlane, 1976), Limbu (Fitzpatrick, 2011b), Chepang (Sharma, 2011) and Rai (Gaenszle, 2000) and Sherpa[25] (Dhakal, 2000). While there is often a lack of clarity on the actual time periods when it was prevalent, it does give insights into how land and labour were managed, and how it related to the larger mode of production.

With regards to the Gurung of the central hills MacFarlane (1973) notes that traditionally a tract of land would be cleared by a family every nine years or so, with undergrowth cleared in March-April. It would be cultivated with millet or maize for a year, before it was left fallow to regenerate. Gurung (1996) suggests that amongst the Magar an area of land would be cultivated every twelve years.

The length of the cycles would have been highly variable across the hills due to differences in the availability of land and prevalence of alternative livelihood activities. For instance, there were relatively short cycles amongst the Tamang of the central hills as described by Hodgson in the mid-19th century (cf. Fricke, 1984). After three to four years of farming the land (or longer for more productive plots), Hodgson suggests that the vegetation would be allowed to restore for around two years, after which it would be burnt and cultivated again with crops such as maize, millet, buckwheat, dal potatoes and yams. A tax (thek) of 1-10 rupees was paid for areas cultivated (Ibid.). Macfarlane (1973) suggests that the cycle was longer for the Gurung as they had alternative livelihoods from sheep and hunting, (later to be replaced by army recruitment income from mid-19th century), meaning that land could be used less intensively. Dhakal

---

[25] Stevens (1996) suggests that the Sherpa who originally were engaged in high altitude agro-pastoralism, adopted shifting cultivation from neigbouring Rai and other communities as the population spread south into the hills.

Figure 7: Fields used for shifting cultivation by the Chepang community in Gorkha in the early 2000s. Shifting cultivation or swidden was once central to Adivasi livelihoods.

Photo: Suresh Dhakal

(2000) also suggests that the Sherpa in the upper Arun would traditionally cultivate on 12 year cycles. It is worth noting that *khoriya* cultivation generally had ritual or spiritual significance (Dhakal, 2000). Sharma (2011) for instance notes how amongst the Chepang, the land used for khoriya is associated with the ancestors and is worshiped once a year through *bhumipooja*.

Alongside shifting cultivation, Adivasi communities were also simultaneously engaged in various forms of pastoralism on lands to which they held customary rights. This often took the form of transhumance, whereby families would move their herds between different altitudinal zones according to the season. Transhumant pastoralism is traditionally associated with high Himalayan communities such as the Sherpa, or those residing in the trans-Himalaya, as part of an agroecological economy. Stevens (1996) refers to this as high altitude agropastoralism. Under this system the main settlements are above 3000m, generally in high glacial valleys which are partially sheltered from the full force of the monsoon.

Most agricultural production would also take place in this domain – which is limited to hardy crops such as barley, buckwheat, and potatoes. Herds, of mainly yak or yak-cow cross breeds, known in different parts of Nepal as *dzo/dzomo, chauri* or *chamri,* would travel up to high pastures above 4000m during the summer (Ibid.).

However, transhumance is also widespread historically in the hills where the majority of Nepal's upland Adivasi communities reside, as part of a system Stevens (1996) refers to as middle altitude agropastoralism. The herding of livestock such as sheep, buffalo goats or cattle on more marginal land was combined with the production of crops such as millet, maize (and later, rice or wheat) (Stevens, 1996). For livestock, many hill Adivasi communities would make use of the high ridges or *lekhs* in the summer, often at altitudes of between 2500 and 4000m, in the high rainfall transitional zone between the hills and mountains. Naturally, the groups who practice this were most commonly those residing at higher altitudes. This includes the Kham Magar who live in the northern upper altitudes in the central hills, and the Gurung (Messerschmidt, 1976), and Kulunge Rai (MdDougal, 1979). For the Gurung and even some Limbu, Hodgson, writing in the 19th century suggested that transhumant farming, particularly of sheep, known as *barwal*, was central to livelihoods (Hamilton, 2007 [1819]). This went alongside shifting cultivation, and some cultivation of fixed rainfed fields (Messerschmidt, 1981a). The Gurung would reside in the summer in *goths* or seasonal pastures, producing ghee, wool (Ibid.) and cottage cheese (Hamilton, 2007 [1819]). Yak-Cow cross breeds were reportedly also herded by the Gurung, although this was abandoned with Sanskritization (Messerschmidt, 1976). However, yak and chauri/dzo husbandry has long been central to the culture of Tibetan influenced communities in central and eastern hills, such as the Yolmo of Sindupalchok (Bishop, 1989) and the Sherpa of the eastern hills (as noted above). Hunting would have also historically been an important livelihood activity for hill Adivasi (Russel, 1992, Macfarlane, 1976).

Associated with an agricultural system grounded in shifting cultivation or semi-itinerant pastoralism, is the lack of a concept of private land ownership, although rather than land being de facto common property, as was described with regards to the Tarai Adivasi groups such as the Dhimal, it appears that most of the hill region had some customary delineation of 'boundaries' with regards to the rights to use land. Communal customary ownership appears more common – with rights to cultivating a set territory of land being linked to one's clan or lineage.

With regards to the central hills there has been limited in-depth research on communal tenure, but it has been documented amongst the Magar (Gurung, 1996), Gurung (Macfarlane, 1976), Tamang (Tamang, 2009) and Chepang (Sharma, 2011). Importantly, communal land denoted a territory rather than specific fields, often bounded by a watershed or a ridge. It would include both forest and farmland, and all members would have rights to exploit the natural resources in each domain. Gurung (1996), with regards to the Magar, notes how access to this communal land for non-clan members could only be secured through marriage. Clan leaders would allocate different areas of land to different clan sub-groups, and individuals were expected to fulfill communal obligations for the clan. These included communal labour regimes, mobilized by the sub-groups to support *khoriya* or shifting cultivation (see below).

Customary tenure has been most rigorously documented amongst the Kirat communities of the eastern hills, including the Sunwar (Egli, 2000), Rai (Gaenszle, 2000, McDougal, 1973) and Limbu (Caplan, 1970). This is likely because communal tenure remained in place for far longer in the east, and was for a period, legally recognised by the state after the Gorkhali conquest, under a system which would become known as *kipat* (Pradhan, 2009). Amongst the Kirat communities of eastern Nepal, wasteland and un-cleared forest as well as cultivated land around a community were all considered as the inalienable property of the clan, and under customary law could not be sold (Regmi, 1965).

Amongst the Rai for instance (Gaenszle, 2000, McDougal, 1973) and Limbu (Sagant, 1996), most of the land in the vicinity of a village was under the customary collective ownership by the clan. Bearing in mind that there was considerable internal migration within the hills, due to population pressure in particular domains, or for political and security reasons, Kirat clans were regularly being fragmented, as new areas of communal land for agriculture were established (Caplan, 1970, McDougal, 1973). As Caplan discusses with regards to the Limbu in Ilam, the 'first settlers' to clear land in a previously uncultivated area would enjoy customary rights to use this land. Their descendants would continue to hold the rights to cultivate the land their forefathers cleared, but not other members of the clan living elsewhere. These localised rights for what Caplan (1970) terms 'local clan segments', would later be recognised by the state as *kipat* tenure following the Gorkha conquest – which will be discussed at length in later chapters.

There is some debate as to whether the land was under the chief's control rather than being held communally by the clan (Whelpton, 2000). Sagant (1996) suggests that the land settled historically by a particular clan segment was indeed owned collectively, and the headman or *subba* was responsible for managing these lands. Land would be allocated by the village chief to households which appeared to be the basic unit of production (Regmi, 1978). Sagant (1996) notes that should anyone want to clear some uncultivated forest land, the subba would be given a gift of liquor or meat, after which the household in question would choose the plot to be cleared – and could continue to do so indefinitely with rights passing on to the younger generation. It could be used for multiple purposes including shifting cultivation, pastoralism, and later, sedentary agriculture (Gaenszle, 2000). How this household level allocation of land operated in the context of shifting cultivation is not clear, although Sagant (1996) notes that if a plot taken by a household for cultivation reverted to forest, then the *subba* could reacquire it into the collective lands of the clan, for later reassignment. It may be therefore, that households would receive rights to use the land for one cycle (generally a few years), after which it would return to the clan. Pastures however, were managed communally. Pasturelands or fisheries resources were allocated not at a household level, but clan segments themselves had usufruct rights (Sagant, 1996).

The rules over who could access customary lands were not clear cut and there appeared to be some fluidity. With reference to the Athpahariya Rai in Dhankuta, Dahal (1981) notes that because some clans had surplus land, other sub-groups could be integrated into the clan and provided land, to maintain the size of the collective unit. For instance, Dahal reports how a Yakkha Rai who had migrated over a century ago was integrated into an Athpahariya clan segment.

Other ethnic groups who lived in or had migrated to the area, could also make use of communal land, often for payment of a tribute, as described by McDougal with reference to the Sherpa and Gaenszle (2000) with regards to Tamang, who lived adjacent to Rai domains. In both cases the Sherpa and Tamang inhabited a different agro-ecological niche at higher altitudes, and thus competition for resources did not appear to be a critical issue.

These higher altitude communities likely had their own form of customary tenure, although it is not well documented in the literature. The Sherpa for instance, resided not only in the high Himalayan valleys, but gradually spread across the high ridges of eastern Nepal throughout the last few centuries – even before the Gorkha conquest. They also carried out shifting cultivation, which they likely adopted from their Rai neighbours (Stevens, 1996). While there is limited documentation of the land tenure regime, the lands used for transhumant pastoralism of *chauri* or yak-cow cross breeds and other livestock which was important to their livelihoods, appears to have had some form of customary rights (March, 1977). Stevens (1996) suggests that communal rights to pastures were held by both Sherpa and Rai in the Dudh Koshi basin, and Rai could make use of Sherpa pastures on payment of tribute, and vice versa.

It appears that communal tenure and the larger Adivasi mode of production retained relative stability, even as Adivasi groups were integrated into various kingdoms of the pre-Gorkhali era. As noted above, the Kirat retained a large degree of autonomy across eastern Nepal. This also applied to areas of the central hills. Under the Galkot Rajya in Baglung for instance, the Magar retained political and economic autonomy, and continued to farm under customary tenure. Likewise, the Thami of Dholakha paid tax to the Newar Principality of Dolakha, while simultaneously operating their own communal lands (Shneiderman, 2010).

Hill Adivasi mode of production: redistributive ethos and collective labour

One of the clearest parallels of the Adivasi mode of production in the hills when compared with the forested plains was the communal character of this economic formation - most notable of which was the centrality of the clan with a strong ethos of reciprocity, regulated by customary institutions; and, also manifested in the ritualized processes. As Holmberg (2017, 11) notes with regards to the Tamang:

> "Tamang, like many other Tibeto-Burman speaking groups in Nepal, organised relations among themselves and with outsiders primarily according to an ethos, mentioned above, of symmetrical reciprocity, where if you give something, you can expect something of equal value in return. Internally, Tamang were organised into clans and these clans regulated their relations through marriage and these clans had equal status with each other".

As noted above with regards to the Tarai-Madhesh, there were of course some hierarchies within Adivasi society, including not only clan chiefs, but also the stratification associated with proto-state formations, with some clan heads recognised 'kings'[26]. These have been documented amongst the Tamang by Mukta Tamang (2008) who identified 12 Tamang principalities in the northern part of the central hills which fell to the Gorkhas between the late 17th and mid-18th century, bonded together by networks of reciprocal exchange. While there may have been some form of tribute paid to 'kings' and accumulation of surplus, more complex administrative systems were at an emergent stage (see Figure 8) and it was primarily ritual activity which held these polities together (Ibid.).

The important point however, is that within Adivasi society, there is also strong evidence of redistributive mechanisms which moderated the 'accumulation' of surplus (Fricke and Teachman, 1993). Macfarlane (1976), emphasises an ethic of redistribution amongst the Gurung, with social functions and gift giving acting as a mechanism to redistribute

---

[26] For instance, the 12 Tamang principalities were headed by *gyālbo-chyungi* (which translates as the circle of twelve kings) (Tamang, 2008).

wealth. Added to this was a cultural disdain for hoarding wealth i.e. the 'richer' one is, the greater the cultural pressure to share. He gives examples for instance, as to how even at the time of fieldwork in the 1960s, expensive agricultural equipment would be recognised as the property of the community rather than an individual – being readily lent out to those in need. Dahal (1981) similarly notes with regards to the Rai in Dhankuta, that it is a social obligation rather than maximisation of profit which determines what happens to any surplus. For instance, under the 19th century *kipat* system (although this likely predates it), a clan member wishing to cultivate a tract of land needed to pay a fee to the headman known as *kosheli* (English, 1983). This would be redistributed within the clan.

It is worth noting in this context, that while most Adivasi communities would have a traditional leader or headman – due to this redistributive

Figure 8: Ruins of Gol Dzong in Rasuwa, one of 12 forts home to the pre-Gorkha conquest Tamang rulers. Conquered by Prithvi Narayan Shah in 1774.
Photo: Kathryn March and David Holmberg (reproduced with permission)

ethos, there is limited evidence that they accumulated significant wealth. Any cornering of surplus was more likely linked to ritual activity – such as the expectations of raised bride price or higher value gifts during marriages, as shown by Dahal (1981) with regards to the Athpahariya Rai. This wealth would also be frequently redistributed through community functions or other ritual events (Ibid.). At various points in history this was supported by the fact that there were limited ways to dispose of a 'surplus' in the first place, given that there was a limited market for commodities or land – meaning investments to reproduce one's social or ritual status were prioritised (Macfarlane, 1976). It is worth noting that there were some other forms of stratification beyond that associated with political authority. For instance, amongst the Gurung, there were two hierarchical classes, which were broken into multiple exogenous clans. While there were some wealth differences between them, within each clan there was often relative equality (MacFarlane, 1976).

Communal labour appears to have also been an important aspect of Adivasi society. For instance *nogora* was a complex system of labour pooling amongst the Gurung (Messerschmidt, 1981b). Collective labour teams would operate for different periods of the agricultural year, for different agricultural tasks, as well as for reproductive activities such as wood and dung carrying. These would be organised by neighbourhood, and for agricultural tasks such as weeding of rice, they would be organised according to one's clan. This was helped by the fact that the lands of the clan tended to be close together (MacFarlane, 1976). Some forms of communal labour were organised by age group (Ibid). Amongst the Magar of Baglung, communal labour would be mobilized at a clan level to support *khoriya* or shifting cultivation. On agreement within the clan, they would cultivate specific tracts. Grain would be stored in communal granaries and distributed within the group – a system known as *mukhbaro laune*. Some communal hunting and gathering of forest produce took place alongside this (Gurung, 1996).

Cropping systems prior to the Gorkhali conquest

There is limited documentary evidence of the cropping systems in Nepal prior to the Gorkha conquest. It is very difficult to determine with assurance at which time or place – or in which form agriculture was first practiced in Nepal – given the limited archaeological research. Nevertheless, with some conjectural evidence, it can be assumed that the territory which was to become Nepal would have had its first agricultural communities around 3,000 BC, aligning with the development of agriculture on the Gangetic plain alongside Kashmir and other Himalayan regions that bordered Nepal in its south and west and shared a similar ecological context.

Different crops reached the territorial boundary of present-day Nepal from at least three frontiers. First, wheat, barley and some upland rice varieties from the west via Kashmir, rice from the southern plains, and millets and sorghums from the northern and possibly southern border. Thus, diffusion played an important role in the rise to world dominance of agricultural economies and the concepts of 'origins' and 'spread' are inseparably linked (Harris, 2020). The limited evidence on early cropping systems will be dealt with below in turn for the Tarai and hills respectively.

The introduction of agriculture and emergence of the rice and wheat cultivation in the plains

Plains-based kingdoms were arguably engaged in paddy cultivation for millennia. There was a long history of rice cultivation in South Asia which dates back to as early as 6000-8000 BC (Fuller et al., 2010), The rice complex, however, could have entered into the Tarai-Madhesh of Nepal around 3,000-2,500 BC, or even later, as it spread across the Gangetic plains – most likely beginning with the areas under sedentary cultivation in early Vedic kingdoms such as that of Videha. This assumption is largely based on the geographical proximity and ecological similarities with the areas where we have archaeological evidence of crop cultivation (Kajale, 1991). There is evidence of a well-established seasonal rice-wheat cropping pattern and sedentary cultivation on the Gangetic plains as early as 2000-1800 BC (Boivin et al., 2012, Fuller, 2011). While rice was certainly present in Nepal, wheat would have been dependent upon access to irrigation – which was very limited in the Tarai until at least the Rana era, as will be discussed below. It may have been produced in areas adjoining rivers, or where irrigation ponds had been constructed. However, it is unlikely to have been a major crop – and even as late as the 1960s a report from the Kailali and Kanchanpur suggested that wheat production was negligible in the plains (2.89% and 4.17% respectively of the cropped area) – and maize was in fact the major dry season crop (Rana, 1971).

In the Tarai-Madhesh, other than paddy, there was some evidence of sugarcane production historically, although there is no evidence that it was a major crop. Mangos were referred to frequently in Lichhavi era inscriptions dating from between 400 to 750AD (Yadav, 1986). Given that Kathmandu is unsuitable climatically for widespread Mango cultivation, it is likely that these were brought up from the lowlands, suggesting it was cultivated in the Tarai-Madhesh at the time. For the regions under shifting cultivation there is far less information – although amongst numerically dominant groups such as the Tharu, rice appeared to be also important, being cultivated through shifting cultivation in forest clearings (Guneratne, 2002). This may have included dry as well as wet rice (Muller-Boker, 1999). It is likely that coarse grains, roots and tubers also played an important role – although there has been virtually no research on this in the Tarai. Hamilton (2007 [1809]), writing shortly after the Gorkha conquest made an interesting observation that foraging by wild elephants during the monsoon discouraged the production of rice in some heavily forested parts of the Tarai, and farmers instead focused on dry season crops such as wheat, barley and mustard during the winter months when elephants retreated to the hills. He suggested that rivers were used to irrigate these crops.

Cropping systems in the hills and the mode of production

In the course of the evolutionary history of these crops in the hills in a diverse agro-ecological context, not only did the cultivation system develop locally unique characteristics, but so did the harvesting and crop-processing techniques and the ways in which land and labour was managed. Cultivators accumulated advanced indigenous knowledge suited to diverse local variables, including the local climate, land, soil, and terrain. Importantly, one cannot overstate the importance of the mode of production in the hills in shaping the historical evolution of cropping systems. Rice production in particular, is strongly associated with sedentary peasant production, which as indicated above, appeared to be present in much of western Nepal prior to the Gorkhali conquest. This cropping system is dependent upon the availability firstly of *besi khet*, the warmer water abundant fields in the valleys, and secondly on terracing and irrigation technologies (Dhakal, 1997). While paddy is produced in the monsoon, where water is available, it is followed by irrigated wheat for the drier winter months – a system known as a rice-wheat cropping system.

Meanwhile, shifting cultivation or *khoriya* which does not involve terracing, is unsuited for crops requiring irrigation such as wet rice or wheat, yet is associated with the cultivation of dry rice or ghaiya dhan, millets and other coarse grains. Even in areas of sedentary cultivation, such crops remained important beyond the rice growing zone on the dry fields today known as *bari*, which refers to land unsuitable for paddy (Dhakal, 1997).

The division between these two forms of agriculture, and their respective crops, have been perpetuated by divergence in ritual and symbolic aspects of cultivation. Gaenzle (2000) for instance emphasises the ritual significance of millet in Adivasi *kirat* culture in the eastern hills – a core crop of the *khoriya* cultivation cycles, in contrast with the importance of paddy for the incoming sedentary Hindu castes. Rice has been long of ritual importance to upper castes – but its production and the demand for paddy lands is also associated with the acquisition of social status (Hitchcock, 1974). This is due to the rule that Brahmins must not drive a plough. They therefore require land that is productive enough to yield a surplus so they can hire labourers who can be paid a share of the harvest (Ibid.).

Where there is less certainty is with regards to the dates at which these different cropping systems were introduced. We will now explore the limited literature on the history of these cropping systems.

History of rice and wheat production in the hills and terraced sedentary farming

With regards to rice, excavations in the Kathmandu valley dating back to the Licchavi era find evidence of rice grains, suggesting a long history of cultivation (Khanal and Riccardi, 1988). Paddy production was also mentioned frequently in Lichhavi era inscriptions. Land was reportedly measured according to how much paddy it produced, suggesting it has been a major crop by sedentary peasants in the Kathmandu valley for at least 1500 years (Yadav, 1986), just as it is today. Shortly after the Gorkha conquest, it was reportedly common for more than one harvest of rice to be produced in the lower valleys such as Nuwakot on terraced land irrigated by numerous springs (Kirkpatrick, 2007 [1793]).

Beyond the vicinity of Kathmandu however, rice production arguably had a more recent history, arriving with the westward migration of Hindu castes from the 13th century onwards. Its emergence in the western hills dates back to the Khas kingdom (Luintel, 2013). Much of the paddy was initially of the *marsi* variety locally produced in the Karnali up until today – a variety which is suitable for a cooler climate (Ibid.). It is believed that this variety was brought by the sage Chandan Nath from Kashmir in the 13th or 14th century. However, lowland varieties also came with migrants from the plains who brought new irrigable lands alongside rivers into cultivation (Cameron, 1998b). By the time of the Baise Rajya in the west, Subedi (1998) suggests that rice and wheat cultivation was well established. This was aided by the pressure to intensify production, whereby those who would leave the land fallow/barren would be penalized (Subedi, 1998). As noted above, paddy cultivation which depends upon terracing technologies spread eastwards as Khas settlers migrated beyond the confines of the old Khas kingdom into what would become the Chaubise Rajya, and the new more intensive cropping pattern supporting a rise in the population (Pande, 2014). Ramirez (2000 [cf. Aubriot, 2004]) suggested that control of paddy cultivation lands was important for the founding of pre-Gorkhali principalities such as Gulmi.

With regards to the history of wheat, this likely corresponds with rice, with cultivation, dating back to 400BC - 100 AD in the Himalayan region (Knörzer, 2000). It was cultivated during the Lichhavi era in Kathmandu valley (Yadav, 1986), and thereafter was planted widely in the Karnali during the Baise Rajya period, supporting a rice-wheat cropping cycle (Subedi, 1998).

While paddy in the hills can be produced without formal irrigation canals, with water being captured from rain and run-off in bund-divided fields, larger canal networks can significantly boost yields and bring new areas without a local water source under cultivation. Importantly though, canals are essential for wheat to be produced (Figure 9), as it is cultivated during the dry season. The emergence of the rice-wheat cropping cycle which is prevalent in parts of the hills today would have expanded along with the construction of irrigation infrastructure.

There is a long history of irrigation systems in the hills. There was reference to irrigation systems in Lichhavi era inscriptions in the Kathmandu valley (Yadav, 1986). Under the Malla era which followed, further irrigation systems were built by the kings (Raj Kulos), with

Figure 9: Wheat production in Bajhang in the height of the dry season (2012). This depends heavily on an extensive network of irrigation canals, and has a long history in the western hill region.

Photo: Fraser Sugden

complex management regimes (Knörzer, 2000). As well as irrigation canals, Kirkpatrick (2007 [1793]) refers to the extensive production of wheat and barley in the Tadi valley of Nuwakot shortly after the Gorkha conquest – which would suggest the presence of fixed irrigation canals. He also makes reference to other forms of hydrological infrastructure such as stone flood defences to protect the terraced fields from the floods of the Tadi river.

Irrigation also has a long history in the mid- and far- western regions, including the Karnali during the Baise Rajya period (Subedi, 1998). Subedi notes, "People in Karnali were keen on mining, digging irrigation canal and cultivating in the irrigated field, livestock raising, and cottage industries...they had cross-border trade relation with both India and China, with whom they used to barter their products" (pp29-31). Canals which were built include the Kalanga & Sunigadh canals in Bajhang; Jorail & Bogatan canals in Doti; Luham canal in Salyan; Patan canal in Baitadi, Sinja and Lamra canals in Jumla; Gamgadhi & Khumriphant canals in Mugu; Besi & Jahari canals in Rukum; Thalara Pikhet canal in Liwang, Rolpa; Lohoro and Dullu Padukasthan canal, Dailekh.

In the central hills, a number of irrigation systems were established by the kings of the Chaubisi Rajya (Aubriot, 2004), including the Raj Kulo (royal canal) of Argali built by Mukunda Sen of Palpa in the 16th century (Pradhan, 1990). Canals were also built by the rulers of the Newar principality of Dolakha during the medieval period (Bajracharya and Shrestha, 1974). Pradhan (1990) suggests that irrigation canals were built often to serve *guthi* lands associated with temples (including the Argali canal), whereby the water was used to maximise revenue for the shrine. Likewise, some were built by local elites and others by communities themselves. In central Nepal, Royal edicts by Ram Shah of Gorkha in the early 17th century also make reference to irrigation canals, making it clear that local disputes over irrigation had to be dealt with at a community level and without the involvement of the state authorities (Riccardi Jr, 1977). Pradhan (2000a) suggests this edict by the nascent Gorkha state, set the precedent for the many farmer managed irrigation systems, which dominate hill agriculture today.

Upland and unirrigated cropping systems

In large tracts of the hills including the upper valleys of the Karnali home to the so called Matwali Chettri or Pawai and the Adivasi domains of the central and eastern hills, non-terraced, rainfed farming was likely predominant. This was in part because the climate was unsuitable for rice, but more commonly because rice or wheat required terracing, irrigation and fixed fields, which was incompatible with the shifting cultivation which dominated the Adivasi mode of production. Kirkpatrick's (2007 [1793]) 18th century account from Kathmandu and Nuwakot points clearly to the emergence of parallel cropping systems dominated by irrigated *khet* lands, fixed *bari* fields and *khoriya* plots used for shifting cultivation. The latter fields were used for unirrigated dryland crops which could be grown on steeper slopes (in particular coarse grains such as millet, maize, and buckwheat as well as root crops like taro and dry rice) (Ibid.). These cropping systems likely persisted as part of a rainfed system, beyond the shift towards sedentary cultivation. The history of these major dry field crops will now be reviewed.

At some stage, dry rice or *ghaiya dhan* which is planted without bund separated fields or terraces, was adopted in the hills of Nepal and is associated traditionally with *khoriya* (shifting cultivation), grown on higher unirrigated fields (Hamilton, 2007 [1819]). In Kirkpatrick's travelogue from shortly after the Gorkhali conquest (2007 [1793]), he suggests that *ghaiya dhan*, and in particular, two varieties known as *towli* or *ikaro*, were major crops on the steep northern slopes of the Kathmandu valley. Other studies have suggested that *towli* cultivation is still widespread amongst Lohorung Rai communities in eastern Nepal and has important ritual significance (Adams, 2010)[27], suggesting that this has for many generations been an important crop.

While it has generally been produced under shifting cultivation on steep slopes, it was not restricted to such fields. For instance Hodgson reports the cultivation of *towli* by Newars on fertile ridgetop or plateau lands of present day Kavrepalanchok district (Hodgson, 1988 [1848]). It

---

[27] Adams (2010) notes that it plays an important role in the *nuagi* ceremony which has kept its cultivation alive.

was reportedly particularly suited to *tars* or elevated river terraces which lacked reliable irrigation (Ibid), alongside barley, millet and wheat. It has until relatively recently still been produced on *tars* (Joshi et al., 2001).

Other than *ghaiya dhan*, coarse grains likely dominated rainfed and swidden systems, including crops such as millet and sorghum. Like rice, the cultivation of these crops in Nepal likely dates back millennia. Millet and sorghum could have entered Nepal from its northern border, via Tibet, through the silk road. China had developed a direct trade route with Arabia by the third century AD. That was the trade route through which sorghum reached China (Kajale 1991:176). However, it could have also entered from the South. While finger millet originated in Africa, *kodo* millet, which is one of the most popular forms of millet in Nepal is a South Asian variety which was domesticated in India three millennia ago (House, 1995). Similarly the presence of sorghum (*sorghum bicolor*) appears to have been equally well established in South Asia for several millenia, with evidence that it was cultivated in Harappan sites at the Indus valley, dating back to ca 2000 BC. Haaland (1999) suggests that domestication of sorghum first occurred in Asia, and the intensified use of resources led to the cultivation of morphologically wild sorghum as early as the 6th millenium.

Other coarse grains with a long history in Nepal include buckwheat and barley. Archaeological excavations in the Jhong Valley (3000-4000m) in the Himalayan region of Mustang, undertaken between 1990 and 1995, showed evidence of alternating crops of buckwheat and barley from the 1st millennium B.C, with evidence of millet and legume cultivation from 400BC - 100 AD (Knörzer, 2000). There was also evidence of sub-tropical crops which were likely imported from lower down, including – as would be expected – rice, as well as lentils and hemp. There was limited change in the cropping diversities discovered in samples up until after the 1600s. Coarse grains produced in the Karnali at the time of the Baise Rajya include naked barley (*uwa*), millets, sorghum, and legumes (Subedi, 1998).

Alongside coarse grains, farmers likely combined these with pulses and oil crops, and a limited variety of vegetables or root crops. There is evidence that pulses and oil crops, as well as onion and garlic, were produced in the Kathmandu valley as early as the Lichhavi era after 450AD (Yadav, 1986).

The Colombian exchange and other crops

Importantly, a large share of Nepal's current crops for both shifting cultivation on dry fields and irrigated sedentary cultivation, including maize, potatoes, and common vegetables or fruits such as chayote (*iskus*), capsicum, tomatoes, bananas and chilli peppers originate in the Americas, and thus date back only to the Colombian Exchange. While the exact date of the introduction of these crops to Nepal is not clear, it was likely a gradual process which occurred between the 17th and 19th centuries – when these crops were introduced to South Asia by European traders (Whelpton, 2005). Regmi (1972) estimates that Maize was introduced in the early 17th century and was reportedly so widespread by the late 18th century around the time of the Gorkha conquest, that land areas in some locales were measured by the volume of maize seeds required during sowing. Bhattarai (2003a) suggests that maize was highly significant in supporting population growth in the hills, as it allowed a pre-monsoon harvest on unirrigated lands prior to the plantation of millet.

Potato (which would go on to become a major crop) likely came later – possibly around the time of the Gorkha conquest. Regmi (1999) estimates that it was introduced between the late 18th and early 19th century (Regmi, 1999). This corroborates reports in Kirkpatrick's (2007 [1793]) travelogue which mentions that potato was available as of the late 18th century in the central hills, although he noted that new seed potatoes needed to be brought in from Patna before each season, suggesting it was a relatively new crop at the time. It likely took longer for it to reach peripheral regions, and with reference to Solu Khumbu, Stevens (1996, 217) using oral histories and other sources, estimates that it reached the Sherpa domains by the 1850s, supporting a rapid population growth.

There was also evidence of cotton production (Yadav, 1986). Stiller (1975) suggests it was the main cash crop in the hills prior to the Gorkha conquest, although other studies have suggested there were many others. These include walnut, which was suggested by Kirkpatrick (2007 [1793]) to be a famous crop from Chitlang, the valley to the south of Kathmandu in the late 18th century. With reference to the low lying fertile Tadi valley of Nuwakot, just north of the Kathmandu valley, he makes reference to a somewhat dynamic cropping system whereby alongside paddy in the monsoon and wheat in the winter, there was production of crops for the market, including high quality garlic, orange, guava and pineapple. Other products produced for the market include sisau oil and turpentine which was produced from pine trees in surrounding forests and sugarcane. Half a century earlier in the early 17th century, the Jesuit traveller Ippolito Desideri reported the production of sugarcane in the Kathmandu valley, alongside paddy, wheat, millet, oranges, lemons, and pineapples suggesting these were all well-established cash crops in the hills before the Gorkha conquest (Desideri, 1937). In the Tarai, there are few sources from the pre-Gorkhali period, yet revenue records from Morang and Mahottari in the early 19th century just after the conquest, point to the production of cotton, tobacco and mustard – with sugarcane also in Morang (Hamilton, 2007 [1819]).

Chapter 3

Gorkha conquest (1750s – 1900s) and early Rana rule

The Gorkha conquest of the Baise Rajya, Chaubisi Rajya and Sen Kingdoms in the second half of the 18th century, which is generally considered a process of 'political unification' into a single contiguous empire, marked the formation of the state of Nepal. This was a defining moment in the region's agrarian history. The foundation of a stronger agrarian bureaucracy were being laid in the Gorkha principality before its rapid expansion. Pande (2014) notes how under Ram Shah in the 16th century, there was a standardisation of weights and measures, the setting of official interest rates, regulations on forest, pasture and irrigation management (Riccardi Jr, 1977), and formalisation of caste hierarchy and rules (Pande, 2014). By the time of Prithvi Narayan Shah, the Gorkha state had emerged into a military power, with armament factories and a growing standing army, making possible its campaign to found the Gorkha empire in the late 18th century (Ibid.).

It is notable that at the time, smaller states had faced many barriers to expansion and their natural tendency was actually to fragment, due to the challenges of administering territory, competing interests of local level nobility and inability to finance military expansion (Stiller 1975). Gorkha however, differed not only in the strong military leadership of Prithvi Narayan Shah, but also in their successful model of using land to consolidate political authority to a much greater extent than earlier states. This included for instance, the gifting of personal *jagirs* to each soldier who fought for the king (rather than just for officers, as some states had done). It also extended to the expanded distribution of *birta* grants to high ranking nobility from outlying regions and the reconfirmation of earlier grants from the smaller principalities which had been given to loyal nobles. These processes will be discussed at several points in the subsequent pages.

There is also evidence that the new empire had a strong bureaucracy and efficient revenue generating machinery which surpassed earlier state formations (Regmi, 1976). Nevertheless, Stiller's (1975) suggests at several points that there was limited change initially to the lives of the peasantry – tenants would still be expected to surrender at least half of their crop as tax or provide labour tribute, regardless of the overlord who ruled them. It is true also that immediately following the conquest, the new Gorkhali rulers avoided measures which might disturb traditional land management institutions and undermine the loyalty of local elites to the new regime (Regmi, 1972). The initial priorities of the empire were the control of territory, and cross border trade routes (Pande, 2014). In this context, existing systems of revenue administration remained in place and nobles who pledged loyalty retained their estates, saw their holdings protected.

Nevertheless, this continuity was likely only relevant to areas which were already strongly under the revenue administration of the state, and which were dominated by a sedentary peasantry. The primary change under the Gorkhas, we argue, was the extension of the state administration and its land tenure policies into peripheral regions which had until then, retained relative autonomy. An important part of this process included the dissolution of the Adivasi mode of production. As will be shown, this was accelerated by the growing bureaucracy and military which contributed to a surging demand for revenue. Charting the impact of this change, alongside other political, ecological and demographic shifts, is the focus of this chapter.

The first section looks at the Tarai-Madhesh. The clearing of the forest frontier, creation of an indigenous functionary class, and distribution of land grants, led to the rapid subjugation of the Adivasi economic formation of the Tharu, Rajbanshi and other indigenous groups. It was replaced by sedentary farming under a largely feudal mode of production. In the caste Hindu domains of the central and parts of the western plains, one saw intensified inequalities, and an expansion of this economic formation with migration from the Gangetic plains to the south as the state sought to maximise tax revenue. The second section looks at the hills after the Gorkha conquest. While there was some continuity in the case of the western hills, like in the Tarai, migrations of Hindu castes across Nepal (in this case the Khas), supported the expansion of sedentary cultivation under either centralised or localised feudalism. Change within the Adivasi mode of production in the hills (particularly amongst Tibeto-Burmese speaking communities of the central and eastern hills) was much more uneven and drawn out. The latter were initially given relative autonomy as the state sought to maintain political stability in the rugged uplands. However, over time, this mode of production was also undermined. Like in the Tarai, this emerged in part from the creation of an indigenous functionary class. However, more significantly, this stemmed from the gradual erosion of customary forms of land tenure (including *kipat* whereby the state protected clan based communal land rights), and the growing shortage of land which went alongside the eastward migration of Khas castes. This, alongside population pressures made shifting cultivation increasingly less viable, and paved the way for a growing ethnic inequality between an indigenous and settler peasantry. The older Adivasi mode of production grounded in redistribution of surplus and shifting cultivation/ transhumance on clan operated lands, did however, persist in more remote domains where the influence of the state was less prominent.

The third section of this chapter explored some significant changes in the late Rana era – most notably the confirmation of private property rights to land and the reduction in tax revenue. The latter was of particular importance for the consolidation of *localised* feudal landlord-tenant relations in large tracts of the Tarai-Madhesh and pockets of the hills. It also covers the early efforts to resettle the plains. The final section of this chapter looks at the change in cropping patterns – which included early irrigation initiatives and the huge expansion of the rice-wheat cropping system alongside the increase in sedentary farming.

Mode of production and tax collection hierarchy in Tarai-Madhesh

The tax collection system and land tenure

The Tarai-Madhesh in was prized by the new Gorkhali rulers, given its flat and fertile land and high revenue generation potential, which could help fund the regime's military campaigns (Gaige, 1976, Michael, 2012). Shortly after the conquest, there was already considerable revenue from the sale and processing of timber, elephants and other forest produce (Regmi, 1972), as well as levies on seasonal herders from India (Guneratne, 2002). It also offered plentiful lands which could be bestowed to military officers in lieu of salary (see below) (Pande, 2014), and most notably for the generation of land tax. The latter represented Rs600,000 in revenue by 1834, as compared to Rs300,000 for timber, Rs71,000 for elephants and ivory and Rs20,000 for pasturage fees (Guneratne, 2002).

The primary change throughout the subsequent centuries was the gradual contraction of the forest frontier as the state sought to clear land for tax paying farmers, and a transition towards sedentary agriculture under feudal conditions. Nevertheless, this was a gradual process, and the new regime had to balance out military strategic interests with revenue generation goals, given that the malarial plains offered a natural defence against invasion from the south (Mørch, 2023).

At the dawn of the Gorkha conquest, the Tarai still included vast tracts of forest home predominantly to Adivasi groups. However, there were also areas which were already cleared and under sedentary cultivation – particularly in the central plains of Mithila[1], which encompasses mostly caste Hindu but also some Tharu domains such as Saptari. The landscape of the Tarai at this time has been characterised as an ever changing patchwork of intermittent forests and fields (Michael, 2007). In spite of

---

[1] For instance, in Saptari and Mahottari in the first decade of the 19th century, revenue from land tax was Rs68,957 whereas revenue from sale of timber was just Rs4687. This stands in contrast to Morang which was known to have been more forested. In the latter, revenue from the sale of timber was a substantial Rs38,000 and from land revenue it was Rs54,025. This suggests that there was a considerably larger area under cultivation already in Saptari and Mahottari at the start of the 19th century.

the need to protect some forests which offered strategic defence, with occasional forest protection decrees (Mørch, 2023), the demands for revenue meant that increased settlement and clearing of the forest was encouraged (Gaige, 1976), particularly given that many cultivators had fled to Indian territories after the Gorkhali conquest (Michael, 2007)[2]. A decree issued to local land revenue functionaries between Parsa and Jhapa in 1798 encourages the clearing of land, under the leadership of Kaji Abhiman Singh (Regmi, 1978b), with subsidies and temporary tax rebates offered as incentives (Dahal, 1983b).

Permanently settled land in the Tarai, and across Nepal, was legally classified under a tenure known as *raikar*, which allows individual households to operate personal plots while the state was the ultimate landlord, with tax being paid to a local functionary who in the Tarai was known as a *Chaudhari* (Regmi, 1978c). Earlier zamindars from the pre-Gorkha periods, some of whom had de facto property rights to their holdings, including the ability to rent it out to tenants, saw their power undermined, as the state rather than title holder for the land emerged as the ultimate landlord and surplus appropriating entity (Regmi, 1978d). Regmi suggests that landed families became de facto 'tenants' on state owned land, with the exception of *birta* estates (see below) (Ibid.). This also meant that pre-existing tenants for landed elites, in effect became sub-tenants.

Land tax represented a significant share of the surplus which the state appropriated from the peasantry – estimated to vary initially from around a third to 40% of the crop (Karky, 1981). These rates were comparable to Mughal India, and the share was subsequently converted into cash (Regmi, 1972). It was extracted through several mechanisms (Regmi, 1988a), which varied according to the pre-Gorkha administrative system and local agro-ecological context. In the more settled tracts along the southern border of the plains, which included large parts of the Maithili and Bhojpuri speaking belt in the Central Tarai-Madhesh, the crop tax system entailed the calculation of revenue on the basis of the crops produced for

---

[2] Numerous incentives were offered to encourage these cultivators back (Michael, 2007).

each bigha³ of land. In more forested areas, where plots were dispersed, another system known as the *mouja* system was dominant. Under this system, the entire *mouja*, a much larger unit, was the basis of calculating revenue – with the rates varying according to the productivity of the land rather than the specific crop (Regmi, 1988a). This was however, gradually replaced by the crop tax system as settlement and cropping intensity increased (Ibid.). Another system was the *hal* system, whereby tax would be collected from individual cultivators, but according to a *hal* – which is the area equal to the tillage of an ox drawn plough unit, and didn't necessarily correspond with cultivable area. This was common in parts of Morang-Jhapa and the western Tarai-Madhesh (Regmi, 1988a). The *hal* system in the western Tarai-Madhesh was later replaced with taxation based upon a fixed unit of land in 1837.

Regardless of the system for calculating tax, the state depended upon a hierarchy of functionaries to collect taxes for the regime, building upon the administrative foundations of pre-Gorkhali principalities (Regmi, 1988a). Functionaries at all levels were granted salaries and land assignments for their services (Regmi, 1988a, 1970c) and were also entitled to receive 'labour rents' or corvée from the peasants under their jurisdiction.

The top-level posts was the *subba* who administered a district. This was taken by powerful members of the Gorkha elite. For instance, a brother of Prithvi Narayan Shah was appointed as administrator of the central Tarai districts of Bara, Parsa and Rautahat in 1786 (Regmi, 1971a). Below the *subba* was a *fouzdar* (also from the ruling circle) who was responsible for coordinating revenue collection at the next geographical unit down, the *taluk*. Each *taluk* was divided into *pargannas*, (made up of a collection of villages⁴). In Morang for instance, there were eight *pargannas* across the three *taluks* which made up the district, in Saptari there were thirteen and in Mahottari just four (Hamilton, 2007 [1819]). A *chaudhari*, usually from the local elite (again a continuation of the pre-Gorkha system) was

---

³ The bigha is a unit varying from around 8100 to 19600 square yards depending on the part of the country

⁴ In Chitwan they would control 10-15 villages (Muller-Boker, 1999).

placed in charge of extracting tax in-kind from the peasantry on *raikar* land (Regmi, 1988a, 1970c)[5]. Below the *chaudhari* the *qanungoe* (also spelt as *kanugoya*) would maintain records of revenue rates at the parganna level, while the *mokadam* was a village-level functionary who would assist in the collection of revenue (known as *mandal* in some districts such as Morang). They would be assisted by a village level clerk or *patwari* who maintained accounts of revenue collections and rates (Regmi, 1970c, Hamilton, 2007 [1819]). There were however local and culturally specific variations to these different intermediary roles. For instance, amongst the Tharu of Dang, the *Chaudhari* was assisted by a *mahdtahwa* who would support them in collecting tax, mediating village disputes, mobilising labour for public works and organizing collective religious rituals (Krauskopff, 1989). Other locally specific roles include the *mahato* in Chitwan, who would be responsible for 5-7 villages in a parganna to support the *chaudhari* (Boker-Muller, 1999).

After the 1820s, tax was collected in the Tarai-Madhesh through a variation of the *thekbandi* system used in the hills, whereby appointed *Chaudharis* would be given responsibility to collect revenue for a specific period of time. The system was known as *panchasala-thek*, under which a local *chaudhari* would set a stipulated tax for the *parganna* under his jurisdiction, payable on a contractual basis by the peasantry, usually for up to 5 years at a time (Regmi, 1978d). *Chaudharis* were encouraged to promote settlement and clear new land from the forest (Krauskopff, 1989, Regmi, 1976).

The revenue generation apparatus during the early Gorkha period was inefficient. Michael (2012) suggests that there were frequent disputes between officials, and regional administrators would often abuse their power, collecting higher tax or cornering a greater share than was allowed. While functionaries at all levels were encouraged to clear forest land and promote settlement – labour shortages made this a significant challenge.

---

[5] There were also alternative arrangements, although the degree to which these operated separately or as part of the same system is unclear. Under the *ijara* system, Gorkha officials would enter into contracts directly with the old pre-existing elite who were given the role of *ijaradar*. An alternative system was the *anamat* system, a Gorkha official would be given the role of collecting taxes directly (Michael, 2012).

Michael (2012), with reference to the central Tarai bordering onto Champaran and the western Tarai bordering Gorkahpur, noted that the process of settlement was uneven. Areas would be cleared but then abandoned again due to lack of labour or exploitative taxation (Michael, 2007). He notes that the agricultural land in this belt in the early 19th century, transitioned between cultivation, common land and wasteland depending upon the availability of labour (Michael, 2012).

To compensate for labour shortages on newly cleared forest land and to maximize tax revenue, local functionaries encouraged the migration of farmers from India to the south, many of whom were from lower castes. They joined the ranks of poor tax or rent paying peasants (Gaige, 1976). This was because bringing settlers from adjacent *raikar* lands which had already been cleared, or from elsewhere in Nepal, would potentially result in a loss of revenue from existing taxable holdings (Ojha, 1983). It is perhaps set against this context that the aforementioned 1798 decree to settle the Eastern and Central Tarai requested functionaries to: "Continue cultivating the lands that are already under cultivation, and retain their cultivators there as usual, so that revenue may not decline. Attract settlers from birta and jagir lands, as well as from the Moglan [India], and reclaim and settle Kalabanjar [uncultivated] lands" (Regmi, 1978b).

Land grants

Alongside the *raikar* system of state landlordism the Gorkhas continued to recognise two forms of tax free tenure, *birta* and *guthi*, both of which had been present under the preceding state formations. Firstly, *guthi* was a type of tenure where the state passes ownership of land over to some charitable, religious, or philanthropic institutions – and the origin of this form of tenure appears to date back to long before the Gorkha conquest, and possibly to as early as the Lichchhavi period (Pradhan, 2009). The term *guthi* is possibly derived from "*gosthi*" or council (Pradhan, 2009). Guthi lands were administered by the state or by the institutions themselves. The income from such land would be used for religious and charitable purposes, and as some *guthi* land was used for agricultural production, farmed by tenants who would surrender a share of the harvest (Regmi, 1988a).

The second form of tenure was *jagir* which represented a form of taxable land offered in lieu of salary to high ranking members of the civil service or military and as noted earlier, was already prevalent under earlier state formations (Regmi, 1972). Given the abundance of forest land which was uncultivated and fiscal pressures on the regime, offering land instead of payment was a sensible choice, and presented an opportunity to reward loyal and victorious military officers (Mørch, 2023). Recipients were often expected to encourage settlement, while fulfilling other obligations for the state such as equipping or supporting the army with grain, supplying soldiers from the estate, or maintaining forts and trade routes (Regmi, 1972). *Jagir* estates under Gorkha rule appeared to vary considerably in size, and the larger estates would have many farmers cultivating as tenants. The owners had various privileges, including the right to extract additional unpaid labour tribute from tenants or dispense justice (Regmi, 1972, Stiller, 1975). A notable functionary who was given *jagir* estates during the early Gorkha era was the *umra*, who would oversee a unit of irregular soldiers who could be mobilized as and when required. They would be allocated paddy fields as a private estate as payment, with the size varying according to the number of men to be mobilised (Regmi, 1988b), and examples were reported from Gorkha, Nuwakot, and Makwanpur (the latter described by Kirkpatrick, 2007 [1793]). This irregular army supplemented the regular Gorkha army for its military campaigns in the west (Regmi, 1988b).

The third form of tenure, which was likely far more significant in shaping the agrarian structure in the Tarai in later years was that of *birta*. Grants of *birta* land were the most prestigious, were tax free and were generally given to high level members of the ruling elite (Regmi, 1976). The distribution of *birta* grants had started under pre-Gorkha state formations. While many of these pre-existing bestowments were initially confiscated following the conquest, in 1787 efforts were made to scrutinise earlier *birta* (and *guthi*) endowments and many earlier grants were restored. Title holders who had collaborated with the Gorkhas were likely to keep their estates. Owners had to provide evidence that the grant was given by the reigning king, queen or crown prince at the time, and could have them restored so long as they accepted the authority of the conquerors (Regmi,

1976). The Dang rajas for instance, gave land grants to Brahmins of the hills (Krauskopff, 1989), and these practices were continued when it was annexed into the principality of Salyan, an early tributary state of the Gorkhas in the mid-18th century (Mishra, 2007). Regmi (1989a) also records the distribution of *birta* grants to Maithili Brahmins in the Mahottari-Dhanusha region in the late Sen period which were reconfirmed by the Gorkha king Rana Bahadur Shah in 1794. Many of the *birta* grants distributed in this region were to abbots of monasteries in the area around Janakpur and their reconfirmation was in respect for the religious authorities of the town (Burghart, 2016).

New grants of *birta* land were also distributed in the Tarai-Madhesh to members of the hill bureaucratic elite (largely Brahmins Chettris and Thakuris), including family members of the ruling elite, priests, and high ranking bureaucrats (Regmi, 1972). Examples included loyal generals following the conquest, as well as former rulers of the Baise Rajyas in the west, who had pledged allegiance to the Gorkhas – all of whom were recorded as receiving *birta* land (Regmi, 1964). Reconfirming older grants or offering new grants was particularly important for the Gorkhas to award nobles who had helped them during the military campaign (Stiller, 1975). Mishra (1987) adds that land grants such as this effectively incorporated loyal feudal lords within the state-bureaucratic alliance and were highly effective in extending the states' political reach across the plains.

Most of the actual *birta* landlords were based in the hills, only visiting during the harvest (Feldman and Fournier, 1976, Lal, 2002), with the exception of the *birta* estates which continued to be endowed to abbots of monasteries and priests in Janakpur (Burghart, 2016). The grants were often of forested land in the plains, and had the added value for the state in that the recipients could encourage settlement and conversion of jungle into farmland (Regmi, 1989a, 1976, Mørch, 2023). Recipients brought in tenants from more settled tracts, including in India, to clear the forest. This was sometimes a condition for receipt of the grant. For instance, in 1798 birta lands were given in Bara and Parsa on the pretext that they would be cleared and put under cultivation. *Birta* owners were able to extract rent from their tenants, as well as revenue from customs/markets, or judicial fines (Regmi, 1976). While most *birta* grants were tax free, a variant known as *tiruwa birta* offered concessional reduced taxation to encourage reclamation – which was notably lower than for *raikar* land.

Regmi (1971b, 38) referred to Birta as 'privileged landownership', as he maintained:

> "Birta system undoubtedly served the social, economic, and political needs of the ruling classes of Nepal during the period before 1951. It was a form of privileged land ownership that enabled them to exploit the land resources of the nation for their personal advantage. From the view point of the nation, therefore, the birta system was synonymous with inequalities and exploitations"

Birta estates were not always permanent, and could be confiscated or redistributed according to the political interests and loyalties at the time (Regmi, 1976). For instance in an unusual episode in 1806 (1862 BS), in order to generate money to finance military campaigns in the far west in Jamuna-Sutlej region, General Bhimsen Thapa, with a permission from the then King Rana Bahadur Shah seized a large number of tax-free estates which had been given to temples as *guthis* or to individuals as *birta*, in order to convert the land to taxable *raikar* land and fill the empty state coffers (Nepali, 1956). This was later known as *Baisathi Haran*, after the Nepali year when the incident took place. It was also taken as an early 'land reform' initiative to scrutinize the tax-exempt lands without valid documents. Those who could take an oath of validity were not affected (Nepali, 1956). Some land was even converted into *Jagir* for the army, as reported in Dolakha (Regmi, 1981b), and there were also reports of land in Doti being distributed to landless households (Pande, 2014), likely as a means through which to maximise tax revenue. Following his seizing of land, around 1808, Bhimsen Thapa further ordered the reclamation of wasteland in the Tarai-Madhesh region to increase state revenue, and encouraged the development of irrigation facilities there. In places where there were a lack of tenants, farmers were allocated the wasteland with tax exemption, and a loan was provided for new incoming settlers. The wasteland reclamation policy was particularly successful in the Eastern Tarai (Nepali, 1956). Considering the staunchly conservative society of the time, these were somewhat 'radical' reforms. They were therefore unpopular, among the ruling elites, and they were later corrected by Jung Bahadur Rana in the mid-19th century, with new lands being given to those who had lost their estates (Nepal, 1998).

Tax collection and the mode of production in the long-settled tract

The conquest of the Tarai-Madhesh by the Gorkhali state had far reaching implications on the agrarian formation, consolidating a centralised form of feudalism as the primary mode of production. In the long-settled areas already under the firm administrative control of the state with sedentary cultivation – which likely includes much of the caste Hindu heartland of the central and parts of the western Tarai (which encompassed some Tharu domains such as Saptari) – two parallel forms of feudalism had emerged with two surplus appropriating classes – one on *raikar* land, and another on lands given as *birta* or *jagir*. We refer to both systems as a form of feudalism, although the former (state appropriation of surplus) has also been characterised by Mishra (1987) as the 'tributary mode of production', or by Regmi (1976) 'state landlordism'[6].

State appropriation of surplus on raikar lands

We start with a discussion of the state appropriation of surplus on *raikar* land. On *raikar* lands, the state appropriated a large share of the annual harvest. Records from late 18th century Mahottari compiled by Burghart (2016), suggests that the percentage of the market value of the crop which the peasantry retained after paying tax, varied from 64% in a good year, to just 22% on a bad year.

Other than the bureaucracy, the revenue collectors themselves emerged as the surplus appropriating class locally (Burghart, 2016), including both the Chaudharis and lower-level functionaries. This appeared initially to be through their ability to corner a share of the revenue rather than via the leasing out of land and extraction of rent. Revenue collection

---

[6] See Sugden (2019) for a discussion on the characterisation and terminology surrounding 'feudalism' versus 'state landlordism'

intermediaries were not able to accumulate large areas of land in the early Gorkha era due to weaker property rights for land after the conquest. However, the process of revenue collection allowed intermediaries to accumulate a share of the harvest for the locality under their jurisdiction, and they could maximise this surplus through attempts to extend their revenue collection rights to new areas (Ibid.). Functionaries were also able to extract additional 'rents' through the extraction of labour tribute or corvée. Documents compiled by Regmi (1971a) for example from 1810, note how the village level revenue administrator or *mokkadam* in the Mahottari-Dhanusha region was entitled to one labour day of a ploughman and field worker per year from every family. In Dang, the *Chaudhari* was entitled to several days of labour per year from each family (Krauskopff, 1989).

These inequalities between the administrative apparatus and the peasantry supported a reproduction but also reconfiguration of caste and ethnic relations. It is probable that those who were functionaries for earlier pre-Gorkha states such as the Sen kingdom, were integrated into the new tax collection apparatus. In the belts of the Tarai-Madhesh home to caste Hindus such as the Maithili and Bhojpuri speaking belt between the Koshi river and the Chitwan hills, plains upper castes were given the role of *chaudhari*, as well as intermediate functionary positions (Sugden, 2019). Similarly, in the Tharu domains of northern Saptari which were already under the administrative reach of the Chaudandi Sen kingdom, former Tharu functionaries became Chaudharis for the Gorkhas (Krauskopff, 2018). The transfer of power does not however, appear to have been straightforward. For instance, with reference to the Tharu functionaries of Saptari, Krauskopff (2018) note how they lost some of the privileges they had enjoyed under the Sen kingdom, whereby they had a more personalised relationship with the Sen Kings and relative political autonomy. They were subject now to a more centralised and bureaucratic state apparatus, with an intermediary (a *subba*) between them and the King in distant Kathmandu, with shifts in the tax revenue collection method[7]. Documents from the Panjiyar collection showed that this shift caused some Tharu functionaries to flee to India with the population of their villages (Ibid).

Appropriation of surplus on birta and other private estates

With regards to lands bestowed as grants, surplus appropriation took place primarily via rent – and the agrarian relations appeared to represent more classical landlord-tenant type relationship. The majority of *jagir* and *birta* holdings were far too big to be cultivated by individual households (Regmi, 1972), and thus they were cultivated by tenants. In this case it would be the landlord, not the state who would corner the agricultural surplus – and given that *birta* grants were tax free, this would amount to the entire agricultural surplus going to the *birtawala* or title holder. Rent on *birta* or *jagir* estates was usually on a sharecropping basis or *adhiya*, whereby the landlord would take half of the harvest (Regmi, 1972), although there were variations. In Dang for instance, the share to be paid to landlords was just a quarter, but the tenants needed to cover all the cultivation costs and also had to provide 24 days of corvée labour on the landlord's private holding (Mishra, 2007). There was in some cases a fixed rate system whereby a fixed amount of grain had to be given each year.

It was common for landlords to be absentee, and based in the hills, as noted above. In Mishra's (2007) study from Dang for example, absentee landlords living in Salyan would descend on the valley in the malaria-free winter to collect the rent, although some would be sold as grain at the Indian border market and converted into cash to then pass on to the landlords in the hills.

Burghart (2016) offers crucial insights into the status of tenants on *birta* lands in his study of the estates bestowed upon abbots around Janakpur. He notes that some landlords arranged cultivation themselves, and employed permanent labourers or *nokar* who were paid monthly, or casual workers (*jan*) to work on the estate, being paid in kind, including

---

[7] At this time in Saptari there was a shift in the method to calculate tax whereby instead of giving a share of the produce Chaudharis needed to give a fixed sum to the state.

meals. Such workers lived in extreme poverty – and were often in perpetual indebtedness. Giving the land out to sharecroppers was however, by far the most popular way through which *birta* lands could be cultivated. The sharecroppers situation would be slightly better off than labourers (with a net income estimated to be 1.5 times higher), although lacking any tenure security, they had no incentives to invest on the land, including the expansion of irrigation (Ibid.) – a situation which persists even in the present day (Sugden, 2014). While some tenants were given fixed rate contracts, whether this was advantageous or not compared to sharecroppers, depended on the harvest in a given year – but the majority of both form of tenant were, like labourers, in chronic food insecurity (Burghart, 2016).

Birta owners had de facto private property rights to their estates, which essentially operated as self contained feudal vassals (Regmi, 1976), with tenants often having no direct relationship with the state and dealing with the landowner for almost all affairs. The estates sometimes even had its own administration (Regmi, 1976), with the *birtawala* extracting rent and labour service obligations from the population. Less is known about the situation of tenants on *jagir* lands, but there were likely close similarities in terms of the mechanisms of surplus appropriation – albeit with the owners lacking the autonomy and tenure security of the *birtawalas*. Some peasants would cultivate *birta* or *jagir* land as tenants alongside personal *raikar* holdings which were often too small to sustain a family – and thus they would experience parallel surplus appropriation by both state and landlord (Regmi, 1972).

Burghart (2016), with reference to the *birta* lands in the name of Janakpur abbots, suggests that in general, it was preferable for a peasant to be a tax paying cultivator on *raikar* lands rather than being a *birta* tenant – particularly if the peasant had capital to invest. This suggests that becoming a *birta* sharecropper or fixed rent tenant was a last resort due to the absence of alternative options. In theory competition for surplus between revenue collectors on *raikar* land and *birta* landlords, would set a limit to the levels that rents could be raised – particularly when land was abundant and labour was scarce. There was indeed competition between *birta* owners who sought the tenants' surplus via rent and the revenue collectors at a *mauja* level – who depended upon a share of the tax. However, the availability of migrants from East India Company lands in the South offset this – and helped defuse competition (Ibid.) – and by implication, also minimised downward pressure on rents and land tax[8]. It thus appears that immigration to the Tarai-Madhesh was in part driven by the need for both *birtawala* and revenue collectors to guarantee their share of the agricultural surplus.

While there were evidently three classes appropriating surplus (local revenue functionaries, the centralized state and *birta* and *jagir* landlords), official documents from the period point to conflicts over spoils between the two groups. In Saptari and Dhanusha of Nepal in the early 19th century for example, records point to efforts by the centralized feudal state to clamp down on additional taxes and unpaid corvée labour obligations being levied by local functionaries (Regmi, 1982c). This suggests that aside from official land tax and rent, the local landed elite took advantage of administrative weaknesses to maximize the appropriation of surplus from the peasant majority. This parallels events on the Indian side of the border. The District Gazetteer of Darbhanga reports very similar incidences throughout the 19th century, with zamindars beyond the control of colonial authorities not only retaining a greater share of the tax revenue than they were entitled, but extracting additional labour rents to work for land owners (Chaudhury, 1964).

Tax collection and the subordination of the Adivasi mode of production in the forest belt

As discussed above, in the settled tracts home to sedentary caste Hindu cultivators as well as Tharu domains such as Saptari which were already within the administrative net of the state, the Gorkha conquest likely supported the emergence of a more centralised form of feudalism and propped up a local upper caste (or Tharu) nobility already established since the time of the Sen or earlier kingdoms. However, for the largely

---

[8] Although Burghart also notes that land was set aside for orchards and other purposes if tenants were unavailable – this may have been considered preferable than setting more favourable rents.

Adivasi domains of the Tarai-Madhesh which were still heavily forested, the change after the Gorkha conquest was far more significant.

As noted in the last chapter, the degree to which the state apparatus could exercise influence over isolated forest dwelling communities is questionable, and it is likely that they were still under Adivasi modes of production with shifting cultivation as the dominant form of farming. In the century following the Gorkha conquest, this mode of production had been undermined and subordinated to the same system of centralised feudalism and local landlordism which characterised the settled tracts of the lowlands (see Sugden, 2013). In chapter 2 we touched upon three parallel and interconnected processes which supported this process of subjugation.

The first was the *creation of an indigenous functionary class*. This process may have begun in localities already under the influence of early state formations, yet the expanded tax generation apparatus under the Gorkha state and its efforts to bring new areas under cultivation (including relatively autonomous Adivasi domains) consolidated the rise of an Adivasi nobility. Positions such as *Chaudharis*, and the subordinate roles of *Kanugoyes, Mokaddams* or *Patwaris*, which were discussed above, were generally appointed to those with the ability to expand land reclamation and coordinate the collection of revenue from the peasantry (Regmi, 1970c), not to mention intermediary roles in the harvesting of timber (Guneratne, 2002). This in particular, included the Tharu and Rajbanshi chieftains, gradually creating the foundations of what would become an indigenous landed class.

The second process of subordination was surplus appropriation by taxation and rent. As noted earlier, it was not easy to extract revenue from remote forest dwelling communities, but with the imposition of a more rigorous tax collection apparatus (Regmi, 1976) – it is probable that far more Adivasi cultivators were subsumed within the tax appropriation net. However, it is unlikely that the state would be able to set up a complex land administration and extract a significant share of the harvest immediately in the forested belt. The process was gradual, and may have included 'transitional' forms of taxation suited to forest dwelling itinerant cultivators.

There is limited data on early taxation of forest dwelling communities in the Tarai, although insights can be gained from the Meche and Garo in North Bengal, who – like their counterparts in Nepal in the late 18th century – were shifting cultivators under the overlordship of a hill-based kingdom (in this case Bhutan). Following the annexation of the Dooars by Bhutan they would offer labour services such as portering for government officials and also were charged taxes for residing in the forest, plying and trading boats and for operating weaving looms (Grunning, 2007 [1911]). How they paid was unclear, although Ray (2002), suggested that cotton would be produced on their swidden plots and exchanged for cash. Similarly, with regards to the Darjeeling Tarai lands under the rule of the Sikkim raja, Hodgson (1880 [1847]) notes how the Dhimal and Meche would annually pay the Raja 1 rupee per agricultural implement[9] and a corvée labour contribution (of 18 days per year, or the equivalent value in cash), usually for porterage between the hills and plains. It is probable that similar forms of revenue generation were applied in Nepal.

At a later stage, as farmers made a transition towards sedentary cultivation and lands were formally registered as being under *raikar* (state ownership), then tax could be more easily appropriated as a share of the harvest through the *mauja* and later the *crop tax* system. There were likely local variations as the state sought to balance political and economic considerations in the newly conquered domains. A locally specific form of tenure amongst the Tharu of Dang described by Krasukopff (1989) was known as *potet*. Under this system peasants would have a right to consume the harvest, except a share (usually 1/5th of the harvest) which would be paid to the Chaudhari (tax collection functionary) as tax (Krauskopff, 1989). Land rights were defined by one's right to consume the harvest rather than official ownership over the land itself, and they did not consider themselves as 'tenants' in the traditional sense. McDougal's (1968) study from the adjacent Deukhuri valley suggests that *potet* tenants paid tax themselves, and provided a (generally modest) labour tribute to the functionary, either by cultivating a share of their demesne or *jirayat* lands, or through providing a certain number of days of labour. What does

---

[9] Hodgson's respondents estimated that Rs40 could be produced with one implement, and thus this was a modest tax burden at this stage.

appear apparent from both studies was that *potet* gave the tenant full usufruct rights to land which was under the jurisdiction of a Tharu *Chaudharis*. It is suggested by Kraupskopff (1989) that this was a transitional system emerging from a time when land was de facto common property. Whether *potet* was a recognised system of tenure in parallel to *raikar*, or was a customary system used by the Tharu within the framework of the *raikar* revenue generation apparatus, is not clear.

The third intervention which was central to feudal subordination in forested Adivasi domains, were the efforts to expand the cultivable area and encourage settlement. It was only the clearing of the forest frontier which effectively compelled the Adivasi population of the Tarai to become tax paying sedentary farmers. It would interrupt the traditional pattern of nomadic shifting cultivation while simultaneously increasing the reach of the state apparatus from more populated regions into the remote forested belt. Historical documents suggest that revenue functionaries in the plains were encouraged to clear tracts of forest and distribute land to tenants soon after the Gorkha conquest, particularly in the eastern and central Tarai (Regmi, 1978b, 1976, Dahal, 1983b). The forest in this context, was no longer considered a necessary defensive barrier as it had been under earlier state formations (Stiller, 1975). The forests which were cleared would have included not only the forests adjacent to caste Hindu domains with a longer history of settlement, but also the more sparsely populated Adivasi belt which included the northern belt of the central plains, much of the far-eastern lowlands and eventually, the western plains.

While some tracts of forest may have been cleared by local Adivasi *Chaudharis* on lands under their jurisdiction, it appears that outsiders (particularly from the hills) also cleared the forest and encouraged settlement, taking up the position of tax collector on these new estates. For instance, the *mouja* system of revenue calculation which was predominant in Adivasi dominated forest tracts in the first half of the 19th century was conducive to the creation of new estates (Regmi, 1988a). Unlike the later crop-tax system whereby revenue was calculated on a plot-by-plot basis according to crop type, the *mouja* system saw revenue fixed for a large area. This incentivized the clearing of forest, as with more cultivators, the share of the output being absorbed as tax was lower, offering an incentive for enterprising members of the hill aristocracy to clear new areas of forest (Ibid.). Outsiders were also incentivised to clear land also through being offered a portion of the cleared estate as tax free *birta* (Regmi, 1989a, 1976)[10].

It has been established that a large share of the Tarai's Adivasi peasantry were under the government's tax generation apparatus by the 19th century – consolidating the dissolution of the Adivasi Mode of Production. The tax burden combined with the clearing of the forest frontier intensified the drive towards sedentary production. Fixed plots of land were the norm in newly settled tracts, which were easier to administer and collect revenue, and as forests became scarce, finding land for shifting cultivation became challenging. More fundamentally, the internal redistributive and communal nature of Adivasi society had been transformed – with a new tax collection hierarchy and rising vertical segmentation within Adivasi society. This encouraged accumulation of wealth, and broke down some of the indigenous mechanisms of surplus appropriation (see Singh, 2023). These three processes of subordination thus contributed to the emergence of new agricultural communities of Adivasis farming under the centralized feudalism of the state, on fixed plots, with surplus being appropriated via taxation – and revenue being paid to their own tribal chieftains.

It is important to note however there were always large frontier zones which had yet to be cleared, allowing the Adivasi mode of production to persist for much longer in some locales. Muller-Boker (1999) also suggests that Tharus were carrying out shifting cultivation in the Chitwan valley during much of the Gorkha and Rana era. Before large scale resettlement from the 1950s onwards, large areas of Chitwan remained as forest as it was used as a hunting reserve (Guneratne, 2010), used by the Rana aristocracy and even British royalty (see Figure 10). Land was therefore sufficiently 'available' for this type of extensive land use in spite of the expanding reach of the state. Slightly elevated tracts of river terraces were preferred, whereas lower areas within the flood plain were avoided because

---

[10] There were several categories of Birta in practice; for example, Bakas, Bakas-Mafi, Bakas-pot, Bekh, Bitalab, Chhap, Daijo, Dukha, Farmaisi, Gharbari, Guthi-Birta, Guthi-Bakas-Birta, Halbandi-Manachamal, Jiuni, Kharidi, Kush, Mafi Birta, etc. (See Regmi 1978).

Figure 10: Hunting trip during the Prince of Wales' visit to Nepal in Thori of Chitwan, 1921. Much of the Chitwan region was used by the Rana elite as a hunting reserve until the latter part of the Rana era, resulting in it remaining heavily forested for longer than other parts of the Tarai.
Photo: Madan Puraskar Pustakalaya, Reproduced with permission

of the risk of flooding and the excessive moisture of the soil, but also because crops would have been destroyed by the wild animals (Muller-Boker, 1999).

Importantly though, the Adivasi of the Tarai were not passive in their subordination to the central state, and communities had strategies to avoid subjugation in areas still under forest. For instance, Rai (2015) observed that in the north of Morang and Jhapa, parts of which remained forested as late as the mid-20th century, the Dhimal were not official title holders to any land, and actively avoided registering their plots. They were able to continue their forest-based livelihood for decades, using the abundant forest land without the need to register it under their names with the bureaucracy – thus avoiding the tax burden. The high prevalence of malaria further weakened the hold of the state power over the malaria-resistance indigenous groups such as the Dhimal (Rai 2013).

Similarly, when new areas began to come under the control of the state and be cleared for permanent cultivation – some Adivasi were able to avoid subjugation through moving to more remote locales. This echoes James

Scott's concept of 'escape agriculture' pursued in mainland Southeast Asia, whereby shifting cultivators would relocate to evade the extractive state apparatus (Scott, 2010). Attempts by the state to enforce land registration resulted in some Dhimal communities migrating to forest regions over the border in India as the forest contracted (Rai, 2015). This paralleled similar eastward migration of the Meche who migrated into Assam to escape subordination by the British colonial state in North Bengal (Debnath, 2010)[11]. Westward migration into virgin forest land was also a widespread trend amongst the Tharu of Dang in the western Tarai-Madhesh (Krauskopff, 1989). This allowed them to escape the excesses of landlordism and taxation under the Gorkhali and Rana regime. There were also reports of entire villages being abandoned during the transition from the Sen to Gorkha rule, when Tharu Chaudharis who had enjoyed certain privileges under the Sen kingdom, unhappy with changes to their political and economic status, would flee with the peasants (Krauskopff, 2018).

Escape agriculture of a different kind was even reported from caste Hindu domains. In Mithila, the pressure placed on the peasantry by the multitude of rents and taxes resulted in families fleeing to India, or launching complaints to the central government[12], particularly when local functionaries appropriated levies beyond their state sanctioned entitlements. Regmi notes how *ryots* (peasants) from Mahottari and Saptari came to Kathmandu in 1809 to complain of "over-taxation and oppression" (Regmi, 1971a), and records a separate incident of over taxation in Saptari in the 1830s which resulted in 300 families fleeing to neighbouring regions (Regmi, 1989b). For a majority of farmers however, 'escape agriculture' was not an option, because of the speed at which

---

[11] The population of Mech in the Western Dooars reportedly declined from 21,608 in 1891 to 10,777 by 1921 as they moved to Assam (where many became known as *Bodo*) to escape subjugation and the tax burden of the colonial state (Debnath, 2010, 53).

[12] Regmi notes how *ryots* (peasants) from Mahottari and Saptari came to Kathmandu in 1809 to complain of "over-taxation and oppression" (Regmi, 1971a), and records a separate incident of over taxation in Saptari in the 1830s which resulted in 300 families fleeing to neighboring regions (Regmi, 1989b).

forests were cleared - and as soon as lands were cleared, they became designated as either *raikar* or *birta* (Regmi, 1972).

Onset of Rana rule in Tarai-Madhesh

After Rana rule started in 1846, the economic importance of the Tarai to fund the regime continued to grow (Guneratne, 2002). While trade with the emerging British colonial regime to the south, with whom the comprador Ranas were to build a strong alliance, offered new sources of revenue, land tax remained critical for the state – particularly in the second half of the 19th century. Mishra (1987) estimates that land tax made up 68% of government revenue as of 1853, eclipsing what was provided by fines, custom duties and the sale of timber. Notably, with the more limited conflict in the latter parts of the 19th century, military expenditure dropped and a greater share of revenue than before went directly to the state-bureaucratic alliance, and Mishra estimates that in the mid-19th century, 25-30% of state revenue went directly to the Rana prime minister (Ibid.).

In this context, a more efficient tax collection system was introduced to regularize the collection of revenue, with pressure to maximize surplus to fund the conspicuous consumption of the elite in Kathmandu (Regmi, 1976) (see Figure 11). The Ranas intensified efforts to measure the cultivated area, and expanded the crop-tax system which specified revenue according to crop on a bigha by bigha basis (Regmi, 1988a). Unlike older systems such as the *mouja* system which often led to underestimates, this offered a more accurate and generally higher flow of revenue for the regime. The *hal* system, was carried over into the Rana era in some areas, while the *serma* system of the hills was introduced in some parts of the western Tarai-Madhesh where landholdings were not measured (Ibid.). There were also intensified efforts to register land which had not been declared and had up until then been untaxed (Regmi, 1988a) – which likely included remoter tracts.

In 1861 Jang Bahadur Rana turned his attention to improving the process of actually collecting tax and administering the land in the Tarai (Regmi 1976). The prevailing unit of land, namely the *pargana* was too

Figure 11: Residence of Commanding General Rudra Shumsher Jung Bahadur Rana. The Rana rulers invested considerable sums in opulent palaces for their inner circle.
Photo: Madan Puraskar Pustakalaya, Reproduced with permission

large a unit for the Chaudhari, the revenue collector, to be able to effectively collect revenue (Regmi 1978:78-79). The *pargana* was therefore sub-divided into a number of *mauja* (a village or smaller groups of villages), a new functionary known as *jimidar*[13], would oversee each *mauja*, replacing the *chaudhari* to collect revenue (see Figure 12). In forested tracts, *jimidars* could also be appointed to clear land, settle it with tenants and administer these new villages. However, because the development of new *maujas* from the forest required a certain amount of capital, it is likely that they were developed later by families already established locally as *jimidars*, who were more likely to have the resources or access to credit (Regmi, 1976, Guneratne, 1996). As with the earlier system, under each *jimidar* were several *patwaris* or clerks - functionaries to assist in the collection of taxes and maintenance of accounts and records (Regmi, 1978c), and a village level administrator or *mokadam* (also spelled *mokuddum*)[14] (Regmi, 1978d).

---

[13] Regmi (1977) usefully clarifies that *jimidār* which means 'functionary', should not be confused with the term *zamindār*, used in India, which simply refers to a landowner.

[14] The *mokaddam* was normally in charge of settlement operations and allotment of uncultivated lands. While they were appointed in Chitwan District and also a few

Figure 12: Ruins of a Rana era malpot or tax office in morang, from which the jimidar would collect grain and administer revenue.
Photo: Fraser Sugden

Regmi (1988a) notes that while some former *chaudharis* were able to find a position within the new *jimidari* system, preference for the *jimidar* positions was given not to the traditional landed gentry at the *mouja* level, but to elites from the hills with strong connections to the bureaucracy. This supported fiscal discipline, as they were essentially employees of the state who could be dismissed if they failed to perform their duties (Regmi, 1988a). In the Dang valley, there was unease amongst the new Rana rulers at the extent of local economic and political power held by Tharu *Chaudharis* – and this set the rationale to abolish the position entirely (Krauskopff, 1989). Krauskopff's (1989) ethnography suggests that while many Tharu who had been *chaudharis* were also *jimidars* under the Rana regime, many hill upper castes would later take on this role on adjacent tracts of land, although maintaining their estates from afar.

In some districts, where *jimidars* from the hills could not be found, wealthy settlers from India were also brought in to take on the role (Regmi,

---

eastern Tarai-Madhesh districts of Nepal, the position was not common in Dang and other western Tarai-Madhesh districts (Rajaure 1981).

1982a). Oral histories collected in Dhanusha in 2012 suggest that wealthy upper caste families from as far away as West Bengal were brought in to administer the land. Unlike the *jimidārs* however, it was required that *patwaris* be from the local community under their jurisdiction, and thus an indigenous elite retained some power (Regmi, 1978c). Other culturally specific roles were taken up by Adivasi community members including that of the *mahaton* amongst the Dang Tharu who would do village-level administrative jobs which didn't involve revenue collection (Rajaure, 1981)[15]. How the *mahaton* differs to the role of *mahtahwa* described by Krauspkoff (1989) which was also a locally specific role amongst the Dang Tharu is not clear.

Inequality and the prevalence of local landlordism increased during the Rana years. The *mouja* under which a *jimidar* was tasked with collecting revenue was smaller than the *parganna* for which *chaudharis* would collect revenue under the old system – a move aimed at facilitating more rigorous tax collection. Nevertheless, *jimidars*, like the functionaries they replaced, continued to accumulate wealth. They could still retain a percentage of the taxes in compensation for collection activities (Muller-Boker, 1999) as well as extracting additional unauthorized payments from the peasantry (Regmi, 1976). In Mahottari, Burghart (2016) estimates that 1/16th of the tax revenue would be the personal commission of the tax collector.

Importantly, unlike during the early years of conquest when functionaries accumulated wealth primarily through a share of the revenue, *jimidars* also accumulated property - emerging into powerful landlords themselves and money lenders, who had titles to large areas of their own *raikar* land beyond what was needed for themselves, as well as having revenue collecting duties. This paved the way for sub-infeudation, whereby rent paying tenants would be brought in to cultivate the *jimidar's* surplus land (Burghart, 2016), and the functionary would extract surplus as rent as well as through a share of the tax. Sharma and Malla (1957), referring to data collected in the 1950s just after the end of Rana rule, observed that in some *maujas*, the entire land used to be owned by the *jimidar* (i.e. there

---

[15] Rajaure (1981) suggests that the mahaton still functions as a traditional village leader, and they have also been recognized by the local government in recent years.

were no independent *raikar* tenants). They used to keep 5-6 permanent and full-time servants, as bonded laborers, who would receive 5-7 *muris* (a local unit of measurement) of paddy annually. One owned up to 60 bighas of land, but the productivity was low. Every large peasant used to keep up to 100-150 cattle, but of the local breed (Sharma and Malla, 1957).

There were several mechanisms through which functionaries could accumulate land. Firstly, the *raikar* land which they administered was divided into two types, the plots for peasants, and a private demesne for the *jimidar*, also known as *jirayat* (Regmi, 1978d). Secondly, *jimidars* would sometimes appropriate the land of tax or loan defaulting peasants (Regmi, 1976). Thirdly, as noted above, lower-level functionaries were also able to accumulate land. For instance, a *mokuddum* would receive 5% of the land in their jurisdiction free of tax, while *patwaris* would receive a share of the revenue generated (Regmi, 1976; Burghart, 2016). Oral histories collected in Morang suggest that *patwaris* were able to access land through their appointments (Sugden, 2010) – although it is not known whether this was a private holding given as part of their revenue administration duties, or whether land was appropriated from the others at a later stage from peasants who defaulted on tax or debts – a process which became easier after the emergence of private property rights and a land market in the early 20th century. The wealth of these often Tharu functionary-landlords was well known. Tharu *jimidars* and other high level functionaries reportedly kept elephants as status symbols and for transport in Morang (Sugden, 2010), and Dang (Krauskopff, 1989). The tenants meanwhile would be other Tharu, or in Morang, politically weaker Adivasi groups such as the Bantar, Rajbanshi and Santhal (Sugden, 2025).

Jimidars and other functionaries also had the power to appropriate unpaid labour or corvée from the peasantry. For example, to clear jungle from their *jirayat* holdings *jimidārs* reportedly were allowed to appropriate the unpaid labour of one ox team from each settler family each year (Yadav, 1984). In Dang, during the time of sowing or cultivation of paddy, for each *hal* of land (the amount of land ploughed by a pair of bullocks in one morning) cultivated by a household in the village, tenants had to offer one plough team to work the family of the *mahaton*, the Tharu functionary working for the jimidar. Similarly, one female worker from the ploughman's family had to work in the same area for one afternoon (Rajaure 1981). Likewise, they also had to offer the free labour to the *mahatons* during the harvest of paddy. The requirement of a day's free labour to the village head (known still as *mahaton* or *barghar*) continued until relatively recently.

Incentives continued to be given to *jimidars* to accelerate the clearing of the forest frontier (see Figure 13). Yadav (1984) reports that a *jimidar* who clears forest would be given 10 years tax exemption and a tenth of the reclaimed land as a personal tax free *birta* which could be let out to tenants. They were also entitled to further grants of uncultivated *jirayat* lands. The latter did not include full property rights, but allowed the *jimidar*, as well as cultivating them alone, to sub-let lands to new immigrants or local farmers to yield rents, as long as taxes were paid (Regmi, 1976). *Jimidars* were also able to increase their personal holdings of taxable land to sub-let by illegally claiming land which should have been distributed to new settlers (Regmi, 1976).

For entirely uncultivated areas, wealthy settlers with capital from the hills were encouraged to create new estates by being offered the position of

Figure 13: Narayanghat of Chitwan during the Rana era. The Rana state intensified efforts to clear the forest frontier.
Photo: Madan Puraskar Pustakalaya, Reproduced with permission.

jimidar. For instance, in Morang, by clearing more than 100 bighas of land and bringing it under cultivation one could get an additional 25 bighas of land as Jirayat, while being recognized as *jimidar* (Regmi, 1978; DDC Morang, 2059 BS).

The availability of peasants to settle on new estates was a challenge. Provisions in Nepal's first legal code entitled foreign nationals to purchase titles to *raikar* land to speed up the process – supporting migration from India (Kansakar, 1985). This increased the population of Maithili, Bhojpuri and Awadhi speaking castes, particularly in the central Tarai belt. For example an 84 year old Mushahar informant from Tankisinuwari, Morang, interviewed in 2008 by one of the authors, recalled how he came to this place along with his father and many others from India to work for a Pradhan (Newar) landlord originally from Kathmandu, to clear the forest and make the land cultivable (field notes from researchers). There were relatively open immigration policies and incentives to encourage settlement. There were also many peasants driven over the border to Nepal to take up tenancies on new estates by the excesses of landlords in North Bihar after the colonial era Permanent Settlement (Regmi, 1988a).

Birta grants during the Rana era

During the Rana era, *birta* grants continued to be offered directly to members of the nobility both to strengthen the loyalty of the elite and to encourage settlement (Regmi, 1976). It is likely that a number of estates changed hands during the shift in the political balance of power, and Regmi suggests that few of the *birta* (or *guthi*) grants bestowed by the Gorkhali Shah kings prior to 1846 were still in place at the end of Rana rule by 1950. Nevertheless, the institution remained the same, and Rana rule saw an intensification of the distribution of new grants in the Tarai-Madhesh. As a move to enhance their political support, the Rana also made an effort to offer new *birta* grants of forest land in the Tarai-Madhesh to members of the nobility who had them confiscated in 1806 by King Rana Bahadur Shah (Regmi, 1976).

The heavily forested Morang and Sunsari region in particular, was the site of many *birta* grants, and as a result it emerged into a region with severe land inequality, with vast estates belonging to single families from the hills and cultivated by rent paying Adivasi farmers (Sugden, 2013). Records show evidence of land being cleared by General Bhim Shumshere J. B. Rana in Morang in the early 20th century, with tenure being changed to *birta* after the establishment of the settlement (Regmi, 1989a). While *birta* grants were most commonly distributed to member of the hill elite, there were also some cases of Adivasi beneficiaries. For instance, the Ranas gave *birta* donations of 100 bigha to each of the Tharu *Chaudhuris* of the Deokhuri area of Dang (a locale with limited influence of hill people) to thank them for building forts, irrigation canals and roads. This supported their emergence as large local landlords (Krauskopff, 1989).

In areas with a longer history of settlement and sedentary cultivation such as the caste Hindu heartland of Mithilanchal, some lands which were already settled and cultivated were transferred into *birta* tenure in the name of members of the nobility. Early 20th century records of *birta* grants from Mahottari-Dhanusha make it clear that these were 'cultivated lands', with one 182 bigha grant also listing the infrastructure that came with the grant such as residential sites, wells and ponds, (Regmi, 1989c).

As noted above, *birta* estates frequently had their own administration and revenue generation apparatus which differed from the *jimidari* system operating on *raikar* lands – and an extreme case during the Rana era was the far-western Tarai-Madhesh districts of Banke, Bardiya and Kanchanpur. Nepal ceded these territories to the British after the 1814–1816 Nepal–British war and their administration was passed on to the Nawab of Oudh (Regmi, 1981a). The lands were subsequently returned to Nepal in 1860 in appreciation of the military assistance offered by the Ranas during the 1857 mutiny. Thus, the restored territory was called *naya muluk* (new territory). It was recorded that after this, the then King Surendra granted half of the *naya muluk* to Janga Bahadur, while distributing the other half to his six brothers (Karki, 2002). The entire region thus became a personal *birta* for Jang Bahadur Rana's family with its own bureaucracy (Kansakar, 1985).

Prior to the Naya Mulak being transferred back to Nepal, the Nawab of Oudh had collected tax via a network of functionaries known as *Talukdars* (Regmi, 1981a), which included Kathariya Tharu chieftains (Johnson,

2023). After the region fell under *birta* tenure within the state of Nepal, the *talukdars* lost their role, and new functionaries known as *chaudhuris* (not to be confused with the pre-Rana position) were placed in charge of each *tappa* (or district) which would include a large number of villages (Regmi, 1981a). At some later stage, it appears that the land was possibly parcelled into smaller *birta* estates, as Karki (2002, 204) observes,

> "subsequently, Rana rulers granted land in Tarai-Madhesh to Shaha, Thakuris and Brahmins who were in the upper echelons of government ranks, army generals and members of nobility with a view to strengthening their power base in the remote villages in the Tarai-Madhesh, in general, and Banke and Bardiya, in particular. Land grants were thus made to the ruling elite in increasing number throughout the Rana regimes".

Cropping systems in Tarai-Madhesh (1750s-1900s)

After the Gorkha conquest, the primary divergence in cropping systems was between the lands under shifting cultivation and the land under permanent settled cultivation. The expansion of the latter was by far the most significant change taking place during this period.

In areas under shifting cultivation Hodgson (1880 [1847]) writing as of the mid 1980s with reference to the Dhimal (in the eastern Tarai and North Bengal), suggests that there was no irrigation yet a surprisingly diverse series of crops were farmed, cultivated once a year over the monsoon. Grain staples were dry rice (ghaiya dhan), millet, maize and pulses. However, farmers also produced oilseeds such as mustard; root crops such as yam; gourds, including popular Nepali vegetables today *karala* (bitter goard), lauka (bottle gourd) and *kakra* (cucumber); as well as peas, red pepper and cotton. Significantly, cotton was reported to be possibly the most important crop – as it was sold to procure rice to make up production shortfalls, suggesting that a rice-based food culture was well established, even amongst swidden cultivators by the 19th century[16] (Hodgson, 1880 [1847]). Later correspondences with Hodgson specifically with reference to Morang, points to the presence of Opium cultivation,

---

[16] As his study was focused mainly on data from Dhimal of North Bengal – this may not have been the case in the remoter communities of Nepal.

suggesting that cash crops were of emerging importance, even for forest dwelling communities (Campbell, 1841).

Elsewhere, with regards to the Tharu cultivators of the Chitwan valley, rice and mustard were also known to be common crops in the 19th century (Müller-Böker, 1999). There was some irrigation by diverting water from small streams. On these irrigated fields they would plant *jhinuwa dhaan*, a long grain rice, whereas in the dry fields, dry rice or mustard were cultivated. Both, direct sowing or transplantation was in practice. In any case, only one harvest a year was possible (Ibid.).

In the areas under permanent cultivation, paddy was, as one would expect, the predominant crop in the early Gorkha period – although the rice-wheat cropping system which had emerged in the western hills was constrained by the lack of irrigation for wheat. Other crops mentioned by Hamilton (2007 [1819]) from the early 19th century include tobacco, mustard and lentils. Government records from the early 19th century do make numerous mentions of irrigation infrastructure in Bara, Parsa and Rautahat - including disputes over water allocation. This includes irrigation channels and canals commissioned by the local Chaudhuris (tax collectors) (Regmi, 1978a). In most cases, irrigation was dependent upon private investment by enterprising farmers and landowners. While incentives were offered, such as meeting half the costs (Pradhan, 1990), the coverage of canals remained very limited. Burghart (2016), with reference to Mahottari notes that revenue collectors had limited incentives to encourage or invest in the construction of irrigation canals as they would not be in power long enough to benefit – and preferred to maximise their income by expanding their revenue collection rights to new areas of land, through for instance, seeking a higher rank which would increase the area of one's jurisdiction.

After the Rana takeover there was increased agricultural output. While this may have been driven in part by Rana policies, population growth and the rising cultivable area appears a more likely explanation (Seddon, 1987). Nevertheless, there was some modest development of the productive forces which likely contributed to greater cropping diversity as well as new cultivation techniques (Ibid.).

Paddy, millet and lentils were reported in government taxation records as the major crops from the Rana period (Regmi, 1988a)[17]. While wheat may have been produced as part of a rice-wheat cycle – most records of wheat production were from the hills where irrigation was widespread. Wheat is largely dependent upon some form of irrigation which remained limited in the plains at this time.

Only a few larger irrigation schemes were constructed during the Rana era, such as the Chattis Mauja irrigation network which was built during the time of Jang Bahadur. This was built by Tharu leaders (likely tax functionaries) – and the local Tharu continued to manage the system even after a large share of the land in the command area was given as *birta* to several hill upper caste families (Yoder, 1994), although whether they did so as tenants or as tax paying peasants operating irrigated plots in parallel to the landed estates, is not recorded. Later on, two further large irrigation systems were constructed. One was Chandra Nahar in Saptari, built in 1923. The other was the Judha Nahar, built in the 1940s (Pradhan and Belbase, 2018, Pradhan, 1989b). However, the reach of these canals was limited, and groundwater pumping technologies were yet to be widely available (Aubriot and Bruslé, 2023). The only alternative were village ponds (see Figure 14), which were particularly common in the Mithila region. Interviews carried out in four villages of Saptari and Dhanusha in 2012 suggested that many were constructed by *jimidars* during the Rana period. Few were linked up with a canal network, and water had to be physically transferred to fields manually using a paddle device, and thus large-scale irrigation was challenging. Ponds were also used as the primary source of household water use, as well as being used for livestock. In this context, it is likely that for a majority of the peasantry in the Tarai-Madhesh, the land was rainfed.

There were some efforts to establish commercial production in the plains during the Rana era – including some large-scale, state-run

---

[17] Records of prescribed land tax attest to the production of three categories of crops. Tax varied according to the crop, with lower rates for millets and lentils (12 annas per bigha) and higher rates for tobacco (6 rupees and 8 annas) (Regmi, 1988a). The latter was likely one of the few commercial crops produced on a small scale locally. Land tax for rice was around the middle (6-8 annas).

Figure 14: Irrigation pond in Thadi Jijha, Dhanusha (top) and Morang (bottom). These were the primary source of irrigation in the 19th century.
Photo: Fraser Sugden

plantations, with the sole aim of increasing government revenue. However, these were often short lived, and closed if they did not yield the government sufficient profit (Regmi, 1988a). The only commercial crop which appeared to grow in increasing volume was jute in Morang, which was largely cultivated by local farmers without government intervention from the late 19th century onwards. Earlier government efforts to establish jute plantations in the western Tarai-Madhesh failed (Regmi, 1988a). The land tenure system was an impediment to commercial production. Under Ranas, although *jimidārs* were supposed to encourage innovation and development in agriculture, Regmi (1976) asserts that, like under the earlier administration, their operations remained primarily restricted to the parasitic activities of tax collection, rent collection from tenants and usury.

Mode of production and tax collection hierarchy in the hills after the Gorkha conquest

Tax collection hierarchy and mode of production in areas under sedentary cultivation

As noted above, there was a significant difference in the agrarian mode of production between areas home to a predominantly Adivasi peasantry with livelihoods grounded in shifting cultivation and customary tenure, and areas with a sedentary peasantry – composed of tax paying Hindu castes and Adivasi groups which had already been 'subordinated' to feudalism. This section focuses on the latter domains, which includes much of the western hills and areas of the central and eastern hills close to state power. These regions were already under sedentary peasant farming at the time of annexation, with terraced farming, particularly of rice. While the mode of production could be characterised as 'feudal' even at the time of conquest, both localised and centralised feudalism prevailed depending upon the land tenure arrangements. A large share of the peasantry in these sedentary farming domains were tax paying proprietors, and the Gorkhas classified much of this land as *raikar*, like in the plains, while other lands were classified as *jagir* or *birta* (bestowed as land grant to individuals), and to a lesser extent as *guthi* (bestowed to a religious institution).

While the hills were a less important source of revenue for the state when compared to the lowlands (Regmi, 1988a) a large share of the peasantry still surrendered a significant share of their surplus either as tax directly to the state, or to the local landlords on large *birta* or *jagir* estates, which were under a localised form of feudalism. In the areas close to Kathmandu for instance, Kirkpatrick (2007 [1793]), reporting from shortly after the Gorkha conquest makes reference to an agrarian system dominated by both sharecropping on *jagir* and *birta* lands (particularly in the valleys such as Kathmandu itself and Nuwakot), as well as a tax paying peasantry (presumably on *raikar* holdings) in the surrounding hills. He suggests that there were different classifications of peasant on the basis of the number of ploughs they own, varying from those owning more than five ploughs, and those without ploughs, who were largely dependent upon labour. This suggests there was already considerable differentiation within the *raikar* farming peasantry in accessible parts of the central hills, although how this corresponds with ethno-caste divisions is unclear[18]. In the western hills, Pande (2014) also alludes to two parallel economic formations – one concerning peasant cultivation of taxable lands and another which involved cultivation of *birta* and *jagir* estates.

Taxable raikar lands in the hills

The share of the cultivable area under *birta*, *jagir* or *guthi* land grants compared to the area under *raikar* tenure, is not known and seems to vary by district. In Jajarkot for instance, which was under the tributary rule of a local raja, all the land was reportedly under *raikar* (Fortier, 1995). By contrast, Hamilton 2007 [1819] implies that further east, a notable share of the land in the old state of Makwanpur was under *jagir*, although given that he likely primarily visited selected areas close to state power, this is probably an overestimate. Taxable *raikar* land appears to have emerged as the most significant form of tenure across the hills in the decades after the

---

[18] Kirkpatrick's account is a travelogue from an Anglo-Irish East India Company (EIC) representative following the 1793 EIC mission to Nepal and makes numerous observations about the economic and political context in the format of a travelogue, yet the details were far from comprehensive with many inaccuracies.

Gorkha conquest as it sought to bring new areas under cultivation and maximise tax revenue. In the former Chaubisi and Baise Rajya where former petty kings were often tasked with tax collection, the pressure to raise revenues would have been high at a time when large areas of the Tarai were uncultivated. For instance, in the former principality of Khachi (present day Aragakhachi) the Raja in the early 19th century, would procure 4000 rupees a year from the hills in revenue as compared to just Rs500-1500 from the plains (Hamilton, 2007 [1819]).

While private property rights and a market for these taxable lands had already emerged in some domains such as the west – this was likely undermined as the Gorkhali state asserted its position as the ultimate landlord (Regmi, 1972). Regardless of ownership rights, taxation continued to be collected from peasant proprietors via a network of intermediaries, as it was in the pre-Gorkhali period, although there was considerable complexity due to the Gorkhas building upon the administrative foundations set by the multiple principalities which they conquered. This diversity also continued into the Rana era, unlike the Tarai which was placed under the relatively uniform *jimidari* system.

Regmi (1988) identifies three broad types of tax which were collected in the hills after conquest. First was tax on the house itself or 'roof tax', known as *saunefagu*. The *saunefagu* tax was fixed irrespective of family size or land size – although it was higher in the Kathmandu valley and lower in more remote areas (Regmi, 1988a). The second was the homestead tax or *serma*, on land around the home which usually included cattle sheds, kitchen gardens, and non-water retaining holdings or *pakho* used for dryland crops such as millet. Tax was assessed according to the number of ox teams required to plough the land. There were exemptions or ceilings on *serma* and *saunefagu* taxation for some privileged castes such as Rajputs and Thakuris (Regmi, 1988a). Finally, tax on more productive rice holdings or *khet* lands was the third type of revenue. The latter had the highest taxes, which were originally around 50% of the crop (Karky, 1981), although it later shifted to a fixed rate contract system in some parts of the hills. At a later stage land was graded according to four subcategories based upon productivity (Regmi, 1988, Karky, 1981).

Other than tax on crops, there were numerous other forms of tribute paid by farmers, particularly in the vicinity of the Kathmandu valley. These are described by Tamang (2008, 138): "Included among the varieties of random tax levied directly for the royal House of Gorkha were: chumāwan for the sacred-thread-investiture ceremony of the king or the crown prince, gadimubārak for the royal coronation, goddhuwa for the wedding ceremony of a royal princess, saunefāgu, a biannual tribute to the royal house from the rural households in the hill region..." Given that many of the upper castes holding jagir or birta lands paid little tax (particularly under the latter), the intense tax burdens in the areas close to the capital were disproportionately borne by the Tamang (Tamang, 2008).

In terms of the mechanisms to collect tax, systems included firstly, the *amanat* system in central hills (Karky, 1981), whereby like in the Tarai, a state functionary or *dware* was appointed to collect taxes and maintain peace and justice. The second was the *thekbandi* system which was widespread across the hills, where a *mukhiya* (who could include an Adivasi headman or member of the local landed upper castes) was fully responsible for collecting taxes from community members and had a contractual obligation in their personal capacity to do so (Regmi, 1978d).

The third was the *ijara* system (which often went alongside the *amanat* system) which placed a local individual in charge of tax collection. Rather than being a permanent government employee, an individual was appointed on a temporary basis to collect revenue. *Ijaras* were given based upon one's ability to make revenue payments in advance if the government required funds – and thus it normally went to wealthy individuals with capital (Regmi, 1984). Often those who generated more revenue for the government were able to take on *ijaras* – a process which often involved the government bypassing pre-existing mukhiyas under the *thekbandi* system to give *ijaras* to elites who could promise to meet higher revenue targets. *Ijaras* also had a right to dispense justice, and thus gave them the power to extract labour service and other concessions from the peasantry. This encouraged wealthy individuals to take up *ijaras* for personal enrichment (Regmi, 1978d)

A fourth form was the *thekthiti* (also known as *theka-thiti*) system in the former Baisi Rajya region which included less accessible parts of the western hills such as Jumla (with *thekbandi* being more popular in the lower hills of the west) (Pande, 2014), although *thekthiti* was also the main form of tax collection later in the Majh Kirat, which will be discussed in the next section (Russel, 1992; Gaenzle, 2000) and possibly other parts of the east. An individual, also known as a *mukhiya* or *jimmawalla* represented the community and would collect revenue equally from all members. The tax contract was given not to individuals but to the whole community for which a fixed amount was paid. Unlike *thekbandi* system full responsibility for tax payment lay with the community, not with the individual tax collector (Karky, 1981).

All the above forms of revenue generation likely led to growing inequalities in the areas of sedentary peasant proprietorship – like in the lowlands. For example, Regmi (1978d) reports how *mukhiyas* were under obligation to allot vacant land to landless peasants. However, if there was nobody to take the land immediately they were allowed to retain it temporarily as a personal holding. However, this often became permanent, even when tenants were available. They were also able to extract labour tribute (Holmberg et al 1999). However, it is likely that the tax collectors didn't accumulate the same quantities of land as in the Tarai-Madhesh, particularly under the Rana era where *jimidars* would receive tax free personal allotments of land alongside their responsibilities to collect tax.

There were also some mechanisms which limited internal inequality within the tax paying peasantry. The *raibandi* system was applied in some parts of the eastern and central hills after the 1830s (Regmi, 1976), at times replacing the *kipat* system which was widespread amongst some hill Adivasi groups (see below) (English, 1983). Under this system, the government would periodically redistribute *raikar* rice lands according to family size. This system while appearing 'equitable' at face value, supported the maximization of revenue in the hills, as it ensured each peasant had enough land for subsistence, and the likelihood of default on taxes was reduced. As a result, it was conducive to reproducing an agrarian structure in parts of the central or eastern hills dominated by small cultivators, with variations in wealth according to family size (Regmi, 1978d). However, it only applied to rice lands, so farmers could still accumulate large non-water retaining *bari* holdings. Also, farmers without rice lands at all were often not counted as eligible peasants, and thus were left out of the system. Likewise some farmers could also hold titles to large areas of non *raikar* lands simultaneously (Regmi, 1978d). Whelpton (1987) suggests that *raibandi* was not actually widespread and was often on *rakam* land – a form of *raikar* tenure where the tenant was expected to contribute labour. The *raibandi* system became redundant in the second half of the 19th century after Rana regime revised revenue records listing the cultivator, area of land held and tax due. Those on the record, which often included those who had invested capital to clear forest land, were in a long-term advantage, securing their long-term rights to the land. Only waste lands were left to redistribute to households who needed holdings (Regmi, 1976).

Birta and jagir lands in the hills

As noted above, *birta* and *jagir* lands were home to a parallel mode of production, with rent as the primary mechanism of surplus appropriation. While *birta* grants were less widespread than in the lowlands, they still played a critical role as part of the state building process. Grants were often gifted to local chieftains or nobility of old hill principalities – particularly in newly annexed lands such as Jumla, Dailekh and Baglung (Regmi, 1972). They were particularly valuable to reward rulers who had defected to support the Gorkhalis, and many recipients were allowed to retain their feudal titles albeit under the overlordship of Gorkhalis (Regmi, 1976). As noted above for the Tarai, *birta* grants which were provided by earlier rulers were restored so long as they pledged loyalty. The distribution of *birta* grants increased substantially during the Rana era, but their purpose was changing. Like in the Tarai-Madhesh, they were increasingly oriented around enriching the Ranas and their inner circle, rather than being a tool to win the loyalty of local nobles (Regmi, 1976). Peasants worked as tenants on *birta* lands, and would pay rent alongside the provision of forced labour for the landlord, known in the hills as *beth* (Tamang, 2008).

Jagir grants were particularly important in the hills[19]. Stiller (1975) suggests that large tracts of newly conquered hill land were parcelled out as *jagirs* to high ranking soldiers who had served in the Gorkha army in lieu of salary. *Jagirdars* emerged as small landlords. They had a right to appropriate 50% of the surplus from peasants working the land as tenants as well as collect non-agricultural levies and to evict peasants. They were often absentee landlords given that military duties often assigned them elsewhere (Ibid.). Many continued to farm these lands in the western hills as small landlords even after they were disbanded from the army following the end of the Anglo-Gorkha war (Pande, 2014).

The distribution of *jagir* grants was also widespread in the Kathmandu valley and surrounding fertile valleys of the central hills, and writing in the late 18th century, Kirkpatrick (2007 [1793]) implied that they took up a large share of the paddy growing land in the valleys of Kathmandu and Nuwakot, with peasants working as tenants on these lands, while cultivating the drier steeper slopes independently. Reporting in the early 19th century, Hamilton (2007 [1809]) also suggested that a large share of lands (at least those under the control of the state) in the old Sen territories of Makwanpur, Chaudandi and Vijayapur, were under *jagir*. Stiller (1975) suggests that the distribution of *jagir* grants and the pressure for new lands which this system created, contributed to the opening up of new areas to cultivation.

While there was a landlord class with extensive private holdings due to these various land endowments, their power was more localised when compared to their Tarai counterparts (Müller-Böker and Seeland, 1986). It is in the western hills where the greatest inequalities were likely to be present – given the presence of private property rights during the pre-Gorkha period, and the legacy of the Khas kingdom, and the smaller states which it disintegrated into (Regmi, 1972), and the large numbers of *jagirs* given out to members of the Gorkha army (Pande, 2014).

In terms of the relations of production on *birta* and *jagir* lands, like in the Tarai, they were dominated by localised feudal landlord-tenant

---

[19] Jagirs offered a way of paying the army, while the demand for such lands itself incentivised further military expansion (Stiller, 1975).

relations with surplus being appropriated in rent, in parallel to the tax paying peasants on *raikar* land. Sharecropping was the preferred mechanism of surplus appropriation, like in the plains (Regmi, 1972). Kirkpatrick (2007 [1793]) with reference to the Kathmandu valley and Nuwakot suggests that the *jagirdar* would generally just manage the cultivation of a small area independently (with labourers) to produce fruit and vegetables, with the remainder being handed over to sharecroppers[20].

At various points fixed rate tenancies were introduced in the hills. Kirkpatrick (2007 [1793]) suggests that while sharecropping was preferred on jagir estates, fixed rent tenancies in cash or a share of grain were sometimes used instead, which could offer a favourable share to the tenant. It is worth noting that this also put the tenant in a situation of extreme risk in the case of a failed harvest. In Doti for instance, the *kut* system was introduced in the late 19th century whereby *jagirdars* could receive a fixed amount of the harvest, guaranteeing them an income, even in the case of a failed harvest (Pande, 2014). However, this was counterproductive, and the hardship it caused the tenants forced many to flee their lands (Pande, 2014).

A hill land-owning class also emerged in the Rana era through the acquisition of land through means other than *jagir* and *birta* grants, particularly when there were already locally powerful tax collecting functionaries. This appeared particularly prominent in the west where the market for land was relatively well developed, allowing the emergence of an intermediary landowner class who could buy up holdings from smaller owners (Pande, 2014). It also emerged however in the central and eastern hills as upper caste landlords appropriated former *kipat* land from Adivasi communities, a process which will be discussed below. In the Arun basin for instance, tracts of fertile land on the valley floor which had once been under *kipat* tenure was in control of Brahmin and Chettri landlords by the Rana era (Sugden et al 2018).

---

[20] He refers to share tenancies as *buttye*, which corresponds with the term *bhattaiya* which is used in the Tarai-Madhesh and Gangetic Plains today to refer to sharecropping.

A related political intervention in the context of the annexation of smaller principalities, which often went alongside the distribution of birta grants, was the *rajya* system of the western hills. To win support of local rajas, they were granted varying levels of economic and political rights over their domains, while maintaining allegiance to and paying tribute to the state. They were given responsibility to collect taxes within the territory, and sometimes received *birta* grants alongside it (Regmi, 1978d). In these regions, landlords were often descended from local nobility who retained nominal political and economic power after the Gorkha conquest. Cameron's (1998b) study from Bhajang for instance, suggests that the largest landlords included the descendants of the Bhalara raja.

Caste and landownership

The body of evidence from the period suggests that the largest landlords were predominantly upper castes, although the relationship between caste and land ownership was different from the caste Hindu belt of the central Tarai-Madhesh (Hamilton, 2007 [1819], Stiller, 1975, Pradhan, 2009). In Mithila of the central plains for instance, the emerging inequality was between largely upper and middle caste tax functionary landlords or land grant recipients, and tenants were predominantly from the Dalit community (Sugden, 2019a). In the hills by contrast, the tenants included occupational Dalit castes, but also many Adivasi groups (see for instance Hitchcock, 1966 on the Magar), who had already become sedentary farmers and were integrated into the caste system by the Ranas (Höfer, 1979). The exception was in the Kathmandu valley whereby the Newar caste system facilitated the emergence of a clear land owning and tenant class which corresponded with the internal Newar caste hierarchy (Müller-Böker and Seeland, 1986), although even here it was complicated by the large tracts of land belonging to Khas castes which was under *birta* and *jagir* tenure, not to mention *guthi* lands (Müller, 1981, Webster, 1983).

In the western hills there were further complexities in the relationship between caste and land. This region was dominated almost entirely by Khas Chettris, Brahmins and Thakuri castes. Local landlords were entirely upper caste, particularly Thakuri, who made up a large share of the local nobility, and the majority of Dalits were landless. For instance, Cameron (1998b) suggests that the majority of the Dalit in her study site were tenants for the Bhalara raja. There were however, also likely many upper castes who lacked political connections who were also tenants – particularly when one considers that upper castes were the majority given the history of Sanskritization whereby a large share of the Khas peasantry adopted upper caste titles.

There were also localised landlord-tenant relations between upper caste large farmers and Dalit occupational castes (Cameron, 1998b) – linked to the *riti-bhagya* system of inter-caste exchange. Occupational castes would produce clothing, tools, metalwork and other commodities for the upper castes, facing limited market competition, and in return they would receive a share of the harvest, known as *khalo*. This system is similar to the *jajmani* exchange between castes in the plains. However, as will be described in the next section, this could also occur between Dalits and medium to large farmers and was not necessarily restricted to those who would be classified as 'landlords'

Internal migration in the hills

Following the Gorkhali conquest, there was a substantial rise in internal movement within the hills. In the wake of the westward expansion of the Gorkhali empire was a gradual migration of Khas Chettri and Brahmins who were carrying out sedentary, terraced rice farming, into Adivasi domains. While there was already a substantial Hindu caste population in the central hills[21] and smaller populations in pockets of the east before the 1770s, this migration appeared to have increased substantially following the Gorkha victory. As in the Tarai-Madhesh, to maximize tax revenue, it was necessary to increase the cultivable area by clearing hill forests, so the state actively encouraged this migration as it sought to bring new lands under cultivation (Regmi, 1976).

---

[21] For instance, Khas families from the Thapa clan who worked for Jaya Prakash Malla had lands in Tamang domains close to Kathmandu, and Brahmins held land in Ramechhap and Sindhuli under the patronage of the Sen kings of Makwanpur (Tamang, 2008).

The Tamang domains of the central hills saw Brahmin and Chettri farmers increasingly populating the fertile valleys, a process intensified by the distribution of *birta* and *jagir* grants and indebtedness amongst the Tamang (Tamang, 2008). The demographic change was perhaps most rapid in the Kirat region of the eastern hills (Gaenszle, 2000; Caplan, 1970). Migration to the east was primarily of upper caste Brahmin and Chettri, but they were also usually accompanied by Dalit occupational castes who would provide services to the upper castes as well as the Rai in return for grain, via the *jajmani* system (Gaenszle, 2000). While the occupational castes were often landless, the numerically and economically dominant Brahmin and Chettri were mostly peasant cultivators with varying sizes of holding, farming permanent fields. They would pay tax directly to the state, and were not directly subordinate to the local chieftains (Rai or others) (Gaenszle, 2000).

There was also continued smaller scale eastwards movement of Adivasi groups from the central hills such as Gurung and Tamang. Writings from Brian Hodgson in the 1830s for instance, from the main trade route east of the Dhud Koshi, point to quite ethnically diverse country, with villages of not only Kirat (Rai and Limbu) and Khas (presumably Brahmin, Chettri and occupational castes), but also Magar, Gurung and Tamang (Hodgson, circa 1830sa). The degree to which this emerging cultural diversity preceded, or succeeded, the Gorkha conquest is not clear, particularly for the Tamang who are well established in the region. Hamilton (2007 [1819]), writing in the early 19th century suggests there had been a movement of Tamang (referred to as Murmi) into more remote areas, including an eastward migration into areas still controlled by Sikkim (which includes parts of NE Nepal), to escape subordination to the Gorkhas[22]. Migrant Adivasi tended to exploit different ecological resources than the indigenous Kirat groups of the east. The Tamang farmed land high above the subtropical valley slopes inhabited by the Kirat (Gaenzle,

---

[22] Hamilton refers to their mistreatment by the new rulers in lieu of cultural practices such as cow slaughter as being behind their eastwards migration, although in reality, given the proximity of the Tamang homeland with Kathmandu and their disproportionate subjection to forced labour (Holmberg, 1999), there were likely clear economic reasons, including so called 'escape agriculture'.

2000), while the Gurung's livelihood in eastern Nepal were (like in their central hill homeland) more closely oriented around sheep herding rather than cultivation of crops (Northey and Morris, 1928). There were also localised populations of Magar in the central and eastern hills, particularly around forts – and it has been speculated that some were the remnants of the Gorkha army (Hamilton, 2007 [1819]). Hitchcock (1965) suggests this may also apply to the Gurung. Other migrations were associated with occupation, with the Majhi for instance, migrating up the major river valleys from the central Tarai into the hills to operate ferries and fish in the rivers (Sugden et al. 2018).

Forced labour and slavery

An important form of surplus appropriation by the state, particularly in the hills, other than tax, was a form of corvée labour – or 'labour rent', which became widespread in the middle hills following the Gorkha conquest, although it appeared to have increased considerably during the Rana era. Extracting labour rent was one of the few ways through which surplus could be appropriated from some of the remoter domains which were yet to fall under sedentary peasant cultivation. Mishra (1987) goes as far as to suggest that the lower levels of revenue extracted from the hills compared to the Tarai, were compensated for by the fact that the hills was a source of labour for the regime[23].

There were several mechanisms of labour rent extraction. Certain *raikar* lands were placed under a tenure known as *rakam*, whereby the users had obligations to provide unpaid labour to the state (Regmi, 1976). This was prevalent in the central hills around Kathmandu, in particular (Holmberg et al., 1999), and groups classified as *praaja* (which included Tamang, Rai, Limbu, Sunwar, Thangmi and Chepang) were obliged to provide labour service in order for them to continue to cultivate their land.

Within this region, the Tamang appeared to have borne a disproportionate share of the forced labour burden. They had been

---

[23] While Mishra refers largely to military recruitment and later wage labour with regards to the latter, one may also add the importance of the hills as a source of feudal 'labour rent' or *begar* (Holmberg et al., 1999).

relegated to a lower caste status in the Rana civil code than other Adivasi groups, and were categorised as *masinya*, or 'enslavable' (Holmberg, 2017). They also resided close to state political power in the capital. The Tamang headman or *mukhiya* was responsible for mobilising large groups on a regular basis to provide unpaid labour to serve the Rana elite. This included herding animals for the Royal dairies or work on fruit orchards. *Hulak* service was another form of regular compulsory labour which involved porterage of goods for the state (Regmi, 1982b), although who was required to provide this labour and for how long, is not clear. Royal orders to Danuwar and Kumal headmen from Nuwakot suggest that it was (like *rakam*) tied to land tenure – with cultivators of crown lands being required to provide porterage for the Royal palace.

Jhara or *begar* was a more occasional labour obligation which applied to all regardless of the land they were cultivating. *Begar* was labour mobilised on an emergency basis, whereas *jhara* was labour mobilised for public works projects (Singh, 1997). To give an example, government documents in the Dingla area of Bhojpur in the mid-19th century note how labourers were drafted in for a number of state projects including the construction of a fort, and even to support an elephant hunt (Regmi, 1987). Other examples include the construction of dams and embankments in Nuwakot (Regmi, 1982b).

While *Jhara/begar* teams were mobilised by members of the local tax administration, including Adivasi headman (Ibid.), there were also suggestions in royal orders from the mid-19th century, that *birta* estate owners in the eastern hills would be responsible for mobilising forced labour of their tenants on behalf of the state when needed (Regmi, 1982b).

It appears that the forced labour obligations of the peasantry frequently changed, and at times when forced labour was required for higher priority activities in particular locales, the peasantry were temporarily exempt from providing labour services elsewhere. For instance, royal orders from the eastern hills (Ibid.) suggest that provision of *jhara* for particularly large projects, would temporarily exempt workers from other labour services until further notice. Sagant (1996) provides evidence of this in Pallo Kirat or Limbuwan as part of an agreement with Subbas, whereby a tax of Rs1 would exempt households from being subject to *jhara* duties. Similarly, those providing *hulak* services or work in mines would also be sometimes *exempt* from *jhara/begar*, as would those living in border areas – possibly in case they were needed for defence.

While a lot of the research on forced labour is from the Adivasi domains in the central and eastern hills, there is less literature on the forced labour system in the western hills, but Chataut & Chataut (2013) suggests it was also widespread – whereby various forms of compulsory labour were provided by the peasantry, including in agriculture.

The state was not the only entity collecting forced labour. Corvée, whereby farmers would provide a labour tribute to local feudal nobility as a part of the rent on land, was prevalent across all cultures and regions. Amongst the Magar of Tara Khola valley in Baglung, the region was allotted to the King of Galkot as *rajya birta*. The indigenous Magar, while carrying out shifting cultivation and following customary tenure with some autonomy, still had to provide tribute as well as unpaid labor services for farm work, portering, construction and livestock (Gurung, 1996). *Birta* owners also had the rights at certain times to extract labour service from their tenants, like in the plains (Tamang, 2008). For instance, a royal order from Nuwakot appears to exempt *birta* owners from provision of *jhara*, but allows the latter to "obtain payments and services" from tenants instead (Regmi, 1982b).

Forced labour likely had a significant financial and demographic hardship on the peasantry. For example, people enlisted for portering were often expected to provide their own food for the months they were away, as well as tools which would otherwise be used in agriculture (Regmi, 1972). Even children were drawn into portering and other activities. The shortage of labour could even lead to the peasants' own land being left untilled (Tamang, 2008). Forced labour may have also contributed to depopulation of territories. Kirkpatrick 2007 [1793] suggests that labour obligations to porter goods between Kathmandu and Hetauda had contributed to the falling population of Chitlang of Makwanpur, as the peasantry fled to escape the labour burden[24].

---

[24] Given that this account was written shortly after the Gorkha conquest, this may have even started under the earlier Malla rulers (Chitlang was ruled by the Patan

Other than forced labour, slavery was also widespread at various points across Nepal. Accurate records are not known. British colonial records estimated that there were around 20-30,000 slaves in Nepal as of 1877 (Sen, 1973), although this was likely higher in the past. For instance colonial sources also suggested that 200,000 individuals were enslaved during the Gorkha rule in Garhwal (Regmi, 1972) – and while this may have been an exaggeration (particularly as the British were keen to justify their own annexation of the territory) – Regmi (1972) suggests that the number was still considerable.

Enslavement has received comparatively limited research – but Sen (1973) suggests there were three types of slave ownership in the 19th century. The first included members of the nobility who inherited slaves as ancestral property, the second included farmers who kept slaves to work on the land (although whether these were individuals 'bought' for the purpose, or were indebted bonded labourers as discussed below, is not clear). A third type related to actual traders of slaves, who would raise families in enslavement, and sell the members – although how this worked in practice was unclear. Bajracharya and Shrestha (1974) with reference to Dolakha, suggest that inhabitants of some *birta* lands were treated as de facto slaves, being offered as collateral for loans.

There appeared to be several mechanisms through which an individual became enslaved. For instance, some children were born into slavery, although the child of an enslaved women and a free-born master would be considered free (Sen, 1973). Enslavement appeared in some contexts to be as a punishment, for crimes ranging from rebellion to cow slaughter (Regmi, 1972). In Jumla, Pande (2014) reports that political adversaries or rebels, or individuals charged with certain crimes would sometimes be enslaved as punishment. One of the privileges granted to some *jagirdars* (recipients of *jagir* lands) was the right to enslave criminals, and the possibility to sell these slaves on to others (Pande, 2014).

There were likely economic elements as well, and as indicated above, debt was often one reason people would be enslaved. The lack of property rights to land meant that land could not be furnished as collateral, creating

---

kings), as Kirkpatrick himself notes as a possibility.

ripe conditions for bondage if the money couldn't be repaid (Regmi, 1972). The same also reportedly applied to unpaid taxes (Regmi, 1972). However, freedom could be provided once loans were repaid – and thus this arguably represents a form of indentured servitude rather than slavery per se – and was possibly a pre-cursor to the kaamaiya system which emerged in the western Tarai after the 1950s.

Sen (1973) also noted that impoverished Dalit families from the Newar and Khas populations, would sometimes sell children into slavery due to economic hardship. There was also cross border trade, with families in the North Indian plains selling children into slavery during times of hardship or famine (Sen, 1973), with similar cases of children from the western hills being sold in India and even Tibet. There were also cases of traders deceiving and trafficking individuals as slaves (Regmi, 1972, Sen 1972). While Jang Bahadur Rana legislated against the trade in free born individuals as slaves in the 19th century, he allowed those who were already enslaved to remain in slavery. The importance of slavery for agriculture is not clear – and while it appears that some landlords such as *jagirdars* held slaves (Pande, 2014), it is likely that many were also engaged in domestic labour by various members of the nobility. Slavery was only formally abolished in the 1920s.

Subordination of Adivasi modes of production

A significant change in the hills, was the gradual subordination of the hill Adivasi mode of production to the centralized state, and the process largely paralleled that which occurred amongst Tharu and other ethnic communities of the Tarai-Madhesh, albeit with some subtle differences. The Adivasi mode of production of the hills was dominated by shifting cultivation, customary tenure, and redistribution of surplus – yet its dissolution was a temporally and spatially uneven pattern. Like in the Tarai, there were areas in the southern belt of the hills where the Adivasi mode of production had already been partially dissolved or had given way to sedentary farming before or shortly after the Gorkha conquest – particularly in areas with robust state control and a revenue collection apparatus - see for instance Hitchcock, (1966) on the southern Magar, some of whom were already sedentary. English (1983) also gives the examples of Rai communities who were working as tenants on *jagir* and *birta* estates (some of which predate the Gorkha era) and carrying out the sedentary agriculture for their landlords, representing an entirely different agrarian formation from other Kirat.

However, much of the literature cited thus far suggests that many Adivasi domains of the hills retained relative autonomy under pre-Gorkha state formations – given the difficulties of collecting revenue from isolated valleys, or political decisions by earlier rulers to protect indigenous autonomy in return for military favours (as noted above). These factors continued to remain important as the Gorkha state consolidated its control and sought the loyalty from indigenous chieftains in the late 18th century. However, other than some more remote domains, it is likely that the Adivasi mode of production experienced an unprecedented wave of subordination throughout the 19th and early 20th century.

As landed estates were less prevalent in the hills when compared to the plains, a large share of the subordinated Adivasi peasantry appear to have become small tax paying proprietors of *raikar* lands (much like their caste Hindu neighbours), albeit with pockets of localised landlord-tenant relations. The processes through which this transition took place in large tracts of the hills during the Gorkha and Rana era are outlined below.

Creation of functionary class

As occurred across Nepal, the Gorkhali state preserved and intensified existing indigenous hierarchies to support the state revenue generation apparatus. This intensified following the capture of state power by the Rana clan in the mid-19th century. Adivasi chieftains in particular, saw their political and economic power increase, as the Gorkha and Rana rulers required their loyalty not only to maintain and legitimise central rule, but to manage the collection of revenue and mobilise forced labour. While in the Tarai, this contributed to the emergence of an Adivasi landed class and was a key process through which the Adivasi mode of production was subordinated to centralised feudalism, in the hills this played a more complex role.

Amongst the Tamang for instance, the state created a two tier division between village headman or *mukhia*, and ordinary peasants, who became known as *raiti* which referred to a kind of tenant (Holmberg, 2017). The headman was responsible for mobilising forced labour, dispensing administrative justice and collecting tax. There were two tax collection roles, that of the *jimwal* (also referred to elsewhere as jimmawala) who collected tax on paddy fields, and who took care of judicial matters, and the *talukdar* who collected tax on dry fields (Holmberg, 2017). There were also several subordinate roles to support them, which were also drawn from pre-existing indigenous hierarchies - including *badhauli* (elder), or *thari* (clan chief) (Holmberg et al., 1999). These positions existed alongside other state enforced administrative roles taken almost exclusively by Brahmins and Chettris such as overseers of state herding operations. The power of the *mukhiyas* were ritually upheld by the Buddhist lamas, who managed village religious affairs. Tamang peasants were also obliged to offer unpaid corvée labour to the mukhiya. There is evidence therefore that there was growing differentiation within Tamang society.

In the east, internal stratification appeared slower and more modest. Like elsewhere, the traditional *Kirat* political structure was integrated into the state administration system, and the responsibilities for tax collection, administration and dispute resolution was superimposed onto the position of clan headman (McDougal, 1973, Fitzpatrick, 2011, Gaenszle, 2000, Russel, 1992, Sagant, 1996). The Gorkhas were late to impose taxes initially in Pallo and Majh Kirat as they consolidated their empire, yet a taxation system was eventually imposed several decades after the conquest (Russel, 1992). Hodgson (1988 [1848]) in his discussion on taxation in the Dhankuta region, confirms that Rai chieftains were being taxed by the mid-19th century, although he suggested it was lower than elsewhere in Nepal. The taxation system in the eastern hills, was from 1820 the *thekka thiti* (or *thekthiti*) system (which replaced the *ijara* system initially imposed). Under the thek-thiti system in Pallo Kirat (Limbuwan), tax was composed of three fees, the fixed sum of Rs5 to be paid by all households or *thek*; a fee of Rs1 which exempted one from forced labour or *jhara*, and a fee of Rs 0.5 for a waiver of caste rules (Sagant, 1996). Tax would be paid on kipat according to the number of households rather than the area of land (Gaenszle, 2000). The Kirat clan headman was responsible for collecting this revenue from *kipat* and *raikar* land (Russel, 1992, Sagant, 1996). The reinforced headman role had different names including *talukdar* or *jimmawala* in the Majh Kirat (Russel, 1992, Gaenszle, 2000) or Rai itself and parts of the central hills (Holmberg, 1999) the *subba* in the Limbu domains of Ilam (Caplan, 1970), and the *majhiya* amongst the Yakha in Sankhuswabha (Russel, 1992).

It does not appear that they were able to appropriate a significant share of the tax revenue or any commission on this (Sagant, 1996). Nevertheless, other than tax collection, Kirat chiefs were offered strengthened judicial power, and the right to collect fines from the local population (Gaenszle, 2000), which would be transferred to the state along with tax (Russel, 1992), and also extract labour tribute (Sagant, 1996). This allowed them to accumulate some wealth, and was possibly more significant than as a source of personal revenue for the headman than one's tax collection role (Gaenszle, 2000). They were also entitled to a share of some of the resources from the *kipat* area including from hunting, as well as receiving gifts from migrants from outside of the area who wanted to farm the clan's kipat lands. There was some labour service required for the headmen, although this was often modest, at a few days a year, with most of the burden being borne by migrants from outside of the area (Ibid.).

The degree to which significant 'accumulation' took place was variable depending on a range of agro-ecological, cultural and economic factors. Nevertheless, it will have to some extent undermined the redistributive and egalitarian ethos within Adivasi society, although not to the same extent as in the plains where a robust Adivasi landlord class had been established. The next process – the loss of communal lands, was likely the most significant contributing factor to the subordination of the Adivasi mode of production.

The protection and dissolution of customary tenure

The second process through which the Adivasi mode of production was dissolved was through their growing alienation from land. This process has been complex and entails a multifold process of customary tenure being dissolved in favour of household-based titles to *raikar* land, and subsequent dispossession due to debt, not to mention the growing physical shortage of land due to rising population and growing competition for resources with upper caste settlers and land grant recipients.

We will start with a discussion of the loss of customary tenure. What was unique in some parts of the hills was that customary communal tenure which was emblematic of the Adivasi mode of production, was actually protected initially by the state, as a means to maintain the loyalty of the clan leaders. The tenure of these lands were known as *kipat*. While *kipat* as a term is closely associated with the Kirat of eastern Nepal where the tenure was most widespread, the term itself is not indigenous, but is derived from a Sanskrit term *kripatra*, which referred to a grant given to a particular clan or group (Regmi, 1972). As well as amongst the Kirat, *kipat* tenure was also recognised for other ethnic groups in the central hills including the Tamang (Tamang, 2008) Chepang (Regmi, 1970b) and Thami (Shneiderman, 2015)[25].

There is a possibility that the confirmation of *kipat* titles to the Adivasi peasantry goes back to the pre-Gorkha states. For instance, Tamang (2008) notes that *kipat* titles were given to Tamang in Kavrepalanchok district by the Malla kings who had control of the region, and the Gorkhas reconfirmed these rights (Tamang, 2008). Some lands which were also initially confiscated were returned as kipat after a Tamang revolt in the Nuwakot region in 1791-93 (Tamang, 2008). However, *kipat* lands when restored often reinforced unpaid labour obligations. Throughout the 19th century, these lands were gradually reappropriated. Various land surveys reduced the *kipat* area to a minimum, often being re-classified as *rakam* (a form of tenure which included a compulsory labor tax for the state), and there are few records of *kipat* amongst the Tamang after the end of the 19th century (Tamang, 2008).

It is in the east however, where the dissolution of *kipat* was most drawn out, and is also the most well documented. When Kipat tenure first

---

[25] Shneiderman (2015) suggest that kipat may have been present in earlier state formations – including the Newar principality of Dolakha, which gave kipat rights to the Thami.

emerged in the eastern hills, it was offered not initially in a specific legislation but through an agreement that Limbu communities could continue to enjoy the customary rights they held prior to conquest – much like their Tamang counterparts described above. This was a critical means through which to subdue potential rebellion. This was summed up in a much quoted edict to Limbu chieftains by Prithvi Narayan Shah: "Enjoy your land from generation to generation, as long as it remains in existence... In case we confiscate your land, may our ancestral gods destroy our kingdom." (Regmi, 1972, 50).

With reference to Pallo Kirat (Limbuwan), Caplan (1970) records the first written evidence of a Limbu *subba* (chieftain or headman) being given formal *kipat* rights in 1825. Such land could not be alienated to non-Limbus as per the law (Fitzpatrick, 2011). *Subbas* were responsible for collecting taxes from both their own clan as well as other ethnic groups who had migrated into the region (Ibid.). As noted above, tax was imposed on each homestead rather than on plots of land – which would have been much easier to collect from farmers still engaged in shifting cultivation. In the Majh Kirat region between the Dudh Koshi and Tamur rivers where the Rai were predominant, this homestead tax was known as *serma* and was imposed on each user of *kipat* lands (Gaenszle, 2000).

While protecting customary tenure was important on a political level, it yielded much less revenue than *raikar* lands which were under sedentary cultivation (Sundas, 2020). This created the conditions whereby the state encouraged the conversion of *kipat* lands to *raikar* in spite of earlier commitments to protect the tenure. This applied particularly to low altitude forested valleys which could become high yielding paddy lands. Part of this process entailed the state encouraging the settlement of rice cultivating caste Hindus (Regmi, 1972). The westwards migration of Khas-Chettri and Brahmins, which expanded the tax paying peasantry, paved the way for the end of the protection offered by *kipat* tenure, and in turn, contributed to a long-term trend of dispossession.

The erosion of *kipat* which ensued did not take place overnight, but was a gradual process which took place between the middle of the 19th and early 20th centuries. There is also evidence that some groups such as the Limbu were able to hold onto Kipat rights for longer (even up until the mid 20th century), yet discussions on *kipat* amongst the Rai (English, 1983) imply that the tenure was dissolved relatively quickly. The processes described below largely refers to the Rai and Limbu domains of the east where the dissolution has been most well documented.

As a first stage in the erosion of communal tenure, the Rai and Limbu were encouraged to settle immigrants on their own *kipat* land (Gaenszle, 2000, Caplan, 1970). In Pallo Kirat or Limbuwan, the holdings given to settlers were known as *soranni* (Caplan, 1970). While land was abundant, the Rai and Limbu tolerated this migration, given that they exploited different agro-ecological niches and brought new agricultural skills. The incoming caste Hindus brought with them paddy cultivation, as well as associated technologies such as terracing (see Figure 15 and Figure 16) (Gaenszle, 2000, Caplan, 1970, English, 1983). While still subject to surplus appropriation to the state through tax, the Hindu castes were part of a quite different mode of production from the indigenous population, grounded in the cultivation of individual fixed family plots.

English (1983), with reference to the Rai, suggests that Kirat headmen actually profited from allowing settlers. This was because Brahmin and Chettri migrants of influence were granted a sub-headman role or *thari* and they would collect tax on the newly settled lands within the *kipat* area, including revenue from any later settlers. They would in turn pay a tribute to the Rai headman. This echoes an observation by Sagant (1996) from Pallok Kirat (Limbuwan), who suggests that the powers bestowed by the state to the clan headman or subba meant they increasingly saw the *kipat* lands as their 'personal' holding – rather than the collective lands of the clan segment, paving the way for decisions driven by self interest, which ultimately contributed to the alienation of Limbu land.

Resentment and struggles over resources grew as the number of migrants rose and land scarcity became more widespread (McDougal, 1979). Communities often came into direct conflict with the state for failing to allow incomers to take up lands (Sundas, 2020). Nevertheless, by the late 19th century, the eastern hills had experienced a demographic and agricultural transformation due to in-migration, and the clearing of new land paved the way for gradual erosion of communal *kipat* tenure, and the rising power of a new upper peasantry.

Figure 15: Paddy fields in the Pokhara valley. This valley was for several centuries, home to some of the richest rice growing lands in the hills.

Photo source: Harold L Dusenberry Collection, Madan Puraskar Pustakalaya. Reproduced with permission.

Figure 16: Terraced agriculture in the Rai village of Moli, Okhaldhunga. Terraced paddy cultivation was adopted by the Rai relatively late following the in-migration of caste Hindus from further west

Photo: Fraser Sugden

Although, in 1883 it was specifically decreed that *kipat* land could not be alienated, twenty years later (in 1903) orders were issued to permit the alienation of *kipat* jungle or waste lands to other settlers, on condition that it was converted into paddy fields (Regmi, 1965). State policy thus dictated that land brought under permanent cultivation within the *kipat* area was automatically converted into *raikar* tenure[26] (Gaenszle, 2000, Fitzpatrick 2011), even though the Kirat headman retained tax collection and judicial responsibilities over the settlers (Sagant, 1996).

This dissolved the remaining rights that the Kirat had to holdings of kipat land they had earlier given to new settlers, such as the Limbu's *sorrani* holdings. The change was permanent, and such land could not ever be converted back to *kipat* again (Regmi, 1965). While local Kirat could also clear forest land and claim it as *raikar*, incomers had the advantage due to their greater wealth and capital, setting the seeds for future ethnic disparities in landownership (Gaenszle, 2000).

As noted above, it was uncultivated yet highly productive valley land within the kipat area which was suitable for rice cultivation (*khet*), which tended to be appropriated by incomers. The migrant Hindu castes had resources and technology to clear the jungle, after which it could be claimed as personal *raikar* land (Gaenzle, 2000). The fact that the Kirat had not cultivated the lower valleys has a long history. Colonial accounts from the late 18th century (Kirkpatrick, 1796) and 19th century (Hodgson, 1988 [1848]) make frequent reference to low valley lands or *besi* being dangerous due to malaria or *aul*, and notes that for this reason the Kirat rarely "dwell in" the lower valleys (Hodgson, 1880 [1847]). While later accounts of Rai villages alongside the Arun River contradict this claim, it does appear from the larger literature (e.g. Gaenzle, 2000) that the primary agro-ecological belt for the Kirat was the temperate middle valley slopes (see Figure 17). As their swidden-based cropping system of millet and other coarse grains was suitable for the rainfed fields on the upper slopes and land was plentiful, it is quite possible that they had limited need to cultivate the lower valleys given the risks of doing so.

---

[26] These newly cleared lands would sometimes become part of the *raibandi* system (English, 1983).

Set against this context, it appears that upper caste settlers with resources began to clear the forest and create rice fields, while residing in villages higher up on the valley slopes, above the malarial zone. Hodgson (1988 [1848]) for instance refers to fertile lands on the edge of the Dhud Koshi belonging to Brahmins living higher up, suggesting that the appropriation of besi land by upper castes was already well underway on the fringes of Majh Kirat during the mid-19th century[27]. He also refers to the village of Mangmaya in Dhankuta (which includes a large area of irrigated land suitable for paddy) in the mid-19th century as being a Rai and Limbu village, yet research carried out by one of the authors in 2004 (Sugden, 2004) in the same settlement found it to be home predominantly to Brahmin and Chettri castes. This points to a *possible* transfer of land in the preceding century and a half of fertile lands of the lower Mangmaya Khola valley from Rai/Limbu families to upper castes.

Other ways in which *kipat* land was converted to *raikar* in Caplan's (1970) study of the Limbus included the appropriation of land for public works, or failure to identify a Limbu heir following the death of a landowner. Alienation was facilitated by a legal process biased against Limbus during disputes. Kipat lands could also be directly seized as a form of collective punishment for misdemeanours. For instance, a notice from Jang Bahadur Rana in 1847 urged a community of Chepang who had fled to return to their holdings, threatening the confiscation of the communities' *kipat* (alongside enslavement), should they fail to cooperate (Regmi, 1970b).

Debt and the mortgaging out of land to outsiders was however, one of the greatest factors contributing to alienation of land and conversion of *kipat* holdings to *raikar*. While settlers were quick to achieve *raikar* rights to the lands they had cleared, as land became scarce, expanding one's holdings was dependent upon buying up mortgages on lands which were often still under kipat (Sagant, 1996). Gaenszle (2000) reported Rai

---

[27] As an aside it is worth mentioning that Hodgson suggests this area was under the control of a local Chettri overlord. Whether they were a *birtawala, jagirdar* or simply a powerful local administrator is not known, and thus the land may not have been *raikar*, although it demonstrates a trend of caste-based control over land which would become more prevalent across the eastern hills in the years ahead.

Figure 17: Highly fertile besi (valley) land at the base one of the Arun tributary basins in Bhojpur (top) and the Rawa Khola valley of Khotang (bottom). This land was cleared relatively later, often by Brahmin and Chettri settlers, who remain the primary population at these lower altitudes today.
Photos: Fraser Sugden

households offering their *kipat* plots on which they have customary rights, to an incomer in return for loans, with it being appropriated if the debt remained unpaid, and converted to *raikar* tenure. Lower levels of literacy, and weaker political connections amongst Kirat when compared to upper caste incomers meant that the former were often vulnerable to loss of *kipat* holdings due to deception when the loans became unrepayable (Caplan, 1970). There was also widespread deception during the repayment of loans, with tricks including the addition of extra zeros to credit agreements. Similarly, government demands for documentary evidence of *kipat* titles, which many farmers often did not have, were often used to the advantage of incomers to legally justify the seizure of their lands (Caplan, 1970). While *kipat* rights to paddy growing lands were abolished entirely in 1907 (at least in Majh Kirat) with all land being registered as *raikar*, this made little difference as most land had already been cleared and converted to *raikar* (Gaenzle, 2000). *Kipat* tenure on dry upland fields was formally dissolved much later, and this will be described in the next section.

It is important to note that not all of the alienated *kipat* land went to 'outsiders'. Gaenszle's (2000) study suggest there were many transfers of land to local Rai, who became *raikar* title holders. However, the government had attempted to control and dilute the authority of Rai chieftains by placing limits on their authority and by providing titles and privileges to a broad set of families to limit the concentration of political power (Gaenszle, 2000). For this reason, control over large tracts of land was rare and they never developed into the indigenous landlords which were present in the Tarai-Madhesh – instead becoming tax paying peasant farmers as the *kipat* system fell apart (Gaenszle, 2000). Likewise for the Limbu elite, with reduced access to land, the economic benefits of being a *subba* dissipated, particularly when many had social obligations (Caplan, 1970).

It is important to note that while *kipat* was a formally protected form of customary clan-based ownership, as noted above, there were many other forms of communal, customary tenure systems across the hills, which were central to Adivasi livelihoods, and as Gurung (1996) notes, not all of these lands were legally recognised as *kipat*. Customary tenure of these clan lands was dissolved through the same mechanisms outlined above –

namely clearing of valley land by caste Hindu settlers and deception. There is however, very limited research on this topic. The evidence of this process is clear however, when looking at the distribution of land. Hitchcock's study in Magar settlements in Syangja for instance in the 1950s, indicates how Brahmins came to control the best land due to higher levels of education and close relation with historic state formations under the Chaubisi Rajya and Gorkha regime (Hitchcock, 1974). There is a good chance that some of these lands were under some form of informal customary tenure like Magar elsewhere (Gurung, 1996), yet were gradually alienated throughout the 18th and 19th centuries.

Alienation of Adivasi lands and Land grants

The distribution of land grants was another mechanism through which kipat lands were lost. While the distribution of *jagir* and *birta* lands was widespread in the hills (Regmi, 1972), unlike in the Tarai, the degree to which this included customary lands cultivated by local Adivasi groups has received limited research. Gaenzle (2000) suggests that there were *jagir* lands in the Majh Kirat region, with *jagirdars* playing a role in the collection of tax from *kipat* holdings in the vicinity – although the data is not clear.

Land grants do appear to have been particularly significant in contributing to land alienation amongst the Tamang in the central hills. As noted above, the Tamang had legally sanctioned *kipat* lands which were gradually withdrawn throughout the 19th century (Tamang, 2008). Perhaps the most significant way in which they lost their land however, was via the distribution of land grants. The fertile valleys of the former Tamang principalities were particularly sought after for land grants due to their proximity to Kathmandu (Tamang, 2008, Tamang, 2009). These included firstly *jagir* estates which were awarded to the army – and the distribution of *jagirs* continued until the 1950s in some locales of Sindupalchok and Kavrepalanchok[28] (Mahat et al., 1986). *Jagirs* in this

---

[28] Mahat (1986) suggested that giving out jagir grants close to the capital was important to incentivise recruitment from the central hills at a time when many were joining the British army.

region initially often just involved the tax being paid by the existing peasant to the *jagir* holder instead of the government, but as the demand for resources to support the military increased, then land was often alienated from the existing title holders and given directly to the *jagirdar* (Tamang, 2008).

Birta distribution to a small group of Brahmin, Chettri and Thakuri families was also significant in the low-lying valleys in districts such as Sindupalchok, Dolakha and Sindhuli[29], and the pre-existing Tamang peasantry would often become immediate tenants, obliged to surrender 50% of their crop as rent (Tamang, 2008). For instance, fertile paddy growing domains such as the Melamchi valley also saw large tracts of *kipat* land being given as *birta* or *jagir* to Brahmins (Pokharel, 2010). High profile grants include 10,000ha awarded to a colonel, which eventually extended to around 35,094ha of land across Dholakha and Sindupalchok, including vast areas of forest. Local herders who used this land were expected to pay in kind rent in the form of agricultural produce, wool, ghee and other forest produce (Mahat et al., 1986). Enclosure also extended to the enclosure of common lands for which Tamang peasants once had customary access to. For instance, the creation of pastures for royal dairies north of Kathmandu by the Ranas, for which the Tamang were drawn in for forced labour or *rakam*, also resulted in communities losing access to valuable pasturelands which in the past would have been used for their own herds (Holmberg et al., 1999).

Debt, differentiation and the emerging landlord class

Even once customary lands had been converted into *raikar* following the eventual dissolution of the Kipat system – losses of land amongst the Adivasi communities of the hills continued, due to debt, deception or tax default, like the processes described above – and this contributed to an emerging non-Adivasi landlord class.

---

[29] For example, Tamang (2018) recounts how in 1806, a high level officer Ujir Singh Thapa was rewarded with a grant of villages and plots of irrigated lands stretching from the east of the Indrawati River to Dolakha by King Girban Yudda Shah.

In the Arun valley for instance in Majh Kirat, there was an emerging Brahmin and Chettri landlord class (Sugden et al., 2018). Other than those who had received *birta* and *jagir* grants, incomers who had taken on tax collection roles such as *thari* (English, 1983) on non-kipat lands, were able to accumulate wealth, for instance through appropriating *raikar* land from farmers who failed to keep up with tax payments (Sugden et al 2018). They also emerged into a money lending class (English, 1983), and could appropriate land from poorer farmers due to unpaid debts. In Sugden et al's (2018) study, these landlords came to control a large area of land at the base of the fertile Chirkhuwa valley. Similarly, amongst Thami, land was lost to high caste settlers, who loaned money at high interest, with subsequent debt resulting in the loss of holdings (Shneiderman, 2010).

Similarly, amongst Tamang who had secured plots of private *raikar* tenure following the dissolution of customary systems, encounters between wealthier Brahmin and Chettri farmers, combined with the impoverishment brought about by decades of forced labour for the state, led to a cycle of debt, which often resulted in the dispossession of land (Holmberg et al., 1999, Tamang, 2008). Like in the east, it was common for Tamang families to lose fertile valley land through taking large loans from Brahmin and Chettri settlers, yet have their land seized when they defaulted. Sometimes this process of dispossession also involved direct deception at the hands of predatory landlords (Holmberg et al., 1999). Similar findings were evident in the Melamchi valley, where the Tamang sold a large share of the best paddy land to Brahmins throughout the Rana era (Pokharel, 2010).

The process through which the Adivasi of the hills were dispossessed was a slow one which took place over a number of decades, including a combination of legislation biased against the Adivasi peasantry by a feudal state and in-migration, as Uprety (2021, 185), sums up, with reference to the Limbu domains of Pallo Kirat:

> "inequitable agrarian policies adopted by the Gorkhali state of predatory nature during the process of territorial or political unification and its successive governments since the last quarter of the 18th century until the late 1960s were primarily responsible for the accumulation of resources

(land, forest, and revenues from them) traditionally held under communal ownership for the entrenchment of political and economic interest of the ruling elites, and loyalists of the regimes at the state level and the embourgeoisement of a select group of immigrant people belonging to Hindu high caste social structure through the dispossession and the consequent pauperization of the generality of indigenous Limbus peasantry at the individual household level".

Search for new land and Adivasi internal migration

As noted above, there has been an eastward migration of Adivasi groups within the hills over the last few centuries. While some of this movement may have been linked to the settlement of soldiers of the Gorkha army, some Adivasi movement may have represented a form of 'escape agriculture'. As already discussed above, the eastward movement of the Tamang, who increasingly cultivated the high ground above the Rai and Limbu, may have been connected with an attempt to escape subordination (Hamilton, 2007 [1819]). Adivasi migration may also have been simply linked to population pressure and a search for land to cultivate as *raikar* or as a tenant on landed estates – no doubt facilitated by the introduction of new cereal crops such as maize, and potatoes (Sugden et al 2018).

Another form of internal migration in the east included Kirat sub-groups from other parts of the eastern hills who settled on more marginal land above or around the established settlements (Gaenszle, 2000). The Chirkhuwa sub-basin for instance, is traditionally home to the Sampang Rai, but over the decades there has been migration of sub-groups such as the Kulunge and Bantawa Rai, mostly from the Dudh Koshi basin in the west (Sugden et al 2018) – an eastwards migration described by McDougal (1979). As noted above, Dahal (1981) reported migrant Rai from other regions being integrated into the clans in the areas where they settled and having access to the *kipat* land – and this was useful for clans at a time when labour was scarce. Similarly, Caplan also notes that at times when land was abundant, Limbus from other areas were given rights to use *kipat* lands in the areas they settled (Caplan, 1970).

However, Dahal (1981) notes that this flexibility became less tenable as land became scarce – reminding one of the importance of abundant land, to facilitate an equitable distribution of resources. Following this, it was likely that migrant Adivasi farmers would use the *kipat* land belonging to the clan who were established in an area, on payment of an in-kind tribute, as shown by Gaenszle (2000) in the upper Arun valley. In his case study, these dependent *kipat* users were termed *dhaakre* and would purchase the right to use the land with a symbolic gift paid twice a year to the headmen – this may for instance include sheep for those who used the high pastures. Their position appeared heavily subordinate, particularly as land became scarce and their dependence increased, and *dhaakre*[30] were often expected to conduct labour service for the headmen (Ibid.).

Following the dissolution of *kipat* and other customary tenure systems, what this meant for these dependent Adivasi groups is not known. Some may have had their lands converted into *raikar*. Some may have also become tenants on landed estates which were an outcome of the alienation of *kipat* lands – for instance, many of the sharecroppers in the Bhojpur case study by Sugden et al (2018) were in fact Magar living below the Rai on the latter's former *kipat* lands, albeit paying rent to new Brahmin overlords.

End to shifting cultivation

The alienation of customary lands and the dissolution of *kipat* tenure also contributed to the demise of shifting cultivation. The latter depended on large areas of forest land against which farmers had use rights. Even after the conversion of most farmland to *raikar*, shifting cultivation will have persisted on state owned forests where looser customary rights existed (Sugden et al 2018, Gurung, 1996). However, with the population continuing to rise with in-migration as well as natural population growth within Adivasi society, and with a contracting forest frontier as former *kipat* lands were converted into fixed permanent fields, shifting cultivation became an increasingly less viable livelihood strategy, and farmers had no choice except to intensify production on fixed sedentary fields (Sugden et al., 2018), particularly in the lower segment of the middle hills. Contact

---

[30] The term *dhaakre* refers to the carrier of a *dhoko* or basket, implying that the position of these migrants was servile in nature Gaenzle, 2000).

with Hindu castes meant that Kirat farmers had learned the techniques of terraced paddy cultivation, and this was increasingly adopted in low lying valleys, with terraced production of maize and coarse grains on the drier *bari* fields (ibid.).

Uneven dissolution of the Adivasi mode of production

As noted above, the process through which Adivasi modes of production were dissolved was uneven across Nepal. Some groups such as the southern Magar sub-tribes were likely some of the first to experience subordination to the state and transition to sedentary rice cultivation, possibly even before the Gorkhali conquest (Hitchcock, 1965). Elsewhere, the process of subordination between the Gorkha conquest and mid-20th century was highly uneven across time and space. If one takes shifting cultivation as a proxy, there is evidence that this was widespread across the hills, even in the Tamang domains in the vicinity of the Kathmandu valley[31]. Hodgson (1988 [1848]) suggested that as of the mid-19th century Murmi (reference to Tamang) and Magar were sedentary cultivators while Rai and Limbu were still shifting cultivators. This was however, likely a sweeping generalisation. Anthropological research from the hills, including research on upland Magar (Hitchcock, 1974) (particularly so called Kham Magar) and Gurung settlements (Macfarlane, 1976) and Tamang (Fricke, 1984) has found that economic, political, ecological, cultural and demographic factors, all shaped the degree to which the elements described in this book as the 'Adivasi mode of production' persist.

---

[31] Kirkpatrick's (2007[1793]) report from his visit to Kathmandu, Chitlang and Nuwakot in the late 18th century, makes reference to three land types – (i) *Kaith* (a mis-romanization of *khet*), which like today refers to low lying irrigated fixed fields – and he suggests was mainly under sharecropping tenancy; (ii) *Bari*, which referred like today, to upland unirrigated fixed fields used for vegetables and other crops; and (iii) *Kohrya*, which is less productive forest land used to cultivate crops such as maize, dry rice (ghaiya dhan) and millet, and was cultivated by 'lower classes'. The use of the term *kohrya*, which will have been the incorrect romanization of the commonly used term for shifting cultivation *khoriya*, indicates that this form of agriculture was widespread, possibly amongst the local Tamang, even directly north and south of the Kathmandu valley in the trade corridor running from Chitlang to Nuwakot.

As noted above, loss of customary land (often to settlers), taxation and the creation of an indigenous functionary class were central processes of subordination. However, in areas where land was abundant or competition with upper castes was limited, and the administrative reach of the state was poor, then evidence suggests that the Adivasi mode of production persisted throughout the 19th and even 20th centuries. For instance, taxation was levied on Adivasi groups carrying out shifting cultivation at an early stage in locales where the state had a strong administrative apparatus.

To give one example, Kirkpatrick (2007 [1793]) suggests that *khoriya* lands yielded limited revenue for the government due to the low value of the crops produced, yet were nevertheless still taxed according to the 'number of ploughs' used. However, this refers to the (most likely Tamang) lands close to Kathmandu, and taxation likely came much later to more remote Tamang villages in the higher hills. By contrast, Gurung's (1996) study of the Magar in the Tara Khola valley in Baglung showed that while the valley was designated as *rajya* with the Galkot Raja maintaining some level of political control over the region in the 19th century – many Magar were living beyond the effective control of the central state and its official land revenue system (Gurung, 1996). The Magar in this region continued to carry out shifting cultivation on customary lands and retained relative political autonomy throughout the Rana era.

In the Gurung settlements studied by Macfarlane (1976), he notes that while tax had been levied on paddy lands for some time, it was only applied to unirrigated fields after cadastral surveys in the 1930s. These are the fields which had traditionally been used for shifting cultivation. Even then, the abundance of land which could be cleared for dry hillslope cultivation placed a limit on the levels of internal differentiation. Those who did not have access to sufficient paddy land, could clear and register new upland fields for maize cultivation throughout subsequent decades, even as shifting cultivation became less tenable – and it appears that the area under cultivation only reached its limit by the 1960s. Macfarlane and Gurung's studies didn't look into internal differentiation (due to the tax administration) in detail. Nevertheless, there is evidence that the degree to which Adivasi functionaries were able to accumulate significant wealth in such domains was limited when compared to their counterparts in the

Figure 18: The Rai communities of the Hongu valley (photo taken, 2010) in Solu Khumbu likely retained relative autonomy until much later than their counterparts in the lower hills

Photo: Fraser Sugden

Tarai and in areas of the hills which were more productive and where there was a higher demand for resources.

McDougal (1973) suggests that amongst the Rai in the Hongu valley (see Figure 18) in the 1960s, an area which at the time had relative abundance of land, the *talukdars*, who were appointed from within the clan leadership, received limited days of labour tribute, yet were able to accumulate only limited wealth – even after a century of Rana rule. There was also some 'redistribution' of wealth via the offering of feasts for the community. The same cannot be said of the Limbu communities in Ilam covered in Caplan's (1970) study, which was indicative of much higher levels of internal differentiation – something which is unsurprising given that it is a lower lying more fertile region with high competition for resources from upper caste settlers.

Importantly, in remoter areas, even with the loss of the *kipat* system, many Adivasi farmers continued to maintain control of their land and rely heavily on customary tenure and shifting cultivation in isolated valleys well into the 19th and even 20th century, cultivating land on a customary basis, even if it wasn't encouraged by the state. As noted above, Gurung (1996) showed that there was a persistence of the customary land management practices of the Magar of the Tara Khola valley,– even though these rights were not officially recognised. Although they didn't have formal *kipat* rights and land was mostly under *raikar* tenure, they continued to cultivate it communally for shifting cultivation, as it was considered as common property by communities. Similarly, Macfarlane (1976) shows that there was a decline in transhumant sheep farming throughout the 19th and 20th centuries as many Gurung had shifted their settlements to lower altitudes to take advantage of more productive lands. However, shifting cultivation on land which was held communally by the clan around these lower communities, remained important to livelihoods.

With regards to transhumance, unlike shifting cultivation, this persisted throughout the upper reaches of the central and eastern hills in the Rana era (Sugden et al 2018), particularly amongst the Sherpa community (March, 1977), Kulunge Rai (McDougal, 1979) and also

Figure 19: Herds of Sheep in the Ankhu Khola region, Dhading, 1977
Photo – Kathryn March and David Holmberg (reproduced with permission)

Tamang (Figure 19). There also appears to have been some long distance transhumance in the hills, perhaps brought about by land scarcity in the lower valleys. For instance Northey and Morris (1928), writing from the late Rana era, document the movement of Rai from the lower hills of Dhankuta to *goths* (seasonal settlements) in the upper Arun basin near the Tibetan border, many days walk away, to raise herds of livestock. Whether they paid tribute to access the customary lands of the local Sherpa or made use of de facto common property forests is not known.

While elements of the Adivasi mode of production were to persist until well into the 20th century in the case studies outlined above, in general, shifting cultivation, (and to a lesser extent) transhumant pastoralism and communal tenure did appear to be in decline by the latter part of the Rana era, and certainly by the early Panchayat era (see below). However, with few outside settlers, decline in remoter locales appears to have taken place in the context of population pressure within the hills rather than being due to direct subordination by the state, as has been described in the case studies above of Tamang, Rai and Limbu communities living further south. For instance, Macfarlane (1976) notes how at least at the start of 19th century the Gurung in his study had begun terraced wet rice cultivation, driven by population pressure and migration to lower altitudes, although this emerged without the demise of shifting cultivation, which was reserved for secondary crops of coarse grains. At this time, labour rather than land was the key asset which would give farmers economic advantage, as anyone with workers could access forest land for shifting cultivation of maize and millet. However, there was a six-fold increase in population between 1821 and 1961 in part due to in-migration but also due to natural growth in population with improved public health, and this contributed to the eventual dissolution of shifting cultivation by the Panchayat era, with coarse grain cultivation continuing, yet on fixed *bari* fields (see Figure 20). The need to intensify production and clear the remaining unprotected forests meant that shifting cultivation was no longer feasible – a process which has taken place much earlier in other Adivasi domains. The demise was hastened also by the conversion of formerly communal land into privately owned land between the 1940s and 60s (Ibid.).

Figure 20: Millet production on fixed yet unirrigated fields or bari, in the Hongu valley in 2010. In past generations, millet in the Hongu valley was produced via shifting cultivation on temporary plots. The Kulunge Rai of this valley made the transition to sedentary agriculture later than in other regions.

Photo: Fraser Sugden

Fricke's study (1984) from the Tamang homelands in the north of the central hills, suggest that shortages of land due to population pressure had as of the 1970s already resulted in livelihood adaptation, with a reduction in the size of herds for agro-pastoralism and an end to shifting cultivation. Farmers had also increased the number of harvests – and thus intensification of agriculture was the solution to resource scarcity, once the forest frontier which would allow 'extensive' growth was closed, with no new cultivable land left to be cleared.

The key message was that the process of 'dissolution' outlined above was gradual but also uneven, depending on the local context. The era whereby transition out of shifting cultivation took place offers a useful metric to understand these differences. For instance, it persisted longer where the competition for resources was lower. Other reasons for a delayed transition include whether there were alternative livelihood options which reduce the need for a grain surplus, such as pastoralism.

International Migration

With pressures of surplus appropriation via rents and taxes, long term and even permanent outward migration to India from the hills was widespread. Migration occurred initially through the recruitment of men from Nepal's indigenous hill communities (notably Gurungs, Magars and Tamangs) from the western and central hills to the Gurkha regiments of the British army, following the 1814-16 Anglo-Gorkha war, to serve British imperial expansion (Kansakar, 2012).

This began later in the eastern hills, alongside more permanent migration to Northeast India, both for the purposes of settlement (for agriculture, labour and for livestock keeping). Pressure on land in Eastern Nepal was a prime cause of migration to Sikkim as early in the 1890s where farmers found new lands (Caplan, 1970). In the 19th century, the British also began building roads and tea plantations in North East India, and Darjeeling and Assam both began to see a rising tide of Nepalese migration, most of whom were from hill areas of Eastern Nepal (O'Malley, 1907). Tamang (2008) estimates that in the late 19th century, around a third of the population of the eastern part of the Tamang homeland were driven to Darjeeling and Sikkim due to scarcity of land and the feudal excesses of the state. Emigration to Sikkim reached such proportions eventually that laws were passed by the Sikkim authorities to check the flow (Nakane, 1966, cf. Sugden et al., 2018).

With the exception of migration for the military, it is likely that most migration was a process of resettlement, whereby households would permanently resettle in India, and it is questionable whether households maintained a link to their farms in Nepal – facilitating an articulation between the mode of production in the hills (as we see today), and capitalist and other formations outside of Nepal.

Cropping systems in the hills

One of the most striking observations from historical records was the sheer diversity in crops by the time of the Gorkha conquest, particularly in terms of the different types of grain. Hand-written records by the former

British Resident Brian Hodgson from 1846 for instance, identifies other than several varieties of rice, wheat, barley, millet and maize, an additional 32 grains and pulses. He also records 17 textile crops, (including jute and hemp), 16 varieties of oil crops, 77 spices and other agricultural products used for flavouring[32], 28 crops which are used for colours or dyes and 61 vegetable and root crops (Hodgson, 1846). Of course, it is likely that not all were 'cultivated' and others may have been gathered from the forest and other uncultivated lands. There was also likely considerable genetic diversity in terms of local seed varieties. By the early 20th century, there were 61 recorded varieties of rice (Chataut, 2017).

While there was clearly considerable diversity, the cropping systems in the hills remained roughly divided between unterraced, rainfed production, generally associated with the shifting cultivation (swidden) of the Adivasi economic formation, and the terraced sedentary cultivation associated with Hindu castes. The former was focused largely on coarse grains, pulses and roots whereas the latter was focused on paddy and wheat (although both systems likely included a range of vegetables and other crops at different times of the year).

A notable change however in the 19th and early 20th century, was the expansion of the rice-wheat cropping system at the expense of the coarse grain/swidden system – particularly into central and eastern Nepal, paralleling the gradual dissolution of the Adivasi mode of production. With the growth of sedentary terraced agriculture there was also an expansion of irrigation, which likely supported a notable rise in cropping intensity. We will explore the evolution of irrigation and cropping systems in the western hills and central/eastern hills separately below.

Rice-wheat cropping system and irrigation in western Nepal

Unlike in the central and eastern hills, a rice-wheat cropping system appears to have a long history in the western hills, dating back to the pre-Gorkha era (Subedi, 1998), and therefore, the pattern of change was likely

---

[32] Note that some products such as limes and raisins are erroneously classified under 'spices'.

less dramatic here throughout the 19th and early 20th century. Other than paddy and wheat, oil seeds such as sesame were reported in Doti in the early 19th century, alongside pulses and barley on drier land. In addition, Adhikary (1997) notes that during the 18th century the Karnali used to export wool, woolen clothes, herbs, horses, falcons and musk (from deer) towards the plains of India; as well as pepper, chilli and some items to Tibet. There was likely less notable change in the cropping system of the region therefore after the Gorkha conquest – although what was more significant was the expansion of the cultivable area alongside a rising population (Bishop, 1978). For this to happen however, the expansion of irrigation – on which wheat in particular depends – was essential, and western Nepal had arguably had the most extensive irrigation network during the Gorkha and Rana era.

As noted in the previous chapter, irrigation in the west under the domains of the Baise Rajyas dates back to the medieval period (Subedi, 1998), yet new canals were built throughout the 18th, 19th and 20th century. Across Nepal during this period, the construction of canals was often carried out under the command of local revenue functionaries for *raikar* lands or *birta* owners, using free labour service from the peasantry, as well as occasionally the use of slaves (Pradhan, 2000b). Access to water from canals were bound with *raikar* or *birta* tenancy rights, and failure to provide unpaid labour to build and maintain the canals – could result in possible eviction. While this implies that the construction of new canals was a centralised process led by landlords or revenue functionaries – this was likely not the only mechanism through which the irrigated area was expanded. Pradhan (2000b) also notes that to encourage land reclamation, the 1854 Muluki Ain allowed tenants on *raikar* land to construct new canals themselves (including those passing over the land of others) so long as it helped expand the cultivable area.

More specifically with regards to the western hills, interviews carried out in Bajhang in 2012 suggested that most canals originated from the time when particular villages were founded, with estimates varying from 100 to 400 years, suggesting that most were constructed as the population spread out across the hills between the times of the Baise Rajya and the Rana era. Whether canals were built by tenants or on a more coordinated basis by revenue functionaries is not known, but it was likely a combination of both, and this may explain the different water rights which persist to the present day. For instance, while most canals were considered the property of the community as a whole, regardless as to whose land the canal passes through, others were lineage based, usually owned by the descendants of the families who originally built the canal (Sugden, 2012a) – hinting that these were canals built independently without the involvement of the village administration.

Over time, sophisticated water allocation and maintenance institutions developed – including customary roles such as the *kulalo* who would be paid a share of the harvest as compensation to coordinate the maintenance of the system (Sugden, 2012a). Another study from a different part of Bajhang (Rana, 1992) referred to the role as a *kulachya*, noting that they would be elected by the community, and would be responsible for ensuring the equal distribution of water, overseeing small repairs, and mobilising labour for larger ones.

As another example, Ludku and Diyar village of Jumla had canals which date back to the Rana era (Shrestha, 1993). They had a *kumthi*, a management committee. In general, three community members would be elected, known as *kumthel*, and during the main agricultural seasons they were responsible for the smooth operation of the canal and equitable distribution of water. If someone was found guilty of stealing water or any misconduct against the agreed rules, a fine would be paid to the committee. For the maintenance of the canal, each household was expected to contribute compulsory labor. After each harvest, the owner of the irrigated land, would give 0.5 percent of the total production (paddy) to the *kumthi*; which they would divide among the *kumthels*, Usually, they would select a member of such management committee on the basis of first, the ability to take responsibility; and second, whether one has land to produce by himself and needs to buy the grains (Shrestha, 1993, and interview with author)[33].

---

[33] These complex irrigation management regimes echo those documented in the high Himalaya region. In the Kali Gandaki valley of Mustang for instance, a leader to manage the irrigation system known as a *rolo* would be chosen by election, and they would be endowed with the power to control the water supply. The customary method

Rice-wheat cropping system and intensification of agriculture in central and eastern Nepal

In central and eastern Nepal, there was a slightly different trajectory of change. Paddy cultivation, including associated irrigation and terracing technologies was likely widespread in central Nepal even in the pre-Gorkha era. As indicated earlier, it was the primary crop in the Kathmandu valley. Hodgson, writing in the mid 19th century, suggests that on the highest grade of land in the valley, 1 patti (3.2kg) of seed would produce 4 muri (approx. 288kg) per ropani of paddy. This declined to 1 muri (approx. 72kg) of rice on poorer grade land (Hodgson, circa 1843), pointing to a reasonably high yield by contemporary standards[34].

Elsewhere in the central hills, rice was brought in by early Khas and Brahmin settlers – as noted in the last chapter. For instance, as of the early 19th century it was the main crop in lower hill districts such as Arghakhanchi, Gulmi and Palpa, which had particularly high Khas and Brahmin populations (Hamilton, 2007 [1819]). Irrigation systems also have a reasonably long history, particularly in central Nepal. However, as has happened throughout Nepal's agrarian history, the spread of new cropping systems and technologies has been uneven across space, and large tracts of land, particularly in the eastern hills, were still under shifting cultivation at the dawn of the Gorkha conquest, with lands suitable for paddy often under forest.

As the eastward migration of Hindu castes accelerated following the Gorkha conquest, so did the expansion of paddy cultivation into Adivasi domains which had previously been dominated by dryland rainfed coarse grains (Liebrand, 2014), including associated technologies such as ploughing, terracing (Gaenszle, 2000) and irrigation (Aubriot, 2004). This new form of agriculture expanded in the forested valleys which were cleared by settlers, creating the water retaining lands which today are

---

in most villages for irrigation is to allow the water to flow from upper fields to the successively lower fields, the water would flow to the land through a small cut in the levee (Kihara, 1956).

[34] This would translate to approximately 1414kg to 5662kg per hectare, assuming the unit conversions were the same as used today, which is not far off the average yield of 3700kg per hectare in Nepal today.

known as *khet*. However, initially it was a single season cropping cycle dominated by monsoon paddy. The expansion of winter grains, most notably wheat, was much slower in the central and eastern hills, unlike in the west where it appears to have a longer history. In the west, cultivation of wheat was supported by higher winter rainfall and the presence of year-round irrigation.

The development of much more extensive irrigation systems which can provide water in the peak dry season was thus a necessary prerequisite for a rice-wheat cropping system in the eastern and western hills. The construction of irrigation canals across the hills increased after the Gorkha conquest, and into the Rana era (Aubriot, 2004), with the state viewing irrigation as an opportunity to intensify production and increase tax revenue. While there were a small number of state sanctioned canals or so called 'raj kulos', some of which used forced labour for their construction, incentives were also given to farmers to construct their own canals (Pradhan, 1990). The 1854 Muluki Ain clarified the rules of water allocation including recognition that the benefits of any canals would go to the farmer who invested, while clarifying the rights and responsibilities for canal users, and giving recognition to customary rules of management (Pradhan, 1990). While a majority of canals remained largely under community control (Liebrand, 2014, Aubriot, 2004), it appears that the state regularly intervened in their management, for instance in mobilising forced labour for maintenance, particularly for canals constructed under the initiative of the state (Pradhan, 1990).

This irrigation expansion paved the way for the introduction of wheat and other winter grains beyond the wheat production belt of the western hills. Regmi (1978d) suggests that there were some efforts by the state to increase cropping diversity in Gulmi and Agarkanchi districts in 1866-67 by introducing winter wheat and barley, incentivising it by banning the winter grazing of livestock after the paddy harvest – although this had limited success. Aubriot's (2004) study from Gulmi suggests that wheat cultivation only started in the 1920s. It is suggested that dry season free grazing of livestock remained a constraint for agricultural intensification during the 19th century. However, as the caste Hindu migrations slowed down in the early 20th century as the opportunity to expand the cultivable area reached its limit, the peasantry were compelled to increase cropping intensity to support a rising population (Ibid). This encouraged the extension of a multi-harvest rice-wheat cropping system into central and eastern Nepal, and with this, the associated irrigation technologies which were a necessity to keep up with population growth.

Despite the spread of terraced cultivation and irrigation, and the move to a more intensive arable cropping system, chemical fertiliser use was rare, only being officially introduced to Nepal in 1951 (Manandhar and Khanal, 2005). Even in the Kathmandu valley, prior to the 1960s the account of Bhaktapur peasant leader, Krishna Bhakta Caguthi, documented by Raj (2010), suggests that 95% of land was fertilised using a mix of household compost and clay soils (which were sourced in numerous mines surrounding the city).

Coarse grains and other rainfed crops during the Gorkha and Rana era

Lands under *khoriya* or shifting cultivation will have been under similar cropping systems as in the pre-Gorkha period as described above – and oriented around the production of coarse grains and other rainfed crops. In the Kali Gandaki valley of the central hills, Hamilton (2007 [1819]) for instance, describes the cropping system amongst the largely Gurung cultivators, as being dominated by buckwheat (*phapar*), naked barley (*uya*), foxtail millet (*kanguni*) and finger millet (*maruya*). Similarly, Hodgson, writing in 1880 from the Kirat region of the eastern hills noted that on land under shifting cultivation, buckwheat, millet, legumes, dry rice and cotton were produced (cited from Russel, 1992). Legumes were produced across the hills on rainfed land (although these could also be grown in the dry season on *khet* lands) including *masuri* (red lentil) and *urad* (black gram) (Hamilton, 2007 [1819]).

However, a range of new crops which don't necessarily depend on irrigation and could be integrated into shifting cultivation based agrarian formations, increased from east to west across the hills throughout the Gorkha and Rana era. Potato, which was discussed above, supported population growth across the eastern hills throughout the 19th century

Figure 21: Marginal rainfed lands just beyond the Kathmandu valley in the early 20th century. These lands were disproportionately farmed by hill Adivasi groups such as the Tamang, even after the demise of shifting cultivation.
Photo: Madan Puraskar Pustakalaya (Reproduced with permission)

(Seddon, 2012). Maize likely became an important part of the cropping system throughout the Gorkha and Rana era – being planted on unirrigable *bari* lands during the monsoon. There is limited data on when maize was produced – in some areas of the central hills it appeared only in the early 20th century (Aubriot, 2004), although it was mentioned by Kirkpatrick (2007[1793]) as being cultivated in the hills between Kathmandu and Nuwakot in the late 18th century and by Hodgson in 1880 (cf Russel, 1992).

Even after farmers began to shift towards sedentary cultivation, it is important to note that only lower lying lands could be converted into *khet* (irrigable rice-wheat land). As noted above, on higher altitude lands or lower lying yet marginal slopes, the same *khoriya* crops as listed above, were produced on fixed *bari* fields which were entirely rainfed. Thus, a cropping system oriented around coarse grains continued to be associated with Adivasi society well after the transition away from swidden farming – and this was all the more relevant given the disproportionate control of the best paddy lands by Nepali speaking upper castes (see Figure 21).

Cash crop production

There was some limited cash crop production in the hills, although exports were not on a large scale and the state held a monopoly in the trade of most agricultural commodities, including indigo and cardamom. Although these monopolies were operated through individual contractors, efforts were made to promote the cultivation of new crops (Regmi, 1999). Cardamom was one of the first crops to be exported at a large scale. Cultivation techniques and seeds were thought to have been brought from Sikkim, and Regmi (1983) suggests that its production dates back to even before the Gorkha conquest, with colonial sources reporting imports of cardamom from Nepal in the late 18th century. It was certainly recognised as an important niche crop in the early 19th century (Hamilton, 2007 [1819]). There was even a government run cardamom plantation in Kaski in the Rana era (Regmi, 1983), although it was in the east where production was most widespread. It was not however, until the second half of the 20th century that it emerged as a major commercial crop for the peasantry (Fitzpatrick, 2011).

In terms of other forms of plantation agriculture, tea cultivation emerged from the third quarter of the 19th century alongside its growth in Darjeeling (Regmi, 1988a). This was initially in Ilam, on plantations which were state managed, and later under the *ijara* system of taxation. Later plantations were established in Baitadi and Udayapur. However, the latter two struggled with low productivity and a weak market. There were also attempts at cotton plantations in Nuwakot, but these were largely unsuccessful (Regmi, 1988a).

Other agricultural products which were reported to have been traded through the Birgunj-Raxual border in the late 19th century included spices, ghee and wax, as well as sugarcane and ginger, which were produced in the Tarai and central hill districts such as Palpa (Hamilton, 2007 [1819]). Hodgson's note on agricultural products suggests that a diversity of spices were produced including methi, dhaniya, dalchini (cinnamon), cumin (jeera), camphor, hing (Hodgson, 1846). How many were produced commercially is not known, although a letter by Ram Tanu to Brian Hodgson in the 1830s on crops exported to the lowlands and India, mentions cinnamon as an export, alongside cow tails, musk, wax and woolen cloth (Tanu, 1830).

While most of the records relate to crops which were produced for export, it is highly probable that there was also an emerging local market for agricultural commodities, particularly as small towns emerged across the hills. The extensive collection of routes and itineraries across hill Nepal from the early to mid-19th century compiled by Brian Hodgson provide some insights into this process of change. Most 'towns' appeared to have emerged around a network of military encampments or forts. Campbell's (circa 1830s) itineraries in the west, suggest that the town of Doti for instance, which was to go on to become Dipayal, was home to around 400 houses and several hundred soldiers, situated below the fort in Silgadhi. Meanwhile, Salyan was home to around 1000 soldiers. These were reasonably large settlements, and would have required a sizable agricultural surplus and some level of trade and commerce to support the many military personnel present there.

Also supporting the emergence of new settlements, was the expansion of cottage industries. Some of the fort towns were emerging as centers of small scale manufacturing. For instance, Pokhara (Hodgson, circa 1830s c) and Dolakha (circa 1830s, c) were centers for copper manufacture, with the latter also being a site of paper production. More specialized metalwork towns such as Taksar of Bhojpur, home to 1000 inhabitants, were also established in the mid 19th century, supported by the migration of Newar metalworkers from Patan (Shrestha, 2020).

Notably, these emerging towns were linked up by a network of north-south and east-west military roads, some passable in part by horses (or in lower regions) by elephants (Campbell, circa. 1830s). Multiple references to *buniahs* along the trails between Kathmandu and Dolakha (likely a reference to *baniyas* or merchants) is a reminder that these trails were of commercial as well as military importance (Hodgson circa 1830s d). Thus it is probable that improved transportation infrastructure facilitated the trade in agricultural commodities (including those for both local markets and export) as well as manufactured goods. Hodgson (circa 1830s b) also reports on an emerging network of iron and wooden bridges which would have further reduced journey times.

While regular periodic markets were yet to emerge, trade fares or *melas* also appeared as a feature of commercial activity in the hills in the 19th century – including one in Rerighat[35] of Palpa held during the winter which would be visited by traders from across the hills. Canoes were used to transport commodities up and down the Narayani (Hamilton, 2007 [1819]), suggesting that river corridors facilitated trade in commodities as well as military roads.

An area where there appeared to be relatively more limited production of cash crops and commerce more broadly was the western hills – which was emerging into what would become a food deficit region. There are multiple explanations, that likely extend beyond the drier climate (which by any means does not apply to the entire region). For instance, following the Anglo-Gorkha war, this area became the periphery of the Gorkha empire, and there was limited investment in infrastructure, in part because the Gorkhas wanted to maintain this region as military buffer zone with the East India Company acquisitions in Kumaon (Pande, 2014). This undermined trade, while the large area of land under *jagir* tenure and the high rents, meant that there was limited agricultural surplus (Pande, 2014).

Late rana era: Rise in owner cultivation and local landlord-tenant relations

From the narratives above, it appears that throughout the 19th and early 20th century, rural Nepal was comprised of multiple localised modes of production, situated within a larger feudal social formation, with surplus being split between local landlords or intermediaries and the central state and ruling aristocracy. The modes of production on the ground included firstly, independent peasant production, which was particularly prevalent in the hills amongst the caste Hindu peasantry and a large share of the Adivasi farmers who had shifted to sedentary cultivation. There was

---

[35] This likely refers to Ridi Bazaar, known also as Ruru Kshetra, on the banks of the Kali Gandaki, a tributary of the Narayani, a town with a long history as a religious centre and which still hosts a mela, albeit one which is religious rather than trade focused.

notable class differentiation according to caste and ethnicity. Secondly, there were localised landlord-tenant relations, particularly in the Tarai-Madhesh, and pockets of the hills. Finally, Adivasi modes of production likely persisted, albeit in increasingly remote and land abundant locales within the forest belts of both the hills and Tarai-Madhesh.

A notable change in the early 20th century was a change in the distribution of agricultural surplus. By the end of the Rana era, a substantial 36.3% of land was under *birta* tenure, with a further 7.7% under *jagir*, *rajya* and related systems (see Table 1). Within these systems, a substantial share of the agricultural surplus would be appropriated from tenants and would be transferred to the local landlord such as the *birtawala* or *jagirdar* as ground rent or other form of tribute. Approximately half of the land was under *raikar*, whereby titleholders of these land were de facto tenants to the state under centralised feudalism, although as noted above, there was rising sub-infeudation with landlords (particularly *jimidars* and other functionaries) holding large areas of *raikar* land. For these large *raikar* holdings however, while these 'sub-tenants' would have been paying rent, a substantial share of the surplus would still have gone ultimately, as tax – at least in the earlier Rana era.

However, there were two major changes in the late Rana era which changed the position of peasants working on *raikar* land – firstly, the emergence of private property rights and secondly, the declining value of land tax. These two changes transformed 'sub-tenants' on *raikar* land (i.e. those leasing out land from a *raikar* titleholder) into ordinary tenants working on private estates, with the *raikar* landlord rather than the state emerging as the primary surplus appropriating class. On a positive note however, it also transformed individual titleholders of *raikar* land into de-facto independent owner cultivators, who (with falling taxation) retained most of their surplus for themselves. This facilitated an evolution from centralised feudalism to what we call an 'independent peasant' mode of production. This change was to become of huge significance following the post-Rana rolling out of *raikar* as the dominant form of tenure across Nepal, which we discuss in the next chapter.

A third major change in the late Rana era was the emergence of early resettlement schemes which paved the way for a massive population movement within Nepal during the later Panchayat era. This also contributed to a significant rise in the population of an independent owner cultivating peasantry. These three changes are explored in detail below.

Table 1: Approximate share of land under different forms of land tenure before 1950

Tenure	Area in Hectares	Percentage
Raikar	963,500	50.0
Birta	700,080	36.3
Guthi	40,000	2.0
Kipat	77,000	4.0
Rajya, Jagir, Rakam and Others	146,330	7.7
Total area	1,927,000	100

(Zaman, 1973)

Emergence of private property rights for raikar land

While private property rights for land had been historically present in the western hills, they had been undermined following the Gorkha conquest with the classification of all land as *raikar* which was property of the state (Regmi, 1972). While some forms of tenure such as *birta*[36] could be considered as 'private' property with the right to sell holdings (Pradhan, 2000b), the significant change in the late Rana era was the extension of these rights to *raikar* land also.

This was a gradual process. The revenue settlement between 1854 and 1868 offered more secure tenure to a plot of land, yet it was still officially the state's property with restrictions on its sale (Regmi, 1976). However, an 1888 legislation allowed the relinquishment of land with the approval of the local administration. Regmi (1976) notes that while it didn't explicitly state that land could be sold, it supported the emergence of a de facto land market. The right to buy or sell *raikar* land was finally codified in law in 1921 – consolidating private property rights. Any individual

---

[36] Pradhan (2000) suggests that while *birta* holdings could be sold, *jagir* rights were more temporary and such land could not be bought or sold.

could buy, sell or mortgage land so long as taxes were still paid. The 1957 Lands Act changed the name from *raikar* land holder to land owner, and mentioned the ability to draw rent as one of the land ownership rights (Ibid.). The difference between *birta* and *raikar* tenure began to decline during this period, and a 1906 legislation brought some of the laws regarding *birta* and *raikar* in synergy (Regmi, 1976). Similarly, this change meant that *jimidars* and other revenue functionaries who had been accumulating large areas of *raikar* land were in a situation similar to *birta* landlords.

Meanwhile, cadastral surveys (see Tamrakar, 2012) during the late Rana era served to further entrench inequalities as they could be used to consolidate the power of existing landed elites where there was ambiguity over the title holders for existing *raikar* lands. This process has been recorded in the Dang valley in particular where a lot of land had been unregistered. In this inner Tarai valley, the cadastral surveys of 1896 and 1912 were weakly implemented, and served to reinforce the control over land by the Tharu landlord-functionary class (Krauskopff, 1989). Furthermore, as noted above, many Tharu had during the earlier period of Gorkha and Rana rule, cultivated land under a system known as *potet*, whereby they would have the right to consume the harvest on payment of a share as tax to the functionary who had jurisdiction over the area (Krauskopff, 1989). *Potet* rights were defined by one's right to consume the harvest rather than to the land itself. Farmers on *potet* lands were vulnerable to dispossession as private property rights were consolidated, as they lacked land titles, and as a result, at the end of the Rana era, there were many Tharu farmers who lacked ownership of land. McDougal (1968) suggests that *jimidars* who had jurisdiction for an area under *potet* came to be recognised as the title holder for the land[37]. He further notes that while the system (whereby surplus appropriation was mainly via labour tribute or a modest rent payment) worked well at a time when there

---

[37] He also notes however, that even following the end of Rana rule, the rent paid on now privatised *potet* land for the landlord was relatively low and usually included a limited number of days of labour tribute. However, with the decline in the Tharu *jimidar* class, many of these tenants would go on to become ordinary tenants for hill origin landlords.

was abundant land but a shortage of labour, as competition for land increased, it gave way to sharecropping whereby a substantial share of the harvest would need to be surrendered as rent.

While it is clear that some Tharu *jimidars* benefitted from the enforcement of property rights in Dang, for the Tharu peasantry the cadastral surveys also contributed to the loss of land to hill people. Krauskopff (1989) suggests that a subset of Tharu households, which even included former functionaries, lost their estates to upper caste hill origin *jimidars* due to deception during these surveys – a process aggravated by debt or inability to pay tax. Mishra (2007) cites the 1900 and 1932 surveys in Dang in particular, which were used to undermine the power of the Tharu land owning class by absentee landlords from Salyan. The ability to more easily buy land intensified land alienation as many hill origin *jimidars* also purchased large tracts of land in Dang.

The emergence of private property rights also consolidated the demise of the *kipat* system in the east – and contributing to a further alienation of Adivasi lands. As noted above, *kipat* rights on paddy lands were dissolved in 1907, yet the upland *bari* lands were still under communal tenure (Gaenszle, 2000). By 1952, only 4 percent of the land in the eastern hills remained under the *kipat* system (van Driem, 2001, 608) and this was restricted to pastures and uncultivated forest land. Sugden et al (2018) in a study from Bhojpur, noted that government survey teams allocated former *kipat* holdings to the existing farmers of the plots, although influential individuals, often from upper castes, were able to deceive the teams into claiming certain lands as their own, or were able to use political influence to get titles in their name.

As noted earlier, in some remote hilly regions, land had remained under de facto customary tenure, even if it was officially *raikar*. In these locales also however, the consolidation of private property rights also contributed to growing alienation from land. Gurung's (1996) study of the Tara Khola valley noted that tracts of land remained under customary land management practices of the Magar, with extensive areas under shifting cultivation throughout the 19th and early 20th century. However, by the late Rana era, a revenue office was established in Galkot, and property rights for fixed *raikar* plots in the name of individual cultivators began to be enforced. Meanwhile misuse of authority by local elites, mostly from upper castes, during the land registration process, and indebtedness to outsiders contributed to growing inequality in the distribution of holdings, and concentration of the best land amongst non-Magar communities such as Brahmin, Chettri and Thakali (Gurung, 1996).

Monetisation of and declining value of land tax

The second significant state intervention was the monetisation of land tax for *raikar* lands. In the late 19th and early 20th century, government revenue diversified, and the dependence on land tax had declined. For instance, trade from the Tarai-Madhesh boomed during this period, providing new sources of tax for the regime. Forest products in particular, were a lucrative source of revenue. Mishra (1987) notes that the value of trade rose from Rs 9.8 million in 1879-90 to Rs30 million in 1890-91. By 1920-21, trade had reached Rs87.9 million. Exports were dominated by timber, and cash crops such as opium, jute, indigo and tobacco. Imports included gold and other precious metals for the elite – as well as consumer goods for the peasantry including cigarettes, machine made cotton textiles, metal and glassware – which would eventually disintegrate local cottage industries – a topic discussed in the next section (Mishra, 1987). Border towns such as Birganj and Nepalganj emerged during this period as state protected trade hubs. Local traders were required to sell their goods there for export to maximise revenue for the state, with punishment for those who would try to sell independently across the border (Mørch, 2023).

The flow of primary products such as timber to the south and imported manufactured goods from India to the north accelerated after the 1923 Anglo-Nepal Treaty (Blaikie et al., 2001). Timber was a particularly lucrative export, to support the expansion of the British colonial railways, and the export of 200,000 railway sleepers to India in the 1920s brought considerable wealth to the Rana regime (Chaudhary et al., 2023). The state also received payment from the British for military service provided by the hill peasantry – although this was considered by Mishra (1987)[38] as compensation for the loss in land revenue due to army recruitment – particularly considering that an estimated 20% of the adult male population served the British during World War One.

Land taxes which became monetised by the start of the 20th century continued to be increased in line with the rising price of grain for a few years, particularly as railways brought local grain prices in line with those in India (Burghart, 2016). However, after 1910, they remained static despite continually rising prices of the agricultural commodities against which tax rates had been calculated (Thapa, 2000). This parallels a broader trend, echoed in India, where land tax slipped from being 70% of government revenues in the late 18th century to less than a quarter in the 1920s. The establishment of fixed rates of land tax under the Permanent Settlement in Bengal and Bihar meant it declined in value over time with the increase in crop prices, while it became increasingly politically difficult to re-assess the rates (Ibid.). Similarly, in Mahottari district of Nepal, for instance, Regmi (1976) notes how paddy prices increased nine-fold between 1940 and 1961 despite static monetary tax rates. This drop meant that the *raikar* landowner needed a smaller quantity of grain to meet tax obligations (Regmi, 1976).

Impact on the mode of production

This dual process of falling tax and private property rights had a positive impact on *raikar* tenants, who became the owners of their land and were able to retain a growing share of the surplus – this saw the emergence of an independent peasant mode of production. In the hills, where large landed estates were less prevalent, independent peasants emerged as the largest segment of the peasantry (Seddon, 1987) – in spite of notable differentiation within this group.

However, this expansion of the independent peasantry was arguably much more constrained in the Tarai-Madhesh where sub-infeudation

---

[38] An annual payment of 1 million rupees was made to the Rana state by the British (Mishra, 1987).

under the *raikar* system was much more prevalent. For example, as of 1948 it was estimated that 23% of farmers in rural Morang owned less than one bighā each (of *raikar* land), while some *jimidārs* possessed up to 22,000 bighā (Regmi, 1976). Only a small number were fortunate enough to have sufficient *raikar* land to become independent owner cultivators. In the Tarai-Madhesh, therefore, as well as pockets of the hills where landlord-tenant relations were established - rent rather than tax began to emerge as the primary form of surplus appropriation, benefitting those with larger holdings – consolidating *localised* rather than centralised feudalism as the primary mode of production. *Raikar* landlords, like *birta* landlords, were now able to appropriate a significant share of the harvest as their own rent. Data from Thapa's (2000) study suggests that in the 1950s *raikar* landowners in the eastern Tarai who yielded 30 maund from the land (1 maund=40kg) would only be obligated to pay 0.75 maund as tax (just 2.5%), while they could charge 20 maunds in rent – well over half of the harvest.

These very changes contributed to rising concentration of land. The confirmation of private land ownership rights encouraged *jimidārs* to further expand their holdings (Regmi, 1976). However, it also provided an incentive for other wealthy individuals both from the hills and local communities to buy land. The rewards of expanding one's holdings were also higher, as with falling tax it was easier for landlords to rent out excess holdings, as tenants could more easily produce surplus beyond what was needed for their subsistence needs after covering tax and yielding a profit which the landlord could extract via rent (Ibid.). As Regmi (1976, 192) argues: "Raikar landownership rights were now prized not because they yielded an opportunity for personal labour and subsistence, but because they created a new avenue for profitable investment and were therefore a source of unearned income."

The rising inequality in the Tarai-Madhesh and areas of the hills where there were landed estates, can be better understood when one observes that the monetisation of land tax also brought rising debt, a new form of subordination. Although the value of tax was declining, its monetisation created a need for cash, encouraging further monetisation of livelihoods (such as commercial production) amongst the tax paying peasantry and often increasing levels of indebtedness to money lenders (Regmi, 1976). The simultaneous destruction of cottage industries by Indian imports was, however, likely to have been equally important in intensifying commercialisation and indebtedness – with economic distress and rising needs for money to purchase goods from the market – processes explored in the next chapter.

The emergence of property rights for land also meant that land could now be left as collateral for loans, causing many peasants to lose their land if they defaulted (Regmi, 1976). Sugden's (2013) study from Morang showed how *jimidārs* and even lower level *patwaris* were able to expand their holdings by confiscating land from those tenants who were unable to pay back loans. Regmi (1976) suggests that transfers of land also occurred through deception and coercion, turning many marginal farmers into tenants for the growing landlord class. Growing landlessness and debt in this context spawned the emergence of new axes of feudal exploitation – in particular in the form of bonded labour such as the Kaamaiya system of the western Tarai-Madhesh or Haruwa system of the central Tarai-Madhesh (Dhakal et al., 2020).

In sum, by the late Rana era, the primary mechanism of surplus appropriation in the Tarai-Madhesh was through rent, usury and low wage labour, rather than taxation. The surplus appropriating class was by the end of the Rana era dominated by the owners of *birta* estates, mostly from the hill elite, as well as indigenous functionary-landlords in the Adivasi domains, and upper or middle caste functionary-landlords in the caste Hindu belt in the central Tarai.

Early resettlement schemes and rising owner cultivation

While feudal relations remained predominant in the Tarai-Madhesh at the end of the Rana era, and vast tracts of land had been brought under cultivation, a considerable share of the land was still under forest. Ghimire (2017) suggests that 48% of the inner Tarai valleys (like Dang and Chitwan), 79% of the Bhabar (the alluvial slope between the Tarai and hills) and 30% of the Tarai-proper, was still under forest as of 1954. The remaining forested tracts remained sparsely populated due to endemic malaria (Kansakar, 1985), although there were a large number of semi-nomadic communities such as the Dhimal as well as some western Tharu communities who continued to live deep within the forested belt with relative autonomy (Kansakar, 1985, Rai, 2013). A change however, was taking place due to the migration of peasants from the hills – which would lead to a substantial expansion in an owner-cultivating independent peasantry – a trend which would become widespread after the 1950s and 60s when large scale resettlement took place.

Nepal's first official resettlement scheme followed the provision of land to freed slaves in 1925, for which the Prime Minister Chandra Sumsher Rana had established a department, which estimated that there were 59,873 slaves. The government paid 3,670,000 Rs to free 51,782 slaves and resettle them in Bikchskhori, in the Tarai-Madhesh belt of Makwanpur district, which was later named as Amlekhgunj, after *Amlekh*, 'the freed'. These resettled freed slaves were also allowed to cultivate the surrounding jungle areas for their livelihood (Sharma, 1951).

This extended to include other hill migrants in 1931 following the declaration of the *Punarbas Karyakram* (resettlement programs), in 1931. The government's aim was to clear forest, earn money from timber supply, and to collect more land tax by expanding the cultivable area. The government decided to clear 50-60,000 bigha of forest east of the Koshi river, in what is today Morang district. Anyone could apply to the Badahaakim, the local government functionary and chief administrator of the region, to acquire a grant of land (DDC Morang, 2059 BS). Even the person charged for committing various crimes was given the opportunity to settle there by clearing the forest. This supported the emergence of a free owner cultivating peasantry – who would be paying tax, which itself formed a dwindling share of the harvest – a group which would expand considerably following the fall of the Rana regime.

The expansion of this class was however, still relatively low during the Rana era with an unwillingness of farmers to settle in the lowlands. The often cited causes were the presence of malaria in this belt, although Ojha (1983) pointed also to other factors including the excesses of the extractive Rana state, which encouraged migration to outside regions instead such as Assam which offered more favourable conditions for farmers.

Chapter 4

1951-1991: Early democratic period and panchayat era

The second half of the 20th century was a time of global flux – with the emergence of a new world order after the end of WW2, including complex cold war geopolitics, and the wave of decolonisation across the periphery – and associated political mobilisation. This era saw Nepal pursue a so called 'modernisation' agenda in agriculture and other sectors, including large scale infrastructural works as well as land reforms and resettlement of the lowlands. This was also an era of ultra-nationalism, and consolidated centuries old ethnic inequalities in the distribution of land and assets. In many ways the second half of the 20th century, particularly during the so called 'Panchayat era' from the 1960s up until the 1991 – set the foundations for the agrarian structure and cropping systems which dominate rural Nepal today – which entails both continuity as well as change from the Rana era. The national level policy interventions of the period are explored in the first part of this chapter. The second part focuses on how these changes have impacted the Tarai-Madhesh specifically, while the third part looks at their impact in the hills.

Land reform

The Rana regime was overthrown in 1951, in an event which paralleled the anti-colonial movement across the global periphery. At the time of the Rana downfall and the establishment of Nepal's first (short lived) democratically elected government, it is unlikely that there were significant immediate changes to the agrarian structure and rural mode of production. Tax had by this point already become an insignificant share of the agrarian output, and surplus was appropriated primarily through landlord-tenant relations. However, this was also an era of land reforms, as governments globally sought to address the inequalities perpetuated during the century of colonialism, not to mention pressure by the USA to curtail the growth of communism (Kapstein, 2017).

The interim constitution of 1951 confirmed individual ownership rights for land. The constitution made the rights to acquire, use, and sell land property into fundamental ones – thus paving the way for the end of the *kipat* system (UN-HABITAT, 2018). However, faced with the severe inequalities of the Rana era, and growing peasant unrest, some form of redistributive land reform was a major agenda for all the emerging political parties (Dhakal, 2020). The first five-year plan (1956-61) also outlined several land reform policies. These included for example, the protection of tenants, the protection of hired workers, the resettlement of landless farmers, *birta* reform, the provision of agricultural credit, and importantly the consolidation of fragmented holdings. A Royal Land Reform Commission was set up in 1952 to examine problems relating to land tenure and agricultural credit. Around the same time *jagir* tenure was abolished in 1952, being converted into *raikar* land or state property – although most of this land was still registered in the name of individual owners (Dhakal, 2020). The next major land issue was the persistence of *birta* tenure. The abolition of *birta* was met with some reluctance, not only from landlords with whom the monarchy were sympathetic, but even from some leaders within the new political parties (Gill, 2009), who – in spite of their role in the anti-Rana struggle, were closely aligned with the old landed class (Tamang, 2008).

Nevertheless, it was considered a political necessity for the monarchy and emerging political parties to demonstrate their commitment to reform[1] (not to mention the fiscal consequences of having large areas of land untaxed), and in 1959 the Birta Abolition Act was finally

---

[1] Gill (2009) suggested that there was much disagreement over the act. For some, converting *birta* to *raikar* would break the patron-client relationships between large landowners and the Ranas, a change which would be politically advantageous to the

implemented (Gill, 2009). Regmi (1976) notes how the act classified *birta* land into two categories. Type A lands (which appears to have included tracts of uncultivated forest or wasteland) were those whereby the owner was receiving income only equivalent to the land tax on adjoining *raikar* lands, while type B lands were those where the owner was yielding rents from tenants, or cultivating it themselves. Class A lands were re-nationalised on payment of compensation to the owner, calculated in accordance with loss of income from the land (Shrestha, 1967). Class B lands however, were simply converted into *raikar* and were subject to tax. For this reason, the act did not actually facilitate any change in landlord-tenant relations or culminate in any actual redistribution of holdings (Gill, 2009, Shrestha, 1967). As noted above, much of the *birta* land under tenancy appears to have remained with the owners, and as the tax was just a small share of the appropriated surplus, this was likely a small burden for the landlords, and rents continued to be appropriated as before.

Other measures taken during this period included the Tenancy Rights Acquisition Act (TRAA) in 1951 to provide land titles to those tenants who had paid taxes and rent for the land they cultivated. However, it actually had the opposite effect and ended up strengthening the landed elite. The taxes and rents collected were usually registered under the name of landlords rather than the tenants who had paid them, and therefore titles were mostly given to the land owner, thus strengthening their legal claim to the land and creating a more 'permanent' landed elite (Sugden and Gurung, 2012). It was only in 1957 that an act to protect tenants' rights was passed, although these were weakly enforced. Tenants who had cultivated land for over a year were entitled to tenancy rights so they could not be evicted, and rent was set at 50% of the crop. However, the government didn't have the required records on landlords or tenants and implementation was weak (Gill, 2009).

Land reforms were largely ineffective in changing the agrarian structure during the 1950s, and despite the populist rhetoric, new legislations were not effectively applied. The primary outcome was modernisation of the

---

Nepali Congress. However, some segments with conservative leanings were reluctant to see the act implemented.

land tenure system, which allowed *birta* and *raikar* lands to become private property. This streamlining of the system in fact benefitted the government. It increased their control over landlords and helped to ensure that tax was paid, yet it also helped landlords by securing their property rights. Almost no progress was made with regards to tenancy conditions (Wily et al, 2008). In sum, there was little evidence of a significant structural transformation in the character of agriculture during the 1950s in the areas where localised feudal agrarian relations were predominant – particularly in the Tarai-Madhesh.

The democratically elected government was overthrown in a Royal coup in 1960, and King Mahendra founded the Panchayat System of absolute monarchy which was to continue for another three decades. The land reform programme continued after the ascendancy of the monarchy – as the new regime sought legitimacy (Gaige, 1976). In 1962, a Land Survey and Measurement Act was implemented to measure and classify land resources, improve land use and maintain a map-based land record system. Provision of up-to-date information about land ownership was critical for the administration of land and the collection of revenues (Sugden and Gurung, 2012).

However, the most significant ruling by the new regime was the 1964 Land Related Act. The Act in theory, aimed to change existing agrarian relations by actually *redistributing* excess land, and diverting unproductive capital and surplus human resources from agriculture to support the development of the non-agricultural sector (Regmi, 1976). The Land Reform program was implemented in different phases over three years in 16, 25 and then 34 districts (Alden-Wily et al., 2008). The act also upheld and strengthened the rulings of the 1957 tenancy act[2] to set agricultural rents at a maximum ceiling of 50% of the crop and made efforts to enforce tenancy rights (Adhikari, 2006).

It introduced maximum ceilings on landholdings, with the intention of redistributing any excess owned land. The ceiling was set at 10 bighas of agricultural land in the Tarai-Madhesh in addition to prescribed areas for

---

[2] For instance, instead of one year as indicated in the 1957 act, cultivators who had cultivated for just one season were entitled to tenancy rights (Gill, 2009).

residential purposes (The Lands Act, 1964). Lands in excess were acquired by the government after payment of compensation. This was fixed at ten times the annual tax for agricultural lands, and five times the taxes paid for non-agricultural lands. In theory this surplus land was then to be redistributed to the tillers or landless people (Regmi, 1976). The control over taxes and administration was also transferred from local *jimidars* to government District Land Revenue Offices and Village Development Committees (VDCs), and was overseen by the newly established Ministry of Land Reform and Management (Regmi, 1976). While the *jimidars* saw their political authority withdrawn, this came at a time when the revenue collection apparatus was already losing its relevance as agrarian tax became a less significant part of the overall harvest.

Another significant change in the wake of the land reforms was the abolition of *kipat* tenure in 1966. While officially only 2% of land in Nepal was still under this tenure at the time it was abolished (Alden-Wily et al., 2008), this represented the end of any legal protections for customary forms of tenure which was once central to the Adivasi mode of production – although it persisted on an informal basis in later years, albeit to a declining extent.

A final part of the land reform programme was a reform of the *guthi* system of land tenure linked to religious sites. Prior to 1950, there were three major types of Guthi: *amanata guthi, chhut guthi,* and *niji guthi*. After 1950, the Ministry of Finance had taken over the administration of all types of Guthis; and in the 1960s, the government promulgated a '*Guthi Sansthan Ain 2021*' (Guthi Corporation Act 1964). The Guthi Corporation took charge of all other *guthi*s except *niji guthi*, the private *guthi*, which was taken care of by the members who established it.

Zaman (1973), supported by FAO, was commissioned by the government to evaluate the land reform program across Nepal. While he acknowledged that the central and eastern Tarai should have been priority areas for reform, he observed very limited change in the disparity of holdings, while assessing the success of the reforms under four major categories; i. effects of the land ceiling and allotment measures, ii. The effects of the new tenancy regulation, iii. the effects of the credit and savings schemes, and iv. the effects of the land administration. On all four grounds, it was observed that the land reform program faced several constraints in implementation. The discussion below, while focusing on the Tarai-Madhesh, had relevance for the whole of Nepal.

Impact of land reforms

Tenancy rights

In terms of tenancy rights introduced by the land reform programme, these were weakly enforced. Few tenants were able to independently take up legal cases against landlords, and there was even widespread eviction of tenants before legislation came into effect (Gill, 2009). If anything, the efforts to regulate tenancy simply moved it underground (Bhandari, 2006) and into the informal word of mouth contracts which appear to be prevalent today (Sugden and Gurung, 2012). As Basnet (2018) notes with regards to a study in Dang and Banke, registering tenancy rights required the will of the landlords. Any efforts to file cases by tenants would take up to a decade to be processed. During visits of Panchayat officials, they would receive hospitality from landlords, to keep them on their side.

Even for those who did get tenancy rights, 50% still represented a considerable share of the agricultural surplus and was much higher than the one third originally proposed (Adhikari, 2011). This rendered farmers highly vulnerable to climatic or other shocks (Basnet, 2018). Gaige (1970) suggests that the reforms legally sanctioned the exploitative sharecropping system whereby the tenant must surrender half of their harvest. Tenants could also be easily evicted due to non-payment of rent, or spurious reasons such as a failure to look after the holdings (Basnet, 2018). In his study from the western Tarai-Madhesh, Basnet (2018) notes that many landlords also had influence over the distribution of citizenship documents or recommendations from the chairperson of the Panchayat which would be required to register their rights (Basnet, 2018). Other than 'transforming' agrarian relations, tenancy reforms simply served to formalize existing landlord-tenant relationships.

Land redistribution

Land redistribution – which could have resulted in the biggest changes in the relations of production on the ground through dissolving feudal landed property, was similarly weak in implementation. By 1972, the government had ruled that 50,580 hectares of land across Nepal was above the ceiling (Zaman, 1973). However, Regmi (1976) highlights that the official figures for excess land represented only 3% of the cultivable area (Regmi, 1976). Zaman (1973) suggested 34,705ha were 'acquired', affecting 9136 landowners, with just 10,522 beneficiaries. Much later, the Badal Commission which looked into land reform options in 1995 suggested that less than 2% of land was acquired by the government and just 1.5% was redistributed. Regardless of the exact figure, it points to a limited actual redistribution of land – particularly with regards to the large areas formerly under *birta* tenure.

Nepal wide data compiled in Adhikari (2006) does note an almost 10% decrease in the area of land under tenancy between 1964/5 and the 1971/2 National Sample Census of Agriculture (NSCA), from 24.15% to 15.76%. Some of this decline may have been due to a redistribution of holdings from landlords to owner cultivators. However, the migration of hill people to the Tarai-Madhesh throughout the 1960s may have also affected the figures as this represented a significant area of reclaimed forest land which was now under owner cultivation – likely affecting the national level figures.

When looking at the overall data from Nepal, it was clear that land poverty remained a critical issue for agrarian production and livelihoods. Zaman's (1973) survey after the reforms suggested that 4.6% of households with more than 10ha owned 39.1% of agricultural holdings. Those with more than 5ha (10.4%) meanwhile, owned a substantial 60.5% of the land. 63.1% of farmers owned less than 1ha, with the total holdings amounting to just 10.6% of the land, pointing to severe concentration of holdings.

We will now consider the reason for this persisting disparity. Firstly, land which had been seized needed to be purchased by the tillers, with prices set at between Rs140 and 280 rupees per bigha depending on the quality (Basnet, 2018). Prospective buyers had to take government loans, but many could not keep up with payments and thus, ended up having to take private loans at usurious rates. A default on these loans resulted in land going back into the hands of landlords.

Secondly, in the run up to the 1964 reforms some landlords sold off their estates (Gill, 2009, Krauskopff, 1989). However, those buying up this land were often other wealthy individuals with capital rather than poor tenants. It has been argued that the reforms actually supported the emergence of a new landed class as by fixing the rent at half of the crop, they made land a profitable source of investment by those other than the traditional Rana era landlord class (Adhikari, 2011). Regmi's (1976) observes that the emergence of de facto ownership rights in land had made 'ascriptive' rights less important as the source of landed power. An outcome was that the traditional landed elite were increasingly joined by a 'non-ascriptive' land owning class using personal wealth to make investments. Although the relations of production were still 'feudal', this absentee landlord class was becoming increasingly diverse, and was increasingly encompassing urban professionals as well as the traditional landed elite. National Sample Census of Agriculture data suggested that big landlords with more than 10ha owned on average 19ha in 1961, while by 1981 it had reached 22ha (Basnet, 2018), suggesting that they had continued to purchase land even after the land reforms.

Thirdly, the phased implementation of the reforms across different districts gave landlords the opportunity to prepare in advance so they could take advantage of loopholes (Basnet, 2018). Zaman (1972) for instance notes that rather than the twenty Tarai districts which had the most severe inequalities being chosen first, only seven were chosen for the first phase of the programme, allowing landlords in the remaining Tarai districts to take anticipatory steps to avoid the reforms. There were multiple ways to achieve this. For instance, some landlords registered themselves as cultivators while renting out the land to tenants unofficially (Regmi, 1976). Most commonly in such cases, land was registered in the name of different family members to avoid the ceilings (Basnet, 2018). Interviews by the research team in southern Dhanusha, reported that many landlords registered their land in the name of tenants or even controlled large plots of government land and claimed it as their own without any legal claim. These were merely oral claims, which were respected by the villagers given their feudal power. This may explain why the survey area for Zaman's study suggested 0.1% of landlords had excess holdings totalling 653ha. However, only 52ha 8% of this land, had actually been reallocated. The remainder was still in the control of landlords.

More broadly it is important to emphasise, that the landlords often had the land reform officials on their side. For instance, *birtā* grants had incorporated feudal lords within the state bureaucratic alliance (Mishra, 2007). Landlords were important support bases of the king, often influencing implementation agencies and personnel (Khanal et al., 2005, Gill, 2009), and one of the reasons for the failure was the bargaining capacity of the tenants vis-a-vis the landlords (Zaman 1973). A case study from Siraha (Deuja, 2008), suggested that landlords were able to influence land reform officers, who would actually help them conceal their holdings, while confiscating a small part to appear to be working in the interests of the poor. In many areas the cadastral records were weak, meaning that reform officials had to depend on verbal assurances from landlords as to the extent of their property (Zaman, 1973).

The fact that landlords were able to safeguard their property or wealth in advance of the act's implementation, through selling off their estates or transferring ownership within the extended family, was likely a crucial failure of the reforms. Shrestha (1967) makes the important comparative observation that the success of the Japanese land reform was only possible because the government enforced the act in October 1946 with retrospective effect from November 1945 – with all transfer of ownerships taking place in the intervening period ruled as void. Meanwhile, control of rents meant that incentives to buy up land by others in the context of the reforms were low (Ibid.). All of these lessons could have been extremely valuable for Nepal in the 1960s.

A final reason for the limited success of Nepal's land reforms, was that Zaman (1973) points to ambiguities in the content of the Lands Act itself. He cites the preamble of the Land Act which states, *inter alia*, that the main objective of the reform is... *"to improve the standard of living of the actual tillers......through the equitable distribution of cultivable land".* However, nowhere in the Act are the operative words "actual tiller" defined. These ambiguities opened up a number of loopholes which could easily be exploited by landlords. Failures were bolstered by what Khanal et al (2005) observes - namely a lack of commitment and sincerity of the government and ineffective institutional arrangements for the implementation of land reforms. This is in contrast to later successful land reforms such as those in West Bengal the success of which was driven by a committed communist government and mass scale campaign and grassroots mobilization (Banerjee et al., 2002).

Centralised planning and agricultural development
Foreign aid and development plans

By the end of Rana rule, the agricultural situation across Nepal was precarious. With regards to the hills, it appears that by the 1950s, any expansion of the cultivated area had reached its limit. During a Japanese expedition of 1952-53, the team observed that the central Nepal Himalayas was heavily populated, with every patch of ground which has potential for cultivation being used. Most sloping lands, below 30 degrees, were under cultivation, and even the narrow basins on the lower reaches of rivers such as the alluvial fans, were farmed (Kihara, 1956). The report also refers to widespread use of irrigation, but also the presence of large tracts of rainfed land which would be fallow for extended periods. It also reports that a winter cropping cycle was rare outside of the Kathmandu valley due to the absence of year round irrigation (Kihara, 1956), although as noted above, winter cropping of wheat was well established in the Karnali basin, where some of the most extensive farmer managed irrigation systems could be found (see for example, Sugden, 2012a).

Within this context, agricultural policy makers had to consider ways to limit population pressure in the hills (which set the context for resettlement in the Tarai-Madhesh), while also intensifying production, improving irrigation and nutrient management, and introducing improved seeds. In the Tarai-Madhesh by contrast, there was huge scope for increased cultivation with a vast yet to be cleared forest frontier (Gaige,

1976), although existing cultivated lands lacked irrigation and access to advanced technologies, in spite of the huge productive potential of the soil.

These two diverse contexts, set the scene for a wave of state led national development planning, which was to last until the mid-1980s. This coincided with an influx of foreign aid into Nepal (Dangi et al., 2021). With the collapse of colonialism in India to the South, foreign governments increasingly sought to exert their influence through aid. India began sending aid to Nepal in 1952, and became the largest donor by the 1966-81 (Dangi et al., 2021). However, by the 1980s, the inflows had diversified to include China, the USA, the Soviet Union and a range of European countries, not to mention a wide range of multilateral development partners such as United Nations agencies. It also increased from just 2% of GDP in 1960, to a substantial 17.8% in 1986 (Dangi et al., 2021). Figures based on successive Economic Surveys and Reports by the Ministry of Finance and the Nepal Rastra Bank suggest that a total of NRs 95 million was provided by foreign 'aid' to Nepal in the period from 1951-52 to 1955-56, all of which was in the form of grants. Approximately 5.2 billion dollars had been received by the end of the 20th century with donors having a major influence on the succession of development plans for the remainder of the century (Whelpton, 2005). The share of aid in development expenditure meanwhile, varied from 82.1% in 1961/62 to just over 60% by the end of 1990/91 (Dangi et al., 2021).

A cornerstone of aid driven development planning was a series of five-year plans, the first of which was launched in 1956 under Nepal's first democratically elected government (Whelpton, 2005). Increasing agricultural production and food security were important in this, and all subsequent plans. In the first five-year period, it was estimated that out of 8.4 million, 95 percent of the population of Nepal was engaged in agriculture; but crop and livestock production were of inferior quality, and food shortages in many places were becoming acute (Government of Nepal, 2020). The plan, which was financed almost entirely by foreign aid (Dangi et al., 2021), envisioned a range of interventions in fields including agronomy and demonstration farms, horticulture, plant breeding, plant and animal protection, soil sciences, agricultural tools, implementation and machines, agricultural marketing, livestock development, dairy, fisheries development, and soil and water conservation. Likewise, agricultural extension and education were also priorities (Government of Nepal, 2020).

State led development planning continued following the establishment of the Panchayat system in the 1960s, after the King dissolved Nepal's nascent parliamentary democracy and assumed absolute powers. For the authoritarian Panchayat state, rural development was an important means through which it could maintain its legitimacy. The second (1962-65) and third (1965-1970) plans were launched, with the third plan in particular containing ambitious agricultural goals and aimed to increase food grain production by 15% and cash crops by 73% (Seddon, 1987). There were also concerted efforts to increase the dissemination of improved seeds, fertiliser and farm equipment. The Agricultural Supply Corporation was established to distribute improved inputs in 1966 (Seddon, 1987).

An important change in the post-Rana era was a significant increase in the irrigated areas. The three main canal systems built during the Rana era (Chandra, Jagadish and Judha canals) had a command area of just 50,000ha (Shrestha, 1967). The first five-year plan also highlighted that one of the strongest means of expanding food production was by increasing the availability of assured, abundant water supply, improvement and extension of existing irrigation work, and the development of new irrigation projects (Government of Nepal, 2020). The Department of Irrigation[3] was established in 1952 and this was to become a key institution to oversee the construction of large surface irrigation schemes (Pradhan and Belbase, 2018). The Department[4] had a mandate to manage systems that were more than 500 hectares in the Tarai and 50 hectares in the hills – systems which came to be known as Agency Managed Irrigation Schemes

---

[3] In 1972 it became The Department of Irrigation and Meteorology, and in 1987, it was renamed the Department of Irrigation, Hydrology, and Meteorology (Pradhan, 1990).

[4] This was the name of the main department to manage new agency managed irrigation schemes as of the 1980s, although it changed multiple times as different departments merged and split (Pradhan, 1990).

Figure 22 Tara Prasad Bhod, the water divider distributing irrigation water to Chhatis Mauja and Sohara Mauja irrigation schemes, Rupandehi, in 1985
Photo: Prachanda Pradhan (reproduced with permission)

– which became predominant in the Tarai-Madhesh, unlike the Farmer Managed Irrigation Schemes of the hills (Pradhan, 1989a).

Goals in the first five year plan included reconditioning two of the larger pre-existing irrigation works (Jagdishpur and Judha) capable of watering about 9000 acres of paddy, while completing seven projects currently underway with Indian and American aid (which, when finished, would irrigate about 45,000 acres) while constructing additional projects which would cover some 200,000 acres of arable land (Government of Nepal, 2020).

Irrigation expansion continued to be a priority throughout the Panchayat era (see Figure 22) and major schemes included the Sunsari-Morang irrigation system, which was the largest in Nepal (Valadaud, 2023, Aubriot and Bruslé, 2023). In the Tarai there was also a rise in the use of shallow tubewell irrigation between the 1960s and 1980s, which required private investment by farmers (see Figure 23), facilitated by new credit agencies such as the Agricultural Development Bank (Pradhan, 1990), although overall levels of uptake were low.

While the Department of Irrigation managed and built larger schemes in the Tarai, The Ministry of Panchayat and Local Development (MPLD) managed smaller scale irrigation schemes at the district and village levels, mostly in the hills. While there were some larger irrigation schemes in the hills built by the government such as the 120ha Kallaritar scheme in Dhading (Pradhan et al., 2023), most government support for hill irrigation entailed offering technical and financial assistance to pre-existing farmer-managed irrigation systems rather than building new schemes (Pradhan, 1990). The latter systems, including complex management regimes, continued to function throughout the Panchayat period across the hills (Pradhan, 1990, Sugden, 2012a).

Set against this backdrop, the irrigated area increased from less than 200,000ha in the 1950s to over 1,100,000ha by the 1980s (Seddon 1987). The area irrigated by government managed systems meanwhile, increased from just 6500 ha prior to the first plan in 1956 to 84,427 ha by 1980, with 4210ha being situated in the hills and 9856ha being in the Tarai-Madhesh (Pradhan, 1990). Expanding the irrigation coverage to catch up with rising demand for food was a continued challenge, and under the Basic Needs Programme in the 1980s, the government estimated that

Figure 23: Groundwater irrigation in Chitwan, late Panchayat era
Photo: Prachanda Pradhan (reproduced with permission)

irrigation needed to increase by 68,000 ha per year to meet projected food demand (Pradhan, 1990).

Persisting agricultural crisis

In spite of the ambitious plans, the agricultural situation remained precarious – particularly in the hills. Even with the modest investment in irrigation programmes in the hills, by the beginning of the 1980s, most hill and mountain agricultural systems were rain fed, with only 0.7 percent of farm land being perennially irrigated (Green, 1980, cf Schroeder, 1985), a figure which appears plausible given that even many old farmer managed irrigation systems only supplied water for part of the year. Water availability was a major constraining factor on farming systems and agricultural output because of the strong seasonality of rainfall (Schroeder, 1985).

The 1970s also saw the emergence of 'food aid'. Poor harvests in the hills between 1970 and 1973 and the resulting subsistence crisis, prompted the government to establish the Nepal Food Corporation, to distribute subsidized rice – and Nepal around the same time became a recipient of World Food Programme food aid – which focused on the Karnali (Gautam, 2019).

Efforts were initiated to support commercialisation and improve the productivity of small farmers, particularly in the latter decades of the Panchayat era, through sajhas (cooperatives) to support access to credit and markets and associated programmes such as the 1977 Small Farmer Development Programme which targeted the poorest farmers. However, persisting and worsening land inequalities impeded these programmes from reaching out to the poorest cultivators. Landless farmers were unable to procure credit, and the inputs were too costly for the majority of farmers (Seddon, 1987).

Depleting foreign currency reserves and a growing trade deficit due to rising middle class demand for consumer goods, meant that the first structural adjustment loan was negotiated in 1985 (Whelpton, 2005). A 1987 'Basic Needs' programme was launched in line with popular development discourses of the 1980s, aimed to target the poor so they could meet their basic subsistence needs as well as focusing on national level economic growth. However, this largely failed in its objectives, and by the end of the Panchayat era an estimated 7 to 9 million households were unable to meet their minimum calorific needs (Whelpton, 2005). Meanwhile, an increasing share of foreign aid was given in loans throughout the Panchayat Era, rising to three quarters of total aid by the late 1980s, contributing to a rising debt crisis (Dangi et al., 2021). This set the scene for the economic restructuring which would define economic policy from the 1990s onwards.

Resettlement programmes

While some resettlement schemes which sought farmers from the hills had been attempted during the late Rana period, as described above, these were not as successful as planned. However, an important component of Nepal's post 1950s development strategy was a far larger scale programme to resettle hill people in the Tarai-Madhesh – which still had large areas under forest. In-migration to the Tarai-Madhesh would help maintain social harmony in the hills, where population pressure, soil erosion, deforestation, land degradation and declining agricultural yields were making it increasingly difficult for rural populations to subsist (Ojha, 1983). Shrestha (1990) further argued that "there is no doubt that land settlement schemes have both economic and demographic goals, it also entails an underlying socio-political motivation in that it is politically more desirable and safer to execute that aggressive land reform measures" (Shrestha 1990, p. 139). He viewed the resettlement plan as a project of 'land colonization', and a 'sound agrarian strategy', but in essence a 'political move', to pacify potential peasant movements, and to garner the support from the hill population whose livelihoods were under growing economic and ecological stress. According to Shrestha (1990), "such a policy has a populist appeal among the peasant masses as it is viewed by them as a vehicle to acquire land and start a new life" (p 146). The resettlement scheme thus, arguably had much in common with other forms of 'settler colonialism' whereby the state-facilitated horizontal expansion of the peasantry from ecologically and demographically stressed homelands into less populated domains, was used as a tool to maintain social order.

A second advantage for the regime of resettlement was that it simultaneously facilitated the spread of 'hill' culture in the Tarai-Madhesh. Ethnic nationalism was central to Panchayat rule – based upon the dominant Nepali caste Hindu culture of the hills. The Tarai-Madhesh had up until now been dominated demographically by the Tharu, as well as Maithili, Bhojpuri and Abadhi speaking castes. Increasing the migration of hill people to the lowlands was believed to support national integration by shifting the demographic balance of the region in favour of the dominant hill community (Gaige, 1976). The resettlement programme combined with the malaria eradication campaign was in many ways an embodiment of the Panchayat state's ideology of nationalism and modernisation (Johnson, 2023).

The first major resettlement programme was in Chitwan in the wake of the Rapti Valley Development Project (RVDP) in the mid-1950s, funded by the US government, which in collaboration with the WHO supported DDT spraying to eradicate malaria, which up until then had deterred many hill settlers (Robertson, 2018). The US government saw their ability to support the transformation of the Rapti valley as an opportunity to increase their geopolitical influence during the Cold War (Robertson, 2018).

In 1964, the resettlement programme was expanded with the formation of the Punarvas Company (Nepal Resettlement Company) (Shrestha and Velu, 1993), with the support of an Israeli advisor. The first formal scheme of the company was the Nawalparasi Resettlement Project. The project settled 1,504 households on 3,200 ha of land, and included Nepali households evicted from Myanmar. It was later expanded to Banke in 1965 (Mørch, 2023). It was replaced in 1968 with the Department of Resettlement, and formal programmes were implemented in Bardiya, Jhapa, Kanchanpur and Kailali in the 1970s (Mørch, 2023). An estimated 77,000ha was distributed through these schemes since the 1960s (Ibid.). It is estimated that 607,000ha of forest was cleared for the resettlement programmes, and the revenue for timber was highly lucrative for the state, and $104,800,000 was reportedly generated in tax revenue from the sale of timber between 1966-7 and 1999-2000 (Mørch, 2023).

It is important to note that aside from the formal resettlement programmes, the 1960s and 70s also saw significant 'spontaneous' migration to the Tarai. The supply of new land being distributed by the formal schemes rapidly outstripped demand given the persisting ecological pressures in the hills, encouraging unregulated internal migration (Shrestha and Velu, 1993). The numbers are difficult to pinpoint. A World Bank study in the late 1970s placed the figure at around 7000 migrants a year (Mørch, 2023). It appears to have in fact been the predominant form of internal migration to regions such as the far eastern Tarai districts of Morang, Sunsari and Jhapa (Gaige, 1976). This kind of internal migration was mostly unplanned, resulting in a massive contraction of the remaining forest frontier (Shrestha and Velu, 1993). In spite of this, the establishment of new settlements was tolerated by the government and the Department of Resettlement regulated informal and arbitrary settlements by issuing land titles. Inevitably, those already with land and resources were in a much more favourable position to successfully secure rights, due to the cost of clearing the land and rent-seeking by officials (Alden-Wily et al., 2008), and settlers were often able to acquire large tracts of personal land (Shrestha and Velu, 1993).

First generation hill migrants who were interviewed in Morang, were attracted by the abundance of resources, land, in particular, and found the plains more livable than the place of their origin (interview by research team). In many cases, new migrants (particularly better off settlers) encouraged family and other residents to migrate with them – as Dahal et al (1977) shows with regards to migration from the far western hills to the plains of Kanchanpur. This would sometimes even extend to old social relations being replicated, such as leasing out surplus land to tenants from their home community, or taking up the same political positions that they held in the hills such as that of Pradhan Pancha. This meant also that settlements which were previously unplanned were gradually integrated into the political mainstream as elites from within them sought to replicate the institutions of their home communities of the hills in the plains (Ibid.).

Malaria eradication continued well into the 1960s across the Tarai-Madhesh, and this meant that spontaneous migration remained relatively easy throughout the next two decades. Dahal (1977) however, cautions against overstating the eradication of malaria and formal government programmes as a primary driver of migration to these new lands in the plains – noting that migration outside had always been a solution for households coping with demographic pressures, economic distress and land scarcity. The opening of the Tarai merely channelled people who would have left anyway towards a particular locale. With regards to the far west, he argues that the absence of this pressure valve would have led to social unrest, particularly as the land in the far western hills had already reached the limits to cultivation in the 1960s and there was no 'frontier' left to settle (Dahal et al., 1977).

The resettlement process drove a demographic transformation in parts of the Tarai. There had been less than 19 inhabitants per square meter in Chitwan in 1952-54. This had increased to 160 persons per square meters by 1991 (Müller-Böker, 1991b). Sharma & Malla (1957, 16-17) describe their observation made in the early 1950s that "Chitwan, including some parts of the Makwanpur district, then has an estimated household of 16,000 and a population of 40,000, of whom, Tharus are in the majority, and some Darais, Danuwar, Chepangs, Magar, and Tamangs; and, sporadically, there was some Brahmin and Chettris, as well, in a few numbers, though" (pp. 16-17). According to the Census (2011), Chitwan now has the highest population of Brahmin (28.56%) followed by Chhetris (11.36%); with Tharus comes third at 10.92 percent (Central Bureau of Statistics, 2011b). Such a dramatic change in the demographic structure is attributed mainly to the resettlement programs, and successive informal migration from the hill districts of central Nepal over the last six decades.

In-migration was naturally highest in the regions with large areas of forest, where there was plentiful land to be claimed (Gaige, 1976). As most of this land lay further north along the foot of the hills, this was naturally where the highest levels of in-migration took place. There were however, pockets of such as Jhapa in the east and Kailali and Kanchanpur in the west, where vast tracts of the district were under forest, even as far south as the border with India. While the process of forest clearance in the west was relatively slow, the contraction of the forest frontier in Jhapa and neighbouring Morang and Sunsari was swift. Gaige's sample in the late 1960s from Jhapa showed that 32.8% were migrants, with some settling even in the far south of the district. In neighbouring Morang, most hill migrants were concentrated to the north by clearing the forest and fallow land and settling there, a popular colloquium term for which was Jhoda Phadani (field notes by authors). The construction of East-West highways during the decades of the 1960s, and 70s accelerated the process further, where laborers on the project could settle in any given public land, often clearing the forest nearby. Hill migrants had the opportunity to independently clear the forest, (*Jhoda Phadani*) accumulate as much land as possible and secure their livelihood (Dhakal, 2015).

There was a relatively slower change in the central Tarai-Madhesh, including the Mithilanchal region, where much of the forest had been cleared during the Rana period and before. The survey by Gaige (1976) showed that in a village adjacent to the forest belt of northern Mahottari-Dhanusha and in Bara, only 2.7% and 2.8% respectively were migrants. Even where there were migrants, not all of them were from the hills. While the government's specific aim was to encourage migration from the north, the unplanned nature of resettlement meant that there were also opportunities for the pre-existing Tarai-Madhesh populations to acquire new lands. Gaige (1976) challenged the common perception of the period that most migrants were from the hills, as his survey from across the Tarai-Madhesh showed that more than half of migrants were themselves of plains origin, thus not affecting the overall composition of the region. This movement entailed mostly caste Hindu populations migrating from more densely populated tracts further south, to the forest belt in the north. This was reportedly particularly significant in the Mithilanchal belt. In Gaige's 1967—8 survey, in Mahottari-Dhanusha, hill migrants constituted just 4.3% of the sample, yet plains origin migrants constituted 94%. This was similarly high at 71% in Bara further west (Gaige, 1976).

There was also a notable migration on an east-west basis from the densely populated districts of Mithilanchal in the central Tarai-Madhesh to the more forested districts in the east and west. Gaige (1976) reports significant westwards movement from Mahottari, Dhanusha, Siraha and Saptari, towards Sarlahi and Rautahat. Family histories gathered in Sunsari during interviews in 2015 also suggested that there had been a large eastwards migration from Mithilanchal west of the Koshi during the 1960s and 70s. In the region south of Inarwa, where many of the communities are home to Madheshi middle and high castes, it was found that the caste Hindu population had actually migrated from Siraha and Saptari in the 1960s and cleared former forest land, whereas hill people had settled further north (interview by research team, 2014). Intra-Tarai migration appears to have continued well into the 1980s – and Ghimire's (1998) study of illegal settlements on forest land in Nawalparasi (based upon fieldwork in late 1980s) suggested that while the majority were from the hills, 30% were from other Tarai communities.

This migration of Tarai communities from long settled villages where land scarcity and feudal relations were entrenched to the forested lands to the north, was during the 1960s and 70s often mistaken for movement from India (Gaige, 1976). This contributed to a political narrative during the Panchayat era of an imminent flood of Indian migrants, which the state used to justify draconian citizenship laws (see below). These rumours of an influx of migrants were found to have been unfounded or over-exaggerated. While there was some limited migration from India in the 1960s, it was not as significant as in the Rana era, and again, it varied by region. In newly settled districts such as Jhapa, Gaige's 1967-8 survey of some villages, showed that just over a third of migrants were from India, including Nepali speakers from the northeast, a third were from the hills, while the remainder were from other Tarai-Madhesh districts. In the northern districts in Mahottari-Dhanusha, those from India represented 27% of the total. Many of these migrants were however low caste and joined the existing class of tenants or marginal owner cultivators, and thus they were not actively clearing new land from the jungle (Ibid).

Importantly, there was also a large westwards migration of Tharu from the Dang valley to clear virgin forest land in Bardiya and Kailali – which is why there is a large population of Danguara Tharu today in those districts (Krauskopff, 1989). Largely driven by the high level of landlessness in Dang and subordination to hill migrant landlords, relocating offered Tharu communities access to their own land. Rajapur island in Bardiya for instance which has a Tharu majority, was gradually settled by Tharu farmers in the latter years of Rana rule, but the population increased rapidly in the 1960s with the in-migration of dispossessed Tharu farmers from Dang. The new settlers built a large irrigation system which was central to the success of the new settlement (Gladfelter, 2022, Gill, 2016).

The settling of the Tarai-Madhesh's forest frontier continued into the 1970s and 80s, but growing concerns by the government over rates of deforestation led to frequent confrontation between migrants and the local authorities (Gaige, 1976). Confrontations also took place when migrants settled on privately owned forest land, and this was associated with some violence in Jhapa in the 1970s (Ojha, 1983). By the 1980s, the state had clamped down on the clearance of forest – yet new lands continued to be cleared for cultivation, albeit on a more sporadic basis – with many settlements being illegal, with the *sukumbasi* (landless/squatter) settlers lacking any legal documentation (Ghimire, 1998)[5]. The ecological transformation was dramatic. Ghimire's (2017) study suggests that between 1954 and 1994, forest cover in the inner Tarai had declined from 48% to 29%. In the Bhabar it had declined from 79% to 58%, while in the Tarai-proper it had declined from 30% to 10%.

Agrarian structure in Tarai-Madhesh during Panchayat era: feudalism and the rising owner cultivating peasantry

Three domains of settlement

During the Panchayat era, the Tarai-Madhesh could be roughly divided into three domains – in terms of the pattern of agrarian and social change. The first domain relates to the areas which were very recently settled from the hills – what we term the 'newly settled tract', where the indigenous population was sparse. This included in particular the northernmost tract of former forest land which skirted the hills, and saw the greatest demographic influx of hill settlers. These domains were predominantly home to relatively prosperous owner cultivators.

---

[5] See for instance, Ghimire's (1998) extensive study of spontaneous settlements of impoverished farmers in the 1980s – after the government had finally sealed the forest frontier to further expansion of agriculture.

The second domain was the 'long-settled tract', which included the areas largely under feudal relations since the Rana era, including Madheshi castes (e.g. the Mithila belt) and subordinated Adivasi populations (e.g. Morang, Sunsari, Rupandehi). In the eastern and central Tarai, and the western Tarai up to Kapilvastu, the distinction between the newly settled and long-settled tract was quite distinct, and follows a north-south divide. In Jhapa, and the belt from Dang to Kanchanpur, the geographical division between these two domains are more complex, with hill settlers even living close to the Indian border in some locales. In general, the division between these two domains follows a distinctive north-south divide, particularly in the central Tarai, and from Nawalparasi to Kapilvastu. However, there were exceptions to this pattern, and in Jhapa for instance, hill settlers resided even close to the Indian border in some locales.

The final domain was the 'transitional zone' where there were large pre-existing Adivasi populations living either under feudal relations or still residing autonomously under an Adivasi mode of production, who were living in close proximity to newly settled areas. This domain saw not only existing feudal relations intensified alongside rising owner cultivation, but also emerging inequalities between settlers and the Adivasi population. This geographically included the Chitwan valley and parts of the Dang valley, and large tracts of the Tarai west of Dang (the so called 'Naya Mulak' including Banke, Bardiya, Kailali and Kanchanpur), where the forests were more intact in the 1960s, yet there was also a large indigenous population. As a result, new settlements of hill castes were much more dispersed and were often established in areas with a large Tharu population already, or alongside Tharu settlers from elsewhere in the Tarai (Gaige, 1976). This transitional zone was also present in parts of the east and central Tarai where the long settled and newly settled tracts meet.

Increase in the peasant mode of production in the newly settled tract

In the newly settled tract of the plains, the resettlement of hill people not only led to significant demographic shifts, but also supported the emergence of an entirely new agricultural economy. Settlers from the hills were from across the economic spectrum, including large, medium and near landless farmers (Shrestha, 1990). Nevertheless, regardless of previous wealth, the economic condition of migrants who were landless or near landless in the hills, undoubtedly improved, in spite of the initial challenges and dangers as they adapted to their new environment (Shrestha, 1990).

A large share of the new settlers owned their own land which they had cleared from the forest (see Figure 24). As part of an effort to formalize the resettlement process, in 1968-69, the government set about creating an inventory of new settlements and formalizing land ownership rights (Ojha, 1983). It was reported by local farmers in Dainyia of Morang for example, that this involved a formal survey to identify which newly cleared land belonged to which household (Sugden, forthcoming). This meant that an increasing share of settlers had secure ownership of their plots.

Within this context, the dominant mode of production in the recently settled tract was of owner cultivation by an independent peasantry. Migrant farmers had secure property rights to their new lands and were able to retain any agricultural surplus which was produced. This effectively empowered a large segment of Nepal's peasantry without any 'redistribution' of land. The resettlement schemes itself offered King Mahendra an opportunity to demonstrate a commitment to offering land to marginal farmers, in the context of a lacklustre effort to redistribute landed estates under the land reform programme (Gill, 2009).

While most farmers had their own plots in the newly settled tract, some level of internal inequality was inevitable – particularly with regards to unplanned settlements, given the differential resources settlers had at their disposal to clear new fields. Shrestha (1990), with reference to hill migrants, notes that the areas of land one was able to clear in the plains was generally proportionate to what the settler once had in the hills, given the resources required to clear new tracts of land.

Furthermore, the settlers who came earlier generally acquired larger plots compared to those who came later when regulations were tightening (Shrestha and Velu, 1993). There were also some farmers who were unable to access land. Gaige (1976) notes that there had been a high level of migration of hill Adivasi who had lost their land in the hills for economic or environmental reasons. A study from Morang suggested that some of these settlers, and even some Brahmin migrants, ended up as tenants on the land of absentee landlords (Sugden, 2010).

Having said that, to a large extent, ethnicity and caste did contribute to the reproduction and perpetuation of these inequalities within the newly settled tracts. Gaige's (1970) survey during the late 1960s showed that the largest group of migrants were Brahmins and Chettris and they rapidly managed to consolidate political and economic power in the regions where settlements were concentrated such as east of the Koshi or the mid and far western Tarai-Madhesh – a topic dealt with in more detail below. Of the migrants in Jhapa in the 1960s who had acquired land, Brahmins and Chettris represented 50% of Gaige's sample from 1967/8. On the whole, the Brahmin and Chettri settlers had more capital to acquire land, not to mention higher education as well as the passive support of the local bureaucracy, facilitated by family connections to officials (Gaige, 1976).

As noted earlier, there was also a replication of old social relations from the hills, including tenants from occupational castes migrating with their landlords. This was widespread in the far-west, where Dahal (1977) points to a replication of old social relations in a new location. Field notes from the authors in Borabandh of Morang also found that wealthier Rais from Chinamakhu had migrated followed by their servants from other castes. That was also true in the case of a few Brahmin priest families, as they migrated to Morang alongside their *jajmans* from occupational castes.

There has been some divergence of opinion on whether levels of inequality in the 'planned' resettlement schemes were lower – as holdings were formally allocated by the government rather than being cleared haphazardly according to the resources one had at one's disposal. During the distribution of holdings during the earlier schemes such as the RVDP, Shrestha and Velu (1993) suggests that farmers who applied could be granted lands of between 1 bigha (0.68ha) and 100 bighas (68ha) – implying that it supported the emergence of landlordism in some locales. Nepotism and patronage shaped the distribution of land, with farmers who were already wealthy and influential cornering land meant for flood victims or the landless (Ibid).

However, there is evidence that land distributed later on through the Nepal Punarvas Company was distributed more equitably. A report into the resettlement programme by Elder et al (1976) highlighted that in the areas settled by the company, one could observe relative equality in the distribution of land, regardless of caste. For instance, in the surveyed area, the percentage of Brahmin, Chettris, Magar and Kami with more than 3ha of land was high across groups, at 45%, 53%, 67% and 58% respectively. It was predicted though that inequalities were likely to increase over time once farmers had the right after 10 years (when they received formal ownership of their plots), to sell or mortgage their land. They point to Chitwan which was settled earlier in the 1950s, where there was already a clear differentiation underway within the owner cultivating peasantry by the 1970s (Ibid.). Rising debt amongst poorer settlers who often had limited savings and fallback options following their relocation to the plains, resulted in distress sales (Mørch, 2023)

It is also worth noting, that these tracts of land were not 'empty' prior to their settlement. For instance, Morang and Jhapa was home to the Dhimal who were likely still integrated into an Adivasi mode of production in the early 1960s. However, analysis of historical research (e.g. Gaige, 1976) and the contemporary demographic makeup of the plains, suggests that numbers were relatively small in large tracts of the newly settled belt, and groups such as the Dhimal were rapidly subordinated to the new settlers (Rai, 2013, 2014). The forest on which their itinerant livelihoods depended was cut down, and their culturally embedded rather than legal relationship with the land and resistance to the land registration process, meant that many became rapidly alienated from their means of production (Ibid.).

Throughout the Panchayat era, the resettlement programme contributed to a growing regional divide between the newly settled and long settled tracts. On the one hand, increasingly prosperous settlements of owner cultivators were emerging on the recently settled belt under an independent peasant mode of production. The mode of production contrasted starkly with the domains with a long history of settlement which were under the *jimidari* system or *birta* tenure, and which continued to experience deeply inequitable feudal relations and

Figure 24: Settlement of hill migrants on the forest frontier of Morang: The farmers in these new communities, created in the 1960s and 70s were relatively prosperous owner cultivators.

Photo: Fraser Sugden

landlordism. There was however, as noted above, an area in between which contained both economic systems – and it is to this we now turn.

The Transitional zone and Adivasi-settler interaction

The transitional zone where there was both a large existing Adivasi population and a newly settled population of migrants from the hills and elsewhere in the Tarai, saw the development of a much more complex agrarian system in the Panchayat era. As noted above, this area, which included newly settled lands of Dang, the Naya Mulak (Banke, Bardiya, Kailali and Kanchanpur), Chitwan, and the forest-to-farm transitional belt across the Tarai, was unique in that in-migration and settlement took place on large tracts of forest which were immediately adjacent to areas of permanent cultivation home largely to a sedentary Tharu peasantry. The confluence of these two economic systems gave way to unique forms of subordination.

Prior to the resettlement programme – the Tharu and other Adivasi groups within this transitional zone were part of a mixed economic formation. Some were owner cultivators, particularly in districts such as Chitwan and the Naya Mulak of Banke, Bardiya and Kanchanpur. For example, in the Naya Mulak, a large share of Tharu were the Danguara Tharu escaping feudal subordination in the longer settled parts of the Dang valley and there is evidence that many were owner cultivators at the onset of the Panchayat era. They had been migrating west since the Rana era, and continued to clear new land along with their hill settler neighbours (McDougal, 1968, Krauskopff, 1989). Similarly, Chitwan's former status as a hunting reserve for the aristocracy and buffer zone with colonial territories in India meant that there was not a history of *birta* grants being distributed by the state and landlessness was less common, with owner cultivation being widespread at the end of the Rana era (Guneratne, 2010).

Nevertheless, there were still feudal estates in some locales – with lands belonging to both hill upper caste and Tharu landlords, particularly in Dang and the parts of the Naya Mulak where there were prominent Tharu *jimidars* as well as upper caste hill origin *jimidars* who maintained large estates, yet (unlike their Tharu counterparts) had remained as absentee landlords during the Rana era (Krauskopff, 1989, McDougal, 1968). A study from near Dhangadhi from the early 1960s suggested that one fifth of the land belonged to absentee landlords living in the hills at the time of writing (McDougal, 1968). Basnet (2018) suggested that in Rajapur of Bardiya, there was up to 22,000ha of land controlled by landlords living in Nepalganj or Kathmandu. In Dang, hill origin absentee landlords were also associated with the previous Dang and Salyan rajas (Dang became a vassal kingdom of Salyan in the 17th century) (Krauskopff, 2011, Mishra, 2007), and some landlords were linked to the Kanapatha Yogis with ties to both dynasties, and whose religious institutions were powerful in the valley (Krauskopff, 2011).

In Dang, some Tharu tenants worked as sharecroppers in the traditional sense, while others, particularly in nearby Dheukuri, cultivated land under the *potet* system which by the 1960s appeared to have evolved into a system whereby the former *jimidar* was recognised as landowner, yet tenants still had full usufruct rights to the land and offered only a modest labour tribute as rent (McDougal, 1968).

While the presence of landlordism has been established, even amongst the Tharu, what was unique in this transitional zone was that migration from the hills brought significant changes with the rapid establishment of new settlements of owner cultivating peasants *immediately adjacent to* or *within* existing Tharu settlements. This had two outcomes. Firstly, the pre-existing hill origin landlord class was able to consolidate their control over land in the context of the larger demographic shift underway. Following the control of malaria and the opportunities posed by a rapidly rising population, many formerly absentee landlords moved down to the plains and were able to strengthen their control over the means of production (Krauskopff, 2011). McDougal's (1968) study from Kailali and Dang in the early 1960s showed that many of the former Brahmin/Chettri *jimidars*, took up new political positions in these new mixed ethnicity settlements, such as that of Village Panchayat Chairmen[6] - likely strengthening their control over resources locally. Many also began to edge out the former Tharu *jimidar* landlord class – an issue which would become even more acute following the land reforms (see below). For instance, McDougal (1968) suggests that most landowners in Dang were Tharu at the time of the 1912 revenue settlement. However, this had declined remarkably by the 1960s, and went alongside a rapid rise in the size of the hill origin landlord class. Land reforms had some modest impacts, and Zaman's (1973) sample from Kailali and Dang suggested that 64% of the land above the ceiling was re-allocated, although this did not account for land which was not registered in the first place). Nevertheless, even where reforms were successful, they were balanced out by a second trend outlined below.

Under this second trend, control over land began to be disproportionately in the hands *not only* of established absentee landlords from the hills, but also upper caste peasant settlers from the hills.

---

[6] Tharu former jimidars only took up the new position in the villages of the study where there were no hill settlers (McDougal, 1968).

McDougal (1968) notes that relations between the hill settlers and Tharu[7] were initially amicable, yet the economic gulf between the two intensified over time. There was growing alienation of formerly Tharu controlled land to these incomers (Ibid.). The Tharu were prone to borrowing money from settlers with capital, without understanding the consequences, and many lost their holdings when loans couldn't be repaid (Gaige, 1976). This has been recorded by several studies both across the Naya Mulak (Banke, Bardiya, Kailali and Kanchanpur) and in the Dang valley (Posel, 1995) and Chitwan valley (Müller-Böker, 1999, Robertson, 2018). Guneratne (2002) also notes how some Tharu in Dang were pressurised into selling their land to incomers under threat. Many settlers over time became large landholders, encroaching upon Tharu lands or registering them in their own names through deception during cadastral surveys[8].

Similar accounts of land alienation amongst the Tharu were reported from Chitwan by Guneratne (2002). For instance, a large number of Tharu farmers sold land to mostly Brahmin settlers due to debt, as what was once a relatively closed economy became monetised. However, Guneratne (2002) attests that the levels of alienation were not as severe as in the much more peripheral region of Dang, and there was no equivalent of the *kaamaiya* system in Chitwan. Nevertheless, there was a subset of landless labourers who lost their land through a more complex process. When labour scarcity was high prior to the end of the Rana era, a group of farmers known as *baahaariya* would – rather than taking on *raikar* leases – work as a labourer for another Tharu *raikar* holder, who would provide food and sustenance. The end to labour shortages as the Chitwan valley was opened for settlement and in-migration, resulted in the loss of this

---

[7] This includes both Tharu indigenous to the village in question and those who had migrated from Dang to Kailali/Bardiya.

[8] There was a historic precedent to this. Gaige (1976) notes that hill upper castes preferred to migrate to regions home to plains Adivasi such as Morang, Sunsari and Jhapa, the Chitwan valley, and the western Tarai-Madhesh districts. They would meanwhile, avoid areas home to Tarai-Madhesh high castes and intermediate castes (such as the central Tarai-Madhesh, where most resettlement was from other parts of the plains). This meant that rather than competing for resources with other upper castes, they could more rapidly consolidate their control over economic resources and political power (Gaige, 1976).

livelihood strategy. However, during cadastral surveys, as the government appointed new lands to settlers and reconfirmed existing *raikar* property rights, many *baahaariya* were unable to register lands in their names and thus became landless (Guneratne, 2002).

It is also worth noting that other than land being directly 'lost' to new settlers in the transitional zone, the capacity for local Adivasi themselves to clear forest around their communities and take on land for their own use (particularly as shifting cultivation lost its viability) was far more limited. Oral testimonies from Dainiya in eastern Morang an area at the interface between hill settler and longer established Tarai-Madhesh Adivasi (mainly Gangai) communities reflect some of these unequal power relations. From the 1960s, the jungle to the north of the older Gangai settlement was rapidly cleared and replaced by prosperous settlements of Brahmin and Chettri owner cultivators. New settlers had capital to mobilise labour and clear large areas of land. Some wealthy hill people were able to clear up to 20-25 bigha and thus claim it all as theirs. Even after clearing the land, one had to pay Rs 150 to register the land in one's name, a significant sum at the time. They also had political connections which backed them up in any disputes with authorities. Attempts by the local Gangai to also create new estates were often unsuccessful. Many did not know about the opportunity to clear the forest until the hill people had already begun the resettlement, and few had the relatives or connections to the bureaucracy of their Brahmin and Chettri counterparts. Many worked as wage labourers for the new settlers, but when they also tried to clear some land for themselves, officials would stop them (field interviews by authors, 2012).

Similar challenges were evident in areas such as Kailali and Bardiya where settlers were themselves Tharu from Dang, putting them directly into competition with hill settlers. Krauskopff (1989) does note that the new settlements of Danguara Tharu which were alongside the local Katharya Tharu enjoyed relatively favourable economic conditions and greater political empowerment (Krauskopff, 1989). However, Gaige (1976) further emphasises that Tarai-Madhesh Adivasi groups on the whole had fewer contacts with the bureaucracy, making it more challenging for them to successfully compete for lands, or at least to clear estates of the same size as the hill settlers (Gaige, 1976). Furthermore, many Danguara Tharu who migrated to Kailali, were 'brought' by wealthy hill upper castes in Kailali to work as tenants or labourers (often being recruited by agents) – and thus they were landless and subordinate to hill upper castes from the moment they settled in the district (McDougal, 1968).

Zaman's (1973) post-land reform survey in sample clusters in Kailali and Dang suggested that 20.81% of land belonged to landlords with substantial estates of more than 30 hectares – a group which represented just 2.81% of the sample. While the survey didn't cover landlessness, a number of other studies have analysed this, with a focus on the growing inequalities between the Tharu and hill people, including hill origin landlords since the 1960s. McDougal's (1968) survey of five villages in Kailali in the 1960s suggested that landlessness amongst the Tharu varied from 30.4% in western Kailali to 80.8% in the east, with just 55.2% of Danguara Tharu holding land[9]. In the Dang the situation was particularly bleak, given the longer history of absentee landlordism. Krauskopff (1989) suggests that most of the medium sized Tharu landholders (with lands of up to 15 bighas), had by the 1950s, also lost their land to hill settlers due to debt and deception – with only some of the old Tharu landlords retaining control over their estates. It was suggested that only 23% of Tharu in the survey area had their own land as of 1967.

In the sample from McDougal's (1968) case study in Dang, 87.9% of hill castes owned land, as compared to just 36.3% of Tharu. In one village Tharu only owned just 17% of the land in the village, in spite of them being the majority. Even if one excludes the absentee landlords, 70.6% of resident hill settlers owned more than 5ha of land, with 15.7% owning more than 20 bighas – a substantial holding by Tarai standards. Similar findings were evident in another study from Dang whereby as of 1980, the Tharu who formed around three quarters of the village population owned just 23% of the land. Another 12% belonged to a religious school while 65% belonged to just 15 hill families who represented less than a third of

---

[9] He also notes that land ownership amongst Rana Tharu was higher – yet this was drawn from just a small cluster in one village and requires further research.

the population (McDonaugh, 2012). A large area of land had been *birta* bestowed to a Brahmin, whose descendants had over the years split it amongst family members or sold it to other hill settlers. (Ibid.).

In terms of the mode of production in these areas of high inequality, this appeared to closely resemble the localised feudalism described elsewhere – with a large proportion of farmers working as sharecropping tenants (McDougal, 1968). Tenancy often included corvée labour – whereby Tharu households would be expected to provide unpaid agricultural or domestic labour for Brahmin and Chettri landlords (Limbu, 2018), for tasks such as porterage or domestic work (McDonaugh, 2012). The sharecropping rents also appeared to have risen (likely as competition for land increased) – and in one Dang case study landlords had increased the rent from a fourth or fifth of the crop to half the crop (or a third with the tenant covering input costs) (McDonaugh, 2012). In Dang, feudal excesses by landlords encouraged further westwards migration of Tharu towards Bardiya (Limbu, 2018).

While sharecropping was widespread in more densely populated areas where labour was abundant, elsewhere bonded labour appeared as a more common means through which large farmer settlers and landlords would extract surplus from their excess holdings (McDougal, 1968). The *kamaiya* system of bonded labour was the most well-known outcome of the unequal relationship between settlers and the Tharu community in the western plains (Dhakal, 2001). As noted in the previous chapter, various forms of bonded labour existed historically in Nepal, and the kaamaiya system likely built upon earlier systems of servitude. Dhakal, et. al; (2001) notes that, the term was originally derived from the Tharu dialect, yet is defined in a Nepali Dictionary as a hard tiller of land, earner; manly or obedient person; one who earns along with his family in other's land by borrowing in cash or kind from the land owner or a peasant equivalent to him (Tripathi et al., 1983). However, the definition does not portray the nature of Kamaiya fully as it fails to recognise its bonded nature. Traditionally a Kamaiya has been defined as an agricultural labourer who has life-long involvement in labour for others on an area of land, yet does not have any form of permanent property themselves (Dhakal et al, 2001). Kamaiya would typically be given a small plot (e.g. 1 bigha) to cultivate by the landlord, and would be required to work as a servant simultaneously on the landlord's much larger personal holding, as well as contributing to domestic chores (McDougal, 1968). The relationship is commonly mediated by debt (Maycock, 2012). McDougal (1968), with reference to Kailali suggested that working as a *kamaiya* was actually much more widespread than sharecropping – and for smaller families it was more economical for them to enter a *kamaiya* relationship than take land on lease. However, the author is right to point out that this was at a time when labour was still scarce, so the conditions of employment were better. Conditions deteriorated for *kamaiyas* in subsequent decades as a substantial surplus labour pool emerged, as shown in multiple studies (Maycock, 2012, Giri, 2009).

It is important to note that Tharu zamindars also held *kamaiyas*. For instance Krauskopff (1988) suggests that wealthier Tharu farmers who migrated west from Dang to Kailali between the 1930s and 1940s brought their *kamaiyas* with them (Krauskopff, 1989). McDougal (1968) similarly attests that there were Danguara and Rana Tharus keeping other Tharu as *kamaiya* in Kailali in the 1960s. Maycock (2012) actually suggests that the system most commonly existed within the Tharu community as a form of patron-client relationship between poorer Tharu farmers and landlords before the widespread migration of hill people to the Tarai-Madhesh in the 1960s. Debt or *sauki* was central to the system, and it could be passed between generations, thus assigning a 'cash value' to each worker. However, due to the increasingly unequal relationship between hill settlers and Tharu, and their weakening economic status (see Krauspkopff (1988), most *kamaiyas* by the Panchayat era were working for hill settlers (Giri, 2009). With the predominance of larger farms following the resettlement of hill people in the Tarai-Madhesh with a greater requirements for labour, and the lack of cultural bonds between *kamaiyas* as landowners, the system became increasingly exploitative (Maycock, 2012).

The tradition of Kamaiya was prevalent mainly in the Kanchanpur and Kailali, Bardiya, Banke and Dang districts, the western Tarai-Madhesh. Some versions of this tradition was found also in some of the western Tarai-Madhesh districts, namely Kapilvastu, Rupandehi and Nawalparasi, where significant numbers of Tharus live alongside hill settlers. Though the people from other caste/ethnic groups were also found as *kamaiyas*, they were insignificant in number (Dhakal et.al. 2001).

Why the *kamaiya* system arose primarily in the areas at the frontier of Adivasi and hill settler society in Dang and the Naya Mulak (Banke, Bardiya, Kailali and Kanchanpur) rather than elsewhere is complex. Guneratne (2010) for instance, notes how the Tharu of Chitwan lost land and were reduced to a minority within their district, yet did not experience subjugation as *kamaiyas*. He suggests that this was due to the fact that the district lacked big landlord estates owned by non-Tharu, hill upper castes, as were present in Dang. The remnants of the Tharu landed class also remained more powerful in this region, given that a Rana era landed elite had not established itself there to the same extent (Guneratne, 2010).

As an endnote to the discussion of the transitional zone, it is worth touching upon some more complex processes through which inequities emerged between the settlers and Adivasi peasantry. Yoder (1994) for instance, documents how the original Tharu managers of the Chattis Mauja irrigation system saw their control over water undermined by the expansion of settlement in once forested north of the system. The process whereby the Tharu villages which founded the canal became part of the tail end of the system, led to inevitable conflict over water. The impact of irrigation development is discussed later in this chapter.

The mode of production in the long-settled tract – persisting feudalism and failed land reforms

In the settled tracts to the south of the Tarai-Madhesh, which had been cleared of forest during the Rana era and had not been hit by the waves of in-migration, there was much more limited change after the fall of the Ranas. Agrarian relations remained deeply inequitable throughout the Panchayat era – with a high prevalence of localised feudalism. It was here also that the limited success of the land reforms became apparent. Zaman's (1973) study which included data from Bara and Jhapa after the land reforms pointed out that 21% of the land belonged to just 1.55% of landlords who possessed more than 30ha of the land. This was likely even higher in the areas with deeply entrenched feudalism such as Morang-

Sunsari and Mithilanchal. The survey also suggested that 65.17% of land was held by just 15.45% of landholders possessing more than 5ha, a much smaller proportion than the Dang and Kailali sample where it was more evenly spread across 48.87% of landholders. Zaman's sample from Jhapa and Bara also hints that the land reforms were much less successful in the central and eastern Tarai – with just 5.39% of the land which the survey found to be above the ceiling, being reallocated.

One change in the agrarian structure in the Tarai-Madhesh during the Panchayat era which did take place, was that a segment of the former *birta* owners or other landed classes, migrated to urban centres throughout this period, from where they continued to extract rent - they had become *absentee* landlords (Sugden, 2025, Basnet 2018). This landlord class was generally close to political power, with strong links to the bureaucracy (Basnet, 2018). Surplus extracted by landlords generally was put towards consumption of imported luxuries and speculative investment (Adhikari, 2011).

One element of the agrarian relations which differs in the long settled tract of the eastern and central Tarai when compared to the western Tarai was the absence of the *kamaaiya* system. In places such as Morang and Sunsari, this may have been due to the fact that at the apex of the agrarian structure were large absentee landlords who had an increasingly distant relationship with their tenants, rather than large local landlords. In areas such as the caste Hindu heartland where local landlords were powerful, a similar form of bonded labour known as *haruwa* was present (Dhakal et al., 2020) – and this will be discussed below. We now go on to explore some of the locally specific trends in terms of Panchayat era agrarian relations in the long settled tract of the plains.

The agrarian structure in the Caste Hindu Heartland

In the Tarai-Madhesh districts of Mithilanchal, between Saptari and Sarlahi, there appears to have been limited change in the mode of production after the fall of the Rana regime. While there were some large landlords from the hills who resided in urban areas, most of the powerful landowners resided locally and were usually from the Maithili or Bhojpuri speaking upper or middle castes. Oral histories in Mahottari and Dhanusha collected from elders in 2012 suggested that as of the 1970s, even after the land reforms, there were many households with up to 60 bigha, including Buhimar, Jha and Kyastha landlords. There was limited evidence of the land reforms having any substantial impact, and oral histories collected in the region (Sugden, 2019b, Rinck, 2024) point to an agrarian system not dissimilar to the classical rural feudalism of pre-land reform Bengal described by Bhaduri (1973) whereby a large strata of landless labourers and small peasants would be bonded through ties of interdependence to local landlords through a combination of rent, labour and usurious consumption loans.

Oral histories from Fulgama, Ekrahi and Singya Madan in southern Dhanusha suggested that the power of large landlords was deeply entrenched until the 1980s, although surplus appropriation was not just through rent. While tenancy was present, low caste marginal farmers reportedly also worked extensively as labourers on the estates of landlords, being paid in kind. Land owners included both '*zamindars*', the large landlords from the Rana era (some of whom were hill origin, although most were from Maithili dominant castes), as well as large farmers from dominant castes with excess land (Sugden, 2019b). A *jajmani* system existed whereby tenants or labourers from the Madheshi Dalit community, would work for free for extended periods, in return for grains during festivals. Dependence on landlords was worsened by the inter-linkage of credit-debt relations with land tenure, often leaving farmers with little freedom to leave the village and seek work outside. It was recalled in all the sites, that landlords in the past were also the primary source of credit. Repayments of loans were sometimes the basis on which landlords could extract an unpaid labour rent (Sugden, 2019b). Rinck (2024), in another study on agrarian change from Dhanusha, points to a similar situation marked by perpetual indebtedness, while also noting how access to land markets for the landless majority was virtually impossible. Rinck's (2024) study also showed how many larger landlords in Dhanusha also kept *haruwas* or bonded labourers, a system with some similarities with *kamaiya* in the west.

Harawa-Charawa (HC) is a form of an agricultural labour contract which was prevalent across the central Tarai-Madhesh. It is historically rooted and culturally embedded, and usually tied up with indebtedness (Dhakal et al., 2020). Generally, a Harawa-Charawa can be defined as, "A person coerced to work in the landlord's field as a ploughman or does any other assigned agricultural works for the interest of the loan received, or for grain or the small piece of land cultivated or for shelter in a bonded situation" (Ibid.). It can also refer to "a person who does not have the freedom of leaving the work or has no work choice, does not have fixed working hours, receives insufficient or no wage (i.e., either in cash or in-kind) for his labor" (ibid.). Dhakal (2007) notes that the system as a whole, is an outcome of historically framed patron-client relationships over generations, which had become more exploitative over time.

Farmers across the region noted how poverty was extreme in the 1970s and 80s amongst the small farmer and tenant majority, with subsistence needs pushed down to the physiological minimum, and very limited circulation of cash within the community (Sugden, 2019b). This was a somewhat different situation when compared to the tribal domains of the eastern Tarai-Madhesh, where rent alone appears to have been the predominant mode of surplus appropriation.

There was however, possibly an incremental decline in landlord power throughout the latter Panchayat era – although this did not appear to be due to land reforms (Sugden, 2017b). The fragmentation of estates was a challenge for the landed elite. As land was divided up amongst sons, there was less land to rent out – and while landlords remained powerful, there was a gradual decline in the size of holdings throughout the 1970s and 80s. It was reported in Dhanusha that absentee landlords had also lost land due to fragmentation, but like in Morang-Sunsari, this would not have the same implications, as urban dwelling family members would not have the same interest in agriculture, with some sons not expecting a share of agricultural land (Sugden, 2017b).

Demise of Tharu landed class in Adivasi belt and inter-ethnic transfer of resources

In the Adivasi belt of the Tarai-Madhesh which had been under feudal subordination since the Rana era, including long-settled parts of Chitwan, Morang-Sunsari, Dang, Rupandehi and Nawalparasi – the legacy of the *jimidari* system and subordination of the Adivasi mode of production meant that landlordism and severe inequalities were widespread. The legacy of *birta* distribution in these domains in particular, meant that there were a number of vast estates in this tract belonging to politically connected upper caste landlords.

In the Adivasi belt the land reforms resulted in some internal shifts within the feudal mode of production on the ground – although rather than transforming it, the reforms simply changed the ethnic composition of the landlord class. This change was most notable in the domains with a locally powerful Adivasi landlord class, which included the long-settled parts of the Dang valley (Krauskopff, 1989) western Tarai-Madhesh districts of Rupandehi and Nawalparasi (Sugden, 2012b), and the eastern Tarai-Madhesh districts of Morang and Sunsari (Sugden, 2013), and Jhapa (Gautam, 2005). The estates of the Adivasi landlords in these domains were often adjacent to the lands of Brahmin and Chettri landlords, including *birta* estates which were farmed by Adivasi tenants. Many landlords were absentee (as was common in Morang) collecting rent through a local agent or *kamtiya* (Sugden, 2025) while others resided locally, as in Dang (Krauskopff, 1989).

Studies have shown how a large share of the hill origin landlords in long-settled Adivasi domains were able to bypass land reforms through deception and exercise of political power, often at the expense of the fledgling indigenous landed class (Sugden, 2013, Krauskopff, 1989, Sugden, 2025). From oral histories compiled in southern Morang, it appears that registering land in the name of tenants or splitting titles between different family members was also the most notable mechanism through which absentee landlords avoided the enforcement of ceilings. There were even several rumours of married couples divorcing (on paper only) so some land could be registered in the husband's name and some in the wife's name – a reality verified by the local land revenue office (Sugden,

2010). During the land reforms, a number of landlords even registered their lands as commercial farms. That meant they would not be subject to ceiling rules. Then after the reforms, the landlords would simply lease the land out to sharecroppers. For the few tenants who were able to acquire legal tenancy documents, a few have been able to get half the land. However, a common practice was for landlords to offer some money to tenants so they would give up their claims. Often the tenants were cheated, being given very marginal sums while not knowing the true value of the plots (Sugden, 2025). For the Tharu landlord of Morang however, the capacity to engage in such deception or exploitation of legal loopholes was more limited. They lacked the political connections to the bureaucracy and associated knowledge of legal processes, and thus they were reportedly more likely than their upper caste hill origin counterparts to have their lands seized (Sugden, 2013). Similar findings were noted by Gautam (2005) with regards to the Rajbanshi of Jhapa.

Oral histories from Rupandehi (Sugden, 2012b) and Morang (Sugden, 2025) recount a substantial change of fortune for the former Tharu functionary class. In part the land reforms were responsible. However, the Tharu landlords had also lost considerable tracts of land due to debt. The causes of growing indebtedness are difficult to verify, although the gradual monetisation of the economy and market expansion appear to be partially responsible. There was in this context a growing culture of consumerism and rising expenditures for life cycle ceremonies amongst indigenous landlords. In spite of their falling political and economic power, there continued to be cultural pressure for the former Tharu nobility to spend significant sums on weddings, as well as community level ritual activities (Sugden, 2025). Financial distress amongst dominant groups due to the rising cost of cultural and status associated expenditures, has been a widespread theme in the agrarian history of Nepal. Other examples include the weakening power of the Newar upper castes in Sankhu of Kathmandu (Rankin, 2004), and the decline of the Limbu *subbas* or chieftains (Caplan, 2004).

The power of the landlord class was further undermined as plots were split within growing families. The over-dependence on agriculture and more limited external professional opportunities for Tharu sons to leverage exit from agriculture, may have been one reason that this group was disproportionately affected by the division of holdings, as described in Sugden (2010). By contrast, the absentee Brahmin/Chettri landlords were under less pressure to subdivide their land between sons, as they often had multiple sources of income. In other words, not all the sons were expected to remain engaged in farming (Ibid.).

In the long settled tracts of Dang, it appears from Krauskopff's (1989) ethnography, that the economic and political power of the Tharu landed class was already dissipating before the land reforms, with the rising purchase of and control over land by Brahmin and Chettri landlords (see above). However, for the Tharu landlords who still had estates at the time of the reforms, many sold these off, only for them to be bought up by hill settlers. Only a small number of poorer Tharu households had the cash to buy some of this land, and this became more challenging as the land prices rose (Krauskopff, 1989). Adhikari (2010) also notes that former Tharu functionaries in Dang sold their land to hill people with whom they had strong relations, at the time of the Lands Act. There were only pockets of the district where the Tharu landlords were able to maintain their control over land, largely by dividing them up between brothers (Krauskopff, 1989).

Understanding this shift in the power balance, requires a reiteration of the importance of land to political authority over the last two centuries. Political power was central to the reproduction of feudal relations of production. It is in this context that one can observe the *political* mechanisms through which over time, feudalism was both reproduced and also underwent internal transformation. The indigenous landlords had served their purpose as intermediaries under a centralised form of feudalism or so called state landlordism. Their weaker *political* position after the fall of the Rana regime made it more difficult for them to bypass land reform legislation and maintain their power as a landlord class. Their weaker *economic* position meanwhile, alongside high expenditure, made them vulnerable to debt and hastened their decline as a landed class.

The demise of the Adivasi landed class was of course not uniform across the Tarai, and in some locales they retained relative economic power – including some villages of Morang visited by the authors, and also parts of the Chitwan valley. Muller-Boker's (1999) study of the Chitwan valley towards the latter part of the Panchayat period observed that there was still a notable 'landed' Tharu class, even if their power was weaker than before. The study identifies four distinct strata. Firstly, there were *sukumbasi* or landless workers, who were mostly day labourers or farmhands, including *haruwas*, the bonded agricultural labourers. Secondly, there were so called *yanuriya* (poor farmers), with the very smallest holdings who were largely dependent on outside income, and who also did tenant farming as sharecroppers under *thekka* (fixed in kind rent) or *adhiya* (sharecropping). Secondly, there were *girhat* (landed farmers), who were usually small-to-medium-sized landholders that meet their own needs and may produce a surplus, while employing outside labour (Muller-Boker, 1999). Finally there were the *jimindars* (landlords), who owned medium-to-large-sized holdings with surplus production, employing outside labour, with some employing *haruwas* (Muller-Boker, 1999), although the latter was far more limited when compared to the *kamaiya* system in the far west which is described later. The fact that there was still a Tharu landed class in Chitwan may have been due to the fact that there had never been a large Rana era hill-origin landlord class to edge the former out, unlike other Tharu domains such as Morang. This stems from its history as a hunting reserve, as noted above, whereby it did not see the distribution of large *birta* grants (Guneratne, 2010).

Dispossession of land amongst small landowners

In parallel to the decline in the Adivasi landlord class in large tracts of the Tarai, absentee landlords, usually of hill origin were able to increase their holdings by buying up the land of not only the Adivasi landlords, but also the small owner cultivators who had either received land in the reforms, or had successfully held on to a *raikar* plot during the Rana years. Oral histories collected from rural Morang in 2012 noted how farmers would take loans either from other landlords or money lenders, often for medical or wedding expenses. With land left as collateral, this was often lost if debts could not be repaid. One *Bantar* farmer recalled how his grandfather was cheated by an absentee landlord. Not being able to read, the farmer signed papers for a much bigger loan than he had originally taken –

culminating in the loss of his holdings. Minority Adivasi groups of the eastern plains such as the Bantar, Gangai, Santhal and Musahar appear to have been particularly affected by these processes of debt associated dispossession – and they became functionally landless between the 1960s and 1980s, often retaining just their homesteads or very small plots (Sugden, 2025; Sugden and Gurung, 2012).

In cases such as this in Morang, land was sold both to the traditional landed class of hill origin, as well as a new class of landlords in Biratnagar or other urban outposts buying for speculative purposes (Sugden, 2009b, a). Regmi (1976), suggested that land remained a profitable investment following the land reforms. The Lands Act maintained agricultural rents at a level that ensured landowners continued to receive an income equivalent to that which would be achieved had they invested in other sectors (Regmi, 1976). It therefore encouraged the purchases of land by town dwellers with salaried employment.

Hill nationalism and exclusion from land

While there was an expanding class of functionally landless farmers in the long-settled tract of Madhesh – this groups' exclusion from both land and resources was aggravated by the hill-centric nationalism of the Panchayat era. Ultra-nationalism was important for the Panchayat state to uphold its legitimacy, epitomised by the slogan – *ek bhasha, ek bhesh, ek desh* (Literally one language, one style of dress, one country) (Gaige, 1976).

While the growing dominance of Nepali speaking hill upper castes in control over land in the plains has been documented above, official state policies to uphold 'hill dominance' are most notable with regards to language policy. Nepali had been the functional language of the bureaucracy since the Gorkha conquest[10], yet from the 1960s it was enforced as the medium for education, while the use of indigenous and regional languages were banned (Phyak and Ojha, 2019). Prior to the settlement from the hills, the 1952/3 census suggested that only 4% of the

---

[10] It had previously been termed 'Gorkha bhasa', but was given the name Nepali in the early 20th century, in efforts to strengthen it as a national language. It became the official language of the country though only in 1948 (Phyak and Ojha, 2019).

Tarai spoke Nepali as a mother tongue (Gaige, 1976). While this changed following the resettlement programme, much of the long-settled tract which was far from new settlements had limited contact with Nepali speakers, and thus knowledge of the language was more limited in this belt (Gaige, 1976). This contributed to the inter-generational exclusion from job opportunities (including representation in government) for a generation of youth from this belt.

However, language policy is unlikely to have had a *direct* impact on the ownership of land, and the impacts on agrarian relations were indirect. In general terms, reduced employment opportunities can place a block on upward mobility, particularly amongst a middle peasantry for whom it can contribute to accumulation and even support an exit from agriculture[11]. It also contributed to the further fragmentation of land amongst the old Tharu landed class, as noted above, as the tendency for sons to leave agriculture were less common.

Where hill-centric nationalism impacted access to the means of production for the landless poor was with regards to citizenship. The Panchayat state implemented draconian citizenship policies, influenced not only by its ethnic nationalism, but by an anti-Indianism[12] which was inherent to the Panchayat regime. The more restrictive rules were justified on the basis of state sanctioned hysteria that there would be mass-immigration from India at the time when the Tarai's forest frontier was being settled (Gaige, 1976).

Citizenship was a requirement to own or purchase land. For the large number of individuals in the Tarai who were unable to prove their birth in Nepal or citizenship of their parents, naturalization was an important route to citizenship. However, the 1964 citizenship act defined requirements for naturalization as those who were able to speak and write Nepali, and who were of 'Nepalese origin' (Gaige, 1976). The

---

[11] See discussion in Sunam et al (2025) on routes out of agriculture for youth.

[12] While anti-India sentiment was central to the Panchayat state's ethnic ideology as it sought popular support, on an economic level, the regime remained a comprador state, and the ruling class benefited from deep-seated ties of dependence with India (Blaikie et al 2001).

requirements to write in Nepali was of course impossible for many illiterate tenant farmers, while racist interpretations of the 'Nepalese origin' clause resulted in many Tarai people being denied citizenship by government officials. Nepalese origin was interpreted as those of 'hill descent' on the basis of the government's one-nation-one culture policy.

Denial of citizenship thus contributed to the reproduction of landlessness amongst the base of the Tarai's agrarian structure at a time when the government was carrying out cadastral surveys and reconfirming property rights to lands at the time of the land reforms. Many landless had not previously applied for citizenship, yet such papers were necessary to confirm titles to the plots they farmed. At the same time, land ownership papers were one of the few ways they could prove their residency and claim citizenship papers in the first place (Nepali et al., 2011b). They were thus trapped in a cycle of exclusion. This in particular affected functionally landless Madheshi Dalits and minority Adivasi communities such as the Santhal, Gangai and Bantar. For example, Giri's (2012) study of the Musahar community in the central Tarai-Madhesh showed that they were both disproportionately landless, yet also experienced high levels of exclusion from citizenship (Giri, 2012). Another study from Jhapa district suggested that during the 1960s land reforms, many Santhal did not have citizenship papers to register the land they themselves had cleared from the forest in the past – resulting in the loss of their holdings (UNHCR Nepal, 2011).

Agrarian structure in hills during Panchayat era: Differentiated owner cultivation peasantry and pockets of landlordism

Monetisation and market integration

The nature of agrarian change in the hills differs somewhat from the Tarai-Madhesh. The hills didn't experience the same transformation in agrarian relations and ethnic-caste relations due to resettlement. Nevertheless, there were other drivers of change, most notably of which was the expansion of markets and the cash economy.

As the state underwent its modernisation agenda, with improving infrastructure, foreign aid and growing integration into the global economy – a wave of monetisation swept the hills. As with all processes of agrarian change in Nepal, monetisation was an uneven process, and was connected to (albeit not dependent upon[13]) the transition of the mode of production itself. There was cash circulating in communities as early as the Rana era, including in areas dominated by Adivasi economic formations, through cross border trade and income from army recruitment (see Macfarlane, 1976). However, a notable change in the Panchayat era appears to have been associated with the greater influence of markets for consumer goods, and alongside this, enhanced opportunities to dispose of accumulated savings through investments in land and other assets.

A review of the literature suggests that there were two waves of monetisation. The first was associated with the emergence of bazaar towns across the hills, with greater access to manufactured goods. Small 'towns' and associated trade networks did exist in the 19th and early 20th century (as discussed in the last chapter). However, while in the 19th century, these towns often served a military garrison or fort, with an additional trading function, by the mid-20th century a network of much more commercially oriented 'bazaars' was emerging. For example, Hitchcock (1963) documents the emergence of bazaar towns in Syangja. The first bazaar was established in the 1950s, with several new shops opening at a village level selling commodities such as cigarettes and Indian made cloth (Hitchcock, 1963). Kawakita (1957) also documents the expansion of bazaar towns across the central hills at this time, particularly in strategic locations such as *phedis* (where trails reach the foot of the hill on valley floors), *ghats* (riverside where a ferry would operate), or *bhanjyangs* (passes between hills, often at meeting points of trails). Improved foot trails and a network of suspension bridges also helped catalyse trade (see Figure 25).

---

[13] For instance, Gurung communities studied by Macfarlane (1973) had seen circulation of cash for many decades due to army employment in spite of the persistence of the Adivasi mode of production, whereas many of the fully sedentary peasant tenant farmers in the Kathmandu valley which were the focus of Krishna Bhakta Caguthi's account in Raj's (2010) study, appeared to be integrated into a cashless barter economy up until the 1960s.

Figure 25: Suspension bridge in Dholakha, 1975. Bridge construction accelerated during the Panchayat era, facilitating market integration
Photo – Kathryn March and David Holmberg (reproduced with permission)

Towns in the hills in 1950s were modest in size – for instance, Trisuli Bazaar in Nuwakot had around 200 houses, and Arughat of Gorkha had around 60, and thus were not much larger than the military outposts established the century before (Kawakita, 1957). Nevertheless, these were to expand considerably from the 1960s onwards (see Figure 26), as Caplan (1970) shows with regards to Ilam, where a wage labour economy appeared to be developing to support construction work. Alongside this was an expansion of *haatiyas* or weekly markets across the hills (Dahal, 1981) (see Figure 27) which would give farmers the opportunity to sell small volumes of agricultural produce to convert to cash.

The second wave of monetisation was associated with the expansion of roads (see Figure 29) – which only reached a handful of district centres during the Panchayat era (mainly in the central hills), yet would expand significantly in subsequent decades. This saw much greater levels of

Figure 26: Trisuli Bazaar, Nuwakot in 1988. Markets such as this expanded considerably between the 1960s and 1980s.

Photo – Kathryn March and David Holmberg (reproduced with permission)

Figure 27: Weekly market or Haatiya in Hile of Dhankuta in 2002. Many of these markets which are ubiquitous in the eastern hills, expanded considerably throughout the Panchayat era.

Photo: Fraser Sugden

integration into the cash economy, with higher value bulky commodities now available at a much lower cost (Sugden et al., 2018). This was particularly damaging to local cottage industries (see Figure 28), as shown in Blaikie et al's (2001) comprehensive study of the Butwal to Pokhara road. It meant that mass produced household manufactured goods from India were now easily accessible to large segments of the rural population at a cost which undercut local producers (Blaikie et al 2001).

These waves of monetisation are explained effectively in Dahal's (1981) study of the Athpahariya Rai of Dhankuta. He notes that there was relatively limited circulation of cash prior to fieldwork in the 1970s. Grain was the primary medium of payment during peak times for wages. It took time to convert it to cash (due to the need to travel to the distant market), and this encouraged a cautious use of funds – ensuring that it went to the whole family, rather than being used for 'luxuries' such as cigarettes, soap or liquor. Market forces and demand for cash rose however, with growing availability of new commodities such as kerosene, sugar, and cooking oil, which were available increasingly in *haat bazaars* in the 1970s. The later expansion of the road network to Dhankuta in the 1980s intensified this process of monetisation in the rural areas of the district (Sugden, 2004).

Caplan (1970) with reference to Ilam, also makes reference to similar bundles of commodities (e.g. kerosene, cooking oil, tobacco, soap, tea, salt and meat) – which were now easily available in Ilam bazaar, with demand for these goods driving a rise in the cost of living (Caplan, 1970). Dahal (1983), also with regards to Ilam, also mentions the need to meet expenditures for education and transportation.

There were of course regional divergences to the process of monetisation. Macfarlane (1976) offers an interesting perspective on economic change in the Gurung village of Thak in Kaski, as there was a longer history of monetisation it seems than the eastern case studies discussed above. Even while the Adivasi mode of production was predominant in the 19th and early 20th centuries, it was by no means a 'closed' economy given that there was cash inflow from army recruitment (which was far higher than in the east), and the trade and sale of wool products (linked to the Gurung's transhumant pastoral economy).

Figure 28: Weaving loom in Mhanegang, Nuwakot, 1976. Cottage industries such as this faced increasing pressure from imported goods throughout the Panchayat era
Photo – Kathryn March and David Holmberg (reproduced with permission)

Figure 29: Newly constructed road in the late Panchayat era
(Photo: Prachanda Pradhan, reproduced with permission)

However, the big change was the emerging markets for *consumer goods*, which expanded after the 1960s. Most clothes by the 1960s were bought from the bazaar rather than being produced by local tailors (Macfarlane, 1976). A byproduct of this was the collapse in the production of traditional woolen blankets and robes, which had now been undercut by cheaper imports (Messerschmidt, 1981a). Food prices also increased throughout this period. As noted above, the increase in agricultural output was not keeping up with population growth as agriculture reached the ceiling of cultivation with no 'forest frontier' left to clear (Blaikie et al., 2001, Caplan, 1970). In this context the price of grain increased accordingly (Macfarlane, 1976, Hitchcock, 1963).

Another key change in the central and eastern hills (but less so in the west) was the decline in *jajmani* in-kind exchange between castes, echoing a change across the region (Gellner, 2021). While Hitchcock's study in the 1950s suggested that *jajmani* in-kind exchange persisted even as markets for other commodities emerged, this was to be gradually undermined in subsequent years – as shown in Blaikie et al's (2001) study. As of the 1960s in Ilam, all but two Limbu households still used occupational castes (tailors) to purchase clothes with payment in kind, with most purchasing goods instead from the market. Upper castes with surplus land continued for longer as they had surplus grain which could be committed in advance – while also using the relationship to reproduce their social status. Use of blacksmiths continued but this would decline in years to come (Caplan, 1970).

In sum, the expansion of markets combined with the gradual dissolution of cottage industries, had far reaching impact on rural communities – driving a culture of consumerism and most importantly, a rising demand for cash. There were alternative opportunities for petty trade as markets expanded such as small scale sale of cash crops or livestock products (Dahal, 1981, Messerschmidt, 1981a). However, these were likely insufficient to cover the growing monetary needs or to compensate for the collapse of older cottage industries. As Messerschmidt (1980) notes with regards to the Gurung, monetisation, the loss of income from production of traditional textiles and the growing scarcity of land contributed to rising financial distress and engagement in wage labour, particularly via migration, topics which will be discussed below – and would shape the experience of the hill peasantry throughout the decades to come.

It is worth noting that while the lower hills appear to have seen high levels of market expansion during the Panchayat era, there were many regions where the spread of markets was much slower. For instance, in the Kulunge Rai villages of the remote Hongu valley of Solu Khumbu, the expansion of fixed markets was far more limited during the 1960s (McDougal, 1979). This did not mean that trade did not take place, although it often involved travel over long distances to markets such as Bhojpur or Dharan.

Similarly, in Jumla, there was reportedly no local market for items such as cotton cloth in the early Panchayat era, and few local people had access to basic commodities such as sugar and tea – with the only substantial market being the district headquarters which catered to local government staff (Campbell, 1978). The more limited emergence of markets in the western hills likely had a long history, dating back to the region's peripheralization following the Anglo-Nepal wars of the 18th century (Pande, 2014). After this time, the western hills found themselves at the frontier of the much-reduced Gorkha empire and distant from Kathmandu which was the new centre of political power. There was limited investment in infrastructure and limited agricultural surplus due to the high rents and exploitative agrarian structure (Ibid.). Nevertheless, this did not mean the area had no access to markets, particularly given that wage labour migration to India was well established in lieu of the substantial food insecurity in the region. Migrants would often bring back commodities, or they would be purchased during North-South trading expeditions (Campbell, 1978). In Dahal et al's (1977) case study in Darchula, markets appeared to be more developed, particularly given the road access on the Indian side of the border.

The impact of land reform and persisting inequality in the hills

While inequalities were never as severe in the hills as in the plains[14], the question of land reform impacts is still worth considering. It was particularly in the Kathmandu valley where land reforms appeared to have had a more noticeable impact (Müller-Böker and Seeland, 1986, Zaman, 1973). Elsewhere, studies have pointed to similar patterns of avoidance which were reported above in the Tarai-Madhesh. For instance, like in the plains, tenancies in the hills needed to be registered, and during the land survey, tenants' names were frequently excluded, preventing them from claiming their tenancy rights over the land they had been cultivating, which would entitle them to a share of the property (Müller-Böker and Seeland, 1986). Like in the plains, the cadastral surveys which accompanied the land reforms also paved the way for the alienation of farmers from their lands in cases where property rights were ambiguous (Zaman, 1973). Gurung (1996) reports, with regards to Magar of the Tara Khola valley how those with wealth and power, who had benefitted from the unequal registration of land during the late Rana era, were able to influence or bribe survey teams, and take over large areas of cultivated and forest land.

In the Kathmandu valley by contrast – and in particular, Bhaktapur district – tenants were successful in registering the land they were cultivating. In Bhaktapur, like in West Bengal (see Banerjee et al., 2002), a local leftist party played the role of a catalyst in organizing and alerting the peasants of their rights in the context of the reforms (Hachhethu, 2004, Raj, 2010)[15]. They persuaded the local farmers to demand the formal registration of the *mohiyani hak* (tenants' right) for the *mohis* (tenant farmers), who now had security of tenure and experienced a reduced rent

---

[14] Zaman's (1973) survey identified no land in excess of the ceilings in the hills, but this was based upon a relatively small clustered sample, and most landlordism in the hills appears to be restricted to certain pockets of land in lower valleys.

[15] See Raj (2010) for an in-depth historical account of the peasant movement in Bhaktapur, which spanned the period of the land reforms, through the eyes of peasant leader Krishna Bhakta Caguthi.

burden (Ibid.)[16]. The Land Reform Act 1964 brought substantial improvement in the economic conditions of Bhaktapurians, and the Jyapu caste in particular. As a substantial 95 percent of farming households were tenants, the impact of the Land Reform Act in improving the conditions of the masses in Bhaktapur city was clear (Dhakal and Pokharel, 2010).

However, it is worth noting that the prevalence of feudal landlordism was by no means as widespread as in the Tarai-Madhesh. Out migration to the plains had contributed to growing inequality between settlers and Adivasi in the lowlands, a paradoxical outcome of which was reduced inequality in the hills. This out-migration allowed some moderate redistribution of land during the Panchayat era, particularly with regards to less productive holdings (Sugden et al., 2018).

Nevertheless, importantly, there was also considerable variability in the character of the mode of production across the hills, even within districts. For instance, as is shown in Müller-Böker and Seeland's study of (1986) the Kathmandu valley and Gorkha, there was notable diversity from village to village in the relations of production. Some areas were dominated by owner cultivating small farmers, while others were largely under feudal landlord-tenant relations. The differences were due largely to local historical legacies. A further layer of complexity was the uneven dissolution of the Adivasi mode of production – which was at least partially intact in some parts of the hills.

Three trajectories of change

While the variability in agrarian relations is complex, it appears to map to both the local geography and the competition for resources – and we identify three very rough trajectories. Firstly, in areas of the eastern and central hills with higher population density and where the ceiling of cultivation had been reached, the Adivasi mode of production appears to have been almost entirely dissolved. It had been replaced with either owner cultivation within an increasingly differentiated peasantry, or (on the more

---

[16] For instance, rents in the valley were set at 23 pathis of grain (local unit of volume equivalent to approximately 4.5 litres) per ropani for the first grade of land after the Land Reform Act (Raj, 2010).

fertile valley floors), feudal landlord-tenant relations – a condition itself dependent upon local histories such as the in-migration of upper castes or the distribution of land grants.

Secondly, in locales in the central and eastern hills with more abundant land, where competition for land and resources with upper caste settlers was more limited and where there was still a forest frontier to be cleared, the Adivasi mode of production appeared partially intact with lower overall levels of differentiation. Thirdly, there was the western hills, which has a much longer history of sedentary cultivation and where it appears the ceiling of cultivation was reached long before the Panchayat era. This region followed quite a different trajectory. The mode of production by the Panchayat era was already dominated entirely by sedentary peasant production with high levels of differentiation, and landlordism. These three regions will be dealt with in turn below.

Areas of land scarcity and intensifying or persisting inequalities in the central and eastern hills

Growing land scarcity and internal differentiation within owner cultivating peasantry

By the start of the Panchayat era, large areas of the central and eastern hills were experiencing significant land scarcity – including the tracts of land which were once under the Adivasi mode of production, which had undergone a wave of subjugation in the 150 years after the Gorkhali conquest – as described above. Not only had shifting cultivation ended, the ability to clear new lands for fixed sedentary farming was becoming rapidly curtailed following over a century of in-migration and population growth. Already by the 1960s, there were growing challenges of land degradation and deforestation (Shrestha, 1967), and this went on to intensify throughout the 1970s and 80s (Strickland, 1984).

In many communities, there was growing food insecurity. For instance, a majority of Limbu in Caplan's (1970) study in Ilam could not meet their food needs from the land – with both clearing new fields, or accessing land markets virtually impossible due to the rising prices. Similarly, while Macfarlane's (1976) case study presented a village (Dhap, Kaski) which was still relatively abundant in resources at the dawn of the Panchayat era (as will be discussed in the next section), he notes that many other Gurung villages in the region had already become food deficit. He looks for instance at the village of Mohariya (where an earlier ethnography by Bernard Pignede had been conducted in the 1950s), noting that the expansion of cultivation had reached its limit. With land scarcity, there were a greater share of food deficit households seeking work on the fields of other households, resulting in reduced bargaining power in local labour markets. In this context, payments for farm work (in cash and kind), decreased in proportion to the real productive value of labour. The availability of surplus labour combined with labour saving technologies increased the scope for better off farmers to invest savings in land, and the rise in the price of land further curtailed the poorer segments of the peasantry from accessing the land market driving differentiation (Ibid.).

This transition from an agricultural economy based upon continued expansion of the cultivated area in line with population, to one based upon intensification of production, where ownership of land and assets were much more critical to one's economic security, was a process of transition Macfarlane suggests was widespread in the central hills during the 1960s. This change was also in its early stages in the core field site of Dhap in the duration of his fieldwork. These predictions were supported in a follow up study two decades later, which suggested that the share of households in Dhap who had sufficient rice[17] had declined from 63% in 1969 (as per Macfarlane's data) to 34% (Strickland, 1984) in 1980. Yields of paddy had meanwhile declined by 49.7%, a decline blamed upon land degradation and landslides, as terraced agriculture extended onto even the most marginal slopes.

A by-product of growing land scarcity was a significant decline in the agropastoral economy. Many Gurung villages in the central hills had gradually relocated to lower altitudes to find land which could be more intensively cultivated (e.g. through allowing multiple harvests) as they sought to offset rising population pressure (Messerschmidt, 1976). In this

---

[17] Based upon original calculations by Macfarlane that 15 muri or 750kg of unhusked paddy per year was sufficient for a family to survive.

context, not only shifting cultivation, but also pastoralism was becoming less feasible. Degradation of forest land had meanwhile led to a loss of the remaining lands under clan based customary tenure, which could be used for grazing (not to mention hunting and gathering of forest produce) (Macfarlane, 1976).

It is notable that the case studies covered in Macfarlane's study mainly involved villages where the population was entirely Gurung, with some migrants from other Adivasi groups. However, in areas where there were already notable unequal relations between Hindu castes and now sedentary Adivasi peasants, such as in much of the eastern hills, these processes were intensified – and differentiation within the (now largely sedentary) peasantry was more intense – most notably due to the growing economic gulf between the Adivasi peasantry on the one hand, and sedentary upper caste Nepali speaking settlers on the other.

This was notable in the Limbu villages covered in Caplan's (1970) study from Ilam – as discussed at length in the last section. He notes that the majority of upper castes had food security or were producing a surplus, while most Limbu were food deficit (Caplan, 1970). Following decades of *kipat* lands being converted into *raikar* and alienation at the hands of upper castes, there were many Limbu with no access to *raikar* or *kipat* land. For these families, Caplan (1970) notes that accessing new *raikar* land through the market was out of reach to the majority of Limbus – (particularly paddy lands). Aggravating the situation was rising monetisation which meant that many more households were in debt (Caplan, 1970). By the end of the Panchayat era, Russel (1992) notes with regards to the Rai further west, how many households were already trapped in an intergenerational cycle of unrepayable loans (Russel, 1992).

Debt often culminated in eventual dispossession of land (Caplan, 1970). Even the remaining lands under *kipat* tenure (prior to its abolition) were not spared. For instance, in Caplan's (1970) study from Ilam, upper castes who formed just 3% of the cluster controlled 14.2% of the *kipat* holdings due to these lands being taken on mortgage by the upper castes in return for cash. Half of these lands given on mortgage were subsequently given out to tenant sharecroppers – including *kipat* owners themselves (Ibid.). Whether this was 'feudal' in character is uncertain and depends on the levels of land concentration and wealth of the landowners, but it was emblematic of growing differentiation between a (predominantly upper caste) large peasant class and an increasingly land-poor Adivasi peasantry. In this context, even army income didn't raise their economic prospects. While some Limbu retiree soldiers used their savings to buy plots – the scarcity of land, its price, and competition with outsiders, meant this was not sufficient to stem internal differentiation[18].

Even in more prosperous yet land scarce villages in Ilam such as Pipalbote, studied by Dahal (1983), there was a clear ethnic disparity in the distribution of resources due in-part to the legacy of *kipat* land alienation. As of 1936 42.5% of irrigated land belonged to Limbu who traditionally held *kipat* land in the village, but by 1971 it was just 12%. Out of 93ha of irrigated *khet* lands, 64.86% was held by upper castes, who formed just half of the population. They also held 77.6% of the land used for bamboo and thatch. Similarly, while 35% of upper castes were grain deficit, this figure stood at a substantial 73% for Adivasi (including Limbu, Rai, Gurung, Sunwar and Magar) and Dalit households (Ibid.).

A similar picture emerges from Hitchcock's study of a Magar community in Syangja. He notes that unlike Magar in the higher hills (in particular the so called Kham Magar), in the lower valleys where land was more scarce and sought after, it was land rather than labour which gave households an economic advantage – and controlling rice land was a determinant of one's class power (cf. Mikesell, 2002). He describes with reference to the 1950s-60s, how the disappearance of forest land to clear, combined with a rising population, meant that more farms have been pushed below the level of productivity able to support a family. Set against this context, there was a clear unequal relation between Brahmins and Magar (Hitchcock, 1963). Like in the east, the latter had historically had a greater capacity to clear land due to better education and resources, building upon their position as tax collectors under the Rana regime (Hitchcock, 1974). Brahmins not only had a secure means of subsistence from the land, but access to government jobs also supported their ability

---

[18] This contrasts with Macfarlane's (1976) study where army employment actually moderated inequalities, at least in the early part of the Panchayat era.

to accumulate (Hitchcock, 1963). In this context, they were a source of credit, alongside a small number of Magar headmen. This further upheld Brahman economic power at a time of growing land scarcity, with more Magar households finding themselves experiencing grain deficits (aggravated by rising demand for cash), and seeking loans from better resourced farmers (Hitchcock, 1963). Many Magar in this context lost their land and were working as tenants or providing a labour force to a burgeoning landed class (Hitchcock, 1974). Again, whether these relations were 'feudal' in character is open to debate.

It is worth noting that the relationship between caste and land was not always clear cut. Former headmen often retained some power as a localised large farmer class, as shown in interviews by one of the authors in the Rai villages of the Chirkhuwa valley of Bhojpur (see Sugden et al 2018). Similarly, in Hitchcock's study, he notes how elite Magar such as former headmen were able to use their adoption of Brahmanical religious practices to increase their social, and ultimately economic, status (Hitchcock, 1963). This has to be viewed in the context of a long history of Sanskritization amongst southern Magar groups[19].

Localised feudalism

There were areas of localised landlord-tenant relations within these land scarce domains of the central and eastern hills which could be defined as feudal in character. In the east, the study by Sugden et al (2018) in Bhojpur shows that a large landlord class had consolidated its power on the best land on the fertile valley floor – which persists even in the present day. In this context, these estates emerged not only from the dissolution of the *kipat* system, but from the Rana era tax collection hierarchy and the propping up of upper caste tax collectors (Sugden et al., 2018) – although some may have been the legacy of land grants.

The areas where landed estates in the central and eastern hills were most prevalent (including landlord-tenant relations) were likely the areas

---

[19] This was bolstered by their position as paddy farmers rather than shifting cultivators, and the prestige of having been fighters for both Sen synasty and Gorkha armies (Hitchcock, 1965)

close to the Kathmandu valley, where there was a distribution of a large number of *birta* and *jagir* grants, as noted above (Mahat et al., 1986). These include for instance, the Melamchi valley (Pokharel, 2010). Such land inequality has a distinct legacy in the subjugation of the Tamang community, as discussed in the last chapter.

Areas of the central and eastern hills with abundant land and delayed subordination of Adivasi mode of production

As indicated in the last chapter, there were more remote locales where elements of the Adivasi mode of production remained relatively more intact at the middle of the 20th century and the trajectory of change in the Panchayat era was somewhat different in these domains. While customary tenure was declining in these peripheral regions, there was still relatively limited internal differentiation, and some persistence of shifting cultivation. These however, were generally restricted to areas at higher altitudes, which were above the rice growing zone and where there was still abundant forest cover and natural resources.

Several studies have shown how there was not only still land left to be cleared in these locales, off-setting rising population, there were also more limited competition for resources with Brahmin and Chettri settlers, as most land was above the ecological zone which was favoured by the Khas castes. This divergence is most notable in Hitchcock's comparison of two Magar settlements in the 1950s and 60s (c.f. Mikesell, 2002). A lowland Magar community studied in Syangja had undergone not only cultural Sanskritization, but a complete transition to sedentary cultivation. Individualised imperatives (rather than that of clan or lineage) were driving agricultural production decisions, and there was growing scarcity of land and inequalities between Magar and Brahmin/Chettris. By contrast, the higher altitude Kham Magar villages of Baglung were still heavily dependent upon transhumant agro-pastoralism and some shifting cultivation, while the clan still played an important role in social and economic life (Ibid.). In these upland villages farmers held customary land rights which could be mobilised for swidden farming or pastoralism, and it was labour rather than land which gave households an economic advantage (Hitchcock, 1974). As there was less Brahmin influence or settlement, the distribution of land was less closely connected with caste, and many of the state functionaries were themselves Magar (Ibid.).

Similarly, McDougal (1973, 1979) with reference to the Rai of the Hongu valley, notes how it was only in the lower altitude rice growing areas where there had been some alienation of former *kipat* land to other ethnic groups. In the upper altitude zones not only was there limited competition with settlers, even internally within the local Kulunge Rai, population pressure on the land was yet to be a significant issue, and differentiation was limited[20]. While *kipat* tenure for upland unirrigated fields in the Hongu valley was abolished in the 1940s, this had limited impact on how land was managed on a customary level. The primary change was that tax would now be paid according to the size of the landholding, rather than each house being equally taxed a fixed amount (McDougal, 1979). In some locales there was still land to be cleared – whereby one could do so on payment of a fee to the local clan headman, after which it would be registered as *raikar*, with tax paid through the headman.

With regards to the Gurung village of Dhap, from Macfarlane's (1976) study in Kaski of the central hills, a similar picture was evident from the 1960s, with labour rather than land giving households economic advantage. The village appeared to have entered the Panchayat era experiencing relative equality. While there had been a modest increase in inequality during the late Rana era with emerging private property rights for land, this had reversed by the 1960s, aided not only by land reforms and population growth, but also army recruitment[21] which had allowed poorer farmers to purchase land. There were now no households with

---

[20] This is particularly significant in the context of limited competition with upper castes. Notably there was no money lending class either and most lending was informally between families, in contrast to the Ilam case study from Caplan's study whereby debt to upper caste settlers was a primary driver of land alienation.

[21] Army employment which was available to everyone tended to equalise rather than intensify wealth differences, as it provided an alternative source of income for those with fewer assets and with abundant land, and plots could be purchased to ensure that households had food security.

more than 13 plots of land with the majority holding between 5-8 plots, with 81 out of 100 households owning rice land, compared to 64% in 1933. With markets for consumer goods being yet to emerge, surplus cash would often be used to increase one's social or ritual status through investment in community events, or it was invested in gold or other jewellery. For those who did accumulate savings through army recruitment or other sources, there was limited benefit of investing in land beyond what was needed for one's subsistence due to the shortage of labour. Given the high labour demand, wages were equivalent to what one would earn producing food on one's own land (Ibid.).

In spite of this, with cultivation reaching the limits of expansion, and with growing monetisation and debt, a process of change was already underway throughout the Panchayat era, as observed by Macfarlane during the course of his fieldwork, as well as scholarship from the late Panchayat era (e.g. Russel, 1992). This would see shifting cultivation becoming an increasingly rare form of agriculture, and with growing scarcity of land, and there would be rising differentiation within Adivasi society – a process of change which had already taken place across the hills. This likely accelerated in particular towards the end of the Panchayat era, when resettlement to the Tarai became more challenging, as observed by Russel (1992) in Sankhuswabha, due to the government placing restrictions on the clearing of new farms and spiralling prices of land in the plains.

It is worth mentioning that even though communal or customary tenure had officially been dissolved by the end of the Panchayat era, elements of these systems persisted informally in some locales, even if it was not recognized by state land policy. In this context, one often had legally recognised and customary tenure persisting in parallel (see Table 2).

For instance, McDougal (1979) suggested with regards to the Hongu valley, that *kipat* abolition had limited impact on customary clan-based land management in areas where competition with outsiders was limited. Former *kipat* territories were still used to determine the geographical boundaries within which different clans had the rights to exploit different resources, particularly for uncultivated lands used for grazing, collecting fodder or other forest products. This was particularly significant for the Kulunge Rai given that pastoralism was an important element of the agricultural system. As of the 1960s, some other ethnic groups like Sherpa were also permitted to cultivate land in the *kipat* area of a clan on payment of a fee to the headman of the respective clan.

Likewise, during fieldwork by one of the authors of this book in Panchthar for the UN-HABITAT (2018) report, it was found that several Limbus still recognised *kipat* rights, even after it was formally abolished in 1966. In the 1960s, the *kipat* land which was cultivable and productive was changed to *raikar* land, that is, from communal to private ownership. However, the land which was not cultivable at the time was not reclassified as *raikar* and was still considered *kipat* under the same old jurisdiction of *subbas*. Several documents archived in the land revenue offices in Panchthar illustrate that all those *kipat* lands converted into Raikar had the seal of Subbas (UN-HABITAT, 2018). Paradoxically, it could be argued that the recognition of the role of the clan or lineage chief itself in this transaction legitimised the persistence of the *kipat* type system after it was formally abolished.

The persistence of customary tenure was not necessarily restricted to the Limbu and Rai domains of the east. In many regions it persisted on an informal basis, even in areas where there had not been a history of legal recognition (see Table 2). As Gurung (1996) observed amongst the Magar of the Tara Khola valley, customary tenure existed up until the Panchayat era, even though it had never been legally sanctioned by the state as *kipat*. Hitchcock (1974), with reference to the Kham Magar of the central hills, notes that pastures continued to be controlled by lineages, with those from outside the lineage accessing it on lease.

In the central and eastern hills, amongst Himalayan agro-pastoralist communities, there was also the persistence of various forms of customary collective tenure by the end of the Panchayat era. While Bishop (1989) suggests that pastures amongst the Yolmo of Sindupalchok were already largely private with rights held only by certain lineages, communal tenure persisted elsewhere – such as amongst the Sherpa. March (1977) with reference to the Sherpa in the hills of Solu suggests that community members held collective usufruct rights on the high altitude pastures, with rights being held in the name of the village headman or *mur min* on behalf of the whole community. The headman would be responsible for collecting

Table 2: Customary versus state legal tenure

Customary Institutional Tenure	State's Legal Tenure
* Managed by society or lineages * Land allocated to different people by the community (both individual and cultural ownership), with access often determined by clan, with opportunity for non-clan members to access land on payment of tribute. * Ownership is created /made possible through cultural, ritual and social process. * Culturally embedded rather than legalised relationship with the land. * Transmitted from one generation to the next. * Often associated with itinerant livelihood activities e.g. transhumant agro-pastoralism or swidden cultivation.	* Land ultimately owned by the state. * Ownership bestowed to individuals rather than groups. * Associated with sedentary cultivation on fixed, permanent and clearly delineated fields. * Influenced by a development and modernization agenda under the leadership of the state.

tax and managing access to the pastures, which could extend to neighbouring ethnic groups such as Gurung sheep herders who offered some form of tribute in cash or gifts to the headman.

Customary tenure was also relevant for the limited areas of land which remained under shifting cultivation, even as this form of agriculture was in rapid retreat (UN-HABITAT, 2018). Most of the Chepangs practiced shifting cultivation, and heavily depended upon hunting and gathering for their livelihood during the Panchayat era. Land they cultivated may or may not have had private ownership, but land use was regulated by customary law: shared rules, norms, values and practices that regulate land use and cultivation. Land which was not arable and not good for grain production and that could not be taxed was not recognized as 'land', therefore, shifting cultivation plots remained unrecognized as land, after the Land Reform of 1964.

One relic of the older Adivasi mode of production which persisted until the end of the Panchayat era were various communal labour regimes. Across Nepal more broadly, the pooling of labour remained widespread, taking the form of the *parma* system of labour exchange (Figure 30), whereby households reciprocally worked on each-others land, with each household in the group providing a member a day's labour (Campbell,

Figure 30: Working on paddy fields in Bhojpur. While many more complex labour exchange regimes were on decline by the Panchayat era, parma a straightforward labour exchange remained widespread across the hills
Photo: Fraser Sugden

2018). Nevertheless, while this was widespread in Adivasi villages and had various local terms such as *nangba* amongst the Tamang (Campbell, 2018), it is not an 'Adivasi' system per se but is present amongst hill castes, with it being particularly widespread in the far-western hills (Joshi, 2023). However, parma was linked largely to neighbourhood and amongst farmers with adjacent land, unlike the more complex culturally embedded practices (Russel, 1992) such as *nogar*, described amongst the Gurung, which were community wide and were linked to age, lineage or other social group (Messerschmidt, 1981b), or the *horlenpata* (Russel, 1992) amongst the Yakha. The latter had largely died out by the Panchayat era.

Mode of production in the western hills

In the western hills, there is comparatively less literature, although given that any Adivasi mode of production amongst the Khas had been largely dissolved, the mode of production appeared to be dominated by independent peasant production – amongst a population for whom the majority had adopted an upper caste identity, albeit with a large subpopulation of Dalits. Studies from the far-western hills (Rana, 1971) and Karnali basin (Bishop, 1978) suggest that the limits of cultivation had already been reached in the Panchayat era, with yields suffering from soil exhaustion and land erosion. A large share of households were experiencing a deficit of food, particularly in the drier, more rugged higher elevation valleys (Bishop, 1978, Dahal et al., 1977). The population of Karnali basin for instance, was in a steady state throughout the Rana period, with sufficient land, yet land scarcity increased from the 1930s onwards with the continued expansion of farmland – including the steepest slopes. This increased environmental pressure and degradation (Bishop, 1978).

In terms of the agrarian relations on the ground, the ethnography in Jumla by Campbell (1978) pointed to a sedentary peasantry, with ownership of rice land being the primary signifier of wealth. The growing scarcity of land meant that even the steepest slopes of up to 40 degrees were under cultivation. The majority of households had around half an acre of *jyulaa* or paddy land, with poorer households, including the so called Matawali Chettri or Pawai, largely dependent on rainfed land, owning plots of paddy land as small as one-eighth of an acre (Ibid.). It is important to note that not all households experienced food insecurity, as differentiation within the peasantry was acute in the Karnali. Bishop (1978) suggests that even in food deficit regions, there was a surplus producing subset of households. Those who were in deficit would borrow grain in spring (when their own stocks had finished) and repay it in labour during the summer.

There was also widespread transhumant pastoralism on the vast communal alpine pastures or *patans* during the summer, which was particularly important in the upper Karnali districts (Bishop, 1978), and within these districts to the Pawai in particular, who kept large herds of sheep and goats (Campbell, 1978), and for whom relics of the older Adivasi mode of production persisted. Access to pastures however, did not appear to be associated with customary rights, as was the case amongst the Tibeto-Burmese speaking Adivasi groups of the eastern and central hills, but was more often based upon residence. Campbell (1978) suggests this was a feudal relic from the Baise Rajya period whereby rights to certain natural resources were awarded to individuals or villages in return for services offered.

Further west, Dahal's (1977) study on labour migration from the 1970s offers a picture of the mode of production in the lower valleys of the Mahakali basin. Agriculture appeared to have been again, largely oriented around owner cultivation, and while the region did not appear to experience the same level of environmental and resource stress as the upper Karnali districts, holdings were generally small. In the case study site, 63% of households owned paddy lands, yet holdings were between just 0.05 acre and 7.9 acres. There was notable differentiation in wealth. Like in the upper Karnali, higher altitude villages depended more on pastoralism, and there was less irrigated land. While communities used the different agro-ecological zones for their livestock in line with the changing seasons, large scale transhumance with relocation of herds and populations to summer pastures was not common amongst the largely caste Hindu population of the Mahakali basin, unlike the *Pawai* and culturally Tibetan communities in the Karnali, and a large share of seasonal movement of livestock was associated with trans-Himalayan trade. The exception was the Byanshi, a cross border Tibeto-Burmese community residing at higher altitudes in the Mahakali valley who were engaged in transhumance, relocating each winter to the area close to Darchula town, although the latter also gained a significant income from trade, like their counterparts elsewhere in the high Himalaya (Ibid.).

In terms of landlord-tenant relations in the western hills, the inequalities in land distribution meant that there were localised pockets of feudalism, like in the central and eastern hills. There was for instance a localised class of larger landlords in the Karnali, with Campbell (1978) pointing to the presence of landowners with between 5-20 acres of paddy lands. Dahal (1977) also points to the presence of *jimmawalas*, or former functionaries with larger areas of land in the case study from Darchula.

However, one of the primary axes of inequality which did not necessarily entail 'landlordism', were between the numerically and politically dominant Brahmin, Chettri and Thakuri owner cultivating peasants on the one hand, and occupational castes on the other. While *jajmani* practices associated with this relationship were present elsewhere in Nepal as noted above, they were in decline by the Panchayat era. The system however, appeared to have persisted for much longer in the west. The *lagi-lagitya* system in Jumla for instance, entailed the ritually sanctioned exchange of goods, services and labour for grain between largely landless or land poor occupational castes on the one hand, and a land owning upper caste peasantry on the other (Campbell, 1978). Services offered in exchange for grain included not only traditional caste-based activities such as tailoring, but also general agricultural labour such as harvesting and ploughing. The relationship often extended to sharecropping and taking grain on credit from the same landowners. A similar relationship existed between former slaves[22] – a separate subcaste known as Gharti – and the descendants of their old masters with the former often farming the land of the latter in return for a share of the harvest (Ibid.).

In Bajhang, the *riti-bhagya* system of inter-caste exchange persisted into the Panchayat period, although most Dalit families required land also to subsist in an economy which was seeing increased monetisation (Cameron, 1998b). Dalits generally took land via a form of mortgage known as *maatya*, whereby they would advance money to upper caste landlords, who would allow them to cultivate the land as long as the loan was outstanding. This was interestingly, tied closely with male seasonal migration to India, whereby wages sent home by men would be used by women at home to take out land via the *maatya* system[23]. Cameron's study also showed that it was challenging for Dalit tenants to access the land market, with most upper castes preferring to sell within their own community as it would enhance their political and social networks. Meanwhile, at a time when land titles had not been registered, Brahmin

---

[22] This follows the abolition of slavery in the 1920s.

[23] Interestingly, this was the inverse of the situation in the eastern hills whereby Limbu who had access to customary lands would mortgage it out to upper castes (Caplan, 1970) – yet both cases were imbued with unequal power relations. For the Limbu in the east it was due to a shortage of cash, whereas for the Dalit in the west it was due to constrained access to the land market.

and other upper caste families could use their higher level of education to travel to Kathmandu to register their holdings, supporting their accumulation of land (Cameron, 1998b).

These localised landlord-tenant relations linked to *riti-bhagya* and associated systems of inter-caste exchange and domination could be considered as a form of feudalism if big landlords were involved, although it is worth noting that the size of the landowning upper caste farmers in Cameron's (1998b) sample were extremely small (9 ropani on average versus just under 2 ropani for Dalits). This suggests that the localised upper caste monopoly of land and tenancy relations in this area of Bajhang, represent internal mechanisms of surplus appropriation and domination within the independent peasant mode of production. It may also be the case that population pressure in the higher hills of Bajhang, and subdivision of holdings meant that many of the large landowners of the Rana era were by the latter part of the 20th century simply medium to small peasants.

Convergence in the mode of production by the end of the Panchayat era

For much of the hills across Nepal, it is likely that by the 1980s, the Adivasi mode of production had been largely dissolved, with the exception of elements of customary tenure which persisted in some remoter domains. Lecomte-Tilouine (2017) suggest that by the 1980s to a large extent, sedentary terraced agricultural techniques were carried out by both Adivasi and caste Hindu populations, with cropping systems determined by altitudinal zone rather than ethnic group. Most of the peasantry were part of an independent peasant mode of production oriented around owner cultivation, with some pockets of feudal landlord-tenant relations – and only a few very remote areas still under transhumant agro-pastoralism or swidden farming.

It is important to note however, that while there was a convergence in modes of production within which Adivasi groups and the caste Hindu population were integrated across most of Nepal, there were notable differences with regards to their position within these economic formations

– particularly with regards to ownership of land. The hill Adivasi peasantry (which included the so called Matawali Chettri of the Karnali, as well as Magar, Gurung, Rai, Limbu and Tamang) had a greater involvement in pastoralism and had smaller plots (Lecomte-Tilouine, 2017), usually of rainfed *bari* land – due to the historic processes outlined above. However, for the same reasons the latter were also more likely to experience food insecurity and thus were more likely to be subordinated to localised landlord-tenant relations, as Sugden et al (2018) shows with regards to Bhojpur in the eastern hills. Therefore caste and ethnicity still played a key role in shaping the distribution of the means of production and axes of exploitation.

Growing dependence on wage labour

Local wage labour

A major change in the Panchayat period was the rising engagement in off farm labour – with growing articulations with capitalism. The rising scarcity of land which made it more challenging for households to meet their minimum food needs, combined with a rising demand for cash, had meant that by the 1960s, participation in wage labour was an increasingly important pillar of household livelihoods.

The emergence of new bazaars encouraged a building boom in the 1960s which required labour for construction and portage of building materials (Caplan, 1970). The latter in particular was important as only a small number of district centres were reachable by road. Portering was thus not only a means through which to support the expansion of capitalist markets via a network of hill towns, but provided an important source of income which could cover rising cash demands.

For instance in the Arun valley, portering was one of the main sources of non-farm income throughout the Panchayat era and up until the early 2000s (Sugden et al 2018) (see Figure 31). This firstly entailed the transportation of goods from the plains to the emerging market towns such as Dhankuta, Khadbari, Chainpur, Basantapur and Tumlingtar. As roads penetrated the hills and began to link up bazaars, first to Dhankuta and later to Basantapur in the 1980s, portering became oriented to

Figure 31: Porters in Hile of Dhankuta in 2000, prepare for the multi-day journey up the Arun valley. The porterage economy remained important until the mid-2000s after which it was replaced by mule trains, and finally by roads.
Photo: Fraser Sugden

transporting goods from the roadheads to more remote towns or secondary markets. In a study at the end of the Panchayat era in a Yakha village of Sankuswabha, portering of goods to the roadhead in Basantapur had emerged as an important source of cash, with wages being determined by weight and distance, rather than the number of days – rates which were generally lucrative compared to farm labour (Russel, 1992). This helped to compensate for the growing production shortfalls in agriculture as land became scarce (Russel, 1992), but also offered income through which the consumables brought in from the lowlands could be bought – perpetuating the cycle of monetisation. Porterage was particularly important to the smallest landowners who could not meet their subsistence needs from the land. For instance Upadhyay's study (1990) on porters in Sindhuli and Ramechhap suggested that all the porters were from food deficit households. Over half the porters in the Sindhuli sample owned less than 0.25ha of land, and while porters in Ramechhap had larger holdings (0.75ha on average) it was of marginal rainfed *bari* land, with crops limited to maize, millet and buckwheat. Porterage was a critical source of cash income to compensate for shortages of food, particularly between March and August (Ibid.)

Migrant labour

It was migrant labour which was to increase most notably during the Panchayat era. In the central and eastern hills, it came in two forms. The first was itinerant movement to India or urban centres. In Russel's (1992) study in Sankuswabha from the 1980s, up to a quarter of the men were absent during the winter. This mostly entailed seasonal work in India. Caplan (1970) also noted that many Limbu from Ilam would migrate seasonally to Darjeeling during the dry season.

The most notable form of migrant work however in the Panchayat era in the central and eastern hills was army recruitment. This was most prevalent amongst the Magar and Gurung of the central hills – for both the British and Indian armies. In the case study village of Kaski in Macfarlane's (1976) study, 11.5% of adult males were serving in the army in the mid-1960s. While this had a long history in this community, elsewhere the rise was more recent. For instance, Hitchcock, writing in the early 1960s in Syangja, noted a tripling of the number of soldiers and pensioners (Hitchcock, 1963) (although the time period within which this happened was not clarified), alongside lower levels of wage labour migration to India. In the eastern hills, army recruitment increased in the Panchayat era, but the numbers were lower than in the west (Russel, 1992). It did however allow some farmers to repossess lands which they had given out on mortgage. However, it was restricted by annual quotas and needed to meet certain criteria (Ibid.). In McDougal's (1979) study of the Hongu valley, army recruitment was very low – and in one of the villages just 3 out of 171 households had ex-servicemen[24]. By the late 1980s, army recruitment in the East and across Nepal had dropped substantially to just a few hundred per year (Russel, 1992), with Indian

---

[24] He suggests this is down to geographical isolation as well as the limited competition for land from outsiders, which has given agricultural livelihoods a greater viability.

Gurkha regiments taking on a larger share of recruits than the British army.

In the western hills, army recruitment was rare, yet other articulations with capitalism via migrant labour were much more entrenched. Unlike in the east, the levels of urban development were more limited, and local off farm employment opportunities were scant. At the same time, the limits to cultivation had likely reached their ceiling earlier than in the more fertile centre and east of the country. Therefore there was a well-established pattern of seasonal migration of men to India throughout the Panchayat era (Campbell, 1978, Dahal et al., 1977). In a case study from the far west, seasonal migration, mostly to the Kumaon region in what was to become Uttarakhand, was particularly common in the slack season, especially at higher altitudes where the land was rainfed and unsuitable for wheat cultivation (Dahal et al., 1977). Around a half of active male workers were seasonal migrants (usually for between 2 and 5 months) in the upper altitude case study, where there was no cropping due to snowfall. Work generally involved short term labour (e.g. on government construction projects). The remaining half of the men were engaged in trade and cottage industries such as spinning wool. There was lower migration on the whole in more fertile rice growing lower valleys with greater food security. Just a tenth of active males migrated seasonally in this lower case study site.

There was also substantial long-term labour migration by men, with families remaining at home and receiving remittances. This often involved work such as private security guards, low level civil service jobs, and also army employment albeit for the Indian or Nepalese rather than British army (Dahal et al., 1977). These workers would regularly bring back cash, clothes and other commodities – and would return permanently to the village on retirement. Longer term migration appeared more common amongst wealthier households, given that there were costs associated with securing such work – and the work was often much further afield, including more distant states of India (Ibid.).

Both forms of migration represent a classic 'articulation of modes of production', which would become more common in the 2000s. Under this structural phenomena, employers would benefit from cheaper wages from migrants. This was because they retained a link to the land. The wage would only cover the immediate costs of the worker, and not the longer-term costs of labour reproduction, which includes costs of retirement, bringing up the younger generation, and times spent at home due to illness or while on leave (Meillasoux 1980). This latter component would be covered by agriculture in the migrants' home.

However, as the capitalist sector in India (particularly in Kumaon) was itself in its infancy, a significant share of the labour appeared to be for government projects rather than for capitalism in the traditional sense. Regardless, labour migration in the far west appears to have stimulated the demand for commodities, perhaps accelerating the process which was already underway in the central and eastern hills. Dahal (1977) notes that there was limited demand for commodities such as soap, shoes, kerosene or spices before 1962, yet migration had driven changes in consumption patterns and vice versa.

Cropping systems: 1951-1991

Primary crops during the Panchayat era

By the 1950s, almost all the crops that have a major share in the food stock of Nepali people today had already been introduced. They included rice, corn, wheat, pulses, millet, potatoes, root crops, and oilseed, and less commonly, amaranth, which would be intercropped with maize. Widespread vegetable production was mainly limited to the Kathmandu valley (Kihara, 1956).

Rice by far remained the major food crop, and maintained its economic, social, and cultural/ritual significance, being grown in almost all regions and ecological zones of Nepal. It was grown on more than half the cultivated land, including large areas of the Tarai-Madhesh in the south and the Kathmandu Valley during the monsoon season and by 1988 approximately 3.9 million hectares of land in Nepal were under paddy cultivation (Joshi, 2017).

In the hills however, where rice cultivation was constrained by agro-climatic factors, a division between two distinct agricultural systems persisted – that between the low lying irrigated agriculture of the fertile valley floors on the one hand and upland rainfed agriculture of the upper slopes on the other. In the central and eastern hills, this aligns roughly with the older disjuncture between Adivasi and caste Hindu society. The lower valleys floors were predominantly oriented towards paddy production on fixed fields irrigated by streams and canals – and these *khet* lands were still disproportionately cultivated by Nepali speaking Hindu castes as shown in multiple studies in the central (Gurung, 1996), and eastern hills (Caplan, 1970; Gaenzle, 2000). Wheat, mustard and potato would be planted in the winter as noted in Dahal's (1983) case study from Ilam – although wheat was only introduced in the 1960s (probably due to improved irrigation). Potatoes were also introduced relatively late in the 1960s, having been previously bartered for grain from higher altitude producers (a phenomena also noted in Gaenzle, 2000 in the Arun valley) – although production moved to lower altitudes as food scarcity meant there was insufficient grain to barter (Dahal, 1983a).

On higher slopes and valley sides (where there are a greater share of Adivasi cultivators), even with the end to shifting cultivation, there was some continuity in the cropping systems on the now permanent, yet unirrigated *bari* fields on which the Adivasi of the hills disproportionately depended on. Crops included maize, millet, buckwheat, barley and potatoes (Fricke, 1984, McDougal, 1979) (Figure 32). On valley slopes below 1500m with access to irrigation however, Adivasi communities have made a gradual shift towards paddy cultivation – replicated the agricultural practices of the Hindu castes, as shown in multiple ethnographies, even if most of the farmland is rainfed (Macfarlane, 1976, Caplan, 1976). This has often involved conversion (through construction of irrigation channels) of dry *bari* land to irrigated *khet* land as farmers seek to keep up with population pressure. For instance, in Barbote of Ilam, the total irrigated land area was estimated to have increased from 68ha in 1912 to 493 in 1971 (Dahal, 1983a). For some groups such as the Gurung, this shift towards paddy cultivation had gone alongside a gradual movement south to lower elevations between the Rana and early Panchayat era, whereby pastoralism had reduced in importance, yet households were increasingly clearing valley land for paddy cultivation (Messerschmidt, 1981a).

In western Nepal given the generally drier climate and longer history of irrigation, farmers were more dependent in general on a rice-wheat cropping system. There were however, still large areas which had always been under rainfed cultivation, although the use of these lands didn't align to the same degree with caste – with the exception of the Pawai domains of the Karnali. Major crops on the higher rainfed fields included also millet, maize and barley, like further east (Rana, 1971) and a wide range of legumes. World Food Programme supported rice distribution was blamed for pushing farmers towards a rice consumption culture and neglecting the production of traditional coarse grains and legumes – creating a form of artificial food scarcity (Adhikari, 2008) – a narrative which has not been without critique (see for instance Gautam, 2019).

This division between rainfed and non-rainfed agricultural systems in all areas of the hills was increasingly complicated by the introduction of a range of cash crops which could be grown in a diversity of agro-ecological niches, from the most marginal high altitude *bari* fields to the irrigated valley floors. In high altitude rainfed, yet high rainfall domains of the east, cardamom emerged as an important crop and brought otherwise marginal forest land under cultivation (Dahal, 1983a). While it was present several decades earlier, production only took off in the 1970s, driven in particular by rising monetization and demand for cash (Ibid.). Russel (1992), with regards to Sankhuwasabha however, suggests that production was suitable primarily for richer households who could afford the risk of cultivating a non-subsistence crop, given the risks of market failure. Other high altitude crops included medicinal herbs such as chiraito (Sugden et al 2018), a herb with a long history of cultivation which was of ritual importance for Kirat communities (English, 1983). Lower down, tea cultivation was established around Ilam (Dahal, 1983a), while traditional crops such as rudraksha expanded considerably in the Arun valley (Sugden et al 2018). Rudraksha beads, produced from the seed of the tree Elaeocarpus ganitrus, were particularly important for the Indian, and later the Chinese, religious market.

Figure 32: Tamang women separating grains of finger millet from chaff in Manegaun, Dhading. Millet remained a staple crop on un-irrigable bari fields even after the end of shifting cultivation
Photo: Kathryn March and David Holmberg (reproduced with permission)

There was also a growing market for vegetables and fruits, with niche products in the hills including crops such as tangerines (Dahal, 1983a). While production of fruit and vegetables have a long history, the expansion of towns would have increased opportunities for the marketing of produce. In the western hills however, cash crop production was relatively low with very limited market infrastructure at a village level, and a study from Doti and Dandeldhura found that only mustard was of significance as a commercial crop (Rana, 1971). In the plains, cash crops were limited primarily to jute, tea, tobacco and cotton during the Panchayat era (Seddon, 1987). While most crops were for the domestic markets, a few cash crops such as tea and cardamom, and some pulses, were being exported (Chataut, 2017).

Productivity and yields trends

In sum, the Panchayat era saw rising net output as the cultivable area expanded and irrigation coverage increased, although the process was slow and uneven. The Third plan from 1966-70 aimed to increase food grain production by 15% and cash crops by 73%). Cash crop production increased only marginally – with production of tobacco declining and jute remaining stagnant. Only sugarcane saw a notable increase (Seddon, 1987). Foodgrain production did increase, but by only 7% between 1964/5 and 1971/2, and maize output actually dropped by 11%. Much of the increase was due to a 77% rise in wheat output, although overall production was still very small compared to paddy[25] (Ibid). In terms of yields, these were initially stagnant during the 1960s. While paddy production increased by 7% the actual yields dropped from 2010kg per ha in 1961/2 to 1962kg per ha in 1967/8, with millet dropping from 1312 kg per ha to 1200 kg per ha.

There was nevertheless, rising crop output in later decades of the Panchayat era, particularly in paddy. By 1989 the total production of rice increased to more than 3 million tons[26], up from a little more than 1 million tons in 1966. One can surmise that a large part of the raised grain output was due to the expansion of cultivation alongside the resettlement programme in the Tarai-Madhesh. Added to this was the improvement in irrigation, which contributed to a rising cropping intensity with multiple harvests (Joshi, 2017). For instance, the expansion of irrigation in Chitwan meant that two rice harvests were possible amongst the local Tharu (a pre-monsoon crop as well as a monsoon crop), after which mustard could follow as the winter crop, intercropped with wheat (Müller-Böker, 1999).

The pace of change was of course, uneven. In parts of the Tarai-Madhesh beyond the command of irrigation schemes (including large tracts of the west), cropping intensity remained low between the 1960s and 1980s. In the Dang valley it was reported that many Tharu would 'direct seed' paddy rather than transplant it (McDougal, 1968), practices which would continue in Dang up until the 1980s (McDonaugh, 2012). Nevertheless, even the remoter regions soon transitioned to more intensive cropping systems – particularly as land became scarcer. For instance, by

---

[25] For instance, Seddon (1987) notes that wheat production was just 223,305 metric tons, compared to 2353,871 for paddy.

[26] https://factsanddetails.com/south-asia/Nepal/Economics_and_Agriculture_Nepal/, accessed on 15 December, 2022.

the early 1990s in Dang, most Tharu had shifted to a more intensive methods, which entailed transplantation as well as the use of high yielding seeds and fertiliser – allowing a 3 to 6 fold increase in yields (McDonaugh, 2012).

In the hills, there were also localised increases in output due to the expansion of the cultivable area and improved irrigation. In Ilam for instance, there was a notable rise in paddy output from 73,135 tons in 1967-68 to 77,335 tons in 1970-71, while maize production rose from 123,500 to 130,400 tons. Millet and barley both rose slowly from 30,100 to 31,400 tons, and from 2,825 to 3,176 tons respectively (Caplan, 1970). This was likely to have been due to firstly, improvements in terracing and irrigation, with a 233.7% increase in the irrigated area in Ilam district between 1936 and 1971 (Dahal, 1983a). It is worth noting though that Dahal (1983a) shows that expansion of irrigation, was in part a by-product of the alienation of *kipat* land by Brahmin and Chettri farmers[27], who converted it into the *raikar* lands used for paddy production. Alongside this was a continued expansion of the cultivable area, and out of 313.2ha of cultivable land as of 1981 in one of the case study villages, 108ha had been added in the last 30-35 years (Ibid.).

With regards to fertiliser use, the impact on output is questionable given the tendency for high initial productivity to tail off with overuse. Even in spite of this, chemical input use remained low throughout the Panchayat era. As of the early 1960s, only 10,706 acres (4333ha) of land was estimated to have used fertilisers (Shrestha, 1967). While the rate of fertiliser consumption increased from 0.4kg NPK Nutrient Units per ha in 1962-3 to 3.8 in 1971, its use remained far lower than elsewhere in South Asia (Seddon, 1987). For instance, in the same period in India, the increase had been from 4.7 to 16.5. Most was used in the Kathmandu valley (Ibid.). Studies from the era also suggested that farmers still favoured organic manure due to perceived losses in fertility brought about by fertilisers – although insufficient livestock was also a challenge (Russel, 1992).

---

[27] i.e. As paddy cultivation was central to Brahmin and Chettri livelihoods, it was inevitable that newly acquired former kipat land would immediately be converted to irrigated khet (Dahal, 1983a).

With regards to improved varieties of seeds there was some change. For example, the Taichung variety brought from Nepal was introduced in 1966, yielding potentially 6.6 to 7.9 tonnes per hectare, far higher than local varieties (Paudel, 2017). Like many high yielding varieties, new varieties such as Taichung responded particularly effectively to artificial fertilisers (Webster, 1983), which in the long term would result in rising costs of production. Taichung reportedly made up half the rice crop in Manamaiju just north of Kathmandu in 1978, and was up to 80% of the crop in other settlements (Webster, 1983). For tenants on fixed rent contracts, high yielding crops offered (at least temporally) a greater share for the cultivators (Ibid.). Further afield, a study from the 1970s from Kavrepalanchok, found that most farmers were using improved seed varieties (Bennet, 1981). In Pipalbote of Ilam, improved wheat seeds L-52 were introduced in 1974 and achieved rapid uptake (Dahal, 1983a). One would expect however, that more remote locales made this transition much later, as will be described in the next chapter on the post-1990s context.

Following Taichung there was a wave of imported varieties, most notable of which was Sabitri and Masuli, which were to emerge into one of the most popular forms of rice in Nepal, particularly in the Tarai. New varieties of maize and wheat also followed, and these were disseminated through government extension schemes (Paudel, 2017). Even in remote areas such as Jumla, improved varieties of wheat (Lerma 52) and maize were introduced in 1968 which offered much higher yields than the local varieties (Shrestha, 1993).

In spite of the increased use of improved varieties, it did not appear to have a major impact on per hectare productivity – and thus yield increases are likely less significant than rising cropping area and cropping intensity, in contributing to increased grain output. By 1979/81 paddy yields were 1850kg/ha, and were 1990kg/ha by 1988 (Yadav and Peterson, 1993), only a marginal change from 1962kg in 1967/8. This may be due to the uneven spread of improved varieties, but also because improving yields on some lands were offset by environmental pressures elsewhere. In the Tarai-Madhesh for instance, food grain yields dropped from 1755 per ha in 1974/5 to 1580 per ha in 1977/8. While newly cleared estates of the Tarai saw high initial natural fertility, Seddon (1987) suggests that this had gradually declined by the 1980s. In communities further from the forest fringe, dependence on dung for fuel due to an absence of firewood also had impacts on productivity as it pushed farmers into over-dependence on chemical fertilisers (Seddon, 1987), which would have a detrimental impact on yields in the years ahead (Makaju and Kurunju, 2021).

Declines in yields also took place in the hills, as cultivation expanded onto more marginal land (Seddon, 1987). This was increasing the proportion of lower quality land under cultivation and reducing the overall average yields in national data, while the absorption of all land under cultivation reduced the likelihood that land could be left fallow to recover periodically (as for instance under shifting cultivation). Meanwhile with the cultivation of increasingly steep slopes, land degradation and erosion increased in the hills.

There were early in-roads for mechanisation in agriculture during the Panchayat era, although this was disproportionately a phenomena of the Tarai-Madhesh. The private sector initially played a key role with the growing sale of Indian made two wheel and four wheel tractors for ploughing (Gauchan and Shrestha, 2017). In the hills the rate of change was much slower. A notable change was the transition from hoe to plough agriculture in Adivasi domains such as that of the Gurung, alongside their transition away from shifting cultivation (Macfarlane, 1973). Mechanization in the hills was to come later, although two wheel tractors were introduced to the Kathmandu and Pokhara valleys in the 1970s from South Korea and Japan (Justice et al 2023).

Chapter 5

Liberalisation, agrarian stress and capitalist integration: The 1990s to the present

The 1990s were a period of major political flux. In 1991, the Panchayat era authoritarian government was overthrown and a multi-party system and constitutional monarchy was established. However, any 'peasant' agenda in the pro-democracy movement was limited, and the rapid disillusionment with the new political status quo in Nepal's rural periphery culminated in the Maoist insurrection which would last a decade, paving the way for the eventual abolition of the monarchy.

In spite of these major political events, of perhaps greater significance with regards to the agrarian context was Nepal's economic liberalisation. While Nepal signed its first structural adjustment package in 1985, it set the groundwork for the economic changes which would take place throughout the next three decades – whereby the most isolated communities would be finally integrated into capitalist markets, and articulations of modes of production via wage labour and migration would become a cornerstone of an agrarian system under increased economic and ecological stress.

This chapter reviews the tumultuous political and economic events of the 1990s – 2020s, while exploring what this means for both the contemporary agricultural development trajectory, and most importantly the mode(s) of production on the ground and the increasingly complex matrix of inequalities one observes today.

People's War

There had been a long history of Maoism in Nepal, stretching back to the Jhapa revolt in the 1960s. It was inspired largely by the anti-feudal struggle against landlords over the border in Naxalbari of West Bengal around the same time (Pokhrel, 2018) – and its emergence in the Eastern Tarai is unsurprising given the legacy of feudalism in these districts. Various party splits within the underground communist movement throughout the remainder of the Panchayat era and into the period of early parliamentary democracy, paved the way for the emergence of the Communist Party of Nepal (Maoist), who launched their armed insurgency in 1996.

Interestingly however, the movement originated not in the feudal heartlands of the plains, but in Rolpa in the Kham Magar heartlands of the central hills[1]. The reasons for this are complex and beyond the scope of this book (see Tilzey and Sugden, 2023, for some analysis of this conundrum). Paudel (2019) suggested that a reason the struggle originated in Rolpa, and Thabang village in particular, was due to its long history of locally embedded struggles against the state, which dated back to the 1950s. Maoism thus later became an 'ideological thread' which brought together various acts of resistance against the state at a local level. The idea that this region had an inherent revolutionary consciousness has been critiqued (Zharkevich, 2015) in light of the more complex socio-political reasons for joining the rebellion including cultural obligation to kin and political elites (albeit those with communist leanings). Regardless, it is clear that the struggle was driven in part by a range of proximate material causes rooted in the agrarian economy. These include for instance, the ban on hemp production and the financial pressures associated with agricultural commercialisation as well as historic struggles against taxation, landlords and bureaucratic elites (Paudel, 2019). It is important also to consider the ethnic element to the struggle. While identity and cultural marginalisation of the Kham Magar has been invoked to contextualise the struggle (De Sales, 2003, Ismail and Shah, 2015), the historical

---

[1] While the Rolpa region has historically been considered administratively as part of the western hills, in this book we consider it part of the central hills as per the criteria we outline in the introduction.

subordination of the Adivasi mode of production must also be considered (Lecomte-Tilouine, 2004)[2] – although this is the topic of another book.

At a national level, the war had been quite clearly articulated in the context of Nepal being a semi-colonial, semi-feudal social formation with stagnant industry, and a bureaucracy serving the interests of a comprador bourgeoisie and landlords (Bhattarai, 2003a, Bhattarai, 2003b). The insurrection ended in 2006 following the Comprehensive Peace Accord. Regardless as to the causes of the war and its rationale, other than the abolition of the monarchy and establishment of a federal system – it is questionable whether it led to a concrete and lasting impact on the mode of production on the ground. It did however achieve a decline in landlordism in some pockets due to 'panic selling' of estates by landlords (a theme discussed below), and importantly, contributed to a wave of politicisation amongst marginalised groups. For instance, it catalysed the breakdown of patron-client bonds and challenged concepts of untouchability (Sharma, 2021).

Agricultural development policy

The economic stresses which attracted support for the People's War were arguably intensified by Nepal's neoliberal economic reforms. The first structural adjustment package liberalized industry, exchange and interest rates and trade, while seeking to promote privatisation, export oriented growth and private investment (Uprety, 2021). A second package was implemented in 1989/90, and neo-liberalism continued to shape state development strategy after the restoration of democracy in 1991, including the subsequent development plans and agricultural policy.

In the spirit of neo-liberal thinking, agricultural policy after the 1990s was oriented heavily towards driving the peasantry into so called 'petty commodity production' whereby livelihoods would be grounded in the

---

[2] Maoist leader Lok Bahadur Thapa Magar for instance has in his book discussed many of the same processes of subjugation outlined in this text including a historic agrarian formation dominated by swidden farming and pastoralism, and the migration of upper castes, followed by Sanskritization, seizure of the best lands and the creation of a Magar elite (Cf. Lecomte-Tilouine, 2004).

sale of commodities and purchase of food – with the anticipation that some would emerge into proto-capitalist commercial farmers (see discussion in Uprety, 2021). As a result, strengthening subsistence production and food security at the farm level, received more limited policy interest. A central agricultural strategy of the post-liberalisation context which was emblematic of this shift was the Agriculture Perspective Plan (APP), launched in 1996. The Nepalese government along with its international donors considered this plan as a 20 year strategy for rapid agricultural growth and prosperity (Government of Nepal, 1995).

Agricultural development was particularly dependent upon aid, and the ratio of foreign aid to government development budget for 'agriculture and land reform' was 1.8 as of 1996-6, and for irrigation it was 0.5 (Dangi et al., 2021). Within this context, foreign donors played an important role in shaping the development agenda – and particularly, in mainstreaming the neoliberal principles of entrepreneurship and poverty alleviation through market integration (see Sugden, 2009c). The APP itself was drafted with the support of John Mellor Associates, a consultancy firm led by the economist John Mellor, who sought to model Nepal's agrarian transformation on the success of Punjab and Himachal Pradesh, which according to his study (Mellor, 1976) took advantage of each regions 'comparative advantage' for commercial agriculture to unleeash market led growth (see Cameron, 1998a for a critical debate on the plan). Growth was believed to be possible with a combination of liberal markets and government infrastructural investment (Cameron et al., 2016).

Within this context, the APP aimed to encourage smallholders to shift from subsistence production to the production of high value, market orientated agricultural produce focusing on the niche product which has comparative advantage in the agro-ecological zone in which they reside (Government of Nepal, 1995). The strategy for promoting this form of smallholder commercialisation was focussed on the provision of priority inputs, which included improved transportation infrastructure, alongside technological inputs – including irrigation and extension services to encourage new technologies and commodities (Government of Nepal, 1995, Mellor, 1976).

The APP ended not long after the promulgation of the new constitution in 2015. While some of the APP targets were close to being met such as those associated with transport infrastructure – the transformation in agriculture which it had envisaged remained elusive (Cameron et al., 2016, Uprety, 2021). Economic liberalisation itself had for many farmers undermined the goals of the APP. After Nepal's Structural Adjustment, many of the tariffs and restrictions on imports of agricultural products, which could have supported commercialisation were removed. In the early 2000s, agricultural tariffs in Nepal were actually the lowest in South Asia, with no tariffs at all on grain staples (Pyakuryal et al., 2010). This put farmers at a notable disadvantage when compared to their counterparts over the border in India, where the stronger developmental state in the latter had retained a greater level of support for farmers, even post liberalisation (Sugden, 2009c). Added to this was a substantial drop in public spending in agriculture, from 30% in the 1970s to just 4.87% by 2017/18 (Joshi and Khanal, 2020). The Morang region for instance, saw cutbacks in agricultural extension, with the number of service centres cut by half (Sugden, 2009c).

At the time of writing this book, the fifteenth five-year plan 2019/20-2023/24 period was in operation, with a major focus on agriculture, irrigation, and land management. A strong emphasis was placed on food security, as shown by the quote (Government of Nepal, 2020, 171):

> "by the end of the planning period, the number of households with basic food security will have increased from the current 48 percent to 80 percent. During the planning period, food poverty will decrease to 10 percent, and the current severe food insecurity (according to the food insecurity experience scale) will have declined from 7.8 percent to 2 percent of the population. Similarly, the global food security index will have increased from 46 to 66. The population deprived of the daily minimum calorie intake will have come down from 8.9 percent to 4 percent".

In synergy with the fifteenth plan, the government promulgated the Agricultural Development Strategy (ADS) 2015-2035 to replace the Agricultural Perspective Plan (Ministry of Agricultural Development,

2015). The strategy was in the same market oriented paradigm as the APP, and the main focus was on the commercialization, mechanization, and diversification of agricultural and livestock products to make the sector competitive, while also creating additional employment through the industrialization of the sector. Uprety (2021) suggests that in spite of populist language by the government which emphasises self-sufficiency and protection for domestic producers, the ADS is an extension of the APP's largely neoliberal goals to integrate Nepali producers into global commodity markets. Parallel initiatives including the Prime Minister's Agricultural Modernisation Project divided the country into pockets, blocks, zones and super-zones, with each oriented to a niche product suited to the local agro-ecology, including subsistence, but notably a range of commercial products (Ibid.). In 2021, there was also a directive by the government to open up the agricultural sector for foreign investment (Uprety, 2021). While Nepal has thus far bypassed many of the controversies around global corporate agri-business, including land grabs (McMichael, 2012), this directive signals that change is on the horizon.

The fifteenth plan has rightly pointed out that sustainable irrigation facilities with year-round services are necessary for arable lands to increase agricultural productivity. The ceiling of cultivation had reached its limit in the Panchayat period (and in the western hills, even earlier), and irrigation is one of the only means through which farmers can increase output — either by increasing yields of otherwise rainfed crops, or by allowing additional land to be put to use in the dry season. Irrigation is also increasingly important in the context of climate change which makes even monsoon cultivation risky (see below discussion). As it stands, many existing irrigation systems are poorly maintained, and irrigable and non-irrigable lands are fragmented into different plots (Department of Water Resources and Irrigation, 2019). The 2019 Irrigation Master Plan aims to place an additional 300,000 hectares of land under irrigation through a combination of surface water, groundwater, and inter-watershed transfer projects. It anticipated that year-round irrigation would be available in 50% of the areas where infrastructure had been developed. The strategy has also aimed to rehabilitate and implement sustainable management for

98,500ha of land irrigated under existing schemes (Department of Water Resources and Irrigation, 2019).

But the success of these recent ambitious plans and strategies has already come into question. The average agricultural growth has improved marginally after the implementation of the ADS, but it is still low compared to neighbouring countries (Khanal et al., 2020). When the APP was developed, there was a lack of legislative provisions and institutional arrangements to support effective implementation. This was rectified for the ADS, yet they did not take into account of the new federal structure which was rolled out after 2015, and thus many acts now need to be amended (Khanal et al., 2020).

The constraints which underlined the poor performance of previous plans have not changed. For example, all periodic plans so far highlighted the poor availability of resources and materials which are indispensable for increasing agricultural productivity, not to mention inadequate physical infrastructures such as irrigation, roads, agricultural markets, and the rapid fragmentation of land. Against such a backdrop, the goal set by the 15th five-year plan: "to achieve inclusive and sustainable economic growth through the transformation of the agriculture sector into a competitive, climate-resilient, self-reliant, and export-oriented industry" (Government of Nepal, 2020), appears to be over ambitious. According to one of the government officials interviewed, the goal of the plan, 'to provide sustainable and reliable irrigation facilities for arable lands', was also unattainable. While a range of subsidies have been made available to provide the inputs necessary for these plans, as noted above with regards to irrigation, the reach of many of these programs are poor, and it is often larger landowning farmers who disproportionately benefit due to the complex paperwork required, and favorable social networks within the bureaucracy (Uprety, 2021), as will be shown later in this chapter with regards to groundwater irrigation schemes.

There are also deeper challenges with Nepal's overall agricultural growth strategies, which were identified in much earlier critiques of the Agricultural Perspective Plan (Cameron, 1998a). The APP for instance was driven by the neoliberal assumption that the peasantry is made up of small, independent land owning farmers, whom, with access to markets and infrastructure, could unleash their entrepreneurial potential and accumulate wealth (Sugden, 2009b). This overlooks the deeply entrenched forms of exploitation and the vast inequalities in the distribution of land and assets.

A similar critique can be levelled at the ADS. Roka (2017), in his analysis of Nepal's Agricultural Development Strategy emphasises that it ignores the structural causes of poverty rooted in the unequal distribution of land. Many of the commercial crops it advocates depend on holdings which only the richest farmers possess. The ADS also cites East Asian agricultural growth models which can be replicated in Nepal, such as Japan, However, paradoxically, the success of these models were in fact rooted in the egalitarian distribution of holdings following redistributive land reforms in the second half of the 20th century (Roka, 2017) – something which Nepal has not yet come close to achieving. The strategy also fails to account for persisting challenges in accessing credit, and the fact that many farmers still depend on moneylenders (Roka, 2017). Another reason that agricultural strategy is failing is that while it makes frequent reference to climate change, it doesn't acknowledge that many climate resilient technologies are out of reach to marginal producers (Sugden et al., 2014a). Climate is part of a new wave of agrarian stress which has continued to undermine fragile agrarian livelihoods. These persisting challenges are outlined below.

Agrarian stress
Rural monetisation and rising demand for cash

The ecological crisis in agriculture predicted in studies such as Seddon (1987) and Macfarlane (1976) due to population pressure, the expansion of the cultivable area onto the more marginal land, was fortunately averted (see Sharma, 2021, on this narrative). This is due to multifaceted processes, including permanent out-migration from the hills to the Tarai-Madhesh (Blaikie et al., 2001) and temporary migration to India and more recently overseas – both of which has reduced pressure on natural resources. Similarly, institutional innovations such as Community Forestry (Kanel and Kandel, 2004), and decline in livestock herds (Macfarlane, 2001), had supported a significant recovery in forest cover across Nepal by the 1990s.

However, there is a new wave of stress facing the agricultural sector today. One of the most significant changes has been a rising demand for cash. These are connected to both the rising costs of agricultural production, and secondly a rapid rise in the cost of living.

With regards to the cost of agricultural production, the cost of inputs has been spiralling over the last two decades (Sugden et al., 2014). The removal of state subsidies on chemical inputs following the deregulation of the fertiliser market in the 1990s led to considerable price increases as the private sector took control. Farmers were often forced to use fertiliser of questionable quality due to the spiraling costs (Raut and Sitaula, 2012). Subsidies were re-introduced in 2009, with subsidized fertilizers being distributed through cooperatives or offices of the Agricultural Inputs Corporation Ltd (AICL). However, there are only 40 offices of AICL in 39 districts, and while the remainder is to be distributed through cooperatives, there are ongoing supply shortfalls, with the government only procuring a small share of the annual fertiliser requirements of the country to be distributed through subsidised channels. Added to this is the fact that farmers needed land ownership documents or official tenancy papers, rendering subsidies out of reach to marginal farmers (Raut and Sitaula, 2012).

Spiralling oil prices up until 2014 and again in 2022-2023, have added to the stress on agriculture. In Nepal for example, the price for diesel increased by 352% between 1995/96 and 2009/10, both impacting the price of fertilizer and other inputs (Pant, 2011). This came at a time when dependence on purchased agricultural inputs has been increasing as farmers sought to offset population growth and land fragmentation through intensified use of inputs. Farmers were also required to increase the use of fertiliser due to reduced livestock herds – which translates into reduced supply of organic manure (Gupta et al, 2022).

With regards to costs of living – the processes are complex, yet there are two phenomena which are of significance. Firstly, the real costs of goods have risen rapidly in the last two decades. Retail prices for food soared in the 2000s, due to the rising price of fuel and higher processing costs (Pant, 2011). The Covid 19 crisis (Singh et al., 2020) and war in Ukraine have intensified this trend. This has been aggravated in Nepal by regional events such as a temporary ban in exports of wheat and non-basmati rice by India in the context of a larger regional food shortages, which resulted in the price of chamal (milled rice) increasing from Rs200 to Rs400 for a 20kg bag (Prasain, 2023). The withdrawal of public goods once available prior to liberalisation such as healthcare have also increased living costs significantly for rural households (Gupta et al, 2022).

A second phenomena is enhanced market integration and a greater availability of goods. As noted in the last section, there was a gradual process of monetisation in the hills in the 1960s, as markets and roads expanded – yet there were still vast areas without road access at the dawn of the 1990s – including most of the northern districts of Nepal. However, all districts have now been connected with roads – and even in districts which have been on the road network for decades, there has been an intensification in the expansion of markets. Studies from Dhanusha (Sugden, 2019b, 2017b), Bhojpur (Sugden et al., 2018) (see Figure 35) and the Tamang domains of Nuwakot (Holmberg, 2017) have suggested that even in the latter period of the Panchayat era there were communities with relatively limited circulation of cash. This included the persistence of *jajmani* exchange networks with occupational castes and payment of labour in kind. This certainly persisted in the western hills, although it was in decline elsewhere. Even without *jajmani* relationships, a large share of agricultural transactions were 'in kind'. This included payments for agricultural equipment by surrendering a share of the produce, or more commonly, payments for labour in a fixed volume of grain. In Tharu villages of Morang as recently as 2008, workers for the harvest would receive a share of the crop (Sugden, 2010) and in Dhanusha landless tenants were paid 6kg of rice per day as a wage as of 2013, and thus were entirely dependent upon landlords (Sugden, 2019b, 2017b). This has transformed in the last ten years. Follow up studies to Dhanusha by one of the authors showed that all wages were now paid in cash. In the hills, *jajmani* relations have significantly declined and have almost completely disappeared in some regions such as Kaski (Gupta et al., 2022). More broadly, most commodities are now available in local markets, and alongside the monetisation of wages (Sugden, 2019b, 2017b, Sugden et al., 2018), the levels of cash required in the rural economy have intensified.

The expansion of markets combined with access to the internet, TV and other mediums of communication with the outside world, have also driven an emergent culture of consumerism, even in rural areas (Sugden, 2019b, 2017b, Holmberg, 2017, Sugden et al., 2018) (Figure 33). The lifestyle changes which have gone alongside this have contributed to rising costs as local people purchase phones, recharge cards and mobile internet packages, as well as radios and TVs and solar panels to power them (Sugden et al 2018). Modern consumption practices also signify social status, a process widely documented on the literature from Nepal (Liechty, 2003, Rankin, 2004). Environmental and time pressures as well as availability in markets, also mean that a transition towards the use of cooking gas rather than firewood is underway in the larger villages of the plains and accessible bazaars of the hills. While this has clear health and

Figure 33: Electronics and phone shop in Dingla of Bhojpur, 2022. Such facilities were unthinkable just a decade before when the town was a 2-3 day walk from Hile of Dhankuta, yet these changes are testimony to the growing ability to access commodities due to lower cost transport, as well as shifting culture of consumption.
Photo – Fraser Sugden

Figure 34: Cooking gas ready for sale in Dhanusha, 2022. Its use is already widespread amongst wealthier farmers.

Photo: Fraser Sugden

environmental benefits, it of course comes at a considerable financial cost (see Figure 34).

The change with the greatest implications for household finances however, has been the spiraling costs associated with 'cultural' and lifecycle events. These include ceremonies associated with weddings and births, but also community religious events. Macfarlane's (2001) study of Gurung villages in Kaski offers an interesting perspective as it shows that historically, including the time of the original study in the 1960s (Macfarlane 1976), cultural expenditures, (particulalry those which involved the whole community) were a means through which surplus wealth could be shared. Macfarlane suggests that expenditure was facilitated by the fact that opportunities for accumulation were limited due to the limited market for land or commodities. However, today, in the context of growing differentiation of wealth and land scarcity, they are a key source of financial distress (Ibid.).

With regards to weddings, as well as the cost of the ceremonies themselves, the financial or gift transactions between families associated

Figure 35: Bhojpur Bazaar in 2008 before the road was built, and again in 2024 (bottom). Road construction has transformed rural towns with the extraordinary expansion of commerce and availability of consumer goods.
Photo: Fraser Sugden

with the marriage have also risen in value. Bridewealth, which has traditionally been more common amongst Adivasi groups of the hills, involves a gift being transferred to the family of the bride. Even as early as the late 1980s, Yakha families in eastern hills were experiencing a spiraling cost of bridewealth, with a rise in 10 years from a few gold items to cash sums of up to 10,000 rupees (which at the time was a considerable amount) (Russel, 1992). In the Tarai, dowry is more common, and in regions such as Mithilanchal in particular, the costs have skyrocketed, driven by both the remittances (and the expectations of high amounts if a family member of the bride is abroad) and a rising culture of consumerism (Sugden, 2019b, 2017b, Clement and Sugden, 2021, Sugden, 2025). Dowry was found in a series of studies to be a frequent driver of debt and distress sales of land (Sugden, 2019b, 2017b, Clement and Sugden, 2021). Even amongst the Tharu of Morang, there were expectations that expensive gifts such as motorbikes would be offered to the groom's family, unlike in the past when a gift of livestock would suffice (Sugden, 2010).

It is clear from the above discussion that access to markets (even in ways which improves living standards), combined with rising costs of production, have contributed to rising financial distress across rural Nepal. An almost inevitable outcome has been intensifying debt. In some locales such as Mithilanchal, private lenders still control the moneylending economy (Sugden, 2019a), which has been bolstered in recent years by the demand for loans to go overseas (Sijapati et al., 2017a), a topic discussed below. In other locales such as the eastern Tarai and parts of the hills, microfinance has become a more popular source of credit – epitomising a development strategy of 'neoliberalism from below' (Rankin, 2004). While interest rates are lower, and there are valuable opportunities for female financial empowerment (Karn et al., 2020), the availability of these loans does not stop farmers from falling into cycles of debt. So called 'loan swapping' whereby indebted individuals take on loans from one bank to repay those incurred at another are widespread in rural Nepal (Rankin and Shakya, 2007, Sugden, 2010). The extent of this pressure is noted in Macfarlane's (2001) follow up fieldwork in Dhap of Kaski whereby much of the jewellery and gold which had been an avenue to invest 'surplus' income, had been sold to repay loans by the late 1990s. With fewer fallback options, households experiencing a financial deficit are more likely to sell off some or all of their land, unlike in the past, and distress sales are widespread across rural Nepal (Gupta et al., 2022) – and this will be explored in more detail below.

Climate and agrarian stress

In spite of some positive ecological changes such as a rise in forest cover (Oldekop et al., 2018), agriculture is increasingly facing the stresses of climate change. While the concept of 'climate change' as a global phenomena is an abstract concept for Nepal's farmers, there is a strong consensus that the predictability of the climate has changed – with increased frequency of late monsoons, unseasonal pre-monsoon rains (which damage wheat and other dry season crops), not to mention fog, chilling and extreme heat episodes (Thapa et al., 2015, Gentle and Maraseni, 2012).

A range of studies have identified the mechanisms through which climate is already impacting production. Bhatt et al (2014) for instance, with regards to the Koshi basin in central and eastern Nepal, notes that paddy, maize and wheat cultivated below 1100m, 1340m and 1700m respectively are experiencing stress due to rising temperatures over the last half century, with only some upper altitude domains experiencing improved yields. Temperature rises can accelerate the profusion of pests (Karki and Gurung, 2012) as found during interviews in Bhojpur in 2015 (Sugden et al 2018). Extreme flood events are increasing in frequency, and Karki and Gurung (2012) for instance note how the extreme rain in the mid-western Tarai-Madhesh in 2005/6 reduced crop yields by 30%.

Farmers in Nepal are particularly vulnerable to precipitation fluctuations given that 64% of the cultivated area is estimated to be dependent upon monsoon rainfall (Karki and Gurung, 2012). Frequent droughts or late monsoons in the middle hills (Poudel and Duex, 2017) and Tarai-Madhesh (Sugden et al., 2014a) have meant that farmers cannot plant on time, or experience crop failures at critical times such as directly after paddy transplantation. Precipitation outcomes for farmers are however, complex. Some studies have predicted an increase in net precipitation, although with greater seasonality – in line with the frequently reported farmer concern about growing unpredictability. For instance, in a study from the Babai basin, it was predicted that future rainfall would increase from 15% to 25% and annual streamflow, which is essential for irrigation, would rise by 24% to 27%. However, it is estimated that water deficits would remain high during the dry months (when irrigation is most critical), and shortages will increase with rising demand from farmers (Mishra et al., 2021).

In the hills, where many farmers depend on irrigation, particularly for dry season crops, a growing challenge is the drying up of springs, which form the source for many perennial streams, as well as micro-irrigation systems, not to mention their role as a drinking water supply. Poudel and Duex (2017) showed how in a single watershed in Nuwakot in the central hills, a substantial 73.2% of Springs had decreased their flow, and 12.2% had dried up entirely over the last 10 years – a phenomena which they suggest is connected to localised declines in net precipitation, particularly during the drier months from October to February. Another study found that in two communities (also in the central hills) 29% and 14% of Springs respectively had dried up (Sharma et al., 2016), while a study from the western hills suggested that 70% of Springs had reported reduced flow, particularly over the last 10 years (Adhikari et al., 2021).

Growing articulations with the capitalist sector through wage labour

As noted in the last chapter, outside labour in the capitalist sector, particularly via migration to India, was already well established in the western hills where the physical limits of cultivation had been reached some time ago, and wage work was of rising importance in the centre and east of the country also. However, by the 1990s, with spiralling demand for cash alongside continued pressure on finite land resources and growing inequalities – the articulation between the peasant economy across Nepal's hills and plains, and capitalism via labour, has been intensified. Blaikie et al's (2002b) longitudinal survey in the 1990s from the central hills and Tarai showed a notable rise in off farm labour income since the 1970s for some farmer categories[3].

However, this increase has been eclipsed by a much more significant engagement with capitlaist wage labour via overseas migrant labour –

---

[3] For small peasants-labourers off farm income had increased from 32% to 38%, while for richer peasants it had increased from 51% to 73%, although for middle peasants there was little change.

particularly to the Gulf States and Malaysia – which is increasingly filling in the gap in household cash needs. As of the 1981 census, there were 402,977 Nepalese household members classed as 'absentee', a large share of whom likely included migrants to India from the western hills. Preliminary findings of the 2021 census however, put this figure at 2.1 million, or nearly 7.4% of the population (MoLESS, 2022). While this also included migrants to India, to gain an insight into the extent of migration further afield, the Department of Foreign Employment (DoFE) has issued over 4.7 million new approvals for Nepali workers to overseas employment (not including India) since 2008/09 and renewed over 1.8 million labour approvals since 2011/12.

While labour migration to the Gulf states has increased substantially, and in the eastern and central hills and Tarai-Madhesh has almost entirely replaced migration to India, cross border movement to India persists as the primary form of migration in the western hills and western Tarai Madhesh districts of Dang, Banke, Kailali and Kanchanpur (Poertner et al., 2011). One form of migration which has declined notably is military service. In the east this tailed off with the closure of the Gurkha recruitment camp in Dharan in the late 1980s (Russel, 1992), and while British Gurkha enlistment continues from Pokhara, the numbers are smaller than in the past. In the 1970s there were five battalions of Gurkhas in the UK army with a strength of just 7000 (Rathaur, 2001). Today this has declined to around 4000[4]. The kind of scenario described by Macfarlane (1976) from the 1960s, whereby a large share of young men in a single village are in the military, is increasingly rare.

A common question in the context of high out-migration, is whether remittances could be diverted back into agriculture to support agricultural investment. In terms of how remittances are used, most studies have shown how remittances mainly cover day to day food needs, as well as variable costs on the land such as agricultural inputs (Adhikari and Hobley, 2011, Sugden et al., 2016, Khanal et al., 2015). While remittances have increased incomes, Maharjan et al's study from Syangja suggested that this

---

[4] From British Army data https://www.army.mod.uk/who-we-are/corps-regiments-and-units/brigade-of-gurkhas

had not resulted in greater expenditure on fertilisers and other inputs. Net agricultural productivity has actually declined by 11% per additional migrant (Maharjan et al., 2013a), likely due to labour shortages (see below). As migrants need to take large loans to pay the employment agents to facilitate the migration process, debt servicing often consumes a large share of remittances, or even pushes migrants' families further into poverty and food insecurity if the migration experience does not go according to plan (Sunam, 2020, Gupta et al., 2022, Sunam and McCarthy, 2016).

The ability to invest remittances is also heavily mediated by prior wealth, with successful returnees mainly being those who already had land and assets, and were not burdened with high debt (Sijapati et al., 2017b, Sunam, 2020). A study from Bhojpur and Dhanusha (Gupta et al 2022) found that migrants who were already in a weaker socio-economic position – and in particular those with less land, were more likely to be experiencing food insecurity, with a greater share of remittance income being absorbed by basic food needs, not to mention debt servicing. Land poor households were also more likely to be in debt prior to migration of a family member, or were likely to depend on larger loans to fund the migration process. The study however, also showed that there was a clear difference in the level of remittances between larger and smaller land owners. For instance, in Dhanusha Rs153,178 on average was earned by landless households, compared to Rs 333,300 for farmers with between 1 and 2 hectares. This was because better off farmers could often pay higher fees to agents prior to migration to secure more lucrative jobs overseas, such as service sector positions which offered opportunities for upward mobility. Similarly, poorer households, and in particular marginalised groups such as Dalits, were more likely to be cheated or deceived in the recruitment process, and end up in more precarious or lower paid jobs. Those who did achieve upward mobility as a result of migration appear to be disproportionately the better off households. This group have greater savings to draw upon, had already owned larger holdings of land prior to migration, are less likely to be in debt, while also having the capital and resources to secure more lucrative jobs overseas (Gupta et al 2021). The importance of prior wealth, particularly rooted in land ownership, in shaping migration outcomes, has been cited elsewhere such as Sunam's (2020) study from Sunsari and Fitzpatrick's (2011) from Taplejung.

It is in this context that while migration has offered improvements in living standards, it has not supported 'transformative' livelihood change, and appears to have driven an increase in inequalities within the owner cultivating peasantry. This offers an interesting contrast with the situation described in the Gurung village of Kaski studied by Macfarlane (1976) in the 1960s whereby he notes that remittances from army employment were helping to regulate inequalities by offering the land poor an opportunity to purchase plots. Similar findings were echoed by Caplan (1970) with regards to the Limbu. While army employment has declined to a trickle today, the alternatives through overseas employment are very different – with much lower pay and high upfront costs which drive indebtedness (Campbell, 2018, Sijapati et al., 2017a), and divergent employment pathways which are dependent upon what one can afford to pay agents (Sugden et al., 2022). Migration has also taken place today against a baseline of much greater initial inequality with spiralling prices for land, unlike studies such as Macfarlane's for example, whereby the legacy of the Adivasi mode of production meant that there was relative equality in the distribution of resources at the start of the Panchayat era.

While there is a minority of 'success stories' in the context of migration, the limited opportunities for upward mobility amongst the majority is grounded in the precarity and low wages which underpin the entire migrant labour economy from Nepal. While migration is rooted in agrarian stress and the inability of households to meet their cash needs, the wages that the *majority* of migrants receive, are by no means sufficient to draw households out of agriculture – and they remain embedded in a 'dual' livelihood pattern. This generates exceptional profits for the diverse sectors of the capitalist economy where they are employed overseas. Echoing Meillassoux (1981) and Wolpe (1982), with regards to migrants from West Africa and Southern Africa respectively, the capitalist enterprises in which migrants work, receive *for free*, the cost of feeding the unproductive labourers (children and retired family members), and the costs of the labourers' sustenance while they are on leave, or working the fields at home (in the case of seasonal migrants). The peasant or feudal mode of production at home meanwhile also cover the costs of the workers retirement, or medical costs if they return due to poor health – a widespread phenomena in Nepal (Sugden et al, 2025; Sharma, 2021).

The labour arrangements for workers from Nepal ensure they remain 'temporary' and their families remain home. This is realised through the provision of fixed term work permits and strict employment regulations (Hanieh, 2010), akin to those documented by Meillsassoux (1981) with regards to African migrants in post-war Europe. In the case of migration to urban centres (which also includes non-migrant off-farm labour such as those working in Tarai industries), the low wages and casual nature of work ensures that migrants are obliged to maintain strong links to their home communities, as noted elsewhere (Sugden, 2019a).

This precarity came to the fore during the Covid 19 pandemic, when factories closed overnight with the loss of all daily wage work, and thousands of Nepali migrant workers were forced to return to Nepal en mass under conditions of great distress (Sharma, 2021), as this disposable labour force was temporarily not needed by the capitalist sector.

Permanent migration or resettlement which achieves a 'break' from the land may offer more favourable livelihood outcomes. For instance, Sharma (2021) suggests that some of the first generation of migrants to India from the far-west have settled and established businesses in India, and field research by one of the authors in Doti provided similar conclusions. However, this is rare in the context of the Gulf states. In terms of permanent migration and resettlement within Nepal – this has continued, although resettlement on new farmland in the Tarai is much less common, and as noted above, has declined notably since the peak of the resettlement schemes in the 1960s and 70s. Nevertheless, the population of the Tarai continues to grow due to migration from the hills – with the share of the population residing in the plains rising from 50.27% to 53.66% between the 2011 and 2021 census. However, many of these migrants end up not in rural areas, but in growing plains towns, particularly along the East-West highway (Dahal and Timilsina, 2021), and some have even relocated within the hills to towns such as district headquarters (Gupta et al 2002). This is itself often linked to overseas migration whereby family members of better off migrants relocate to emerging urban centres to access enhanced facilities. Many of these families still maintain a link to their home community which offers them a supplemental source of livelihood through for instance, rent from leased out land at home. Extended families are also often spread out between locations, with the younger generation residing in towns or in the Tarai (often subsisting through remittances from overseas), while agriculture continues to support the elder generation who remain in hill villages (Ibid.). Therefore, it is clear that livelihood strategies and families are increasingly trans-local.

Migration, new stresses on agriculture and mechanisation

Migration itself has generated new patterns of agrarian stress. One of the most significant pressures is a shortage of labour, which is having a significant impact on the allocation of resources in agriculture (Fox, 2018, Maharjan et al., 2013b, Sugden et al., 2016, Sugden et al., 2014b, Adhikari and Hobley, 2011, Devkota, 2016, Tamang et al., 2014). Maharjan et al's study from Syangja for instance, suggested that having one migrant in the household reduces the availability of male farm labour by 44.8% and female labour by 34.5% (Maharjan et al., 2013a). Even on their return from overseas, many young people disengage from the agricultural labour force (Campbell, 2018).

The outcomes of this labour crisis have been multifold. Tamang et al (2014) suggest that migration induced labour shortages have resulted in changing land use – with a shift to less labour-intensive agricultural practices. This includes agro-forestry. For instance, field research by one of the authors in Bhojpur pointed to a rapid increase in commercial plantations of the tree, utis (alnus nepalensis), which have been established by families with migrants on plots above 1700m. Studies have shown that there has also been a decline in livestock, particularly large livestock such as cattle which are labour intensive, due to the need for fodder collection. Instead, farmers are increasingly preferring to keep smaller livestock which require less work, such as goats, poultry, and pigs (Adhikari and Hobley, 2011; Campbell, 2018).

There has also been an increased demand for labour saving equipment such as tractors and threshers. The history of mechanization in the agricultural sector goes back to 1924 when a first single cylinder tractor was introduced to Nepal. In the three decades after the first tractor was introduced, only 64 tractors and 30 pumps were reported to have been imported. From the late 1960s and 1970s, the government directly supported the import of machinery to improve agricultural productivity, as touched upon in the previous chapter (Takeshima and Bhattarai, 2019). However, due to the fragmentary nature of the land ownership, only a few with relatively large holdings benefitted from such government support.

It is only in the last two decades, that mechanization has really taken off – driven by the pressures brought about by out-migration. A 2011 study (Biggs et al., 2011) suggested that there were 30,000 four wheel tractors in the country, mainly imported from India. The use of tractors in the Chitwan valley for instance, have played an important role in helping farmers to cope with migration induced labour shortages (Bhandari and Ghimire, 2016). In the hills, mechanisation was later to start, but increasingly farmers are making use of cheaper Chinese or Japanese two wheel tractors. These, as well as even smaller mini-tillers, have been particularly valuable in the mid-hills due to their portability whereby they can be moved between terraces, and their spread has been charted in detail in Justice et al (2023). The pace of change is notable in Justice et al's (2023) study which suggested that there has been a 300% increase in the number of two wheel tractors in Nepal from an estimated 10,000 to 40,000 between 2010 and 2020. The rise in the use of mini-tillers is even more notable, having risen from just 500 in 2010 to 40,000 in 2020.

In spite of these positive inroads for mechanisation in Nepal, the costs of procuring such equipment is high. The National Land Policy suggests that small sized plots and fragmentation have been a critical constraint (Ministry of Land Management, 2019). Field notes and data by the research team in remoter districts such as Bhojpur, Khotang and Doti as recently as 2023-4 suggest that mechanization, even by mini-tillers, is low at this point in time (see also Gupta et al 2022). The inaccessibility of plots, many of which are located far from each other and don't have access to roads to bring the equipment in makes their use challenging, although there has been some use of two wheel tractors on the low lying *besi* lands.

Furthermore, in districts of the Tarai-Madhesh which experienced the legacy of the *jimidari* system and where inequalities remain acute, purchase of technologies by marginal and tenant farmers is negligible – leaving them dependent upon larger farmers to act as 'service providers', often at monopoly rates. For example, a study from Saptari and Dhanusha (Sugden et al., 2016), suggested that 58% of the tractors in the community belong to farmers with more than 1ha. These are generally rented out to poorer farmers, for profit, with the cost varying according to supply/demand and the bargaining power of the farmer. In villages with few tractors available, the income during the ploughing time can be lucrative. In this context, adaptation to the labour shortages brought about by migration itself increases the cost of production for poorer producers – further increasing the demand for cash. This is intensifying the process of rural monetisation, and reducing the levels of remittances available for reinvestment.

It is important to note that in contexts whereby investment in labour saving technologies are prohibitive, it is women who bear a disproportionate share of the additional labour burden in agriculture in Nepal – a topic on which there is already extensive literature (Adhikari and Hobley, 2011, Gartaula et al., 2010, Tamang et al., 2014). While female migration is increasing, overseas mobility is still largely dominated by men. The literature has shown that while women have always contributed a disproportionate share of agricultural labor, particularly for time intensive tasks such as weeding and transplantation, men were still extensively involved in farm work prior to migrating, and their departure aggravates an already high work burden.

Migration has itself contributed to the monetisation of reciprocal arrangements which women were once heavily dependent upon. Systems of labour exchange in the hills such as *parma* are becoming increasingly financialised, with labourers being increasingly paid in cash (see Campbell, 2018) due to households not having sufficient labour to guarantee that they can return the service. *Parma* is also rarely used for cash crops (Holmelin, 2021). However, more research is required on this topic, as anecdotal evidence suggests that in some locales labour shortages have had the opposite effect, and have made *parma* more popular (Gupta et al 2022).

There have of course been other benefits for women of male out-migration – including greater mobility and control over finances (Sijapati et al., 2017a), benefits which have also been supported by women's engagement in cash crop production (KC et al., 2016) and off-farm micro-enterprises (Karn et al., 2020). However, these changes in gender norms throw up new challenges. Women farmers are now obliged to enter the public sphere more often for work such as collection of remittances, as well as agricultural related social engagements which were once in the male domain, such as arranging irrigation or land to rent from other farmers. This breaking of gender norms, particularly in more conservative social formations such as the central Tarai-Madhesh, has created challenges for women such as negative commentary and mistrust from community members or in laws (Sijapati et al., 2017a). In some cases this can even further restrict women from accessing critical resources to support climate resilience such as groundwater or canal irrigation (Karn et al., 2020, Sugden et al., 2014a).

Land reform failures

In the 1990s there were modest attempts at securing access to land for landless households. For example, the Nepali Congress led government created a Landless People's Problems Resolution Commission (LPPRC) in 1993, and it resettled over 15,000 landless families across 18 districts – mostly on marginal forest land – with plots varying in size from 0.1 to 1ha depending on the size of the family (Conway et al., 2000). A study of Bardiya by Conway et al (2000) suggested that this fostered relatively equitable inter-ethnic relations between Tharu and hill settler farmers, unlike the areas with a longer history of settlement. However, these were very limited in scope given the sheer size of the landless population, and did not involve the redistribution of land, but instead the distribution of wasteland to landless households.

There were discussions of redistributive land reforms following the formation of the Badal Commission under the short-lived Communist government in 1994, which could have undermined feudal agrarian relations. However, these recommendations were not implemented (Alden-

Wily et al, 2008). Various amendments to the 1964 Lands Act were made in the 1990s and early 2000s which recalibrated land ceilings, entitling tenants to half of the land. However, ceilings were not implemented due to pressure from opposition political parties (Nepali and Pyakuryal, 2008) and the guarantee of tenants to half of the land had limited impact when the vast majority of tenants were not formally registered (Basnet, 2018). If anything, it pushed tenancy further underground as landlords had a clear reason not to give out official papers (Alden-Wily et al., 2008, Sugden and Gurung, 2012). Basnet (2018) with reference to a study in Bardiya, suggests that prior to the end of the Panchayat period, political parties (then underground) sought to mobilise farmers' associations to support the implementation of land reforms after the restoration of democracy – yet after 1991, the parties had a change of position, and tended to side with landlords.

Paradoxically, 'scientific land reform' was explicitly discussed in the Constitution of Nepal (2015) (50, e). The constitution emphasises the right of access to land for all, and even mentions the need to 'discourage' absentee landlordism and end dual land ownership. However, the constitution fails to outline any concrete mechanisms through which to achieve this – which are left to subsequent legislations. The likely benefits of later interventions which have been proposed are uncertain. The government for instance, has proposed a so called 'land bank'. The governments' proposals involve landowners depositing their fallow land in a 'bank' which can then be leased out to others. Government owned wasteland or riverbanks can also be accessed by landless farmers through the bank. This in itself can offer an opportunity to match farmers with insufficient labor to cultivate their land, with other households who require additional land on lease, lowering the transaction costs, and builds upon a robust model proposed for the Indian context (see Agarwal and Sharma, 2012). However, CSRC (2021) caution that in the context of the extremes of land inequality in Nepal, over dependence on the land bank idea alone, risks diverting attention from the pro-tiller agenda associated with redistributive reforms, as it protects the land owners' property rights.

A significant set of legislation was the 2019 Land Use Act and 2022 Land Use Regulations (Government of Nepal, 2022). These were largely focused on the classification of land. While there are promising efforts to limit subdivision of holdings and prohibit so called 'plotting' of farmland for residential purposes, the resources which would be required to implement these regulations are huge (CSRC, 2019), and already there have been attempts to loosen the regulations due to pressure from the real estate sector (Fiscal Nepal, 2023).

Discussions on tenancy reforms, or ceilings on land are now rare in mainstream political discourse. The 2022 election manifestos of the mainstream Communist Party of Nepal (United Marxist-Leninist) (2022) and Nepali Congress (2022) for instance, place a strong emphasis on agricultural transformation but with only brief reference to land, and even then, this was largely through the reference to the implementation of land use regulations as well as the aforementioned 'land bank' approach.

Contemporary Agrarian structure and mode of production

In light of the stresses discussed thus far, alongside limited success with land reform, what does this mean for the agrarian structure and mode of production? Out of the total households in Nepal today, the National Land Policy estimates that 74% are peasant farmers dependent on agriculture to varying degrees, of which around 53% own less than a half-hectare of land. Those 53% of households only use the 18% of the total agricultural land (Ministry of Land Management, 2019) – reminding us of the continued inequality in the distribution of holdings. The 2010/11 National Sample Census of Agriculture suggests that the share of households with less than 0.5ha is even higher, at just over 80% (see Table 3). Similar data is evident in the most recent National Living Standards Survey (NLSS) (2022/23), which suggests that the share of agricultural households without land is now 36.4%, up substantially from 16.9% in 1995/6 (National Statistics Office, 2024, Central Bureau of Statistics, 1996). Land fragmentation is a persisting challenge. Data from the Department of Land Management and Archive in Table 5 suggests that a substantial 47.78% of holdings on their records are less than 1 ropani, or around 0.05ha. This is corroborated by the NLSS data in Table 4, which suggests that the share of holdings below 0.1ha is 29.5%. These are extremely small parcels, which likely severely constrain the potential for mechanization or irrigation. There is evidence that the holding size continues to drop. The NLSS data suggests that the average size of holdings (including rented land) has declined from 1.1ha in 1995-96 to 0.4ha in 2022-23 (National Statistics Office, 2024).

While the data above suggests that owned holdings are small, with a clearly skewed distribution, this does not tell us about the mode of production itself – for which we need to look at the Tarai-Madhesh and hills separately.

Table 3: Table Landholding structure in Nepal

Land holding size (ha)	Family (%)	Average size of holdings (ha)	Cultivated area (%)
<0.2	24.36	0.1	4.50
0.2–0.5	30.53	0.34	15.70
0.5–1.0	25.69	0.71	27.50
1.0–2.0	14.33	1.37	29.70
2.0–3.0	3.83	2.39	12.20
3.0–4.0	1.03	3.40	5.30
4.0–5.0	0.39	4.39	2.50
>5.0	0.31	7.2	2.60
Total	100.00	0.66	100.00

Recompiled from National Sample Census of Agriculture, Nepal, 2011/12. (Adapted from Pokharel, 2019)

Table 4: Agricultural holdings by size across Nepal

Land owned (ha)	2022-23	
	Rural (%)	Nepal wide (%)
No land	34.56	16.62
<0.2	19.66	20.30
0.2–1	34.98	48.62
1-2	7.76	10.74
>2	3.04	3.04

Table 5: Number of land plots owned by size (2023)

Area category	Number of Owner	% of total
<4 aana	3,058,926	13.82
>4 and <8 aana	3,397,764	15.35
>8 and <12 aana	2,416,879	10.92
>12 and <1 ropani	1,701,970	7.69
>1 and <=2 Ropani	3,600,935	16.26
>2 and <=3 Ropani	2,337,410	10.56
>3 and <=4 Ropani	1,698,151	7.67
>4 and <=5 Ropani	1,075,394	4.86
>5 and <=10 Ropani	1,929,758	8.72
>10 Ropani	924,160	4.17
	22,141,347	

Source: Department of Land Management and Archive, Kathmandu (Data obtained on 15/09/2023)

Feudalism and owner cultivation in the Tarai-Madhesh

In the Tarai-Madhesh, the evidence thus far suggests that landlessness and landlord-tenant relations remain important features of the contemporary mode of production. While there were some 'seizures' of land during the 10 years of the People's War, much of this land was returned to landlords following the peace agreement (Sharma, 2021), and in other cases landlords sold off their estates, albeit with larger farmers as the beneficiaries – a topic which will be covered below.

The 2010-11 Nepal Living Standards Survey suggests that just over half of households own less than 0.5 ha of land across the central and eastern Tarai-Madhesh (see Table 7). A substantial 36.3% are engaged in some form of tenancy, of which 19.8% are 'pure' tenants who possess no farmland of their own. Meanwhile 30% are landless. A study (Dhakal 2011) carried out in 16 VDCs of 16 districts in the Tarai revealed that 22.7% of families were landless. 6.2 percent of the surveyed households reported that they have 'rented out' excess land for cultivation, whereas 20.6% were renting in land as tenant farmers. Notably, only 2.4 percent of these were registered tenants, who hold legal rights and 14.5 percent of the households were sharecroppers (Dhakal 2011). The latest NLSS data which captures even more recent (2022-23) data on land ownership, points to even higher levels of landlessness, with 39.9% of households lacking any agricultural land (National Statistical Bureau, 2024).

It is important however to re-emphasise that there is a clear divide between the more prosperous belt of the plains home to settlers who cleared the forests in the 1960s and 70s, and the long settled, largely Adivasi and Madheshi domains which bear the legacy of the *jimidari* system. One would expect much higher prevalence of landlordism in the latter. Unfortunately, there is no nationwide disaggregated data with coverage that can provide an accurate picture. Nevertheless, insights can be drawn from a selection of more localised studies from the long-settled domains, within which there are two patterns.

The first pattern points to a continued concentration of land, and classic 'feudal' distribution of the means of production. For instance, a survey in a selection of villages in mostly the southern part of Sunsari and Morang found that 57% and 87% respectively, of land was under tenancy, with surplus being extracted via relations which were feudal in character

Figure 36: In the village of Sitpur in Morang, over three quarters of the land is under tenancy and owned by absentee landlords
Photo: Fraser Sugden

(Sugden, 2017b). Morang and Sunsari themselves appear to be districts with particularly high levels of landlessness given the legacy of absentee landlordism and *birta* grant distribution. For instance, the 2001 census which was the last countrywide record of landlessness[5], showed that of the thirty-four VDCs of southern Morang which had an Adivasi majority, landlessness was over 40% in twenty five of them, and was over 50% in twelve, and over 60% in four (see Figure 36).

Longitudinal data from Morang suggests there is very limited decline in landlord economic power and no evidence of land being sold off, with most purchases of land being from other smallholders. In Morang, the proportion of rented-in land which belonged to absentee, urban-based landlords was 78.85% in 2007-8, and had dropped only marginally to 77.58% in 2019 (Sugden, 2025). Similarly, the proportion of land under tenancy has actually increased during this same period, from 59.9% in 2007 to 64.37% in 2019. 38.46% of households are functionally landless, with less than 0.05ha. A larger sample which included villages in neighbouring Sunsari (Sugden, 2017b) showed that absentee landlords own 53% of the rented land. Only 12.84% of land purchases in the last 10 years were from absentee landlords, with the rest being from local farmers. Tenants farming for absentee landlords in the far eastern plains experience particular challenges. These include a lack of landlord willingness to share costs of inputs, or to offer technical support to tenants (Sugden, 2013). It also extends to the management of the complex Sunsari-Morang irrigation network whereby landowners (who are by default responsible to pay the irrigation fee and take an active role in management), often fail to perform these duties. This contributes to the poor maintenance of the canals or obliges tenants to meet these costs themselves (Valadaud, 2023).

Extreme concentration of land is also prevalent further west, towards the Koshi floodplains – where one still observes a more 'typical' form of South Asian feudalism reproduced by caste, with mainly Rajput landlords sharecropping or leasing out their land to Adivasi and Dalit tenants. A

---

[5] The question on landownership was removed in the 2011 and 2021 census, for unknown reasons.

census of every household in Koiladi VDC found that just under two thirds (62.12%) of households were landless, and a staggering 77% of land was under tenancy (Sugden et al 2016). Landlords maintain strong political as well as economic power, and there is even evidence of corvée or 'labour rent' persisting informally alongside sharecropping, whereby tenants are expected to do unpaid domestic chores for landlords alongside farming their fields (Sugden, 2016).

Another area where landlord-tenant relations are widespread is parts of the Dang valley in the western Tarai – a region which has experienced both historic land grant distribution as well as unequal relations between hill settlers and the Tharu. While exploitative systems such as corvée had died out as tenants are more aware of their rights, the distribution of land remains deeply unequal and is still dominated by landlords (McDonaugh, 2012). A study from one community by Mishra (2007), found that four fifths of the land was under tenancy. It was found that 84% of the land was controlled by hill people, who owned 5.6ha on average, compared to just 1.2ha on average for the Tharu. Elsewhere in the western Tarai, a study from the Tharu belt of southern Rupandehi was also shown to experience high levels of landlordism, particularly closer to the town where a situation similar to Morang was observed (Sugden, 2014).

While it is clear that landlordism is widespread in many domains, there are some parts of the long-settled domain where a second pattern of landownership is increasingly prevalent, with lower levels of tenancy with a decline in the landlord control over property going alongside a rise in the 'middle farmer' class. One area where change appears to have taken place was in the Tarai west of the Dang valley – the old Naya Mulak. While studies using data from the 1990s suggest that a substantial proportion of land in districts such as Bardiya belonged to upper caste landlords (Karki, 2002), this region saw widespread grassroots mobilisation during the People's War and saw substantial land seizures by the CPN(M). Anecdotal evidence suggests that many landlords sold off their estates. One study from Kailali, put the figure for landless households at a relatively modest 24.56% (Nepali et al., 2011a). The National Living Standards Measurement Survey (2010-11) suggests that the proportion of agricultural households who own their own land in the western Tarai (from Dang to Kanchanpur) is 82%, higher than the Tarai-wide average for 2010-11, which is 70%, with 31.2% of households renting in land (as compared to 36.2% average). Another reason which may have contributed to the decline in landlessness in the westernmost Tarai districts is the abolition of the *kamaiya* (bonded labourer) system in 2000, a topic on which there has been considerable research (Fujikura, 2001, Kim and Rawal, 2012, Maycock, 2017, Gahatraj, 2011). Many former *kamaiya* transitioned to become free wage labourers and some had been able to access land through government schemes.

Another area where the concentration of land had declined was in parts of Mithilanchal, particularly around Dhanusha (see Sugden, 2016, Sugden, 2017b, Rinck, 2024), where there appears to have been a notable breakup of landed estates. For instance, in a cluster of villages surveyed in 2013, the area under tenancy was lower than further east in the Koshi floodplains, at 37.5% (Sugden, 2017a). This is because many of the large estates of the Madheshi landlord class have declined. Firstly, there had been a division of holdings amongst sons, a process already well in motion since the 1970s and 80s. Secondly, it was reported that as landlords diversify their income sources, with the younger generation taking up professional employment in the bureaucracy or service sector, they no longer see the value of retaining large estates in the countryside.

Why this has taken place in Dhanusha, but not in other parts of the central Tarai such as the Koshi floodplains is not known, but is likely due to the unique political history of each locality – which saw different levels of mobilisation amongst tenants during the various political struggles of the last few decades. In the case of Dhanusha, political changes since the 1990s have contributed to an undermining of feudal landed authority at a localised level. For example, interviews carried out by one of the authors in Dhanusha in 2012-13 suggested that the restoration of democracy in the 1990s sensitised many villagers, and revolts against the landlords culminated in them eventually selling off their estates. Such instances were amplified during the People's War from 1996-2006, where fear of future land reforms saw many large landlords relocate to the towns while parting with their estates in the countryside. For example, in one Dhanusha village, the tenants agitated against a landlord who they believe had falsely claimed public land in his name. Both incidents eventually culminated in the landlord selling off much of his estate. Even if the land officially seized and redistributed by Maoist themselves was limited at a national scale, the fear this generated resulted in the landowners losing confidence in the security of their property. Coupled with their diversification into new livelihood strategies such as salaried and professional employment, many saw little reason to hold on to their plots. Some landlords reportedly also donated their land to the Janaki mandir, where it became *guthi* land.

Rinck's (2024) study from Dhanusha engages with similar processes, and also shows that many previously landless tenants, often from lower castes, were able to secure plots of land over the last few decades. Nevertheless, the selling off of lands by landlords does not always benefit the landless and land-poor farmers. In Sugden's (2017) study from Dhanusha, it was found that it was middle farmers rather than the landless, who were the primary beneficiary of the break up of big estates, with the latter also purchasing land sold by smaller landowners on a distress basis. The rise of a middle farmer class in some locales is also reflected in Nepal Living Standards Survey data from across the Tarai-Madhesh. It shows that between 1995/6 and 2010/11 there was a significant increase in the proportion of land belonging to farmers in the middle, between 0.5ha and 2ha from 38.81% to 54.7% (see Table 6), despite the fact that this group has declined in number from 47.07% to 42.8% (see Table 9) (Central Bureau of Statistics, 2011a).

This is exemplified by Dhanusha panel data by Gupta et al (2022) which suggests the medium to large farmer class is stable in size (with some selling land, but many also buying land), and is possibly slightly increasing their control over land in the village. The panel data suggests that there is negligible change in the share of middle farmers with 1-2ha and large farmers with 2-5ha, although the percentage of land owned by this group has increased slightly to 61.67% in 2021, up from 57.35% in 2013. Similarly, a sample from across the Tarai-Madhesh and North Bihar suggest that the medium and large farmers with more than 1ha account for 43.08% of the total land purchases over the last 10 years, despite the fact they represent only 17.09% of the sample (Sugden, 2017b). This consolidation of the middle farmer class echoes a much earlier longitudinal study by Blaikie et al (2002b) in a large survey of the central Tarai-Madhesh (and hills) which found that the so called 'middle peasantry' was 44% in the mid-1970s when the authors' seminal book 'Nepal in Crisis' was written, yet had increased to 51% by the mid 1990s.

Field notes collected in a separate cluster of villages in Dhanusha in 2012 suggested that large farmers with 4 to 5 bigha (3-4ha) were now at the apex of the agrarian structure, dominated by middle castes such as the Sah (Teli) and the Yadav. There were some Brahmins, and many had turned to cultivate the land themselves due to economic compulsions rather than rent it out, as was the tradition. Importantly, as shown in the other studies from Dhanusha (Sugden, 2017, 2019), there was limited evidence of any 'proto-capitalist' investment amongst this nascent middle to large farmer class – given the persisting agrarian stress. The relations these middle to large farmers had with tenants who were largely Dalit, represented a continuity of the 'feudal' relations of production which characterised earlier eras, albeit with a smaller, less powerful landed elite. It is worth noting that there are also a large share of medium and small farmers who have benefitted from this break up of estates and are no longer leasing in or out land (Sugden, 2017b). They are effectively independent owner cultivating peasants.

Table 6: Percentage land owned by different land ownership categories in Nepal Tarai-Madhesh 1995/6 – 2010/11

Year	<0.5ha	0.5-2ha	>2ha
2010/11	14.6	54.7	30.7
1995/6	5.8	38.81	55.39

Source: (Central Bureau of Statistics, 1996, 2011a, National Living Standards Survey (NLSS))

The consolidation of middle farmers at the top of the agrarian structures in some parts of the Tarai should not divert attention from the rise in landlessness. This is reflected in the most recent NLSS dataset from 2022-23. Across the Tarai-Madhesh for instance, the proportion of agricultural households owning land declined from 75.59% in 1995/6 to 60.1% in 2022-23 (see Table 7). At the same time, while the proportion of households engaged in tenancy had dropped during this period, the proportion of land under tenancy across the sample had increased from 19.93% to 26.8% (see Table 8).

Other recent studies point to similar trends. For instance, panel data from the community in southern Dhanusha studies by one of the authors, that had otherwise seen a decline in the landlord class (Gupta et al., 2022), showed that the percentage of households who are landless had increased from 24.79% in 2015 to 29% in 2021 – with distress sales of land associated primarily with debt. This was itself contributing to the burgeoning middle to large farmer class. Indebtedness has been aggravated in the context of out-migration, whereby migrants have to pay considerable fees to employment agencies. An unsuccessful migration experience will often result in households returning in a weaker economic position than prior to their departure and being compelled to sell off assets (Sunam, 2020, Gupta et al., 2022).

The distress sale of land is also reflected in the data on the proportion of very marginal farmers, which also appears to be rising. Across the Tarai-Madhesh the percentage of households with less than 0.5ha of land increased from 33.18% in 1995/6 to 50.4% in 2010/11 (see Table 9). At the same time, the average size of plot has declined from 1.29ha in 1995/6 to 0.8ha in 2010/11 (Central Bureau of Statistics, 1996, 2011a). This may be in part also due to the fragmentation of land between sons.

Table 7 % of agricultural households owning land in Nepal 1995/6 – 2010/11

Ecological zone	1995/6	2022/23
Mountains	98.04	89.3
Hills	87.97	69.8
Tarai-Madhesh	75.59	60.1

Source: (Central Bureau of Statistics, 1996, 2011a)

Table 8: Status of tenancy in Nepal 1995/6 – 2022-23

Measure	Ecological zone	1995/6	2022/23
% of households in sample renting in land	Mountains	26.48	26.4
	Hills	22.58	18.2
	Tarai-Madhesh	36.30	22.1
% land owned by sample which is under tenancy	Mountains	10.57	23.24
	Hills	10.91	24.92
	Tarai-Madhesh	19.93	44.38

Source: (Central Bureau of Statistics, 1996, National Statistics Bureau, 2024)

Table 9: percentage households fitting different land ownership categories in Nepal Tarai-Madhesh 1995/6 – 2010/11

Year	<0.5ha	0.5-2ha	>2ha	landless	tenants
2010/11	50.4	42.8	6.8	30	36.3
1995/6	33.18	47.07	19.75	24.41	36.2

Source: (Central Bureau of Statistics, 1996, 2011a)

Feudalism in flux?

It is worth noting though that even in areas where the relations of production and levels of tenancy have remained stable up until the present day, the power of the landlord class has still declined. For instance, it appears increasingly common for land poor farmers to rent land from multiple landlords, including local large farmers. Contracts with landlords have also become more impersonal. In Morang, where there are many absentee landlords, most now manage their estates through an agent, known locally as a *kamtiya*. In Dhanusha and Saptari, patron-client relations between tenants and landlords such as the *jajmani* system have declined (Sugden, 2016, Sugden, 2017b).

In Dang, McDonaugh (2012) notes that while hill upper caste landlords as a demographic, still has a monopoly of land, it was increasingly fragmented amongst several families (due to buying and selling and division within families) – increasing the tenants' bargaining power. Many tenants had been successful in mobilising for tenancy rights or *mohi*, and had refused to offer unpaid corvée labour to landlords. By the 1990s, the area of land owned by the Tharu community had increased from just 23% (in 1980) to 40%, largely as a result of farmers giving up *mohi* rights in return for a quarter of the land. However, this has also meant that many now had to work as casual sharecroppers without legal protection – which is the normal status of tenants in Nepal. The study also notes that in villages where land ownership is still concentrated largely amongst the original landlord families, then the pace of change is slower (McDonaugh, 2012).

Perhaps the most significant change is that there has been a decline in the inter-linkage between landlordism and usury – which was particularly prevalent in the Mithila region (Sugden, 2017; Rinck, 2024). Large farmers and landlords are still the primary lenders, but with surging demand for migration associated loans and greater circulation of cash, a rising number of richer farmers were diversifying into money lending. Poor tenants were therefore less likely to be dependent upon their own landlord to access credit (Sugden, 2016, Sugden, 2017b). This parallels studies from South of the border. Karan's (2009) dataset from Bihar points to a decline in debt associated with bonded labour for landlords between 1982/3 and 1999/00, as does a study from Purnea by Rodgers and Rodgers (2001). Migration itself has also allowed some landless households in Nepal to get a foothold in the land market (even if plots are still below what is needed for subsistence) (Rinck, 2024). It appears thus that even if landlessness is increasing, there are clearly some winners from the migration economy, and this is undermining the authority of the old landlord class.

What is important to emphasise is that despite a decrease in bondage to single landlords and a decline in their political authority, usury has intensified. The overseas migrant economy in particular has increased indebtedness and it is normal for households to take loans of $1500 or above to so called 'manpower agents' to travel overseas (Sijapati et al., 2017b), a process which in turn has bolstered the money lending economy locally amongst the larger farmer class (Sugden, 2019b). Field notes in Dhanusha collected in 2012-13 found that interest rates could be as high as 40% to 50%, although it was normally around 36%. Some take loans from microfinance institutions, while others use a combination of banks and money lenders. One man the authors met during field research had taken a loan of 40,000 from Sano Kishan bank. The rest he took from a rich farmer at 36% interest per year – a Kushuwaha landlord with 10 bigha. He was not paid by his company overseas for 5-6 months. This meant he was struggling to repay his debt and interest was rising.

This creates an interesting phenomena in districts such as Dhanusha whereby our field notes suggest that (as mentioned above) the traditional landlord-tenant relations which emerged from the relics of the *jimidari* system have declined, with medium to large farmers now at the apex of the agrarian structure. However, tenants for these large farmers, and also many owner cultivators who have benefitted from the breakup of landed estates, are subject to increasingly crippling levels of surplus appropriation through usury. Whether interest replaces rent as the primary mechanism of non-capitalist surplus appropriation, remains to be seen. What is particularly interesting however, is that unlike in the past whereby poor farmers would take high interest loans from their landlords, they now have multiple sources of credit to choose from – even if the rates of interest are just as exploitative as in the past, and overall levels of indebtedness have risen.

Alongside these weakened economic ties is a break in the ideological ties between landlords and tenants, bolstered in part by the wave of political mobilisation amongst the Tarai-Madhesh peasantry over the last two decades. Interviews in Dhanusha in 2012 and 2013 noted how tenants and landless farmers felt in a much stronger position to challenge landlord authority or bargain with them, unlike in previous generations. This parallels similar findings across the Mithilanchal region (Sugden, 2017a), and the coupling of declining landlord power with rising debt echoes Sharma's (2021) suggestions for Nepal as a whole, that recent decades have seen traditional feudal authority being undermined just as financial precarity accelerates.

It is worth noting that while interlinkages between landlordism and money lending has declined, bonded labour persists to a smaller extent. The Harawa-Charwa system of bonded labour for example, is still prevalent in the central Tarai-Madhesh, now Madhesh Province (Dhakal 2007). In the western Tarai-Madhesh, the *kaamaiya* system of bonded labour was formally abolished in 2000, yet still persists informally (Giri,

2012). A study conducted in 9 VDCs of three districts revealed that 12.4 families on average across all study villages, were working as Harawa-Charawa, or unfree agricultural labour (Dhakal 2007), a recent study (Dhakal et.al. 2020) shows that the system still persists in the districts of Madhesh Province in varying forms.

Owner cultivation, growing inequality and feudal relics in the hills

With regards to the Nepal's hills in the 1990s and 2000s, the literature suggests that most rural households are today independent land-owning peasants, and while there is still notable differentiation within the peasantry, there are only some areas where a 'feudal' mode of production are present. This represents a notable difference with the Tarai-Madhesh – and the history outlined above helps shed light on the reasons for this. While landlords did emerge in the hills during the Gorkha and Rana era through the *jimidari* system and via *birta* grant distribution, the rugged terrain, and much smaller plots, meant this was far more limited than in the Tarai. There was an Adivasi functionary class, although this was not as powerful as their counterparts in the plains, and in some villages, *internal* inequalities within Adivasi society were limited. Nevertheless, lack of internal stratification was counterbalanced by notable inequalities *between* Adivasi and upper caste settlers, particularly in the eastern and central hills which were the primary cultural interface between these two groups – and at times this extended to landlord-tenant relations.

It is for this reason that it is important to acknowledge the complex diversity in relations of production across the hills. There is a notable geographical and altitudinal pattern to the relations of production. There is compelling evidence that there is lower inequalities in areas with more marginal lands as these lands have historically had less potential for dominant classes to extract surplus via rent or taxation, and these lands were less attractive to upper caste settlers in the years after the Gorkha conquest. A study of land concentration (using the Gini index) in Nepal by Thapa and Chettri (1997), suggested that inequalities were lower in the districts with more rugged terrain, a scarcity of land, and with lower indices of economic and human development. Of course, the reduced capacity of the state to extract surplus in kind was balanced out (historically) by its tendency to appropriate surplus through forced labour tribute.

This difference is evident at a more local level within districts. For example, in the Chirkhuwa valley of Bhojpur, localised feudal relations are present on the fertile valley floor. A substantial 31% of the sample own less than 0.25ha with 77% also engaged in tenancy, and 48.72% owning between 0.25 and 1ha with 75% engaged in tenancy. In this agrarian system, Adivasi (Magar) and Dalit tenants sharecrop the land for upper caste absentee landlords (Gupta et al., 2022). In the same valley, the upper altitude Tamang and Sherpa communities farm much more marginal land, yet are not subject to feudal exploitation, and inequality within the community is only moderate with 92% of farmers owning their own land. The Rai villages in between these two zones is mixed, with some landlord-tenant relations and a moderately differentiated peasantry.

Importantly however, in cases such as this, a lack of 'internal' inequalities in some villages masks much deeper inter-ethnic and inter-village inequalities which follow the contours of caste and ethnicity. In the Chirkuwa valley case, it is upper caste settlers who dominate the best valley land and the Adivasi groups were restricted to the more ecologically vulnerable rainfed higher altitude valley slopes – given the history of in-migration and *kipat* dissolution (Sugden et al., 2018). Similarly, in the central hills, the Tamang peasantry experience tend to live on the more marginal agricultural land (often with just modest internal differentiation, as suggested by Fricke, 1993), with a greater share of fertile valley land in the hands of upper castes labour (Holmberg, 2017). In both the above cases, higher valley slopes may have been suitable for the earlier agrarian system dominated by low intensity shifting cultivation, but for the hill Adivasi today, cultivation of such lands puts them at a considerable disadvantage when it comes to more intensive sedentary terraced agriculture.

The fact many farmers do have their own land, albeit marginal, does not mean they do not experience various forms of subjugation and exploitation. Historically surplus appropriation by an extractive state via labour tax or *begar* or *jhara* would supplement the limited revenue available on more marginal lands, as evident in the case of the Tamang inhabited uplands of central Nepal (Holmberg et al., 1999). Similarly, today, it is these areas which are disproportionately dependent upon overseas labour migration – and this represents by far the most significant form of surplus appropriation (Sugden et al., 2018).

There is also evidence that internal differentiation may be increasing within the owner cultivating peasantry of the hills. On the one hand, the resettlement in the towns and the lowlands continues to act as a pressure valve to reduce competition for land. For instance, the Chirkhuwa valley case study from Bhojpur in 2015 (Sugden et al., 2018) found that many richer farmers had continued to relocate to the lowlands, with the land being bought by farmers who chose to stay, with some also being purchased from other Rai households from remoter domains of Khotang. This points to a some levels of land redistribution across the hills. However, the longitudinal data from this site still records an increase in landlessness between 2015 and 2020 (Gupta et al., 2022).

Looking at the NLSS data from the hills, the percentage of households owning agricultural land declined from 87.97% in 1995/96 to (see Table 7) 69.80% in 2022-23. The decline in the 'mountains' (which for the NLSS includes the northernmost hill districts) is from 98.04% to 89.30%. The percentage of land under tenancy has increased from 10.91% in the hills in 1995/6 to 24.92% in 2022/23 (see Table 8). Like in the Tarai-Madhesh, plot sizes are in decline in the hills also. The average plot size in the hills was 0.89ha in 1996/95, reducing to 0.6ha in 2010/11. The decline in northern districts classified as mountains was from 1.22 ha to 0.7 ha in the same period (Central Bureau of Statistics, 1996, 2011a). The growing influence of market forces through debt (Sugden et al 2018) and cash crop production (Fitzpatrick, 2011) is likely precipitating this trend – with the latter discussed below in more detail in the discussion of 'capitalist' agriculture.

There is less recent concrete data on land ownership and inequality in the western hills. A sample from Doti put the share of landless households at 39.5%, with levels in Bajhang at 24.56% - (Nepali et al., 2011a) figures comparable to the Tarai. Like in the east one would expect concentrated areas of higher landlessness in fertile valleys.

Customary tenure and relics of the adivasi mode of production

While most farmers are owner cultivators today, a remaining question is whether any elements of the Adivasi mode of production – and in particular, 'customary' tenure, persist. As we saw from the discussion so far, Adivasi groups, particularly those who continued to carry out shifting cultivation and transhumant pastoralism during the Panchayat era, continued to relate to land through customary tenure - an extra-legal right over the land, which was neither against the law nor recognized by the law, particularly in isolated regions.

While it is in rapid decline, customary tenure – and with it the relics of the Adivasi mode of production – still persist in Nepal to some extent, outside of the formal legal land ownership system. As noted above with regards to Panchatar, while *kipat* was formally abolished in 1966, customary recognition of rights to formal kipat lands persisted, and this was confirmed in interviews carried out in the early 2000s (UN-HABITAT, 2018). These interviews revealed that development agencies engaged in the conservation efforts related to the 'protected' Kanchenjunga landscape in the 1990s were not allowed to build their offices in some villages, on the basis that the land was traditionally owned by the *Kipatiyas* (the Kipat holders) and the government was not believed to have rights to 'grab' their land. In a similar vein, Fitzpatrick's study (2011) from Taplejung in the 2000s suggested that land which had been farmed by the same lineage for generations without purchase or sale was still recognised culturally as *kipat*, even if in legal terms it was *raikar*.

The legacy of *kipat* abolition and persistence of informal *kipat* has also meant that in some cases land rights remain ambiguous, often to the disadvantage of marginal farmers. For example, interviews by one of the authors in the District Land Revenue Office, Panchthar in the early 2000s reported that about 25 percent of the total land in the Panchthar district was recorded on 'form no 7'. That means no proper measurement of land was done for these lands and plots had not been mapped during cadastral surveys – although individual owners retained some evidence that they were the owner or cultivator. Now there are demands that ownership be recognized formally and legally to ensure their tenure rights.

Another case of interest is that of the Chepangs, a minority indigenous groups of the Mahabharat range of central Nepal, including Gorkha, Dhading, Makwanpur, and Chitwan districts. They still practiced shifting cultivation in the 2000s, and hunting and gathering was important for their livelihood. The land they cultivated for generations may or may not have a land certificate, but the land use and cultivation was regulated by customary law, a shared rule which was collectively inherited. However, in the land record system of the state, this is neither recognized nor recorded (UN-HABITAT, 2018).

Interviews from fieldwork carried out in the central hills by one of the authors showed that because the government did not recognise customary tenure, Chepangs could not register the lands they had been cultivating for generations in their names. Hence, technically they were not the legal owner of the land they themselves occupied for years. A case from Bhumlichowk of Gorkha illustrates this issue, whereby Chepangs were granted tenure rights of a Chiuri tree[6]; but not of the land itself. Hence, the legal tenure rights of a Chiuri tree, which is culturally and economically closely linked with the Chepangs, was granted but the similar rights of the land, usually *Khoirya* land, was not.

Another example of customary tenure is in Manang, a mountainous region, with tradition-bound-land use practices, where the formal ownership of land is (unusually) registered in the name of the 7 villages of upper Manang, now combined to form Manang Rural Municipality. In this region, interviews carried out by one of the authors noted how communities still exercise traditional land use practices governed by customary institutions. Land cannot be sold to an outsider and all seven villages have similar land and resource management practices. Their land and management system coincides with the cropping system and pastoralism cycles. For example, all villagers harvest buckwheat, their staple food, on the same day, and only then can cattle enter the villages. As

---

[6] Chiuri tree (Diploknema butyracea), commonly known as the Indian butter tree, is a multi purpose tree. The main product of the tree is ghee (butter), extracted from the seeds and named chiuri ghee. It is a large tree of the family Sapotaceae. It flowers during cold season and fruit ripens in June-July. This Chiuri tree is considered to be not only economically, but also culturally important for Chepangs.

a customary practice, they have an annual village assembly, called *chongpa*, where a local council of village representatives is elected. Each village has one representative in the council; who is called *Panch-Chongba*, and out of them, a main village head, *Dakp-Serba* is elected. The village assembly fixes the rules regarding grazing, harvesting, and other resource and land-related matters for the year which follows. The day is also marked with a horse race and archery.

Upper Manang is an arid place, and only a few crops can be grown there; making it a food deficit community. To address this, the village head, *Dakp-Serba* of those 7 villages, following the same principle of customary land management, requested the *Dakp-Serba* of nearby Pissang village to grant land in lower Manang for them to produce crops to feed the people of upper Manang. Later the government also approved it and granted the *lalpurja*, the land registration certificate of around 800 *ropanis* of land in the name of those seven upper Manang villages.

These contemporary cases well illustrate that the state's centralised formal land record system is inadequate to record the diversity in the land tenure system in the country. In terms of other forms of tenure, the most famous non-*raikar* form which persists is *guthi* tenure. According to a government's estimation there are altogether 2335 *guthis* in Nepal; out of which 1107, (47.4%) are within the Kathmandu valley (Government of Nepal, 2010). *Guthi* is considered to be one of the most complicated forms of land tenure arrangement in Nepal. However, field observations by the research team show that *guthi* can at times represent a form of institutional landlordism with arbitrary use of power by priests and *mahantas* over the tenants. Again, it is the tenants who suffer, as they do not have any legal authority over the land they have been cultivating for years. Therefore, in practice at times it has closer parallels with feudal economic formations rather than being part of a mode of production in its own right.

Shifting cultivation and pastoralism

Another relic of the Adivasi mode of production, are itinerant forms of production – most notably transhumant pastoralism and shifting cultivation. As noted, this was in decline throughout the Panchayat era – although elements persist today, particularly in the most remote domains. Transhumance continues to persist at upper altitudes of the hills, including the *Kham Magar* country (De Sales, 2003), where farmers move livestock herds up to higher valleys or ridges during the warmer summer months. The seasonal migration with sheep is widespread still in many Rukum communities at the time of writing (personal communication with development workers operating there). However, the general trend across Nepal points to a decline in transhumant pastoralism. While milk products and meat from pastoralism can be profitable, and access to markets has significantly improved due to road construction, out-migration has meant that many households in the hills have reduced their engagement in pastoral activities. For example, in Bhojpur, *chauri* herding on the high ridges during the summer amongst the Sherpa has declined significantly. With labour shortages due to the out-migration of men, many families who stay behind prefer to focus on agricultural production, and have sold off their herds (Gupta et al., 2022). The decline in the pastoral economy in the hills began even earlier in some locales, with Macfarlane's case study from Kaski, noting how the Gurung had made a transition from an economy heavily dependent upon pastoralism in the 1960s to one grounded almost entirely in sedentary cultivation by the 1990s (Macfarlane, 2001).

Metz (2022) traced out the thirty years of agrarian change in the same regions the Japanese expedition of the 1950s (Kihara, 1956) had studied. The study also noted a significant decline in the transhumance economy with falling livestock herds, along with a sophisticated agricultural system utilizing lands across multiple elevations, including distant fields which were farmed on a seasonal basis. Migrant remittances had compensated for this change in livelihoods.

Shifting cultivation continues in some remote domains of the hills – although it is likely that its days are numbered, particularly with the increasing abandonment of coarse grains. Aryal et al (2010) estimate that shifting cultivation is practiced in about 20 districts across Nepal. It was well documented just over two decades ago (Dhakal, 2000, 2002) amongst the Chepang and Magar of the central hills, and Rai, Limbu and Sherpa of the east. How widespread it remains today is difficult to ascertain. Local narratives from Tamang and Sherpa communities in Bhojpur in 2015 suggested it had died out around two decades ago due to stricter community forestry regulations (Sugden et al., 2018).

Shifting cultivation is neither officially recognized as land use by the government nor can the cultivators register the land as such, and there is no specific policy to deal with it. In Dhakal's study (2000, 2002), only 19 percent of farmers had registered plots whereas 81 percent of them were unregistered. The remaining practices of shifting cultivation across the country among many indigenous ethnic populations have further been negatively impacted by various policies regarding forest conservation, land reform, land survey, agriculture and economic change (Arayal et al 2010).

Capitalist agriculture and commercial production

A remaining question is with regards to the emergence of 'capitalist' agriculture. There are three pathways of transition towards capitalist agriculture in a peasant society (see Tilzey and Sugden, 2023). In the first case, there is forced proletarianisation – often involving eviction from the land to make way for large scale capitalist agriculture. Parallels include England, and particularly Scotland which saw large scale dispsosession in a relatively short period of time, followed by mass out-migration (Devine, 2018). Contemporary parallels include 'land grabs' in low and middle income countires (McMichael, 2012), such as the palm oil sector, which releases a huge surplus labour force (Li, 2010). In the second, the peasantry initially retains their land, yet there is gradual differentiation between smaller less profitable producers and the larger farmers with economies of scale, who emerge into a capitalist class – as shown by Byres (1981) in the case of the Punjab. In the third case, farmers retain their land yet are subordinated to capitalism (often to agro-food corporations) via the market which drains a large share of the surplus. These 'petty commodity producers' have been described as 'disguised proletarians' (Bernstein, 1977), although differentiation between more and less successful producers can still occur within this context. A classic example includes 'contract farmers' producing niche commodities for companies (White, 1997), although the presence of a formal link with agro-business is not a prerequisite for commercialised peasants to be entirely dependent upon the market.

With regards to the first transition (enclosure and proletarianisation), this is rare in Nepal, as in much of South Asia (see Tilzey and Sugden, 2023). Nepal lacks the colonial history which established large scale capitalist plantations, and as noted earlier, thus far there has been little interest by agro-food corporations in Nepal's agricultural resources – although this may change with the opening up of the agricultural sector to foreign investment. At the moment though, large scale plantation style agriculture is very limited in scope and restricted to a few pockets such as the tea gardens of the east.

With regards to the second transition, with 'natural' differentiation into capitalist farms and a labouring class, this is similarly limited. Macfarlane (1976) predicted that with new cash crops as of the 1970s, differentiation between farmers would increase in the years ahead. He predicted eventual proletarianization into landless labourers and profit oriented farmers. However, a follow up study (Macfarlane, 2001) suggested that this had not occurred. There are some large family owned farms today producing niche crops such as banana, dragonfruit or tea, which could be considered capitalist or proto-capitalist. For instance a survey of Chitwan banana farms found that over half were above 2ha (Ghimire et al., 2019) which is larger than the average 'peasant' subsistence farm and likely employs a number of labourers. However, the extensive review of contemporary and historical sources on agriculture in Nepal which went into this study, found limited evidence in any locality of a societal wide shift towards a capitalist mode of production with associated differentiation into distinct labouring and capitalist classes. What is clear is that larger capitalist farms exist in isolated pockets alongside pre-capitalist peasant and feudal modes of production as parallel economic formations (alongside other non-farm capitalist enterprises) – akin to what Chaudhuri (1995) describes as capitalist 'enclaves', further east in the tea growing economy of the North Bengal Dooars.

The third transition towards capitalism grounded in peasant-led petty commodity production is in theory a more realistic prospect in Nepal –

particularly in the hills in the context of niche cash crops. To assess whether this matches the reality on the ground requires some analysis of market oriented production. A longitudinal study (Blaikie et al., 2002b) from the central hills and Tarai-Madhesh found that 73% of households sold less than Rs. 1,000 worth of agricultural produce in the mid-1970s during the peak of the Panchayat era. By the mid-1990s the proportion of those selling less than Rs. 10,000 (the equivalent sum given the ten-fold rate of inflation) was over 87% - pointing to lower levels of commercial production. The authors suggest this retreat away from the market was in the context of widespread agrarian stress. Nevertheless, this was before the APP which sought a commercial transformation of agriculture, building upon Nepal's competitive advantage of its diverse agro-ecological niches. With the expansion of road infrastructure there is evidence that market engagement has increased in the first two decades of the 21st century. There was for instance a 12% increase in cash crop production between 2011-2021 (see Table 15).

The entire peasant agrarian sector (regardless of the mode of production) is articulated somehow with capitalism – given that most farmers sell even a small share of goods for the market, and largely depend on cash purchases of inputs (Uprety, 2021). However, the number of farmers who can be considered 'petty commodity producers' who are entirely oriented to the market remains limited. In most cases, subsistence production is the priority, even if cash crop production takes place. For instance, a study in Dolakha, a district which is close to the markets of Kathmandu, suggested that only one fifth of the land had been set aside for cash crops, while 37% do not sell any produce (Holmelin, 2021). Even if some crops are profitable, farmers are unlikely to risk their food security needs in the case of a market or crop failure, and seek to diversify as much as possible (Holmelin, 2021).

Having said that, there are clearly pockets where so called 'petty commodity production' is widespread, and fields of grain staples have been replaced with cash crops. A study from Ilam shows how there was a complete shift from paddy to commercial crops such as cardamom and orange (KC et al., 2016). However, this case study community had a long history of commercial vegetable and ginger production since the 1960s – and is likely atypical.

A more common scenario is that there are pockets with particularly high production of a niche commercial product, whereby it remains an important source of income, yet farmers still set aside a large share of their land for grain staples. In these contexts, the more marginal producers have limited engagement at all in cash crop production due to the prioritisation of staple production – a reality which has been long overlooked by flagship policies such as the Agricultural Perspective Plan and Agricultural Development Strategy. This appears to be the scenario described in Fitzpatrick's (2011) study of cardamom production in Taplejung, whereby farmers produce a market-oriented crop alongside subsistence crops, with the level of market engagement proportionate to one's household food security. While many engage in cardamom production offering a valuable source of cash, profitable cultivation is only feasible for a minority (9%) who produce a medium to large surplus, and together make up the top 10% of cardamom producers, who produced over half of the village output. There was very limited production amongst smaller landholders. Similar findings were evident with regards to rudraksha production in Bhojpur (Sugden et al 2018).

In Fitzpatrick's study of the cardamom economy, this form of commodity production has led to differentiation between richer and poorer producers, but not to the extent that full 'capitalist' social relations were emerging. Those who are losing land are often those in financial distress due to debt which is often unconnected to agricultural production (e.g. linked to migration costs or marriage). Those who are accumulating wealth meanwhile include larger, profitable petty commodity producers. Nevertheless, investments are not necessarily back into cardamom production or other agricultural investments alone given the growing stresses, but also include urban real estate purchases, investment in education with a view to 'exit' from agriculture for youth, and payments to secure more lucrative labour opportunities abroad (Fitzpatrick, 2011), findings echoed from recent studies elsewhere in Nepal (Sunam, 2020; Gupta et al 2022).

This latter point is particularly important as there is evidence across Nepal of a subset of households who have accumulated some capital (from either agricultural or non-agricultural sources) – yet prefer to spend it not on expanding one's holding in the village, or on improving the land through technology investments. Instead they prefer to invest in land in urban areas. This may include for instance purchases of land in district headquarters. In a study from Bhojpur by one of the authors, it was found that many more successful migrant families would use accumulated remittances to purchase land in the district headquarters (Gupta et al 2022). However, an even more desirable investment of capital is in land in the Tarai cities or the Kathmandu valley. This is reflected in Table 10 which explores purchases of land by people from outside of the Kathmandu valley. For instance in Kathmandu district, the number of landowners from outside of the valley has increased from 196,843 in 2018 to 275,665 in 2023.

Interestingly, there has also been a rise in people from within the valley buying land outside of the valley. There were 56,491 residents of Kathmandu with land outside of the valley in 2018, and this had increased to 25,223 by 2023 (see Table 11). This points again to speculative investments in land, albeit by urban dwellers – but is associated with a different trend – the perpetuation of the kind of 'absentee landlordism' visible in the Tarai, whereby urban people with capital buy land in rural areas in the hope that it can be sold off later at a higher price. This is a widespread phenomenon around cities such as Biratnagar where the land has a good market value (Sugden, 2013). While in theory some purchases outside of the valley could have been for agro-enterprises such as plantations – the only modest growth in cash crop production suggests that such investments are the exception rather than the norm.

Both the above two processes point to a trend whereby land increasingly become a commodity to be bought and sold in the speculative market, rather than being used with the purpose of agriculture in mind. Table 12 gives an indication into the rapid increase in the volume of land being bought and sold over the last decade, which alludes to both a rise in speculative investment alongside distress sales.

Table 10. Number of owners of land within the Kathmandu valley by individuals from outside of Kathmandu valley

District with owners	Number of owners					
	2018	2019	2020	2021	2022	2023 Aug
Kathmandu	196843	212881	223766	248040	266394	275665
Bhaktapur	54648	61002	64996	74912	82716	87375
Lalitpur	41966	46765	50125	57675	63801	67096

Source: Department of Land Management and Archive, Kathmandu (Data obtained on 15/09/2023)

Table 11: Number of individuals from the Kathmandu valley owning land outside of the valley

District with owners	Till this Year (Number of Owners)					
	2018	2019	2020	2021	2022	2023 Aug
Lalitpur	15991	17838	19225	21606	23829	25223
Bhaktapur	5944	7188	8003	10227	12019	13015
Kathmandu	56491	62958	66614	74396	81732	86383

Source: Department of Land Management and Archive, Kathmandu (Data obtained on 15/09/2023)

Table 12: Transfer of ownership

Year	Total Ownership
2017	131,080
2018	293,467
2019	635,758
2020	514,669
2021	859,381
2022	650,310
2023 (Till August)	427,259

Source: Department of Land Management and Archive, Kathmandu (Data obtained on 15/09/2023)

Cropping patterns and current trajectory of agricultural development

Cropping patterns

A complex picture

Over the last 30 years since the end of the Panchayat era, the outcomes in terms of cropping patterns has been mixed. As will be described below, there has been a notable increase in the irrigated area, which means that a wider range of dry season crops has become possible. In terms of cropping intensity, recent data suggests that there has been an increase, if modest, from 1.83 in 2000/01 to 1.85 in 2010/11 (see Table 13).

Having said that, there is still fallow land. The current land use data suggests that 1/4th of the cultivable land has been left uncultivated (Ministry of Land Management, 2019). A number of studies suggest out-migration has contributed to falling cropping intensity in some localities – particularly in more accessible regions, in spite of a generalised increase in cropping intensity across the country. Gurung's study from the Pokhara region points to a rise in fallow land (Gurung, 2016), as does Khanal et al's (2015) study from nearby Tanahu and case studies by Uprety (2021) in Panchatar. Fox (2018) also notes that lack of labour has meant that many less-productive fields have been abandoned or converted to tree crops for firewood and fodder.

Table 13: Cropping Intensity

	2000/01	2010/11
Nepal	1.83	1.85
Mountain	1.69	1.74
Hill	1.86	1.85
Tarai-Madhesh	1.83	1.86

(Source: Ministry of Agriculture and Livestock Development, 2022)

There are some areas still with limited use of industrial inputs, including the field site in the central hills by Metz (2022), which was restudied after 30 years. Nevertheless, farmers are to a far greater extent than in the pre-1990s period, dependent upon chemical fertiliser (Tiwari et al., 2008, Uprety, 2021) aggravating the rising costs of production, while also undermining yields through over-use (Macfarlane, 2001). The reduced stocks of livestock due to out-migration has intensified this trend (Sunam and Adhikari, 2016).

Imported hybrid seeds have also become increasingly dominant, with agro-food corporations increasingly controlling the supply (Adhikari, 2014). As a result, the culture of selecting the best yielding traditional crops as seeds for use in the next season has dwindled (Uprety, 2021). While hybrid seeds have supported increased yields, they themselves depend on greater use of fertiliser, which in turn increases dependency on chemical inputs (Tiwari et al., 2008), while the seeds themselves are also increasingly costly (Adhikari, 2014) – further aggravating the growing costs of production. In some cases hybrid seeds have failed, due to unregulated imports of poor quality varieties or defective seeds distributed by international and domestic development agencies (Adhikari, 2014).

A positive outcome of out-migration on land use and cropping systems has been evidence of reduced pressure not only on land but on forest resources next to communities. This has actually supported a regeneration of forest cover (Oldekop et al., 2018), and has reversed the ecological crisis which appeared to be brewing during the Panchayat era. Also significant in supporting this regeneration (particularly since the 1990s) was community forestry rules, which decentralised control over forest adjacent to villages to communities themselves (Smith et al., 2023). The reduced run-off and land degradation, which goes alongside increasing forest cover is likely to have a positive impact on agricultural yields, although it will not reverse the new stresses associated with climate change, labour scarcity and rising costs of agricultural inputs.

Change in cereal production

In spite of the goals of the APP and ADS, the expansion of new crops and intensification of agriculture in Nepal remains limited. Rice remains the predominant crop in the hills up to around 1500m, with an estimated 1,473,474 under paddy as of 2020/21 (see Table 14). Rice constitutes 50% of the cereal crop requirement in Nepal, and is therefore a major source of dietary energy, contributing 30% of the average daily requirements (CDD and ASoN, 2017).

As noted above, improved varieties of seeds from overseas form a large share of rice production. This however, has had a negative impact on genetic diversity, with a loss of local varieties and landraces. There are only 157 landraces which are still grown in Nepal, and these occupy about 10% of the total rice production in the country – with many being superior to the introduced varieties (Joshi, 2017). However, Nepal has not been able to become independent in rice genetic resources for research and development (Joshi 2017). Citing one of the archives of 1903 (1960 BS) from a personal collection of RD Chataut, 61 varieties of rice were grown in Nepal at the start of the 20th century, most of which are no longer in existence now (Chataut, 2017).

As in past years, the rice-wheat cropping pattern is predominant in the Tarai-Madhesh farming system (Chataut, 2017). The expansion of groundwater irrigation has supported an increase in wheat production in some locales and it remains the second most important grain crop in Nepal (see Table 14), although access remains highly unequal (Sugden, 2014). Maize, mustard and potatoes are also grown – although niche cash crop production is more limited – with sugarcane and jute being common crops, although the latter has been in decline for years.

A major change over the last 20 years has been a shift towards rice consumption even outside of the rice growing zone (National Planning Commission, 2013). As noted above, rice consumption has long been a sign of social status in Nepal – with the prestige of a household judged by how much rice they consume. Gaenszle (2000) with reference to the Arun valley, notes how it has long been associated with the Hindu values of the Nepali speaking castes who migrated to the region from the west, bringing with them wet rice cultivation technologies. While rice was of ritual importance to the incomers, crops such as millet had been of greater ritual significance to the indigenous Rai community. While middle hill Adivasi communities such as the Rai adopted paddy cultivation sometime between the 18th and 19th century, rice consumption is now increasing above 1500m, particularly in communities home to the Tamang, Sherpa and other ethnic groups who until relatively recently had not been integrated into rice consumption culture (Sugden et al., 2018). This shift in consumption is taking place at the expense of millet and maize, which had historically been the staple, along with potatoes in the higher altitude villages.

The decline in many of these rainfed coarse grains, which are otherwise more drought tolerant and nutritious than rice and wheat, echoes a trend across South Asia, whereby rice is associated with caste status and Hindu identity (DeFries et al., 2018, Finnis, 2008). In the case of Bhojpur in the eastern hills, this cultural shift, while likely established for decades, has been accelerated following road expansion and greater integration into the market, which has meant lowland rice is easily available for purchase. Migration and the tendency for individuals to spend longer in Kathmandu and other parts of the country has also served to increase upper altitude communities' integration into the national food culture (Sugden et al., 2018). Even villages within the rice growing zone are experiencing change. Uprety (2021) makes reference to a village in Panchatar, which had self-sufficiency in food 25 years ago, yet today is importing white rice from India as maize and millet production decline. Campbell (2018), with regards to Rasuwa, suggests that crops such as millet are also being abandoned due to the poor cash value it offers. While farmers produce for subsistence, a greater awareness of the costs of production versus the market value of the final product if purchased outside, have disincentivised production.

This shift is reflected in national data. An important rainfed coarse grain, maize, has declined over the last ten years by 12%. Another two rainfed coarse grains, millet and buckwheat which were, along with maize, once the staple of many Adivasi communities in the hills, today form a marginal share of the cultivated area (see Table 14), with just an estimated 265,401ha under millet and 13,875ha under buckwheat. Production of both has declined along with the decline in shifting cultivation and shifts in food habits towards rice consumption (Sugden et al., 2018). Millet has declined by 19% over the last decade, buckwheat by an astonishing 40% and barley by 35% (Table 15). Nevertheless, there are likely local variations to these trends. Gautam (2019), in his critique of the 'dependency' narrative in Karnali, suggests that in spite of several decades of food aid

Table 14: Area, Production and Yield by Major Cereal Crops in the Last Ten Years

Year	Paddy			Maize			Millet		
	Area	Production	Yield	Area	Production	Yield	Area	Production	Yield
2011/12	1,531,493	5,072,248	3.31	871,387	2,179,414	2.50	278,030	315,067	1.13
2012/13	1,420,570	4,504,503	3.17	849,635	1,999,010	2.35	274,350	305,588	1.11
2013/14	1,486,951	5,047,047	3.39	928,761	2,283,222	2.46	271,183	304,105	1.12
2014/15	1,425,346	4,788,612	3.36	882,395	2,145,291	2.43	268,050	308,488	1.15
2015/16	1,362,908	4,299,079	3.15	891,583	2,231,517	2.50	266,799	302,397	1.13
2016/17	1,552,469	5,230,327	3.37	900,288	2,300,121	2.55	263,596	306,704	1.16
2017/18	1,469,545	5,151,925	3.51	954,158	2,555,847	2.68	263,497	313,987	1.19
2018/19	1491,744	5,610,011	3.76	956,447	2,713,635	2.84	263,261	314,225	1.19
2019/20	1,458,915	5,550,878	3.80	957,650	2,835,674	2.96	262,547	320,953	1.22
2020/21	1,473,474	5,621,710	3.82	979,776	2,997,773	3.06	265,401	326,443	1.23

Year	Buckwheat			Wheat			Barley		
	Area	Production	Yield	Area	Production	Yield	Area	Production	Yield
2011/12	10,339	10,021	0.97	765,317	1,846,142	2.41	27,966	34,830	1.25
2012/13	10,681	10,056	0.94	759,843	1,882,220	2.48	28,989	36,973	1.28
2013/14	10,510	10,335	0.98	754,474	1,883,147	2.50	28,173	34,824	1.24
2014/15	10,819	10,870	1.01	762,373	1,957,625	2.59	28,053	37,354	1.33
2015/16	11,842	11,641	1.07	745,823	1,736,849	2.33	28,361	32,801	1.16
2016/17	11,090	12,039	1.09	735,850	1,879,191	2.55	27,370	30,510	1.11
2017/18	10,296	11,472	1.11	706,843	1,949,001	2.76	24,648	30,510	1.24
2018/19	10,311	11,464	1.11	703,992	2,005,665	2.85	24,409	30,550	1.25
2019/20	10,369	11,724	1.13	707,505	2,185,289	3.09	24,404	31,147	1.28
2020/21	13,875	15,917	1.15	711,067	2,127,276	2.99	21,862	29,433	1.35

Source: (Ministry of Agriculture and Livestock, 2022: Table 1.1: Area, Production, and Yield of Major Cereal Crops; Last Ten Years, p. 12)

(primarily white rice) being distributed by the World Food Programme, communities still depend disproportionately on coarse grains such as millet, barley and buckwheat. He notes that rice represents just 27% of cereals consumed in the spring and 33% in the autumn. Thus, it is unlikely that the change has been universal across all areas.

In term of other rainfed crops, upland rice or *ghaiya dhan* is still cultivated on rainfed bari lands, particularly in western Nepal. While this is a climate resilient crop, yields are lower than wet rice (paddy) (Sapkota, 2017). Limited data is available on rates of change of this crop.

Interestingly, Table 15 points to a notable decline in major cereal crops over the last decade also such as paddy and wheat. This is likely due to the increase in cultivation of cash crops, although there may be other factors such as the lack of irrigation which is making winter wheat cultivation more challenging (Sugden et al., 2014a). Notwithstanding the changes in the area cultivated the productivity of these major crops has remained almost the same, meaning with the decrease of the area cultivated, the production also decreases; and consequently, the food security situation becomes more precarious.

Table 15: Decrease of the area under the different crops compared to the last ten years: 2011-2021:

Crops	Change in area under cultivation
Cereal Crops	Decreased by 9 %
Paddy	Decreased by 6%
Wheat	Decreased by 6%
Maize	Decrease by 12 %
Millet	Decreased by 19 %
Barley	Decreased by 35
Buckwheat	Decreased by 40 %
Pulses	Decreased by 21 %
Mustard	Increased by 13 %
Potato	Increased by 20%
Other Cash Crops	Increased by 12 %
Species	Increased by 7 %
Vegetables	Increased by 41 %

Source: Ministry of Agriculture and Livestock Development (2022)

Cash crops and commercial production

Market integration has increased across the hills and as noted above there has been a 12% increase in other cash crop production between 2011-2021. Important crops include oilseeds (which are estimated to be cultivated on 259,101ha as of 2020/21), potato, sugarcane, jute and cotton (see Table 16). There are also a number of more localised niche crops such as chiraito, cardamom (see Figure 37), and walnuts (Chataut, 2017, KC et al., 2016). However, as noted above, while such crops can be profitable and have facilitated some levels of differentiation and accumulation, it by no means has contributed to the emergence of capitalist social relations in agriculture, or so called 'petty commodity production, whereby farmers are fully integrated into the market.

Perishable cash crops such as vegetables have brought considerable cash income to communities newly linked to road networks. There has been a 41% increase in vegetable production and 20% increase in potato production – both of which are produced extensively for the market. So

Figure 37: Cardamom processing in Bhojpur
Photo: Fraser Sugden

called 'off season' production whereby hill farmers can sell 'winter' vegetables in the Indian market in the monsoon can be profitable and have supported a local level transformation in livelihoods in some areas with notable accumulation of wealth amongst some farmers, as shown in a case study from Dhankuta (Sugden, 2004, Gahatraj et al., 2019).

Importantly, though the opportunities for accumulation are limited to certain niche crops and are restricted to farmers with land and capital. Commercial production is by no means sufficient to reduce the tendency for out migration for poorer farmers (Gupta et al 2022).

Even for the more successful farmers, the risks are high, especially in the context of climate stress, unpredictable global markets and weak agricultural infrastructure, including extension services and irrigation. There are many examples of commercial crops which are experiencing declining yields or poor market conditions. For example, mandarin production, which was heavily promoted in the APP and ADS for the middle altitudes between 1000m and 1500m has declined notably over the last decade – with production falling from 11.2 metric tons per ha in 2011 to 8.8 in 2014 (Pun, 2018). A study in Parbat by Pun (2018) blames the decline on poor orchard management, pest infestations and inadequate use of manure. Off season vegetable production has been mired by the indiscriminate use of broad spectrum pesticides, with studies showing high levels of residue on crops, carrying significant public health hazards for urban consumers (Tiwari et al., 2008). Cardamom yields have struggled due to disease, worsened by climate change and lack of irrigation (Sugden et al., 2018, Pun, 2018). Blaming increased pest infestations and disease brought about by climatic change, and Rijal's (2013) study from Panchtar found that yields declined from 0.60 metric tons/ha in 2006/7 to 0.42 in 2011/12. The market for other niche crops such as rudraksha, have collapsed in recent years due to falling demand from China (Gupta et al 2022).

The limited scope for accumulation through commercial production, other than climate stress and market fluctuations, also has deeper structural reasons. Lenin's theory of the development of capitalism suggests that the creation of a 'home market' for agricultural goods is central to the development of capitalist commercial agriculture. However this is limited in peripheral contexts when growth is in sectors catering to the urban elite such as construction or the service sector, leading to a disarticulated pattern of development (Lerche, 2013). In Nepal, industry is heavily oriented to agro-processing and has struggled for decades[7].

The most recent agricultural census suggests that consumer non-durable goods represent 60.5% of the value added, with 47.1% being derived from food, beverages and tobacco (Central Bureau of Statistics, 2012). Even despite this and somewhat paradoxically, a large share of processed agricultural products which are consumed by the urban middle class were still being imported from India or elsewhere due to the difficulties of farmers competing with producers in the south (Simkhada, 2020). Evidence of this challenge is the failure of the jute industry in Morang and Sunsari, which has in turn influenced farmer decisions to cultivate the once lucrative crop. As noted above, jute production has been dropping in recent years, due to power shortages or energy costs and the failure to compete with goods imported from India. The removal of government subsidies for electricity for industries and Nepal's power shortages had made it impossible for local industries to compete with Indian and Bangladeshi products, and five out of 11 jute mills in Nepal had closed[8].

Table 16: Area under cultivation of cash crops

Crops	2018/19		2019/20		2020/21	
	Area (ha)	Production (mt)	Area (ha)	Production (mt)	Area (ha)	Production (mt)
Oilseeds	260,307	280,530	258,141	278,325	259,101	287,038
Potato	193,997	3,112,947	188,098	3,131,830	198,788	3,325,231
Sugarcane	71,624	3,557,934	68,565	3,400,176	64,354	3,183,943
Jute	7,285	10,585	7,555	10,165	7,415	10,451
Cotton	97	99	135	140	142	147

---

[7] Industrial production as a share of GDP has declined from 9.29% in 2000/21 to just 6.65% in 2018/18 (Khatri, 2018).

[8] See report in Kathmandu post, Sep 22, 2014. Demand drop leaves jute industry in doldrums and Gorakhpatra article, Aug 24th 2014, Jute industries in eastern region in crisis.

Irrigation expansion, agricultural intensification and climate stress

In the context of growing climate stress, access to irrigation has been critical for farmers to adapt to climate change, as well as being important for farmers to intensify production, enhance food security and where possible increase the saleable surplus. Indeed lack of irrigation has been responsible for the poor performance of many cash crops such as cardamom (Pun, 2018) and mandarin (Prasad and Chandra, 2019). Lack of irrigation has also been one of the primary factors driving food insecurity amongst marginal farmers in the Tarai-Madhesh, already struggling due to the rent burden and rising cash demands. It increases their vulnerability to drought, while impeding the intensification of production during the dry months to make up for small and dwindling holdings (Sugden, 2014, Sugden et al., 2014a).

Only 1.4million ha of agricultural land are irrigated out of the 2.7millon ha of agricultural land in the country (Pradhan and Belbase, 2018), and rivers still provide the primary water source (see Table 17). Since the 1990s, the construction of new large canal systems has been limited, and the focus of the government with regards to surface water irrigation, has been on the revitalisation of the old agency managed systems in the Tarai-Madhesh and modernisation of the farmer managed systems in the hills, including reforms to the management institutions (Pradhan and Belbase, 2018). Table 18 suggests that out of surface water schemes, while farmer managed irrigation systems are predominant in the hills, agency managed schemes remain more common in the Tarai-Madhesh.

Table 17: Sources of irrigation in Nepal

Sources	%
River/ponds/lakes	48
Tube-well/boring	30
Dam/reservoir	16
Others	4
Mixed	2

(Department of Water Resources and Irrigation, 2019)

Table 18 Surface water irrigation coverage

	Farmer managed	Jointly managed	Agency managed
Tarai-Madhesh	240,213ha	350,926ha	367,222ha
Hills/Mountains	131,181ha	6127ha	NA

(Department of Water Resources and Irrigation, 2019)

In terms of the trajectory of change however, this has been positive. The Agricultural Perspective Plan had anticipated that year round irrigation would increase from 459,000ha in 1994/95 to 1.13 million in 2014/15. These targets were nearly met, with 1.227 million ha irrigated by the end of the plan period, suggesting that there has been some success in increasing the irrigated area (Ministry of Agricultural Development, 2015).

However, whether this increase in the area under irrigation accounts for the falling yields of water due to climate change is not clear, and many of the areas of the hills with high water stress are far beyond the command area of surface irrigation schemes, creating the need for smaller scale solutions such as micro-irrigation and pond storage (Sugden et al., 2014b). Furthermore, many of the larger schemes in the Tarai-Madhesh built during the Panchayat era such as the Sunsari-Morang Irrigation System are falling into disrepair or experiencing high sedimentation or unauthorised extraction of water. This is due to a combination of factors including poorly-functioning and politicised WUAs, a disinterest by absentee landlords who own large areas of the command area, combined with an exclusion of tenants from management committees (Valadaud, 2023).

It was groundwater irrigation where most of the policy focus in the Tarai-Madhesh has been centred. The APP had anticipated that there would be 516,000ha under groundwater irrigation by 2014/15, although the target of only 363,000ha was reached. Shallow tubewells, which are small scale investments possible by farmers themselves, made up 318,000ha of the area under groundwater irrigation and deep tuebwells, which generally require government investment, made up 45,000ha (Ministry of Agricultural Development, 2015). The failure to meet targets was officially put down to limited donor investment in irrigation, the conflict, the restructuring of Agricultural Development Bank which reduced its support for irrigation, and the removal of irrigation subsidies (Ministry of Agricultural Development, 2015).

The removal of irrigation subsidies was in part an outcome of economic liberalisation as they were removed following Asian Development Bank pressure as conditions attached to the 1998 Second Agricultural Program Loan (SAPL) (Deraniyagala et al., 2003), although it could be argued that more broadly the shift in emphasis towards groundwater irrigation itself was conducive to the shift towards neoliberal development thinking. The large scale agency managed investments in irrigation canals which were described above, came at a time of higher public spending and centralised planning. The shift towards groundwater was indeed a necessary move in the context of climate stress and underutilisation of existing resources – particularly when vast areas were beyond the command of major river systems. However, with limited subsidies, it was dependent not on state led provision of public goods but private investment by farmers.

This was also in line with neoliberalism which emphasised individual responsibility and investment by farmers to 'lift' themselves out of poverty. It is against this context, that Nepal's existing agrarian structure, particularly in the Tarai-Madhesh, was likely critical in shaping the slower than expected uptake of groundwater irrigation. While the expansion of groundwater irrigation has likely supported an increase in cropping intensity in some locales (see Table 13), access to groundwater remains highly unequal (Sugden, 2014).

Access to shallow tubewells is largely dependent upon one's position in the agrarian structure (Sugden et al., 2014a, Sugden et al., 2015). Firstly, the cost of investing in a pump set and tubewell is high, and is often unfeasible for marginal farmers with only small and fragmented plots of land. Secondly, for the vast number of farmers working as tenants, lack of land ownership and tenure insecurity was an impediment to investment, as they had few incentives to spend money on land which they could have to leave at any time. Various subsidy schemes were later introduced in the 2010s under the purview of the Groundwater Resources Development Board, whereby tubewells would be provided to water user groups (Mccarl, 2013, Sugden, 2014). However, these often required complex paperwork, information was poorly disseminated, and the process of forming a group of willing farmers with land in a contiguous area was often challenging. They were also mostly out of reach for tenants as they required the landowner to apply (Ibid.).

Groundwater markets, whereby farmers rent pump sets and tubewells, have been important in this context for marginal and tenant farmers to access irrigation - although the costs are also high. In spite of the expansion of electrification infrastructure and improved power supply, a large number of farmers still depend on diesel for groundwater irrigation – which have high operating costs, not helped by the use of inefficient and outdated models of pump (Foster et al., 2021). Furthermore, renting a pump is considerably more expensive than operating one's own equipment, as the hourly fee includes not only increasingly costly diesel, but a 'rent' for the owner of the equipment. A study from Morang and Dhanusha showed that pricing was arbitrary, and dependent on one's bargaining power and the level of competition in the groundwater market (Sugden, 2014). Another study by Bhandari and Pandey (2006) from Sarlahi and Banke in the western Tarai-Madhesh noted that the average yield of shallow tube well owners was 25% higher than those who rent wells, and 86% higher than rainfed farmers. Groundwater 'buyers' often receive irrigation water from a well only after the owner has irrigated his or her land. The tube well owner has greater control over where they can irrigate their land, and thus can benefit from a greater quality and quantity of irrigation water, unlike their counterparts who rent wells. These barriers to accessing irrigation in the Tarai-Madhesh mean that marginal and tenant farmers are consistently the most vulnerable to climate stress (Sugden et al., 2014a).

In the hills, where farmers are largely dependent upon surface water irrigation – farmer managed systems continue to play a crucial role in remote communities. These systems are however, themselves vulnerable to climate change, including flood related damage and increased evapotranspiration (Thapa et al., 2016). Furthermore, there is a consistent geography of inequality within the hills – whereby most irrigation is confined to the middle agro-ecological rice growing zone. The farmers living above this zone have weaker livelihoods, and are far more vulnerable to climate stress. As noted in earlier parts of this book, in central and Eastern Nepal in particular, this aligns strongly with ethnic-caste divisions. The legacy of the Gorkha expansion and the dissolution of customary tenure mean that Brahmin and Chettri farmers have taken control of a disproportionate share of this irrigated land. Particular groups such as the Tamang in Eastern Nepal for instance, are dependent disproportionately on rainfed agriculture, which is most likely to be unirrigated and the most vulnerable to climate stress (Sugden et al., 2018).

Conclusions: Learning from the past to shape the future

Throughout Nepal's agrarian history, the pattern of change has been incremental rather than transformative – earlier modes of production have gradually evolved in the context of political interventions by the state, shifting external economic imperatives, as well as struggles over resources and ecological stress. It is for this reason that the successes and failures of contemporary agricultural development initiatives and strategies – including the potential future trajectories of change, can be much better understood by meaningfully engaging with history.

The importance of land

An important overarching lesson when one considers how history has shaped the trajectory of agricultural change in Nepal as a whole, is the critical role played by control over land in shaping the lived reality for Nepal's peasantry – both historically and today. It is important to look beyond simply the distribution of land, but also consider the different relationships between the people and the land under historical and present modes of production – including those which are both cultural and political. One of the most fundamental divergences in Nepal's agrarian history has been between two very different relationships between people and the land. The first is a communally oriented and customary relationship between people and the land. The second is a relationship grounded in legalised individual proprietorship – via either feudal titles to holdings which belong ultimately to the crown, or the de facto 'private' property rights which had become prevalent by the 20th century. The expansion of the latter has been fundamentally linked with the historic expansion of various state formations over the last few centuries.

This divergence between these two relationships towards land has fostered quite different agrarian systems. The prevalence of customary communal tenure historically supported cropping systems oriented around shifting cultivation, transhumant agro-pastoralism, and a relatively equitable distribution of resources which has been central to the so-called Adivasi mode of production. This went alongside the extensive rather than intensive use of land, and the production of rainfed coarse grains in particular, which were often of ritual significance for Adivasi groups.

By contrast, legalised individual ownership has been intricately connected with both independent peasant and feudal modes of production, oriented around sedentary agriculture, particularly of paddy, and is associated with caste Hindu society. The centralised state has also historically played a key part in mediating this relationship between land and society and the historical analysis in this book has demonstrated the inseparable link between land and political power since the Gorkha conquest – with feudalism and sedentary 'owner cultivation' expanding alongside the state itself. Central to this process has been the imposition of a succession of more efficient tax collecting bureaucracies, as well as the use of land bestowments to elites to support the state building process.

The replacement of the first relationship towards land with the second parallels the demise of the Adivasi mode of production. This has occurred in waves over the last millennia. The first wave took place in the western hills with the Sanskritisation and feudalisation of Khas society during the Middle Ages. The second took place in the wake of an expanding centralised state and westward migration of Hindu castes following the Gorkha conquest, which contributed to the dissolution of communal tenure and shifting cultivation, alongside intensified internal stratification amongst the Adivasi groups of the Tarai, eastern and central hills.

Why one may ask, are these complex yet fundamental processes important to understanding the contemporary agrarian system and trajectory of change? Importantly, they offer a more nuanced understanding of contemporary inequalities. Firstly, in the hills, the dissolution of the Adivasi mode of production has contributed to the spatial and geographical inequality in the distribution of resources, with the best irrigable land still disproportionately held by Nepali speaking upper castes. It has been shown that today this continues to shape agricultural investment opportunities, climate change vulnerability and out-migration patterns. The dissolution of the Adivasi mode of production in the hills also has more complex outcomes. It helps explain the continuing cultural devaluation of indigenous coarse grains which are resilient to drought, rich in micronutrients, and require fewer inputs than a wheat-rice cropping system (Adhikari, 2008).

Secondly, within the more fertile paddy growing lands of the Tarai as well as parts of the western, central and eastern hills – there are still landlord-tenant relations and persisting 'feudal' landlordism. These have their origin not only in the subjugation of Adivasi groups such as the Tharu, but in the process of historic state building – whereby land grants and the propping up of local elites to collect tax, were central to the consolidation of the political power of the centre. The life opportunities of Nepal's landless or those who are functionally landless – a large share of whom are in the plains, are directly shaped by this history. Tenure insecurity plays a fundamental role in shaping these farmers' capacity to maintain a sustainable livelihood, adopt new technologies, access irrigation or adapt to climate stress. Importantly though, the entrenched link between land and political power which itself established feudalism in Nepal, continues to set the limit as to what is possible in terms of meaningful land reforms. Several land reform efforts, particularly in the last seven decades, have failed in implementation and delivery as they had promised. Existing power structure and the landed class' hold in politics might be singled out as a major factor for those failures. Added to this are the faulty policy design and implementation strategies, with subsequent reforms rarely learning from the previous failures. Hence, the reform initiatives and the period plans were not adequately informed by past experiences.

The relationship between the spatial and temporal

Another way in which history matters in agricultural development in Nepal is with regards to the intersection between the spatial and temporal. Today, the regional diversity in modes of production and food production systems across Nepal are shaped by a complex series of economic, political, cultural and ecological layers which vary across space. These layers are however shaped by unique and spatially bound histories.

These include firstly, the influence of historical state formations on particular regions, including the interaction between the state and Nepal's ethnically diverse peasantry. The historical influence of the Gorkhali expansion in the late 18th century cannot be understated. While there were local differences in the land tenure system throughout the 18th and 19th century as the Gorkhali rulers inherited older systems of land administration from earlier rulers, this study has shown how these differences became less acute in later years, particularly following the declining significance of land tax in the early 20th century and the 1964 land reforms – which consolidated *raikar* as the primary form of land tenure and regularised land administration across the country. However, the locally specific history of encounters between the state and culturally and economically unique agrarian formations in particular agro-ecological domains, have been critical in shaping the mode of production and the trajectory of change at a local level.

For instance, the *kipat* system of communal tenure emerged from efforts by the Gorkhali conquerors to integrate the Adivasi clan leaders (particularly in the Kirat region of the east) within the state bureaucratic alliance and legitimise rule from Kathmandu, particularly in remoter regions which were more difficult to govern directly. The preservation of this tenure allowed Adivasi modes of production to persist far longer in the east of the country than elsewhere – although it also paved the way for widespread dispossession once the tenure was dissolved. In the central hills, the proximity to the centre of state power in Kathmandu, the state sanctioned caste system, and the importance of this region for Rana era forced labour extraction, also sheds light on the much long history of marginalisation experienced by the Tamang, who experienced alienation from the most fertile paddy lands and a high level of political marginalisation. At the same time, Adivasi communities in the more isolated domains in the higher hills, which yielded limited revenue for the state (e.g. because they were beyond the paddy growing zone) and where the land to population ratio was more favourable – were able to experience relative autonomy for much longer.

Likewise, during the Rana era, the economic value placed upon the Tarai and its fertile low-lying agricultural land and forest as a source of revenue by the state as well as its value as a source of land grants for the political elite, explains why it emerged as the heartland of feudalism in Nepal. By contrast, the lower productivity land of the hills mean that landlord-tenant relations are less prevalent – although the history of dispossession outlined above mean that there are clear inequalities in the distribution of land within the farming population, particularly with regards to the Adivasi peasantry – as noted above.

Another way in which spatially bound histories help explain the locally specific agricultural outcomes are with regards to the struggles over resources which emerge when communities living in particular agro-ecological domains are joined by waves of migrants, who bring with them new technologies and crops, and often entirely new modes of production at a localised level. One of the most notable encounters occurred with the westward migration of Khas communities between the 16th and 19th century, who brought with them paddy cultivation, terraced agriculture and a sedentary peasant mode of production. These movements also have driven changes in food cultures over time, with coarse grains gradually being replaced with rice and wheat. As noted above however, in some domains this cross-cultural encounter was not always equal, particularly in the east.

A second wave of migration was the large-scale movement from the hills to the plains after the 1960s. This paved the way for the creation of an entirely new mode of production free from the remnants of feudalism – whereby settlers acquired their own land, and could retain all of the agricultural surplus. It is for this reason, that there is a clear spatial divide today within the Tarai-Madhesh between the settler belt (largely to the north) and the areas which were already settled and subject to the *jimidari* and *birta* system. To this day as a result, the latter regions still experience high levels of landlessness and tenancy. The settler belt includes some of the most agriculturally dynamic parts of Nepal, with high levels of cash crop production and evidence of accumulation, while the longer settled domains experience high levels of food insecurity due to the feudal rent burden and small, fragmented holdings, as well as more limited cropping diversity. It has been shown however, that at the frontier of these two economic systems there have been locally unique axes of inequality between settlers and the Adivasi population of the plains. These include areas such as parts of Chitwan, the Dang valley, Bardiya, and the parts of the far eastern plains. Adivasi communities who resided in these remote, forested locales, who had been able to retain relative autonomy from the state during earlier eras, and lacked a concept of land ownership, were quick to be dispossessed following the state supported clearing of the forest frontier by hill settlers. As a consequence, there is a clear ethnic disparity in the distribution of land, and the persistence of various forms of bonded labour.

Policy questions

What do these lessons on the importance of history mean for agricultural policy in Nepal today? The recent National Land Policy (2019), Land Use Policy (2015), and the Land Use Act (2019) had lofty objectives to address long-standing issues like tenure security, access to land, proper land use planning, standardizing the land valuation, taxation, and land market, and for the modernization of land administration. These are collective challenges which, as noted above, play a critical role in shaping the agricultural development trajectory, both nationally, but also in shaping regionally diverse outcomes. However, these policies have failed to identify why the past efforts with similar objectives failed – with all previous land reform efforts serving the interests of landlords rather than tenants – a reality with deep historic roots. Contemporary policy around land lacks any truly transformative agenda such as the redistribution of land and assets.

In terms of agricultural policies beyond those concerning land, the Agricultural Perspective Plan (APP), pursued market led growth yet was a failure in many ways. It neglected the structural inequities rooted in land ownership, and historic state-Adivasi relations, which have consistently shaped the localised investment opportunities for farmers in Nepal's diverse agro-ecological zones. A follow-up to it, the Agricultural Development Strategies, ADS (2015-2035) was drafted with the overall objectives of poverty reduction, increasing food and nutrition security, and strengthening farmers' rights, among others. But as discussed above, it has already fallen short of its objectives. One of the major reasons is again, its failure to learn from past experiences. There is also a lack of orchestration between different policy documents. For example, 'food sovereignty' is included as a fundamental right in the constitution of Nepal, 2015, but it is neither reflected in the National Land Policy, nor in the ADS.

Just as the past has shaped the present, envisioning the future of land and agri-food systems depends on how contemporary political actors learn from the failures of the past and address deep seated inequalities through inclusive policies and measures - including genuine redistributive land reform. Until then, equitable redistribution of resources, inclusive growth, and poverty reduction in the future may not be attainable.

References

Acharya, B., 1973. Annexation of the Sen Kingdoms. *Regmi Research Series,* 5, 81-85.

Adams, N., 2010. *The Seed and the Shaman: Encountering diversity in development indigenous Knowledge Production among the Lohorung Rai of Eastern Nepal.* MSc Thesis, Lund University.

Adhikari, B., 2010. *Sharecropping System in Mid-West Tarai. A case study of Gobardiha VDC of Dangdeukhuri district, Nepal.* Master's Thesis, the University of Bergen.

Adhikari, J., 2006. *Land Reform in Nepal: Problems and prospects.* Kathmandu: Nepal Institute of Development Studies.

Adhikari, J., 2008. *Food Crisis in Karnali Zone: A historical and politico-economic perspective.* Kathmandu: Martin Chautari

Adhikari, J., 2011. Contentions and Prospects of Land Reform in Nepal: A historical review. *New Angle: Nepal Journal of Social Science and Public Policy,* 1, 17-31.

Adhikari, J., 2014. Seed Sovereignty: Analysing the debate on hybrid seeds and GMOs and bringing about sustainability in agricultural development. *Journal of Forest and Livelihood,* 12, 33-46.

Adhikari, J. & Hobley, M., 2011. *Everyone is leaving–who will sow our fields? The effects of migration from Khotang District to the Gulf and Malaysia.* Kathmandu: Swiss Agency for Development and Cooperation and Helvetas.

Adhikari, K. P. & Gellner, D. N., 2016. New Identity Politics and the 2012 Collapse of Nepal's Constituent Assembly: When the dominant becomes 'other'. *Modern Asian Studies,* 50, 2009-2040.

Adhikari, S. M., 1988. *The Khasa Kingdom: A Trans-Himalayan Empire of the Middle Age.* New Delhi: Nirala Publication.

Adhikari, S., Gurung, A., Chauhan, R., Rijal, D., Dongol, B. S., Aryal, D. & Talchabhadel, R., 2021. Status of Springs in Mountain Watershed of Western Nepal. *Water Policy,* 23, 142-156.

Agarwal, B. and Sharma, P., 2012. An Idea to Bank On: Innovative solutions can link land demand with supply in a way that protects farmers. *The Times of India.* January 12th, 2012.

Alden-Wily, L., Chapgain, D. & Sharma, S., 2008. *Land Reform in Nepal: Where is it coming from and where is it going?* Kathmandu: DFID.

Althusser, L 1969. *For Marx.* London: Verso.

Althusser, L. & Balibar, E., 1968. *Reading Capital.* London: Redwood Burn Ltd.

Aubriot, O., 2004. Irrigation History in Central Nepal: The interface between agriculture and technology. *Water Nepal,* 11, 19-43.

Aubriot, O. & Bruslé, T., 2023. Agrarian Changes in the Nepalese Lowlands: Local actors and the state. *European Bulletin of Himalayan Research,* 60, 1-23.

Bajracharya, D. & Shrestha, T. B., 1974. *Historical Outline of Dolakha.* Kathmandu: Institute of Nepal and Asian Studies, Tribhuvan University (translated in Regmi Research Series, 1981, 13, 3).

Banerjee, A. V., Gertler, P. J. & G., M., 2002. Empowerment and Efficiency: Tenancy reform in West Bengal. *Journal of Political Economy,* 110, 239-280.

Basnet, J., 2018. Marginalisation of Tenants in Nepal. *In:* Uprety, L. P., Dhakal, S. & Basnet, J. (eds.) *Peasant Studies in Nepal.* New York: Vajra Books Inc.

Beine, D., 2012. An Investigative Look at Healthcare Beliefs and Practices During the Sen Dynasty. *Dhaulagiri Journal of Sociology and Anthropology,* 6, 61-74.

Bennet, L., 1981. The Parbatiya Women of Bakundol. *The Status of Women in Nepal 2 (7)*. Kathmandu: Centre for Economic Development and Administration, Tribhuvan University.

Bernstein, H., 1977. Notes on Capital and Peasantry. *Review of African political economy,* 4, 60-73.

Beteille, A., 1980. On the Concept of Tribe. *International Social Science Journal,* 32, 825-28.

Bhaduri, A., 1973. A Study in Agricultural Backwardness Under Semi-Feudalism. *The Economic Journal,* 83, 120-137.

Bhaduri, A., 1977. On The Formation of Usurious Interest Rates in Backward Agriculture. *Cambridge Journal of Economics,* 1, 341-352.

Bhandari, H. & Pandey, S., 2006. Economics of Groundwater Irrigation in Nepal: Some farm-level evidences. *Journal of Agricultural and Applied Economics,* 38, 185-199.

Bhandari, P. & Ghimire, D., 2016. Rural Agricultural Change and Individual Out-migration. *Rural Sociology,* 81, 572-600.

Bhandari, R., 2006. Searching for a Weapon of Mass Production in Nepal: Can market-assisted land reforms live up to their promise? *Journal of Developing Societies,* 22, 111-143.

Bhatt, D., Maskey, S. B., Mukand S., Uhlenbrook, S. & Prasad, K. C., 2014. Climate Trends and Impacts on Crop Production in the Koshi River Basin of Nepal. *Regional Environmental Change,* 14, 1291-1301.

Bhattarai, B. R., 2003a. *The Nature of Underdevelopment and Regional Structure of Nepal: A Marxist Analysis.* New *Delhi*: Adroit.

Bhattarai, B. R., 2003b. The Political Economy of the People's war. *In:* Karki, A. & Seddon, D. (eds.) *The People's War in Nepal: Left perspectives.* New Delhi: Adroit.

Biggs, S., Justice, S. & Lewis, D., 2011. Patterns of Rural Mechanisation, Energy and Employment in South Asia: Reopening the debate. *Economic and Political Weekly*, 78-82.

Bishop, B. C., 1978. The Changing Geoecology of Karnali Zone, Western Nepal Himalaya: A case of stress. *Arctic and Alpine Research,* 10, 531-548.

Bishop, N. H., 1989. From Zomo to Yak: Change in a Sherpa village. *Human Ecology*, 17, 177-204.

Bista, D. B., 1991. *Fatalism and Development: Nepal's struggle for modernization*. Orient Blackswan.

Blaikie, P., Cameron, J. & Seddon, D., 2001. *Nepal in Crisis: Growth and stagnation at the periphery, Revised and Enlarged Edition*. New Delhi: Adroit Publishers.

Blaikie, P., Cameron, J., & Seddon, D., 2002a. *Peasants and Workers in Nepal*. New Delhi: Adroit Publishers.

Blaikie, P, Cameron, J. & Seddon, D., 2002b. Understanding 20 Years of Change in West-Central Nepal: Continuity and change in lives and ideas. *World Development*, 30, 1255-1270.

Boivin, N., Fuller, D. Q. & Crowther, A., 2012. Old World Globalization and the Columbian Exchange: Comparison and contrast. *World Archaeology*, 44, 452-469.

Bouillier, V., 1993. The Nepalese State and Gorakhnathi Yogis: The case of the former kingdoms of Dang Valley, 18-19th Centuries. *Contributions to Nepalese Studies*, 20, 29-52.

Burghart, R., 2016. *The History of Janakpurdham: A Study of asceticism and the Hindu polity*. Kathmandu: Himal Books.

Burghart, R., 1978. The Disappearance and Reappearance of Janakpur. *Kailash: A Journal of Himalayan Studies, 6 (4), 257-284*

Byres, T. J., 1981. The New Technology, Class Formation and Class Action in The Indian Countryside. *The Journal of Peasant Studies*, 8, 405-454.

Cameron, J., 1998. The Agricultural Perspective Plan: The need for debate. *Himalayan Research Bulletin*, 18, 11-14.

Cameron, J., Pandey, P., & Wagle, B. K., 2016. Assessing the Impact of The Agriculture Perspective Plan (1995 to 2015): The Maoist insurgency on rural lives in Nepal and reflections on the current Agricultural Development Strategy. *New Angle: Nepal Journal of Social Science and Public Policy*, 4, 19-43.

Cameron, M., 1998. *On the Edge of the Auspicious: Gender and caste in Nepal.* Kathmandu: Mandala Publications, University of Illinois Press.

Campbell, A., 1841. Letter from A. Campbell to Hodgson relating to the Nepal Tarai 08-23-1841 *Hodgson Collection, British Library, London,* vol.14 folio 79-81.

Campbell, A. (circa 1830s). Route to Kathmandu and to Frontier forts and military stations. *Hodgson Collection, British Library,* vol2, folio 3-30

Campbell, B., 2018. Moral Ecologies of Subsistence and Labour in a Migration-Affected Community of Nepal. *Journal of the Royal Anthropological Institute,* 24, 151-165.

Campbell, J. G., 1978. *Consultations with Himalayan Gods: A Study of oracular religion and alternative values in Hindu Jumla.* New York: Columbia University.

Caplan, L., 1970. *Land and Social Change in East Nepal: A Study of Hindu-tribal relations.* California: University of California Press.

CDD and ASoN, 2017. Rice, Science and Technology in Nepal (A historical, socio-cultural and technical compendium). Kathmandu: Crop Development Directorate.

Central Bureau of Statistics (CBS), 1996. *Nepal Living Standards Measurement Survey, 1995/1996.* Kathmandu: Government of Nepal.

Central Bureau of Statistics (CBS), 2011a. *Nepal Living Standards Measurement Survey, 2010-11.* Kathmandu: Government of Nepal

Central Bureau of Statistics (CBS), 2011b. *Nepal Population Census 2011.* Kathmandu: Government of Nepal.

Central Bureau of Statistics (CBS), 2012. *National Census of Manufacturing Establishments-2011/12.* Kathmandu: Government of Nepal.

Chandra, N. K., 1974. Farm Efficiency Under Semi-feudalism: A critique of marginalist theories and some Marxist formulations. *Economic and Political weekly,* 10 (13), 1309-1332.

Chataut, R.D., 2017. Where have the rice varieties gone? *Rice, Science and Technology in Nepal (A historical, socio-cultural and technical compendium)*. Kathmandu: Crop Development Directorate and the Agronomy Society of Nepal.

Chataut, R. D. P. & Chataut, R. L., 2013. बेलाको बोली बखतको इतिहास (Vernacular History/History in simple language?). Kathmandu: Nai Prakashan.

Chaudhary, R. P., Uprety, Y., Acharya, H. R., & Rimal, S. K., 2023. Deforestation in Nepal: Status, causes, consequences, and responses. *In:* Shroder, J. F & Sivanpillia, R, (eds.) *Biological and Environmental Hazards, Risks, and Disasters*, 277-318. Elsevier.

Chaudhuri, A., 1995. *Enclaves in a Peasant Society: Political Economy of Tea in Western Dooars and Northern Bengal.* New Delhi: Peoples Publishing House.

Chaudhury, P. C. R., 1964. *Bihar District Gazetteers: Darbhanga.* Patna: Superintendent Secretariat Press.

Cimino, R. M., 1986. Simraongarh: The forgotton city and its art. *Contributions to Nepalese Studies*, 13, 277-288.

Clement, F., & Sugden, F., 2021. Unheard Vulnerability Discourses from Tarai-Madhesh, Nepal. *Geoforum*, 126, 68-79.

Constitution of Nepal 2015. Government of Nepal. *Translation by Nepal Law Commission*, https://lawcommission.gov.np/en/wp-content/uploads/2021/01/Constitution-of-Nepal.pdf.

Conway, D., Bhattarai, K. & Shrestha, N. R., 2000. Population–Environment Relations at the Forested Frontier of Nepal: Tharu and Pahari survival strategies in Bardiya. *Applied Geography*, 20, 221-242.

CPN UML 2022. प्रतिनिधिसभा तथा प्रदेशसभा निर्वाचन-२०७९ नेपाल कम्युनिस्ट पार्टी (एमाले): घोषणापत्र (*Election Manifesto for the Federal and Provincial Election, 2071 VS*). Communist Party of Nepal (United Marxist-Leninist).

CSRC, 2019. *Federal Parliament Passes the Land Use Act.* Kathmandu: Community Self Reliance Centre (CSRC) .

CSRC, 2021. *Land Bank in Nepal: Is it relevant? Is it required? A position Paper*. Kathmandu: Community Self Reliance Centre.

Dahal, D. R., Rai, N. K. & Mansardo, A. E., 1977. *Land and Migration in Far-western Nepal*. Kathmandu: Institute of Nepal and Asian Studies, Tribhuvan University.

Dahal, D. R., 1981. The Concept of Economy in a Peasant Society: A case study of the Athpahariya Rais in east Nepal. *Contributions to Nepalese Studies*, 8, 55-71.

Dahal, D. R., 1983a. *Poverty or Plenty: Innovative responses to population pressure in an Eastern Nepalese hill community*. PhD Dissertation, University of Hawaii.

Dahal, D. R 1983b. Economic development through indigenous means: a case of Indian migration in the Nepal Terai. *Contributions to Nepalese Studies*, 11, 1-20.

Dahal, K. & Timilsina, K. P., 2021. Analyzing Urban Expansion and Spatial Growth Patterns in Barahathawa Municipality of Central Tarai Region, Nepal. *Journal of Geographical Research*, 4, 1-9.

Dangi, M. B, Schoenberger, E., Boland, J. J. & Chaudhary, R. P., 2021. Quest for Development: An examination of more than a half-century of national planning and foreign aid practice in Nepal. *Sustainable Futures*, 3, 100051.

Darnal, P., 2012. Preliminary Report on Khoksar Excavation in 2061/2062 VS (2004/5 ad). *Ancient Nepal*, 180, 6-40.

Das, B. L., 2014. The Sena Dynasty: From Bengal to Nepal. *Academic Voices: A Multidisciplinary Journal*, 4, 9-16.

Das, B. L. 2016. A Study of the Administrative Posts During the Sena Period in the Kingdom of Makawanpur. *Indian Historical Review*, 43, 1-10.

De Sales, A., 2003. The Kham Magar country: between ethnic claims and Maoism. *In:* Gellner, D. N. (ed.) *Resistance and the state: Nepalese experiences* (326-57). New Delhi: Social Science Press.

Debnath, S., 2010. *The Dooars in Historical Transition*. West Bengal: N.L. Publishers.

DeFries, R., Chhatre, A., Davis, K. F., Dutta, A., Fanzo, J., Ghosh-Jerath, S., Myers, S., Rao, N. D. & Smith, M. R., 2018. Impact of Historical Changes in Coarse Cereals Consumption in India on Micronutrient Intake and Anemia Prevalence. *Food and nutrition bulletin*, 39, pp. 377-392.

Department of Water Resources and Irrigation, 2019. *Irrigation Master Plan 2019*. Kathmandu: Government of Nepal.

Deraniyagala, S., Katiwada, Y., Sharma, S., Roy, R & Deshpande, A., 2003. *Pro-Poor Macro Policies in Nepal*. UNDP: Asia-Pacific Regional Programme on Macroeconomics of Poverty Reduction.

Devine, T. M., 2018. *Clanship to Crofters' War: the social transformation of the Scottish Highlands*. Manchester University Press.

Devkota, D., 2016. Occupational Migration: Challenge poses dependency to agriculture in Nepal. *Nepalese Journal of Agricultural Sciences*, 14, 183-190.

Dhakal, S., 1997. *Shifting Cultivation: Technological and Socio-cultural Context. A case ctudy from Arun valley of eastern Nepal*. MPhil Thesis, University of Bergen.

Dhakal, S., 2000. An Anthropological Perspective on Shifting Cultivation: A Case Study of Khoriya Cultivaton in the Arun Valley of Eastern Nepal. *Occasional Papers in Sociology and Anthropology*, VI.

Dhakal, S., Rai, J., Chemjong, D., Pradhan, P., Maharjan, J. & Chaudhari, S., 2001. *Issues and Experiences: Kamaiiya System, Kanara Andolan and Tharus in Bardiya*. Kathmandu SPACE.

Dhakal, S. 2002. Shifting Cultivation in the Arun Valley: An Anthropological Case Study. In Chaudhary, R. P., Subedi, B. P., Vetaas, O. R. &, T. H. Aase (eds.) V*egetation and Society: Their Interactions in the Himalayas*. Kathmandu: Tribhuvan University, University of Bergen.

Dhakal, S., 2015. Getting Into and Out of Poverty: An exploration of poverty dynamics in eastern Tarai-Madhesh of Nepal. *Studies in Nepali History and Society* 20, 178-201.

Dhakal, S., 2020. Peasant as an Anthropological Category and Ethnographic Subject. *In:* Uprety, L. P., Dhakal, S. & Basnet, J. (eds.) *Peasant Studies in Nepal.* New York: Vajra Books Inc.

Dhakal, S. & Pokharel, S., 2010. Local Movements, Political Processes and Transformation: A case study of Bhaktapur municipality. *Occasional Papers in Sociology and Anthropology,* 11, 178-201.

Dhakal, S., Karki, K. & Shrestha, S., 2020. Harawa-Charawa, the Bonded Laborers in Agriculture: A Study of three municipalities of Dhanusha District in eastern Terai. *Contributions to Nepalese Studies,* 34.

Egli, W. M., 2000. Below the Surface of Private Property: Individual rights, common property, and the Nepalese kipat-system in historical perspective . *European Bulletin of Himalayan Research,* 18, 5-19.

Elder, J. W., Ale, M., Evans, M., Gillespie, D., Nepali, R. K., Poudyal, S. P. & Smith, B. P., 1976. *Planned Resettlement in Nepal's Terai,* Kathmandu: Tribhuvan University Press.

English, R. 1983. *Gorkhali and Kirat: Political Economy in the Eastern Hills of Nepal.* PhD Thesis, New School for Social Research.

Feldman, D & Fournier, A., 1976. Social Relations and Agricultural Production in Nepal's Terai. *Journal of Peasant Studies,* 3, 447-464.

Fillippi, F. D. (ed.), 1937. *An account of Tibet, the travels of Ippolito Desideri of Pistoia, 1712-1727.* London: George Routledge and Sons.

Finnis, E., 2008. Economic Wealth, Food Wealth, and Millet Consumption: Shifting notions of food, identity, and development in South India. *Food, Culture & Society,* 11, 463-485.

Fiscal Nepal, 2023. Government relaxes restrictions on land fragmentation. *Fiscal Nepal,* 19th April 2023, https://www.fiscalnepal.com/2023/04/19/12378/government-relaxes-restrictions-on-land-fragmentation/.

Fitzpatrick, I. C., 2011. *Cardamom and Class: A Limbu Village and Its Extensions in East Nepal.* Kathmandu: Vajra Publications, Cinnabaris-Series of Oriental Studies.

Fortier, J., 1995. *Beyond Jajmani: The complexity of indigenous labor relations in Western Nepal.* PhD Dissertation, University of Wisconsin, Madison.

Foster, T., Adhikari, R., Adhikari, S., Justice, S., Tiwari, B., Urfels, A., & Krupnik, T. J., 2021. Improving Pumpset Selection to Support Intensification of Groundwater Irrigation in the Eastern Indo-Gangetic Plains. *Agricultural Water Management,* 256, 107070.

Fox, J., 2018. Community forestry, labor migration and agrarian change in a Nepali village: 1980 to 2010. *The Journal of Peasant Studies,* 45, 610-629.

Fricke, T. E. 1984. *Himalayan Households: Tamang Demography and Domestic Processes.* Michigan: UMI Research Press.

Fricke, T. & Teachman, J. D., 1993. Writing the Names: Marriage style, living arrangements, and first birth interval in a Nepali society. *Demography,* 30, 175-188.

Fujikura, T., 2001. Emancipation of Kamaiyas: Development, social movement, and youth activism in post-Jana Andolan Nepal. *HIMALAYA, the Journal of the Association for Nepal and Himalayan Studies,* 21, 14.

Fuller, D. Q., 2011. Pathways to Asian Civilizations: Tracing the origins and spread of rice and rice cultures. *Rice,* 4, 78-92.

Fuller, D. Q., Sato, Y., Castillo, C., Qin, L., Weisskopf, A. R., Kingwell-Banham, E. J., Song, J., Ahn, S. & Van E., J., 2010. Consilience of Genetics and Archaeobotany in the Entangled History of Rice. *Archaeological and Anthropological Sciences,* 2, 115-131.

Gaenszle, M., 2000. *Origins and Migrations: Kinship, mythology and ethnic identity among the Mewahang Rai of East Nepal.* Kathmandu: Mandala Book Point.

Gahatraj, R. K., 2011. *Socio-Economic Status of The Tharu Freed Kamaiyas: A case study of Dhangadhi Municipality, Kailali District.* Kathmandu: Department of Rural Development, Nepal.

Gahatraj, S., Rai, Hang, H, & Uprety, R., 2019. Assessment of Contribution of Cabbage in Rural Livelihood and Constraints of

Production in Dhankuta, Nepal. *International Journal of Agriculture Environment and Food Sciences*, 3, 150-154.

Gaige, F., 1976. *Regionalism and National Unity in Nepal.* Berkeley: University of California Press.

Gartaula, H. N., Niehof, A. & Visser, L., 2010. Feminisation of Agriculture as an Effect of Male Out-migration: Unexpected outcomes from Jhapa district, Eastern Nepal. *International Journal of Interdisciplinary Social Sciences*, 5.

Gauchan, D. & Shrestha, S., 2017. Agricultural and Rural Mechanisation in Nepal: Status, issues and options for future. *In:* Mandal, M. A. S. (ed.) *Rural Mechanisation: a driver in agricultural change and rural development.* Dhaka: Institute for Inclusive Finance and Development.

Gautam, R., 2005. *Rajbanshis of Nepal.* New Delhi: Adroit Publications

Gautam, Y., 2019. "Food Aid is Killing Himalayan Farms": Debunking the false dependency narrative in Karnali, Nepal. *World Development*, 116, 54-65.

Gellner, D., 2021. Dalits and the Market: Liberation or Oppression? *In:* Kaneff, D. & Endres, K. (eds.) *Explorations in Economic Anthropology: Key Issues and Critical Reflections.* Oxford: Bergahn.

Gellner, D. N., & Quigley, D., 1995. *Contested Hierarchies: A collaborative ethnography of caste among the Newars of the Kathmandu Valley, Nepal.* Oxford University Press.

Gentle, P. & Maraseni, T. N., 2012. Climate Change, Poverty and Livelihoods: Adaptation practices by rural mountain communities in Nepal. *Environmental science & policy*, 21, 24-34.

Ghimire, K., 1998. *Forest or Farm: The politics of poverty and land hunger in Nepal.* Delhi: Manohar.

Ghimire, M., 2017. Historical Land Covers Change in the Chure-Tarai Landscape in the Last Six Decades: Drivers and environmental consequences. *In:* LI, A., Deng, A. & Zhao, W. (eds.). *Land Cover Change and Its Eco-Environmental Responses In Nepal.* Springer.

Ghimire, S., Koirala, B., Devkota, S. & Basnet, G., 2019. Economic Analysis of Commercial Banana Cultivation and Supply Chain Analysis in Chitwan, Nepal. *Journal of Pharmacognosy and Phytochemistry,* 8, 190-195.

Gill, P., 2016. The Water Bringers. *The Record Nepal,* https://www.recordnepal.com/the-water-bringers.

Gill, P., 2009. The Politics of Land Reform in Nepal 1951–1964. *Studies in Nepali History and Society,* 14, 217-59.

Giri, B. R., 2009. The Bonded Labour System in Nepal: Perspectives of Haliya and Kamaiya child workers. *Journal of Asian and African Studies,* 44, 599-623.

Giri, B. R., 2012. The Bonded Labour System in Nepal: Musahar and Tharu communities' assessments of the Haliya And Kamaiya labour contracts. *Journal of Alternative Perspectives in the Social Sciences,* 4, 518-551.

Gladfelter, S., 2022. Imposing Worlds: Ontological marginalization and reclamation through irrigation infrastructure in Rajapur, Nepal. *Annals of the American Association of Geographers,* 112, 1994-2011.

Government of Nepal, 1995. *Nepal Agricultural Perspective Plan.* Kathmandu and Washington DC: Agricultural Projects Services Centre and John Mellor Associates.

Government of Nepal, 2010. *Baigyanik Bhumi Sudhar Sambandhi Uccastariya Aayogko Pratibedan, 2067 (Report of the High Level Commission on the Scientific Land Reform).* Kathmandu: High Level Commission for the Scientific Land Reform).

Government of Nepal 2020. *The Fifteenth Plan (Fiscal Year 2019/20 – 2023/24).* Kathmanmdu: National Planning Commission.

Government of Nepal, 2022. भूउपयोग नियमावली २०७९ (*Land Use Regulations, 2079*). Kathmandu: Ministry of Land Management, Cooperatives and Poverty Alleviation.

Grunning, J. F. 2007 [1911]. *Eastern Bengal and Assam District Gazetteers. Jalpaiguri,* Siliguri: N L Publishers.

Guneratne, A., 1996. The Tax Man Cometh: The impact of revenue collection on subsistence strategies in Chitwan Tharu Society. *Studies in Nepali History and Society,* 1, 5-35.

Guneratne, A., 2002. *Many Tougues, One People: The making of Tharu Identity in Nepal.* Ithaca: Cornell University Press.

Guneratne, A., 2010. Tharu-State Relations in Nepal and India. *HIMALAYA, the Journal of the Association for Nepal and Himalayan Studies,* 29, 2.

Gupta, S., Kharel, A., & Sugden, F., 2022. *Migration and Agricultural Change in Nepal – AGRUMIG final report.* Kathmandu: CESLAM, University of Birmingham.

Gurung, A. B., 2003. Insects–a Mistake in God's creation? Tharu farmers' Perception and Knowledge of Insects: A case study of Gobardiha Village Development Committee, Dang-Deukhuri, Nepal. *Agriculture and Human Values,* 20, 337-370.

Gurung, O. P., 1996. *Customary systems of natural resource management among Tarami Magars of western Nepal.* PhD Thesis, Cornell University.

Gurung, T. B., 2016. Remittance in Rural Phewatal Watershed, Nepal. *Repositioning: the Journal of Business and Hospitality,* 1, 81-90.

Haaland, R., 1999. The Puzzle of the Late Domestication of Sorghum in the Nile Valley. *In:* Gosden, C., & Hather, J. (eds.) *The Prehistory of Food: Appetites for Change.* London: Routledge.

Hachhethu, K., 2004. *Social Change and Leadership Building: A case study of Bhaktapur City.* Paper presented in a Workshop on The Dynamics of Social and Political Change in Nepal, ILCAA, Tokyo.

Hall, S., 1980. Race, articulation and societies structured in dominance. *Sociological Theories: Race and colonialism, pp. 305-345.* Paris: UNESCO.

Hamilton, F. B., 2007 [1819]. *An Account of the Kingdom of Nepal: And of the Territories annexed to this dominion by the House of Gorkha.* New Delhi: Rupa and co.

Hanieh, A., 2010. Temporary Migrant Labour and the Spatial Structuring of Class in the Gulf Cooperation Council. *Spectrum: Journal of Global Studies*, 2, 67-88.

Harris, D. R., 2020. An Evolutionary Continuum of People–Plant Interaction. *In:* Harris D.R. & Hillman, G.C. (eds.) *Foraging and Farming: The Evolution of Plant Exploitation*, pp. 11-27. London: Unwin Hyman.

Hilton, R. H. & Hill, C., 1953. The Transition from Feudalism to Capitalism. *Science & Society*, 17 (4) 340-351.

Hitchcock, J., 1963. Some Effects of Recent Change in Rural Nepal. *Human Organization*, 22, 75-82.

Hitchcock, J. T., 1965. Sub-Tribes in the Magar Community in Nepal. *Asian survey*, 207-215.

Hitchcock, J., 1966. *The Magars of Banyan Hill*. New York: Holt. Reinhart & Winston.

Hitchcock, J., 1974. Himalayan Ecology and Family Religious Variation. *In:* Kurien, G. (ed.) *Family in India-A Regional View*. Hague and Paris: Mouton.

His Majestic Government of Nepal. 1964. *The Land Acts 2022 VS*. Available at https://faolex.fao.org/docs/pdf/nep6239.pdf, Accessed April 2025

Hodgson, B. H., (circa 1830s a). Route from Kathmandu to Limbu Des. *Hodgson Collection, British Library*, vol 2 folios 63-66

Hodgson, B. H., (circa 1830s b). Route from Kathmandu to Mooktinath. *Hodgson Collection, British Library*, vol 2 folio 55

Hodgson, B. H., (circa 1830s c). Letter from B. H. Hodgson to T. H. Maddock submitting the best itinerary of the route from Kathmandu to Western districts of Dang, Salyan and Jajarkot. *Hodgson Collection, British Library*, vol 2, folios 99-111.

Hodgson. B. H., (circa 1830s d). Route from Kathmandu to Dolakha. *Hodgson Collection, British Library*, vol 2

Hodgson, B.H., 1846. Botany, Agriculture and Horticulture. Hand written notes. *Hodgon Collection, British Library*. vol 15 folios 82-127

Hodgson, B. H., 1988 [1848]. From Kathmandu to Darjeeling. *Regmi Research Series,* 20, 2-12.

Hodgson, B. H., 1880[1847]. *Miscellaneous Essays Relating to Indian Subjects: Volume* 1. London: Rubner and Co.

Höfer, A., 1979. *The Caste Hierarchy and the State in Nepal: A study of the Muluki Ain of 1854.* Innsbruck.

Holmberg, D., 2017. *Ethnography, History, Culture: Enduring Oppositions and Creative Dynamism in Nepal.* The Mahesh Chandra Regmi Lecture 2017. Kathmandu: Social Science Baha.

Holmberg, D., March, K., & Tamang, S., 1999. Local Production/Local Knowledge: Forced labour from below. *Studies in Nepali History and Society,* 4, 5-64.

Holmelin, N. B., 2021. National Specialization Policy Versus Farmers' Priorities: Balancing subsistence farming and cash cropping in Nepal. *Journal of Rural Studies,* 83, 71-80.

House, L.R., 1995. Sorghum and Millets: History, taxonomy, and distribution. *In:* Dendy, D. A. V. (ed.) *Sorghum and Millets: Chemistry and Technology.* St. Paul, Minnesota: American Association of Cereal Chemists, Inc.

Ismail, F. & Shah, A., 2015. Class Struggle, the Maoists and the Indigenous Question in Nepal and India. *Economic and Political Weekly,* 50 (35), 112-123.

Johnson, A., 2023. Settler Sensibilities and Environmental Change: Unmaking Malarial Landscapes in Nepal. *The Journal of Asian Studies,* 82, 639-662.

Joshi, B. K., 2017. Local germplasm of rice in Nepal: Diversity, character and uses. *Rice, Science and Technology in Nepal (A historical, sociocultural and technical compendium).* Kathmandu: Crop Development Directorate and the Agronomy Society of Nepal

Joshi, K. & Khanal, Ka., 2020. Neoliberal Globalization, Migration and Food Security: The case of Nepal. *In:* Rasali, D. P., Bhandari, P. B., Karki, U., Parajulee, M. N., Acharya, R. & Adhikari, R. (eds.) *Principles and Practices of Food security: Sustainable, sufficient, and safe food for healthy living in Nepal.* Kathmandu: Association of Nepalese Agricultural Professionals of Americas.

Joshi, K. D., Rana, R. B. & Subedi, A., 2001. *Farmer and Researcher Contribution to the Selection of Landraces of Ghaiya (Upland rice) for Tar areas of Nepal.* Kathmandu: The Local Initiative for Biodiversity, Research and Development (LI-BIRD).

Joshi, R., 2023. Tradition of Cooperation in Sudurpashchim Province of Nepal. *BOHR International Journal of Social Science and Humanities Research.* 2 (1), 66–70.

Justice, S. E., Biggs, S., 2023. *Rural and Agricultural Mechanisation in the Himalayan Rural Economy: The spread of small engines in the Nepal Mid-hills. Economic and Political Weekly.* 58, (25/26), 29-36

Kafle, D. R., 2022. The Historical Development of Settlement by Aryan People in Terai of Nepal. *Historical Journal,* 13, 1-7.

Kajale, M. D., 1991. Current status of Indian Palaeoethnobotany: Introduced and Indigenous Food Plants with a Discussion of the Historical and Evolutionary Development of Indian Agriculture and Agricultural Systems in General. *In:* Renfrew, J. (ed.) *New Light on Farming: Recent Developments in Palaeoethnobotany,* 155-189. Edinburgh: Edinburgh University Press.

Kansakar, V. B. S., 1985. Land Resettlement Policy as a Population Distribution Strategy in Nepal. *In:* Kosiński, L.A., Elahi, K.M. (eds) *Population Redistribution and Development in South Asia,* 111-122. GeoJournal Library, vol 3. Springer.

Kapstein, E. B., 2017. *Seeds of Stability: Land reform and US foreign policy.* Cambridge University Press.

Karan, A., 2009. Changing Land-Caste-Class Relations and Rural Poverty in Bihar. *Agrarian Reforms, Land Markets, and Rural Poor,* 271.

Karki, A. K., 2002. Movements From Below: Land rights movement in Nepal. *Inter-Asia Cultural Studies,* 3, 201-217.

Karki, R. & Gurung, A., 2012. An Overview of Climate Change and Its Impact on Agriculture: A review from least developing country, Nepal. *International Journal of Ecosystem,* 2, 19-24.

Karki, R., Hasson, Shabeh, U., Schickhoff, U., Scholten, T. & Böhner, J., 2017. Rising Precipitation Extremes Across Nepal. *Climate,* 5, 4.

Karky, J.,1981. A Study in Revenue Collection System in Nepal 1846–1923. *Contributions to Nepalese Studies,* 9, 1-2.

Karn, S., Sugden, F., Clement, F., Sah, K., Maharjan, J. & Sah, T. N., 2020. *Shifting Gender Relations in Agriculture and Irrigation in the Nepal Tarai-Madhesh.* Colombo: CGIAR programme for Water, Land and Ecosystems, Research for Development (R4D) Learning Series 10

Kawakita, J., 1957. Ethno-geographical Observations on the Nepal Himalaya. *In:* Kihara, H. (ed.) *Peoples of Nepal Himalaya: Scientific Results of the Japanese Expedition to Nepal Himalaya, 1952-53.* Kyoto: Flora and Fauna Research Society.

KC, S., Upreti, B. R. & Subedi, B. P., 2016. "We Know the Taste of Sugar Because of Cardamom Production": Links among commercial cardamom farming, women's involvement in production and the feminization of Poverty. *Journal of International Women's Studies,* 18, 181-207.

Khanal, D. R., Rajkarnikar, P. R. & Acharya, K., 2005. *Understanding Reforms in Nepal: Political economy and institutional perspective.* Kathmandu: Institute for Policy Research and Development.

Khanal, M. P. & Riccardi, T., 1988. Dumakhal: A brief report on the excavations. *Contributions to Nepalese Studies,* 15, 115-138.

Khanal, N., Shrestha, M. & Ghimire, M., 2007. Flood Hazard, Risk and Vulnerability in Nepal: The physical and socioeconomic environment. *In:* Khanal, N., Shrestha, M. & Ghimire, M. (eds.) *Preparing for Flood Disaster Mapping and Assessing Hazard in the Ratu Watershed, Nepal.* Kathmandu: ICIMOD.

Khanal, N. R., Nepal, P., Zhang, Y., Nepal, G., Paudel, B., Liu, L. & Rai, R., 2020. Policy Provisions for Agricultural Development in Nepal: A review. *Journal of Cleaner Production,* 261, 121-241.

Khanal, U., Alam, K., Khanal, R. C. & Regmi, P. P., 2015. Implications of Out-migration in Rural Agriculture: A case study of Manapang village, Tanahun, Nepal. *The Journal of Developing Areas,* 49, 331-352.

Khatri-Chhetri, A., Poudel, B., Shirsath, P. B. & Chaudhary, P., 2017. *Assessment of Climate-Amart Agriculture (CSA) Options in Nepal.* New Delhi, India: CGIAR Research Program on Climate Change, Agriculture and Food Security (CCAFS).

Khatri, M. B., 2018. Industrial Development in Nepal: Problems and prospects. *Economic Journal of Nepal,* 41, 25-40.

Kihara, H., 1956. *Land and Crops of Nepal Himalaya: Scientific results of the Japanese expeditions to Nepal Himalaya 1952–1953.* Kyoto: Fauna and Flora Research Society, Kyoto University.

Kim, P., & Rawal, V., 2012. Kamaiyas in Nepal and the Role of Ex-Kamaiyas in the Development of Western Nepal. 남아시아연구, 18, 233-263.

Kirkpatrick, W., 2007 [1793]. *An Account of the Kingdom of Nepaul.* New Delhi: Rupa and Co.

Knörzer, K., 2000. 3000 Years of Agriculture in a Valley of the High Himalayas. *Vegetation history and archaeobotany,* 9, 219-222.

Krauskopff, G. 1989. *Maîtres et possédés : les rites et l'ordre social chez les Tharu.* Paris: Eds Du CNRS.

Krauskopff, G., 2011. Fluid Belongings: The weight of places in a valley of Western Nepal. *In:* Pfaff-Czarnecka, J. & Toffin, G. (eds.) *The Politics of Belonging in the Himalayas: Local attachments and boundary dynamics.* SAGE.

Krauskopff, G., 2018. The Silent History of the Tharu Farmers: Peasant mobility and jungle frontiers in the light of written Archives. *Studies in Historical Documents from Nepal and India,* 351.

Lal, C. K., 2002. Cultural Flows Across a Blurred Boundary. *In:* Dixit, K. N. & Ramachandran, S. (eds.) *State of Nepal.* Kathmandu: Himal Books.

Lawoti, M., 2019. Constitution and Conflict: Mono-ethnic federalism in a poly-ethnic Nepal. *In:* Sachdeva, V., Pradhan, Q. & Venugopalan, A. (eds.) *Identities in South Asia.* Routledge India.

Lecomte-Tilouine, M., 2004. Ethnic Demands Within Maoism: Questions of Magar territorial autonomy, nationality and class. *In:* Hutt, M. (ed.) *Himalayan People's War: Nepal's Maoist Rebellion.* Bloomington and Indianapolis: Indiana University Press.

Lecomte-Tilouine, M., 2017. To Be More Natural Than Others: Indigenous self-determination and Hinduism in the Himalayas. *In:* Lecomte-Tilouine, Marie (ed.) *Nature, Culture and Religion at the Crossroads of Asia.* London: Routledge.

Lenin, V. I.,1960 [1899]. The Development of Capitalism in Russia. *In:* Lenin, V. I. (ed.) *Collected Works: Volume 3.* Moscow: Progress Publishers.

Lerche, J., 2013. The Agrarian Question in Neoliberal India: Agrarian Transition Bypassed? *Journal of Agrarian Change,* 13, 382-404.

Li, T. M., 2010. To Make Live or Let Die? Rural Dispossession and The Protection Of Surplus Populations. *Antipode,* 41, 66-93.

Liebrand, J., 2014. *Masculinities Among Irrigation Engineers and Water Professionals in Nepal.* PhD Thesis, Wageningen University.

Liechty, M., 2003. *Suitably Modern: Making Middle-Class Culture in a New Consumer Society.* Princeton University Press.

Limbu, S. T., 2018. Contemporary Dynamics of Post-War Transitions in Nepal: A case of Bardiya (District Mapping Papers: Bardiya, Dolpa, Humla and Saptari). *Borderlands Brokers: War to Peace Transition in Nepal.* Kathmandu: Martin Chautari.

Luintel, Y. R., 2013. Locating Pawai in the Social Hierarchy of the Khasa: A preliminary note on Jumli caste structure. *Dhaulagiri Journal of Sociology and Anthropology,* 7, 31-50.

Macfarlane, A., 1976. *Resources and Population: A study of the Gurungs of Nepal.* Cambridge: Cambridge University Press

Macfarlane, A., 2001. Sliding Down Hill: Some reflections on thirty years of change in a Himalayan village. *European Bulletin of Himalayan Research,* 20, 105-124.

Madhura, R.K., Krishnan, R., Revadekar, J.V., Mujumdar, M. & Goswami, B. N., 2015. Changes In Western Disturbances Over the

Western Himalayas in a Warming Environment. *Climate Dynamics,* 44, 1157-1168.

Maharjan, A., Bauer, S. & Knerr, B., 2013a. International Migration, Remittances and Subsistence Farming: Evidence from Nepal. *International Migration,* 51, 249-263.

Maharjan, A., Bauer, S. & Knerr, B., 2013b. *Migration for labour and its impact on farm production in Nepal.* Kathmandu: Centre for the Study of Labour and Mobility, Nepal.

Mahat, T.B.S., Griffin, D. M. & Shepherd, K. R., 1986. Human Impact on Some Forests of the Middle Hills of Nepal Part 2. Some Major Human Impacts before 1950 on the Forests of Sindhu Palchok and Kabhre Palanchok. *Mountain research and development,* 6 (4) 325-334.

Makaju, S. & Kurunju, K., 2021. A Review on Use of Agrochemical In Agriculture and Need of Organic Farming In Nepal. *Archives of Agriculture and Environmental Science,* 6, 367-372.

Malla, M. B., 1979. The Baise and Chaubise Principalities. *Regmi Research Series,* 77, 276-79.

Manandhar, R. & Khanal, M. P., 2005. Commercial Fertilisers and Their Quality control in Nepal. *In:* Andersen, P. (ed.) *Micronutrients in South and South East Asia.* Kathmandu: ICIMOD.

March, K., 1977. Of People and Yaks: The management and meaning of high altitude herding among contemporary Solu Sherpa. *Contributions to Nepalese Studies,* 4, 83-97.

Maycock, M. W., 2012. *Masculinity, Modernity and Bonded labour: Continuity and change amongst the Kamaiya of Kailali district, Far-West Nepal.* Doctoral Thesis, University of East Anglia.

Maycock, M. W., 2017. Hegemonic at Home and Subaltern Abroad: Kamaiya masculinities and changing mobility in Nepal. *Gender, Place & Culture,* 24, 812-822.

McCarl, B., 2013. *From Plump to Pump: Land, wealth and inequality in Nepal's Groundwater Irrigation Strategy.* MSc Thesis, Kathmandu: International Water Management Institute (IWMI); and Australia: University of Queensland.

McDougal, C., 1968. *Village and Household Economy in Far Western Nepal.* Kathmandu: Tribhuvan University.

McDonaugh, C., 1989. The Mythology of the Tharu: Aspects of cultural identity in Dang, West Nepal, *Kailash* 15 (3/4), 191-205

McDonaugh, C., 2012. Losing Ground, Gaining Ground: Land and change in a Tharu community in Dang, West Nepal. *In:* D. Gellner, J. P.-C., J. Whelpton (eds.) *Nationalism and Ethnicity in a Hindu Kingdom.* Routledge.

McDougal, C., 1973. Structure and Division in Kulunge Rai society. *Kailash,* 1, 205-24.

McDougal, C., 1979. *The Kulunge Rai: A Study in Kinship and Marriage Exchange.* Kathmandu: Ratna Pustak Bhandar.

McMichael, P., 2012. The Land Grab and Corporate Food Regime Restructuring. *The Journal of Peasant Studies,* 39, 681-701.

Meillassoux, C., 1981. *Maidens, Meal and Money: Capitalism and the Domestic Community.* Cambridge: Cambridge University Press.

Mellor, J., 1976. *The New Economics of Growth: A strategy for India and The Developing World.* Ithaca: *Cornell University Press.*

Messerschmidt, D. A., 1976. Ecological Change and Adaptation Among the Gurungs of the Nepal Himalaya. *Human Ecology,* 4, 167-185.

Messerschmidt, D. A., 1981a. *The Gurungs of Nepal: Conflict and Change in a Village Society.* Warminster, England: Aris and Phillips.

Messerschmidt, D. A., 1981b. "Nogar" and Other Traditional Forms of Cooperation in Nepal: Significance for development. *Human organization,* 40 (1), 40-47.

Metz, J., 2022. Thirty Years of Agrarian Change at an Upper Elevation Village in Western Nepal. *Human Ecology,* 50, 817-834.

Michael, B. A., 2007. Land, Labour, Local Power and the Constitution of Agrarian Territories on the Anglo-Gorkha Frontier, 1700-1815 (1). *International Quarterly for Asian Studies.* Arnold Bergsträsser Institut, 38 (3/4)

Michael, B. A., 2012. *Statemaking and Territory in South Asia: Lessons from the Anglo-Gorkha War (1814-1816).* Anthem Press.

Mikesell, S. L., 2002. The Legacy of John Hitchcock's Cultural Ecology in the Anthropology of the Himalayas. *HIMALAYA, the Journal of the Association for Nepal and Himalayan Studies*, 22, (1).

Ministry of Agricultural Development, 2015. *Agriculture Development Strategy (ADS) 2015 to 2035*. Government of Nepal.

Ministry of Agriculture and Livestock Development, 2022. *Statistical Information on Nepalese Agriculture 2077/78*. Kathmandu: Government of Nepal.

Ministry of Land Management, Cooperative and Poverty Alleviation, 2019. *National Land Policy 2019*. Kathmandu: Government of Nepal.

Mishra, C., 2007. *Essays on the Sociology of Nepal*. Kathmandu: Fine Print Inc.

Mishra, C., 1987. Development and Underdevelopment: A preliminary sociological perspective. *Occasional papers in Sociology and Anthropology* 1, 105-135

Mishra, Y., Babel, M. S., Nakamura, T. & Mishra, B., 2021. Impacts of Climate Change on Irrigation Water Management in the Babai River Basin, Nepal. *Hydrology*, 8 (2)

Mørch, M., 2023. *Plains of Discontent: A political history of Nepal's Tarai (1743-2019)*. Kathmandu: Fine Print Books.

Muller-Boker, U., 1999. *The Chitwan Tharus in Southern Nepal: An ethnological approach*. Stuttgart: Franz Steiner Verlag.

Müller-Böker, U., 1991a. Knowledge and Evaluation of the Environment in Traditional Societies of Nepal. *Mountain Research and Development*, 101-114.

Müller-Böker, U., 1991b. Wild Animals and Poor people: Conflicts between conservation and human needs in Chitawan (Nepal). *European Bulletin of Himalayan Research*, 2, 28-31.

Müller-Böker, U. & Seeland, K., 1986. Interpretation of Cadastral Maps and Land Registers: Examples from Kathmandu Valley and Gorkha. In: Seeland, K. (ed.), *Recent Research on Nepal: Proceedings of a*

Conference held at the Universität Konstanz, 27 - 30 March 1984. München: Weltforum Verlag, 141-157.

Müller, U., 1981. *Social and Economic Studies on a Newar Settlement in the Kathmandu Valley*. Geographical Institute the Justus Liebtg University of Giessen.

Narayan, P., 1986. Feudal Developments as Gleaned Through Inscriptions in Early Medieval Nepal (CAD 400—1200). *Proceedings of the Indian History Congress*, 208-213.

National Planning Commission, 2013. *Research into the Long Term Impact of Development Interventions in the Koshi Hills of Nepal*. Kathmandu: National Planning Commission and DFID.

Nayava, J. L., 1980. Rainfall in Nepal. *Himalayan Review*, 12, 1-18.

Nepal, G. M., 1998. नेपालनिरुपण (*Exploration of Nepal*). Kathmandu: Nepal Rajkiya Pragya-Prathisthan.

Nepali Congress, 2022. *Resolution of Nepali Congress: House of Representatives and State Assembly Election 2079*. Kathmandu: Nepali Congress.

Nepali, C. R., 1956. जनरल भिमसेन थापा र तत्कालिन नेपाल (*General Bhimsen Thapa and Nepal at that time*), Kathmandu: Ratna Pustak Bhandar.

Nepali, P. & Pyakuryal, K.N., 2008. Land and power relations. *In:* Upreti, B., Sharma, S. & Basnet, J. (eds.) *Land, Politics and Conflict in Nepal: Realities and potentials for agrarian transformation.* Kathmandu: C CSRC, South Asia Regional Coordination Office of NCCR (North South), Human and Natural Resources Studies Centre, Kathmandu University.

Nepali, P, Shrestha, S., Sing, Adhikari, S. & Pyakuryal, K. N., 2011a. Landlessness and agrarian change. *In:* Pyakuryal, K. N. & Upreti, B. R. (eds.) *Land, Agriculture and Agrarian Transformation.* Kathmandu: Consortium for Land Research and Policy Dialogue (COLARP).

Nepali, P., Pyakurel, K., Sharma, S. & Boeker, U., 2011b. Livelihood Options for the Landless in an Agrarian Society: A case study from far western Nepal. *International Journal of Rural Studies (IJRS)*, 18, 1-8.

Northey, W. B. & Morris, C. J., 1928. *The Gurkhas.* London: John Lane the Bodley Head Ltd.

Ojha, D. P., 1983. History of land settlement in Nepal Tarai. *Contributions to Nepalese Studies*, 11(1), 21-44.

Oldekop, J. A., Sims, K. RE., Whittingham, M. J. & Agrawal, A., 2018. An Upside to Globalization: International outmigration drives reforestation in Nepal. *Global Environmental Change*, 52, 66-74.

Pande, V., 2014. Divergent Historiographical Traditions: A comparative study of Gorkha rule in Kumaun and Far Western Nepal with Particular Reference to Jumla and Doti. *In:* Joshi, M. P., Thapa, S., and Shah, R. (ed.) *Before the Emergence of Nation States.* Almora: Almora Book Depot.

Paudel, D., 2019. Prismatic Village: The margin at the center in the Nepali Maoist Revolution. *Critical Sociology*, 45, 729-743.

Paudel, M. N. 2017. Green Revolution: Global effects and impacts in Nepal. *In:* Directorate, C. D. (ed.) *Rice, Science and Technology in Nepal (A historical, socio-cultural and technical compendium).* Government of Nepal.

Phyak, P. & Ojha, L. P., 2019. Language Education Policy and Inequalities of Multilingualism in Nepal. *The Routledge International Handbook of Language Education Policy in Asia*, 341-354.

Poertner, E., Junginger, M. & Müller-Böker, U., 2011. Migration in Far West Nepal: Intergenerational linkages between internal and international migration of rural-to-urban migrants. *Critical Asian Studies*, 43, 23-47.

Pokharel, B., 2010. Changing Relations Between High Castes and Tamang in Melamchi Valley. *Dhaulagiri Journal of Sociology and Anthropology*, 4, 65-84.

Pokharel, C., 2019. Agricultural Diversification in Nepal. *In:* Kumar, A., Thapa, G. & Joshi, P. K. (eds.) *Agricultural Transformation in Nepal.* Singapore: Springer Nature.

Pokhrel, R., 2018. Naxalbari and Jhapa Revolt: Historical Study. *Tribhuvan University Journal*, 32.

Posel, S., 1995. Kamaiya: Bonded labor in Western Nepal. *Colum. Hum. Rts. L. Rev.,* 27, 123.

Poudel, D. D. & Duex, T. W., 2017. Vanishing Springs in Nepalese Mountains: Assessment of water sources, farmers' perceptions, and climate change adaptation. *Mountain Research and Development,* 37, 35-46.

Pradhan, K., 2009. *The Gorkha Conquests: The process and consequences of the unification of Nepal, with particular reference to Eastern Nepal.* Kathmandu: Himal Books.

Pradhan, P. 2000. *Farmer Managed Irrigation Systems in Nepal at the Crossroad.* Paper presented at the 8th Biennial Conference of the International Association for the Study of Common Property, in Bloomington, Indiana, USA.

Pradhan, R. 2000. Land and Water Rights in Nepal (1854-1992). *In:* Pradhan, R., Benda-Beckmann, F. V. & Benda-Beckmann, K. V. (eds.) *Water, Land and Law: Changing Rights to Land and Water in Nepal.* Kathmandu: Legal Research and Development Forum, Wageningen Agricultural University, and Erasmus University

Pradhan, P. & Belbase, M., 2018. Institutional Reforms in Irrigation Sector for Sustainable Agriculture Water Management Including Water Users Associations in Nepal. *Hydro Nepal: Journal of Water, Energy and Environment,* 23, 58-70.

Pradhan, P., Yoder, R., Meinzen-Dick, R. & Merrey, D. J., 2023. Adaptation to Change in Six Farmer-Managed Irrigation Systems in Nepal: Forty Years of Observations. *London Journal of Research in Humanities and Social Sciences* 23(5), 33-45.

Pradhan, U. P., 1990. *Property Rights and State Intervention In Hill Irrigation Systems in Nepal.* PhD Thesis, Cornell University.

Prasad, P. B. & Chandra, D. S., 2019. Determinants of Mandarin Productivity and Causes of Citrus Decline in Parbat district, Nepal. *Acta Scientific Agriculture,* 3, 14-19.

Prasad, P. H., 1973. Production Relations: Achilles' Heel of Indian Planning. *Economic and Political Weekly,* 869-872.

Prasain, K., 2023. Nepalis hit by rising prices every which way. *Kathmandu Post* https://kathmandupost.com/money/2023/08/27/nepalis-hit-by-rising-prices-every-which-way, 27th Aug 2024.

Pun, A. B., 2018. A Review on Different Factors of Large Cardamom Decline in Nepal. *Asian Journal of Research in Crop Science,* 2, 1-6.

Pyakuryal, B., Roy, D. & Thapa, Y. B., 2010. Trade Liberalization and Food Aecurity in Nepal. *Food Policy,* 35, 20-31.

Rai, J., 2013. Malaria, Tarai Adivasi and the Landlord State in the 19th Century Nepal: A historical-ethnographic analysis. *Dhaulagiri Journal of Sociology and Anthropology,* 7, 87-112.

Rai, J., 2015. "Owning Land was so much of Dukha in the Past: Land and the state-adivasi relations in the Tarai, Nepal". *Studies in Nepali History and Society,* 20, 69-98.

Raj, Y., 2010. *History as Mindscapes: A memory of the peasants' movement of Nepal.* Kathmandu: Martin Chautari

Rana, D. S., 1992. *Irrigation in Bajhang: The role of NGOs.* International Water Management Institute.

Rana, R. S. J. B., 1971. *An Economic Study of the Area Around the Alignment of the Dhangadi-Dandeldhura Road, Nepal.* Kathmandu: Centre for Economic Development and Administration.

Rankin, K. N., 2004. *The Cultural Politics of Markets.* London: Pluto Press.

Rankin, K. N. & Shakya, Y. B., 2007. Neoliberalizing the Grassroots? Microfinance and the Politics of Development in Nepal. In: England & Ward (Eds.) *Neoliberalization: Networks, States and Peoples.* Oxford: Blackwell.

Rathaur, K. R. S., 2001. British Gurkha Recruitment: A historical perspective. *Voice of History,* 16, 19-24.

Raut, N. & Sitaula, B. K., 2012. Assessment of Fertilizer Policy, Farmers' Perceptions and Implications for Future Agricultural Development in Nepal. *Sustainable Agriculture Research,* 1 (2), 188-200.

Ray, S., 2002. *Transformations on the Bengal Frontier: Jalpaiguri, 1765-1948.* London: Routledge-Curzon.

Regmi, D. R., 1952. *Ancient and Medieval Nepal,* Kathmandu: Prem Printing Press.

Regmi, M. C., 1964. *Land Tenure and Taxation in Nepal Vol, 2: The land grant system: Birta Tenure.* Berkeley: Institute of International Studies, University of California.

Regmi, M. C., 1965. *Land Tenure and Taxation in Nepal, Vol 3: The Jagir, Rakam, and Kipat tenure systems.* Berkeley: Institute of International Studies, University of California.

Regmi, M. C., 1970a. A Glossary of Revenue, Administrative and Other Terms Occurring in Nepal Historical Documents. *Regmi Research Series,* 2, 148-150.

Regmi, M. C., 1970b. Order to Kipat-owing Chepangs in Pinda, 1847. *Regmi Research Series,* 2, 46.

Regmi, M. C., 1970c. Revenue Functionaries in the Eastern Tarai Districts. *Regmi Research Series,* 2, 107-109.

Regmi, M. C., 1971a. Taxation in Mahottari District, 1809. *Regmi Research Series,* 3, 28-30.

Regmi, M. C., 1971b. *A Study in Nepali Economic History, 1768-1846.* Mañjuśrī Publishing House.

Regmi, M. C., 1976. *Landownership in Nepal.* New Delhi: Adroit Publishers.

Regmi, M. C., 1978a. Bara, Parsa, and Rautahat in A.D. 1810. *Regmi Research Series,* 10 49-59.

Regmi, M. C., 1978b. Land Reclamation in the Eastern Tarai Region. *Regmi Research Series,* 10.

Regmi, M. C., 1978c. *Land Tenure and Taxation in Nepal.* New Delhi: Bibliotheca Himalaya.

Regmi, M. C., 1978d. *Thatched Huts and Stucco Palaces: Peasants and landlords in 19th-century Nepal.* Vikas Publishing House Private.

Regmi, M. C., 1981a. The Naya Muluk. *Regmi Research Series,* 13, 21-27.

Regmi, M. C., 1981b. The Political History of Dolakha. *Regmi Research Series,* 13, 12-20.

Regmi, M. C., 1982a. Chaudharis and Jimidars. *Regmi Research Series*, 14, 97-99.

Regmi, M. C., 1982b. Remission of Jhara Obligations A.D. 1810-17. *Regmi Research Series*, 41, 45-65.

Regmi, M. C., 1982c. Saptari and Mahottari Affairs, A.D. 1810-11. *Regmi Research Series*, 14, 123-128.

Regmi, M. C., 1983. Cardamom Farming in Nepal. *Regmi Research Series*, 15, 53-55.

Regmi, M. C., 1984. *The State and Economic Surplus: Production, trade, and resource-mobilization in early 19th century Nepal*. Nath Publishing House.

Regmi, M. C., 1987. The Chisapani Fort. *Regmi Research Series*, 19, 160-165.

Regmi, M. C., 1988a. *An Economic History of Nepal*. Varanasi: Nath Publishing House.

Regmi, M. C., 1988b. The Umra. *Regmi Research Series*, 20, 95-97.

Regmi, M. C., 1989a. Confirmation of Birta Grants: AD 1794. *Regmi Research Series*, 21, 68-71.

Regmi, M. C., 1989b. Miscellaneous Royal Orders. *Regmi Research Series*, 21, 95-98.

Regmi, M. C., 1989c. Some Bakas-Birta Grants. *Regmi Research Series*, 21, 91-94.

Riccardi J. T., 1977. The Royal Edicts of King Rama Shah of Gorkha. *Kailash*, 5 (1), 29-65.

Rijal, S. P., 2013. Impact of Climate Change on Large Cardamom-based Livelihoods in Panchthar District, Nepal. *The Third Pole: Journal of Geography Education*, 13, 33-38.

Rinck, J., 2024. Marxist Past to Speculative Futures: Migration, land markets, and political storytelling in Nepal's Tarai. *The Journal of Peasant Studies*, 52 (1), 157–177

Robertson, T. B., 2018. DDT and the Cold War Jungle: American environmental and social engineering in the Rapti valley of Nepal. *Journal of American History*, 104, 904-930.

Rodgers, G. & Rodgers, J., 2001. A Leap across Time: When semi-feudalism met the market in rural Purnia. *Economic and Political Weekly*, 36 (22), 2-8.

Roka, H., 2017. The Status of Smallholder Farmers in Nepal's Agricultural Development Strategy (2015–2035). *Agrarian South: Journal of Political Economy*, 6, 354-372.

Rowley-Conwy, P., 1981. Slash and Burn in the Temperate European Neolithic. *In:* Mercer, R. (ed.) *Farming Practice in British Prehistory.* Edinburgh: Edinburgh University Press.

Rudra, A., 1974. Semi-Feudalism, Usury Capital, Etcetera. *Economic and Political Weekly*, 9 (48) 1996-1997.

Russel, A., 1992. *The Yakha: Culture, Environment and Development in East Nepal.* PhD thesis, Wolfson College, Oxford.

Sagant, P., 1996. *The Dozing Shaman: The Limbus of Eastern Nepal.* Delhi: Oxford University Press.

Sapkota, D., 2017. Upland Rice (Ghaiya dhan) Cultivation in Nepal. *In:* Department Of Agriculture (ed.) *Rice, Science and Technology in Nepal (A historical, socio-cultural and technical compendium).* Crop Development Directorate and the Agronomy Society of Nepal

Sau, R., 1975. Farm Efficiency under Semi-Feudalism: A critique of marginalist theories and some Marxist formulations: A comment. *Economic and Political Weekly*, 10 (13), 18-21.

Schroeder, R. F., 1985. Himalayan Subsistence Systems: Indigenous agriculture in rural Nepal. *Mountain Research and Development*, 5 (10), 31-44.

Scott, J. C., 2010. *The Art of Not Being Governed: An anarchist history of upland Southeast Asia.* NUS Press.

Seddon, D., 1987. *Nepal: A State of Poverty.* New Delhi: Vikash Publishing.

Seddon, D., 2012. *Deep History of the Koshi Hills.* Kathmandu: GRM/DFID.

Sen, J., 1973. Slave Trade on the Indo-Nepal Border in the Nineteenth Century. *Kailash 1 (2), 159-167*

Shah, R., 1989. Ancient and Medieval Nepal. *Kailash*, 15, 21-84.

Shanin, T., 1973. The Nature and Logic of the Peasant Economy: A Generalisation. *Journal of Peasant Studies*, 1 (1), 63-80.

Sharma, B. C., 1951. नेपालको ऐतिहासिक रूपरेखा (Historical Outlines of Nepal). Varanasi: Krishnahuari Devi.

Sharma, B., Nepal, S., Gyawali, D., Pokharel, G. S., Wahid, Shahriar, M., Aditi, Acharya, S. & Shrestha, A. B., 2016. *Springs, Storage Towers, and Water Conservation in the Mid-Hills of Nepal*. Kathmandu: ICIMOD

Sharma, D. P., 2011. Understanding the Chepangs and Shifting Cultivation: A case study from rural village of central Nepal. *Dhaulagiri: Journal of Sociology & Anthropology*, 5, 247-62.

Sharma, D. R., 1988. Archaeological Remains of the Dang valley. *Ancient Nepal*, 88, 8-15.

Sharma, J. L. & Malla, K. B., 1957. राप्ती उपत्यका (The Rapti Valley). Kantipur: Nepal-India Amity League.

Sharma, J. R., 2021. *Political Economy of Social Change and Development in Nepal*. Bloomsbury Publishing, India.

Sharma, P. S., 2015. *Land, Lineage and State: A Study of Newar Society in Mediaeval Nepal*. Kathmandu: Himal Books.

Sharma, P. R., 1977. Caste, Social Mobility and Sanskritization: A study of Nepal's old legal code. *Kailash*, 4, 277–299.

Sharma, P. R., 1978. Nepal: Hindu-Tribal Interface. *Contributions to Nepalese Studies*, 6, 1-14.

Shneiderman, S., 2010. Are the Central Himalayas in Zomia? Some scholarly and political considerations across time and space. *Journal of Global History*, 5, 289-312.

Shneiderman, S., 2015. *Rituals of Ethnicity: Thangmi identities between Nepal and India*. University of Pennsylvania Press.

Shrestha, B. P., 1967. *The Economy of Nepal: A Study in the Problems and Processes of Industrialisation*. Mumbai: Vora Publishers.

Shrestha, B. K., 1993. *A Himalayan Enclave in Transition: A study of change in the western mountains of Nepal*. Kathmandu: ICIMOD.

Shrestha, K. N., 2020. The Newars of the Hills: Migration and Adaptation. *Patan Pragya*, 7 (1), 289-302

Shrestha, N. R., 1990. *Landlessness and Migration in Nepal.* Boulder: Westview Press.

Shrestha, N. R. & Velu, R. P., 1993. Frontier Migration and Upward Mobility: The case of Nepal. *Economic Development and Cultural Change*, 41 (4), 787-816.

Sijapati, B., Lama, A. S., Baniya, J., Rinck, J.,, Jha, K. & Gurung, A., 2017. *Labour Migration and the Remittance Economy: The sociopolitical impact.* Kathmandu: The Centre for the Study of Labour and Mobility.

Simkhada, S., 2020. Review on Nepal's Increasing Agricultural Import. *Acta Scientific Agriculture*, 3, 77-78.

Singh, K. S., 2007. Problematising Proselytisation: A case study from west Nirmar. *Social Science Probings*, 19, 105-148.

Singh, K. S., 2023. Moribund Capital in Tribal Societies. *Seminar*, 265, 47-51.

Singh, N. K., 1997. *Nepal: refugee to ruler: a militant race of Nepal.* APH Publishing.

Singh, S., Nourozi, S., Acharya, L. & Thapa, S., 2020. Estimating the Potential Effects of COVID-19 Pandemic on Food Commodity Prices and Nutrition Security in Nepal. *Journal of Nutritional Science*, 9, e51.

Singh, V. R., 1986. *Land-Use Change in the Tarai region of Uttar Pradesh, India.* Land-use change proceedings of the Asahikawa-Sapporo international symposium. University Press, Hong Kong, 63-76.

Smith, A.C., Hurni, K., Fox, J. and Van Den Hoek, J., 2023. Community Forest Management Led to Rapid Local Forest Gain in Nepal: A 29 year mixed methods retrospective case study. *Land Use Policy*, 126, 106526.

Stevens, S. F., 1996. *Claiming the High Ground: Sherpas, subsistence, and environmental change in the highest Himalaya.* Delhi: Motilal Banarsidass Publisher.

Stiller, L. F., 1975. *The Rise of the House of Gorkha* (1768-1816). Kathmandu: Ratna Pustak Bhandar

Strickland, S. S., 1984. Resources and Population Among the Gurungs: 1958-1980. *Kailash*, 11, 211-252.

Subedi, R., 1998. *Karnali Pradeshko Madhyakalin Itihas (The Middle Age History of Karnali Province)*. Kathmandu: Sajha Prakashan.

Subedi, R. R. 2005. Historical Entity of Vijayapur State. *Voice of History*, 20, 23-28.

Sugden, F., 2004. *Road building and Market Access in Eastern Nepal*. MA Thesis, University of Edinburgh.

Sugden, F., 2009a. From State Landlordism to Contemporary Semi-Feudalism: Understanding the spatial subordination of the far-eastern Terai. *Paper presented at conference Region Formation in South Asia*. Delhi University.

Sugden, F., 2009b. Neo-liberalism, Markets and Class structures on the Nepali lowlands: The political economy of agrarian change. *Geoforum*, 40, 634–644.

Sugden, F., 2010. *Agrarian Change and Pre-Capitalist Reproduction on the Nepal Terai*. PhD Thesis, University of Edinburgh.

Sugden, F. & Gurung, G., 2012. *Absentee Landlordism and Agrarian Stagnation in Nepal: A case from the eastern Tarai*. Kathmandu: Nepal Institute of Development Studies

Sugden, F., 2012a. *Indigenous Irrigation Systems in Bajhang, Nepal*. International Water Management Institute.

Sugden, F., 2012b. *Socio-Economic Constraints to Groundwater Extraction in West-Central Tarai*. CCAFS project report, International Water Management Institute.

Sugden, F., 2013. Pre-capitalist Reproduction on the Nepal Tarai: Semi-feudal agriculture in an era of globalisation. *Journal of Contemporary Asia*, 43, 519-545.

Sugden, F., 2014. *Landlordism, Tenants and the Groundwater Sector: Lessons from the Tarai-Madhesh, Nepal*. Colombo: IWMI Research Report 162.

Sugden, F., Maskey, N., Clement, F., Ramesh, V., Philip, A & Rai, A., 2014a. Agrarian Stress and Climate Change in the Eastern Gangetic Plains: Gendered Vulnerability in a Stratified Social Formation. *Global Environmental Change*, 29, 258-269.

Sugden, F., Shrestha, L., Bharati, L., Gurung, P., Maharjan, L., Janmaat, J., Price, J., Sherpa, T. Y. C., Bhattarai, U. & Koirala, S., 2014b. Climate Change, Out-Migration and Agrarian Stress: The potential for ppscaling small-scale water storage in Nepal. *Research Report- International Water Management Institute*.

Sugden, F., Silva, S de., Saikia, P., Maskey, N. & Kumar, A., 2015. *Irrigation and Water Management Constraints for Marginal and Tenant Farmers in the Eastern Gangetic Plains*. Report compiled for project: Sustainable and Resiliant Farming Systems Intensification.

Sugden, F., 2016a. *Improving Dry Season Irrigation for Marginal and Tenant Farmers in The Eastern Gangetic Plains: Baseline socio-economic report*. Unpublished project report, International Water Management Institute.

Sugden, F., Saikia, P., Maskey, N & Pokharel, P., 2016b. Gender, Agricultural Investment and Productivity in an Era of Out-Migration: A case study from Nepal and Bihar. *In:* Bharati, L., Sharma, B. R., Smakhtin, V. & Mandal, A. S. (eds.) *The Ganges River Basin: Status and challenges in water, environment and livelihoods*. Earthscan.

Sugden, F., 2017. A Mode of Production Flux: The transformation and reproduction of rural class relations in lowland Nepal and north Bihar. *Dialectical Anthropology*, 41, 129–161.

Sugden, F., Seddon, D. & Raut, M., 2018. Mapping Historical and Contemporary Agrarian Transformations and Capitalist Infiltration in a Complex Upland Environment: A case from eastern Nepal. *Journal of Agrarian Change*, 18, 444-472.

Sugden, F., 2019. Labour Migration, Capitalist Accumulation and Feudal reproduction: A historical analysis from the Eastern Gangetic Plains. *Antipode* 51(5), 1600-1639.

Sugden, F., Nigussie, L., Debevec, L. & Nijbroek, R., 2022. Migration, Environmental Change and Agrarian Transition in Upland Regions: Learning from Ethiopia, Kenya and Nepal. *The Journal of Peasant Studies*, 49, 1101-1131.

Sugden F., 2025. *Land, Labour, and Agrarian Change in Nepal's Tarai-Madhesh*. Cambridge University Press

Sugden, F., Crivellaro, F., Kharel, A., Kuznetsova, I., Masotti, M., Pagogna, R., 2025. *Long Term Outcomes of Return Migration: Rural differentiation and class mobility in Nepal, Moldova and Thailand*. Migration Studies. In press.

Sunam, R., Sugden, F. & Kharel, A. 2025. Unpacking Youth Engagement in Agriculture: Land, labour mobility and youth livelihoods in rural Nepal. *Journal of Agrarian Change*, 1-18.

Sunam, R., 2020. *Transnational Labour Migration, Livelihoods and Agrarian Change in Nepal: The remittance village*. Routledge.

Sunam, R., & Adhikari, J., 2016. How Does Transnational Labour Migration Shape Food Security and Food Sovereignty? Evidence from Nepal. *Anthropological Forum*, 26, 248-261.

Sunam, R. K. & McCarthy, J. F. 2016. Reconsidering the Links Between Poverty, International Labour Migration, and Agrarian Change: Critical insights from Nepal. *The Journal of Peasant Studies*, 43, 39-63.

Sundas, B., 2020. The Process of State Formation and its Impact on Social Formation in Eastern Nepal and Sikkim, Sixteenth-Nineteenth Centuries. *In:* Lepcha, C. K., Maiti, S. & Chaudhuri, S. K. (eds.) *The Cultural Heritage of Sikkim*. Routledge.

Sweezy, P. M & Dobb, M., 1950. The Transition from Feudalism to Capitalism. *Science & Society*, 14, 134-167.

Takahashi, H. K. & Mins, H. F., 1952. The Transition from Feudalism to Capitalism: A contribution to the Sweezy-Dobb Controversy. *Science & Society*, 16 (4) 313-345.

Takeshima, H., Bhattarai, M., 2019. Agricultural Mechanization in Nepal—Patterns, Impacts, and Enabling Strategies for Promotion.

In: Thapa, G., Kumar, A., Joshi, P. (eds) *Agricultural Transformation in Nepal,* 261–289. Singapore: Springer

Tamang, M. S., 2009. Tamang Activism, History, and Territorial Consciousness. *In:* Gellner, D. (ed.) *Ethnic Activism and Civil Society In South Asia: Governance, conflict and civil action, Volume 2.* SAGE.

Tamang, M. S., 2008. *Himalayan Indigeneity: Histories, memory, and identity among Tamang in Nepal.* PhD Thesis, Cornell University.

Tamang, S., Paudel, K. P. & Shrestha, K. K., 2014. Feminization of Agriculture and Its Implications for Food Security in Rural Nepal. *Journal of Forest and Livelihood,* 12, 20-32.

Tamrakar, R. M., 2012. A Prospect of Digital Airborne Photogrammetry Approach for Cadastral Mapping in Nepal. *Journal on Geoinformatics, Nepal,* 11, 1-6.

Tanu, R ~1830. A Letter from Ramtanu (Ram Tunnu in original) to Hodgson Regarding Goods from Highlands and Lower Hills Exported to the Tarai and India 1830s. *Hodgson Collection, British Library,* Vol 14 folio 92

Terrenato, L., Shrestha, S., Dixit, K.A. , Luzzatto, L., Modiano, G., Morpurgo, G. & Arese, P., 1988. Decreased Malaria Morbidity in the Tharu people compared to Sympatric Populations in Nepal. *Annals of Tropical Medicine & Parasitology,* 82, 1-11.

Thapa, B., Scott, C., Wester, P. & Varady, R., 2016. Towards Characterizing the Adaptive Capacity of Farmer-Managed Irrigation Systems: Learnings from Nepal. *Current Opinion in Environmental Sustainability,* 21, 37-44.

Thapa, L. B., Thapa, H. & Magar, B. G., 2015. Perception, Trends and Impacts of Climate Change in Kailali District, Far West Nepal. *International Journal of Environment,* 4, 62-76.

Thapa, S., 2000. *Agrarian Relations in Nepal: 1846-1951.* New Delhi: Adroit Publications.

Thapa, S. & Chhetry, D., 1997. Inequality of Landholding in Nepal: Some policy Issues. *Contributions to Nepalese Studies,* 24, 133-145.

Tilzey, M. & Sugden, F., 2023. *Peasants, Capitalism, and Imperialism in an Age of Politico-Ecological Crisis*. Taylor & Francis.

Tiwari, K. R., Nyborg, I. L. P., Sitaula, B. K. & Paudel, G. S., 2008. Analysis of the Sustainability of Upland Farming Systems in the Middle Mountains Region of Nepal. *International Journal of Agricultural Sustainability*, 6, 289-306.

Tripathi, B., Parajuli, K. & Sharma, G. K. 1983. नेपाली बृहत शब्दकोष (*Compressive Nepali Dictionary*). Kathmandu: Royal Nepal Academy.

Tuladhar, S. D., 2002. The Ancient City of Kapilvastu-revisited. *Ancient Nepal*, 151, 1-7.

UN-HABITAT, 2018. *Locally Present Land Tenure Typology in Nepal.* Kathmandu: Ministry of Agriculture, Land Management and Cooperatives, Kathmandu, Nepal Community Self Reliance Centre, Kathmandu, Nepal

UNHCR Nepal, 2011. *State of Stateless Citizens: A case study on citizenship and landlessness issues of the Santhal community.* Kathmandu.

Upadhyay, K. D., 1990. A Socioeconomic Profile of the Porters in the Central Mid-Hills of Nepal. *Occassional Papers In Sociology and Anthropology*, 2, 48-58.

Uprety, L. P., 2021. *Peasantry under Capitalism in Contemporary Nepal:: Macro and micro narratives.* Kathmandu: Bina Khatiwada (Uprety).

Vaidya, T. R., 2020. *Advanced History of Nepal: Expansion of the Gorkha state and the political history from the first battle of Nuwakot to death of Bhimsen Thapa (1737AD to 1839 AD)*. Kathmandu: Educational Publishing House.

Valadaud, R., 2023. The Reproduction of Hydrosocial Dominations: Water user association membership in the eastern Tarai. *European Bulletin of Himalayan Research* 60. https://doi.org/10.4000/ebhr.1259

van der Klei, J. S., 1985. Articulation of Modes of Production and the Beginning of Labour Migration Among the Diola of Senegal. *In:* Van B. W. & Geschiere, P. (eds.) *Old Modes of Production and Capitalist Encroachment: Anthropological explorations in Africa.* Leiden: KPI Limited.

Vansittart, E. & Nicolay, B. U., 1915. *Handbook for the Indian Army: Gurkhas.* Kolkata: Superintendent Government Printing.

Warner, C., 2014. *Shifting States: Mobile subjects, markets, and sovereignty in the India-Nepal Borderland, 1780-1930.* PhD Thesis, University of Washington.

Webster, P., 1983. Peasants and Landlords: Land tenure in the Kathmandu valley, Nepal. *Pacific Viewpoint,* 24, 140-166.

Whelpton, J., 2000. From the Beginning: Themes in the pre-history and ancient history of Nepal. *Voice of History,* XV, 38-69.

Whelpton, J., 2005. *A History of Nepal.* Cambridge University Press.

Whelpton, J., 1987. *Nepali Politics and the Rise of Jang Bahadur Rana, 1830-1857.* University of London, School of Oriental and African Studies (United Kingdom).

White, B., 1997. Agroindustry and Contract Farmers in Upland West Java. *Journal of Peasant Studies,* 24, 100-136.

Wolpe, H., 1982. Capitalism and Cheap Labour-Power in South Africa: From segregation to apartied. In: Wolpe, H. (ed.) *The Articulation of Modes of Production: Essays from Economy and Society.* London: Routledge and Kegan Paul.

Yadav, S. R., 1984. *Nepal: Feudalism and Rural Formation.* New Delhi: Cosmo Publications.

Yadav, S. N., & Peterson, W., 1993. Rice Yields in Nepal: Is the 4-tons per hectare yield goal attainable? *Journal of Asian Economics,* 4, 77-87.

Yadav, S., 1986. *Some Aspects of Economic Life in Nepal in the Licchavi Period (Circa AD 464-800).* Doctoral Dissertation, Banaras Hindu University.

Yoder, R., 1994. *Organization and Management by Farmers in the Chhattis Mauja Irrigation System, Nepal.* International Irrigation Management Institute (IIMI), Research paper no 11.

Zaman, M. A., 1973. *Evaluation of Land Reform in Nepal.* Kathmandu: Ministry of Land Reform, Government of Nepal

Zharkevich, I., 2015. De-mythologizing 'the Village of Resistance': How rebellious were the peasants in the Maoist base area of Nepal? *Dialectical Anthropology,* 39, 353-379.

Index

A

Adivasi vii–xi, 5, 8, 10, 15–18, 23, 25–27, 29–33, 35–37, 39, 41–42, 45, 47–48, 51–55, 57–60, 63, 67, 72–74, 86–87, 89–91, 96–97, 100, 105, 108–109, 112–115, 117–118, 120–121, 123–124, 131–139, 141, 144, 147, 150, 153–154, 157, 161, 167, 185, 187–190, 192–193, 197, 201, 203–205, 207–208, 211, 216–217, 219–220, 222, 224, 226–228, 231–232, 237, 243, 247, 257, 263, 273–274, 283–284, 286, 288, 298–299, 312–317, 344

Adivasi (mode of production) 15-17, 21, 25, 29-31, 35, 37, 39, 40, 45, 48, 51, 57, 58, 67, 72, 73, 86, 87, 90, 120, 121, 123, 124, 137, 138, 141, 144, 154, 167, 185, 188, 201, 211, 216, 217, 222, 226-228, 231, 247, 263, 286, 288, 312-314,

Agrarian change xv, 199, 207, 208, 289

agrarian structure x, 79, 109, 163–165, 184, 198, 207, 214, 270, 278, 282, 307

Agrarian transition vii, xiii, 2-7

Agricultural Development Bank 175, 307

Agricultural Development Strategy 249, 252, 293

Agricultural Perspective Plan 249, 251, 293, 306, 317

Althusser 4

Anglo-Nepal treaty (1923) 158

Arghakhanchi 147

Articulation of modes of production 3, 235, 245,

Arun (valley) 134, 136, 232–233, 237–238, 298,

Asian Development Bank 307

Assam 26, 92, 143, 162

B

Baglung 57, 60, 110, 118, 138, 222

Baise Rajya 9, 39, 43, 46, 64–66, 68, 71, 107, 145, 229

Banke 10, 23, 100–101, 168, 179, 185, 189, 190, 192, 196–197, 261, 308

Bardiya 10, 100–101, 179, 183, 185, 189–190, 192–193, 195–197, 268–269, 275, 316, 324, 326, 337

Barley xviii, 54, 61, 62, 66, 68, 144, 145, 148, 149, 237, 238, 241, 299–301

Bhaktapur 149, 215–216, 295

Bhojpur 117, 130, 136, 152, 157, 214, 221, 227, 232, 254–255, 257, 259, 262, 265–266, 284–285, 289–290, 293–294, 299, 302

Bihar 20, 22, 34, 99, 159, 277, 281

Biratnagar 205, 294

Birgunj 151

Birta viii–ix, 80–81, 85, 90, 99, 110, 118, 133, 155, 164, 222, 274, 283, 316

Bonded labor 97

British Empire 10

Buckwheat 52, 54, 67, 68, 149, 234, 237, 287, 299- 301

C

Capitalism 2–3, 5–6, 29–30, 232, 235–236, 238, 239, 260, 291–292, 293, 302, 303, 305

Cardamom 151, 302–303

caste system 34, 41–42, 113, 314

cattle 54, 97, 107, 265, 287

Chaubisi Rajya 3, 8, 15, 19, 21, 39, 46–47, 66, 71, 132

Chepang 52–53, 55, 116, 124, 129, 181, 226, 287, 289

China 66, 68, 173, 303

Chiraito 238, 302

Chitwan 10, 23, 26, 76, 77, 83, 90–91, 94, 102, 161, 176, 179, 181, 185, 188–189, 190, 192, 197, 201, 204, 240, 266, 287, 291, 316,

climate change 5, 250, 252, 259, 297, 303, 305–306, 308, 313,

Colonialism 164, 173, 178,

Commercial agriculture 248, 303

Communal labour 29, 55, 60, 226

Communal land 55-57, 73, 123

Communist Party of Nepal (Maoist) 246

Communist Party of Nepal (United Marxist-Leninist) 270

Cooch Behar 20, 26

corvée labour 84, 86, 88, 116, 122, 195, 280

Cottage industry 66, 152, 158, 161, 211–213, 235

cropping system 9, 13, 16, 61-63, 67, 70, 73, 101, 102, 128, 144–145, 147–150, 163, 168, 231, 236-238 238, 240, 287, 297, 312, 313

customary tenure ix, 13, 28, 35, 57, 105, 118, 120, 123–125, 131–132, 136, 140, 157, 219, 222, 224–225, 231, 286–287, 309

Index

D
Dailekh 43, 49, 66, 110
Dalits 114, 207, 228, 230–231, 262
Dang 19, 23, 31–32, 77, 80, 83–84, 88, 92, 95–97, 100, 156–157, 161, 168, 183–185, 189–198, 201, 203, 240–241, 261, 275–276, 280, 316
Darbhanga 86
Darchula 214, 229
Darjeeling 88, 143, 151, 234
DDT 179
Debt 97, 115, 119, 124, 129, 131, 133, 134, 157, 160, 161, 178, 188, 192, 194, 196, 202-205, 219, 224, 258, 262, 279, 281, 282, 285, 293
Deforestation 178, 184, 217
Dhading 13, 140, 176, 239, 287
Dandeldhura 239
Dhankuta 56, 59, 122, 129, 141, 210–211, 232–233, 255, 303
Dhanusha 13, 20, 80, 83, 86, 96, 100, 103–104, 170, 182–183, 199–200, 254, 256, 262, 267, 276–279, 280–282, 308
Dharan 20, 31, 214, 261
Dhimal xv, 23, 26–29, 32, 55, 88, 91–92, 101, 162, 188
Dolakha 8, 48, 49, 57, 66, 81, 119, 124, 133, 152, 292
Dolpa 40, 337
Dooars (North Bengal) 27–28, 88, 92, 291

Doti 66, 81, 112, 145, 152, 239, 264, 266, 285
Droughts 10, 259, 299, 305, 313,
Dullu (Dailekh) 31, 43, 49, 66

E
East India Company 86, 106, 153
England 290

F
FAO 167
feudal ix, xii, 2–3, 16–17, 30, 35, 37–38, 42–43, 72–74, 80, 85–86, 89, 105, 110–111, 116, 118, 134, 143, 153, 161, 166, 169–171, 183, 185, 188, 190, 195, 201, 203, 216–217, 219, 221, 229, 231, 246–247, 263, 268, 273, 276, 278, 282, 283, 284, 288, 291, 312–313, 316
Feudalism viii, x–xi, 2, 5–6, 16–17, 29–30, 33–34, 37, 43–46, 73, 82, 86–87, 90, 105–106, 121, 154, 160, 184, 195, 197, 199, 203, 221, 229, 231, 246, 272, 274, 280, 312–313, 315, 232, 247
forced labour 110, 115–119, 121–122, 133–134, 148, 284
Forces of production 4
Foreign aid x, 172, 173, 178, 208, 248

G

Gangai 23, 26, 193, 205, 207
Goats 54, 228, 265
Gorkha viii–ix, 2–3, 7–8, 15, 17, 19, 21–23, 33, 43, 45–49, 51, 53, 56–57, 59, 61–62, 64, 66, 69–71, 73–80, 83, 86–87, 89, 90, 92, 101–102, 105–108, 111, 113–116, 118–121, 124, 132, 135, 137, 143–145, 147–151, 153, 155, 156, 205, 209, 214, 216, 221, 283, 287, 309, 312
Gorkha conquest viii, 2, 15, 17, 19, 21–23, 33, 43, 45, 48, 56–57, 59, 61–62, 64, 66, 69–71, 73–74, 78, 86–87, 89, 101, 105, 106–107, 113, 115–116, 118, 120, 137, 143, 145, 147–148, 151, 155, 205, 283, 312
Gulmi 64, 147, 148
Gurung 8, 25, 32, 35, 48, 52, 54–55, 58, 60, 115–116, 118, 131–132, 136–138, 140–141, 149, 157–158, 165–166, 168, 205, 208, 211, 213, 215, 218–220, 223, 225–227, 232, 234, 237, 243, 256, 259, 263, 269, 289, 296
guthi 38, 44, 66, 78, 79, 81, 99, 105–106, 113, 155, 167, 277, 288

H

Harawa 200, 282–283
High Yielding Varieties (seeds) 242
Hodgson, Brian 26, 28, 115, 144, 151–152
Hongu (valley) 139, 142, 214, 223–224, 234
Hunting 27, 52, 54, 91, 226, 287,
Hunting reserves 90, 91, 190, 204,
Hybrid seeds 297

I

Ilam 8, 56, 123, 139, 151, 209, 211, 213, 217, 219–220, 223–234, 237–238, 241–242, 292
India 2–3, 20, 28, 29, 31, 34, 48–49, 66, 68, 74–75, 78, 80, 84, 86, 92, 94–95, 99, 106, 120, 143, 145, 151, 153, 158, 159, 173, 181, 183, 190, 206, 211, 214, 230, 234, 235–236, 241, 249, 252, 254, 260–261, 264, 266, 299, 304
India (agricultural equipment)
internal migration 55, 114, 135, 180
international migration 143
irrigation ix, 1, 4, 13, 38, 41, 62–63, 65–68, 71, 73, 81, 85, 100–104, 144–149, 172–177, 184, 197, 237–241, 248–251, 259–260, 268, 271, 274, 298, 301, 303, 305–308, 313
Irrigation Master Plan 250

J

Jagir (land tenure) ix, 47, 49–50, 71, 78–79, 81–82, 84–86, 105–106, 108, 110–113, 115, 119, 121, 132–134, 153–155, 164, 222

Jajmani system 115, 199, 280

Janajati (see also Adivasi) 36

Janakpur 10, 20, 33, 80, 84–85, 322

Jhapa 27, 75, 76, 91, 179–185, 187–188, 192, 197–198, 201–202, 207, 246

Jimidari system (Nepal) 95, 100, 107, 188, 201, 267, 273, 282–283

Jumla 39–40, 45, 66, 109–110, 119, 146, 214, 228, 230, 242

Jute 10, 105, 144, 158, 239, 240, 298, 302, 304

K

Kamaiya 195–196, 197, 199, 204, 276

Kanchanpur 10, 23, 26, 62, 100, 179, 180–181, 185, 189–190, 192, 196–197, 261, 276

Kapilvastu 18–19, 21, 23, 185, 196

Karnali 9, 39, 41–42, 44, 64–65, 66–68, 145, 172, 177, 228–229, 232, 238, 299, 319, 321, 329, 350

Kaski 151, 211, 217, 223, 234, 254, 256, 258, 263, 289

Kathmandu valley viii, 8, 10–11, 15, 17, 36–39, 45, 48, 64–67, 69–70, 107–108, 111–113, 137, 147, 149–150, 172, 208, 215–216, 222, 236, 241, 288, 294, 295

Kavrepalanchok 67, 124, 132, 242

Khas 8–9, 17, 19, 21, 31, 36, 39, 41–49, 64, 73, 111, 113–115, 120, 125, 147, 222, 227, 312, 315

Khas kingdom 17, 19, 31, 41, 43, 44, 64, 111

khoriya 51, 53, 55, 60, 63, 67, 137–138, 149–150

kipat 55–56, 59, 73, 109, 112, 122–126, 128–129, 131–136, 139–140, 155, 157, 164, 167, 219–221, 223–225, 241, 284, 286, 314

Kirat 8, 20, 48–51, 55, 57, 63, 109, 115, 117, 121–126, 128–129, 131–132, 134–135, 137, 149, 238, 314

L

labour migration 214, 229, 234–236, 261, 285

Labour tribute 16, 43, 44, 72, 79, 83, 88, 109, 118, 123, 139, 156, 191, 284;

Jhara 43, 117, 118, 122,

Rakam 110, 116, 117, 124, 133, 155

Land inequality 100, 222, 269

Land reform 81, 163-172, 178, 186, 191, 194, 197-207, 215, 216, 223, 248, 252, 268, 269, 270, 276, 290, 313, 314, 316, 317

Land tenure 13, 18, 57, 72, 73, 74, 105, 117, 164, 166, 167, 199, 288,

Land degradation 178, 217–218, 243, 297

Sharecropping 35, 84, 106, 112, 157, 168, 195, 196, 204, 230, 274, 275

Lands Act (1964) 167, 269

Lenin, Vladimir 2, 303

Licchavi period 37, 38, 62, 64, 65, 69,

Limbu 35, 50, 52, 54–56, 115–116, 123, 125–126, 128–129, 131, 134, 135, 137, 139, 141, 195, 202, 213, 217, 219–220, 225, 230, 232, 234, 263, 289

M

Magar 8, 35, 42, 46–48, 50, 52, 54, 55, 57, 60, 113, 115–116, 118, 120, 132, 136–138, 140, 157–158, 181, 188, 215, 220–223, 225, 232, 234, 246–247, 284, 289

Magar (Kham) 8, 54, 137, 220, 222, 225, 246, 287

Mahabharat range 8, 9, 287

Mahaton (Tharu functionary) 96–98

Mahottari 20, 33–34, 70, 74, 76, 80, 82–83, 92, 96, 100, 102, 159, 182–183, 199,

Majhi 29, 116, 123

Makwanpur 8, 13, 19, 21, 30–31, 33, 34, 39, 49, 79, 106, 111, 114, 118, 162, 181, 287

Malaria 128, 129, 162, 179-181

Malla 8, 19, 21, 38, 39, 41, 43, 45, 48, 65, 96, 97, 124, 181

Manang 13, 287, 288

Maoism 246

Marx, Karl 2,

Matwali Chettri 40, 67

MC Regmi xiv, 2, 5, 7, 9, 11–12, 16, 21, 30–31, 33–35, 38, 43–48, 55–56, 69, 72, 74–87, 89–90, 92–103, 105–114, 116–120, 124–125, 128–129, 132, 148, 151, 155–156, 159–161, 165–167, 169–170, 205

Mechanisation 4, 243, 265, 266

Micro-credit

Migration 1, 9, 17, 33, 41, 45, 55, 64, 73, 78, 86, 92, 99, 114, 115, 116, 125, 134-136, 143, 147, 152, 162, 163, 168-170, 179-184, 187, 189, 191, 192, 195, 196, 197, 206, 214, 216, 217, 229, 230, 234-236, 252, 260-267, 279, 281, 284, 289, 290, 293, 296, 297, 299, 303, 312, 313, 315

millet 28, 39–40, 52, 54, 63, 67, 68, 69–70, 101, 103, 107, 128, 137, 141–142, 144, 149, 234, 236–241, 298–301
Mithila 20, 25, 34, 74, 92, 103, 113, 185, 281
mode of production i–vii, viii–xii, 2–5, 12, 15–17, 25, 29, 30–32, 35–39, 43–46, 48–49, 51–52, 57–58, 62–63, 67, 72–73, 82, 86–87, 90, 105, 110, 120–124, 126, 137–138, 141, 143–144, 154, 159–160, 164, 167, 185–186, 188, 195, 197–198, 201, 208, 211, 216–217, 222, • 226–229, 231, 247, 263–264, 270–272, 283, 286, 288, 291–292, 312–315
Mode of production debate 2, 3, 5
Money lending (see also debt) 48, 134, 281, 282
Morang 13, 23–24, 26–27, 34, 70, 74, 76–77, 91, 97, 99–101, 104–105, 160–162, 175, 180, 182, 185–189, 192–193, 197, 198, 200–205, 249, 254, 258, 273–275, 280, 304, 306, 308
Mughal empire 17, 31
Mugu 66
Muluki Ain (Civil Code) 145, 148,
Musahar caste 205, 207,
Mustang 8, 68, 146
Mustard 27, 62, 70, 101, 102, 237, 239, 301

N
Nawalparasi 13, 21, 179, 183, 185, 196, 201
Nepalganj 158, 190
Nepali Congress 268, 270
Newar 8, 36, 38, 48, 49, 57, 66, 99, 113, 120, 124, 152, 202
Nuwakot 64, 66–67, 70, 79, 106, 111–112, 117–118, 124, 137, 150–151, 209–210, 212, 254, 260

O
Occupational castes 36, 41, 45, 114, 115, 187, 213, 230, 254
Okhaldhunga 127

P
paddy xvii, 27, 39, 41, 44, 47–48, 61–65, 70, 79, 97–98, 102–103, 111, 122, 125–129, 131, 133–134, 137–138, 144, 146–148, 150, 157, 159, 175, 218–219, 221, 227–229, 236–238, 240–242, 259, 292, 297, 300–301, 312–313, 315
Palpa 8, 19, 21, 31, 39, 66, 147, 151, 153
Panchayat x–xi, xiv, 3, 7, 12, 141, 155, 163, 166, 168, 174–179, 183–184, 188–191, 196–198, 200, 204–210, 212, 214, 216–220, 222–228, 230–240, 241, 243, 245–246, 250, 254, 263, 269, 286, 289, 292, 296, 297, 306

Panchayat system 166, 174
Parbatiya (see also Khas) 36, 46
pastoralism viii, xii, 11, 26, 37, 42, 51–54, 56–57, 141–142, 219, 222, 224, 226, 228–229, 231–232, 237, 247, 286–289, 312
Pawai (see Matwali Chettri) 42, 43, 67, 228, 229, 238
People's Movement 246, 247, 272, 275, 276,
Permanent Settlement 20, 99, 159
Petty commodity production 247, 290–293, 302
pigs 265
plantations 105, 143, 151, 265, 291, 294
Pokhara 127, 152, 211, 243, 261, 296
Potato 52, 54, 69, 135, 149, 236, 237, 298, 299, 301, 302 304
Potet (tenure) 88, 89, 156, 190

R
Rai v, xiv, xvi, 23, 27–29, 35, 50, 52, 54–57, 59–60, 67, 91–92, 115–116, 121–123, 125–128, 129, 131, 135–137, 139–142, 162, 188, 211, 214, 219–221, 223–225, 232, 284–285, 289, 298, 319, 325–326, 328, 335, 339, 344, 351
Raikar 155, 160, 225

raikar viii, ix, 75, 77–78, 81–82, 85, 88–89, 93, 96–97, 99–100, 105–106, 109–110, 112, 116, 121, 123–125, 128–129, 131, 133–136, 140, 145, 154–160, 164–166, 192–193, 204, 219, 223, 225, 241, 286, 288, 314
railways 158, 159
Rajbanshi 23, 26–27, 32, 72, 87, 97, 202
Rajput (caste) 8–9, 19, 41–42, 45–46, 274
Rajya (political system) 8–9, 15, 19, 21, 31, 39, 43–44, 46–47, 49, 57, 64–66, 68, 71, 107–108, 132, 145, 155, 229
Ramechhap 114, 233
Rana viii, ix, 3, 5, 16, 23, 62, 71, 73, 80–82, 90–96, 98–103, 107, 109–110, 112, 116–117, 120–121, 129, 134, 138–141, 145–146, 148–151, 154–159, 161–164, 170, 172, 174, 178, 182–185, 190, 192, 194, 196, 197–199, 201, 203–204, 208, 215, 220–221, 223, 228, 231, 237–239, 283, 314–315
Rasuwa 59, 299
Rautahat 76, 102, 182, 345
Regmi, Mahesh Chandra xiv, 2, 5, 7, 12, 16
Relations of production 4, 38, 111, 169–170, 203, 216, 278, 280, 283
Religion 39, 40

resettlement ix, 90, 143, 154, 161–164, 172, 178–179, 180–182, 185–188, 190, 192–193, 196, 206–207, 224, 240, 264, 285
Resettlement program (Tarai) 162, 178–181, 188, 190, 206, 240
Rolpa 66, 246
Rudraksha 238, 293, 303
Rukum 66, 289
Rupandehi 21–23, 175, 185, 196, 201, 202, 275

S

Salyan 31, 66, 80, 84, 152, 157, 190, 332
Sankhuwasabha 13, 238
Sano Kishan bank 282
Sanskritization 26, 41–42, 54, 114, 221–222, 247, 312
Saptari 20, 22, 31, 33–34, 74, 76, 82–84, 86, 92, 103, 182–183, 198, 267, 280
Sarlahi 182, 198, 308
Scotland 290
Sen kingdom 3, 8, 15, 21, 31, 39, 46, 49, 50, 71, 83, 92
Shah dynasty 36
Sherpa 52–54, 57, 69, 140–141, 225, 284, 289–290, 298
shifting cultivation viii, xii, 13, 15, 18, 25–28, 30, 32, 35, 37, 39, 48, 51–57, 60, 62, 63, 67, 69, 73, 87, 89, 90, 101, 105, 118, 120, 125, 136, 137, 288–290

Sikkim 26, 49, 88, 115, 143, 151
Simraongarh 324
Sindhuli 114, 133, 233
Sindupalchok 54, 132–133, 225
Slavery 116, 119, 120
Solu Khumbu 69, 139, 214
sorghum 61, 68
Sugar 211, 214
Sunsari 99, 175, 180, 182, 185, 192, 198, 200–201, 263, 273–274, 304, 306
Syangja 132, 208, 220, 222, 234, 261, 265

T

Tamang 8, 35, 36, 52, 55, 57–59, 108, 110, 114–118, 122, 124–125, 132–135, 137–138, 141–143, 150, 164, 222, 227, 232, 239, 254–265, 267, 284–285, 290, 298, 309, 314
Tanahu 296
Taplejung 13, 263, 286, 293
Tar (geographical feature) 334
Tara Khola (valley) 118, 138, 140, 157, 215, 225
Tarai-Madhesh vii–xi, 10, 17–19, 25–30, 32, 34–35, 47, 51, 58, 61–62, 72–77, 80–83, 86–87, 92–93, 95, 99, 100–101, 103, 105, 109–110, 112–114, 120, 131, 154, 158–163, 166, 168–169, 172, 175–176, 178–180, 182–184, 187, 192, 193, 196–198, 200–201, 207,

215–216, 236, 240, 242–243,
252, 259, 261, 267–268,
271–272, 277–280, 282, 283,
285, 292, 296, 298, 305–307,
308, 315
Tax (*amanat*) 108, 167
Tax (*ijara*) 108, 122, 151
Tax (*jimidari system*) 95, 100, 107,
188, 201, 267, 273, 282, 283,
315
Tax (*mouja*) 76, 89, 93, 95, 96
Tax (*saunefagu*) 107, 108
Tax (*serma*) 93, 107, 125,
Tax (*thekbandi*) 77, 108, 109
terracing 39, 63–64, 67, 126,
147, 241
Thakuri (caste) 41–42, 47, 113,
133, 229
Tharu x, 10, 18, 19, 23–26, 29,
31–33, 62, 72, 74, 77, 82–84,
86–89, 92, 95–97, 100,
102–103, 120, 156–157, 162,
179, 183–185, 189–197,
201–204, 206, 240–241, 254,
258, 268, 275, 281, 313
Tibet 68, 120, 145, 327
Tirhut 19
Towli 67
Transhumance 289

U
Uttar Pradesh 22, 349
Uwa 68,

V
vegetable production
236, 302, 303

W
wage labour 116, 161, 209,
213–214, 232, 234, 245, 260,
276
walnut 69, 302,
West Bengal 20, 26, 96, 172, 215,
246, 320, 325
wheat viii, ix, 9, 16, 39, 54,
61–68, 70, 73, 102–103,
144–150, 172, 235–238, 240,
242, 254, 259, 298, 300–301,
313, 315
World Bank 180

Y
Yadav caste 2, 38, 62, 64–65, 69,
97–98, 242, 278,
Yakha 123, 227, 233, 258,
Yaks 54, 57

Z
Zaman, M. A. 155, 167, 169–
171, 191, 194–198, 215